CALL OF THE AMERICAN WILD

Pilot Mountain
Grass Lake
Winter
portage
CABIN
Dog Yard
dam
beaver house
The Lake
to siwashing grounds
Dawn Reade

To the two families: one who let me go,
and the other, who ensured I came back alive.

CALL OF THE AMERICAN WILD

A TENDERFOOT'S ESCAPE TO ALASKA

GUY GRIEVE

SKYHORSE PUBLISHING

Skyhorse Publishing books may be purchased in bulk at special discounts for sales promotion, corporate gifts, fund-raising, or educational purposes. Special editions can also be created to specifications. For details, contact the Special Sales Department, Skyhorse Publishing, 307 West 36th Street, 11th Floor, New York, NY 10018 or info@skyhorsepublishing. com.

Skyhorse® and Skyhorse Publishing® are registered trademarks of Skyhorse Publishing, Inc.®, a Delaware corporation.

Visit our website at www.skyhorsepublishing.com.

10 9 8 7 6 5 4 3 2 1

Library of Congress Cataloging-in-Publication data available on file.

ISBN: 978-1-61608-820-0

Printed in the United States of America

'It matters not how strait the gate
How charged with punishments the scroll
I am the master of my fate:
I am the captain of my soul.'
W.E. HENLEY, *INVICTUS*

A Tribute to Jack London

My desire to experience the wilderness goes back to childhood, and my early reading of Jack London. His stories encapsulated the cruel beauty and mystery of the far north, none more so than *The Call of the Wild*, from which this book takes its name. In the hundred years that have passed since London was writing, our world has been transformed; yet the lands of which he wrote have barely changed at all. Neither has that part of human nature that is restless, that cannot be satisfied by the trappings of modern life. No other words better describe this than the 'call of the wild'.

CONTENTS

PROLOGUE

This is the Law of the Yukon, that only the Strong shall thrive;
That surely the Weak shall perish, and only the Fit survive.
Dissolute, damned and despairful, crippled and palsied and slain,
This is the Will of the Yukon, – Lo, how she makes it plain!

ROBERT W. SERVICE, *SONGS OF A SOURDOUGH,*
THE LAW OF THE YUKON (1907)

As I bend to hoist my overstuffed hiking bag on to my back, I see
the deep impression of a large paw print in the cool mud. My
heart squeezes a beat that almost hurts, and I need no guidebook
to tell me that, shortly before I landed on this beach, a grizzly bear
stood on this spot. As I stare at the print, my tired brain adjusts to
the reality of my situation: I am in the sub-arctic wilderness, a
place where I could be overpowered and eaten by an animal
weighing over one thousand pounds. I touch the deep holes where
five claws have left their mark. Looking along the line of prints,
I realise the bear has disappeared into the same woods that I
now plan to make my home. Unlike him, I am a complete
beginner

Using a flood-bleached tree for support, I pull myself up the
bank towards the trees. I am dripping with sweat, and surrounded
by a halo of buzzing black flies. The bag is too heavy to climb with,
so I heave it over the lip of the bank and into a clump of thorny
bushes before raising one leg over the edge to lever myself into the
greenery. I trample down some of the vegetation and stand on the

edge looking down at my clown-like trail, slipping and smearing its way up from the river.

I stand there for a few minutes, reluctant to take the first step away from the safety of my boat and into the darkness of the woods. Night is coming and I know that I have over a mile of difficult passage through dense trees and undergrowth before I reach the lake where I will make camp. At this moment, I would joyfully undo everything, turn the clock back to a time when life was safe and predictable. Taking a deep breath, I turn away from the beach and walk towards the woods.

PART 1

Reality can destroy the dream,
why shouldn't the dream destroy reality?
GEORGE MOORE

1

UNDERCOVER DREAMER

A laconic, world-weary but nevertheless warm voice answers the phone. '*Scotsman* editor's office, Sonja speaking. Can I help you?'

I stutter into action like a rusty outboard on a wet day. 'Ah yes, um . . . could I possibly speak to Iain? This is Guy from downstairs.' I hope that my cunning tactic of referring to the editor by his first name will get me past the gate-keeper, but she's an old hand.

A slight pause. 'Can I ask what you need from Iain?' She must be wondering what some hapless sod from the sales floor could possibly want with the editor of Scotland's oldest and most august newspaper.

'Well . . . I'm just wondering if I could meet with him at some point?'

'He's really busy at the moment Guy. Can I ask what it's about?'

I feel like telling her that it is about the fact that I am going stir-crazy and have finally reached the point of no return. That the only way I can see of freeing myself from the trap of office life is to head for one of the loneliest and wildest places on earth, where I will be alone and far from my family with a not inconsiderable chance of dying. Instead I say, 'Well Sonja, I know this sounds odd, but can you just tell him I'm sure he will not find a meeting with me a complete waste of his time?'

She laughs. 'Guy – what are you up to?'

'Not really sure to be honest. I just have a feeling that he might be able to help me.'

'Hold on.' There is a long pause as she checks his diary. I hear phones ringing in the background and imagine what the days must look like to a hassled and hardworking man dealing with deadline after deadline, meeting after meeting. I hear rustling and Sonja is back on the phone. 'Right – come up tonight after five-thirty and wait. No guarantees, but I'm pretty sure you will be able to get a bit of time with Iain.'

I hold the phone with two hands and experience a surge of something quite foreign: hope. 'Thank you Sonja – I'll be there.'

I replace the handset and look up. My line manager is looming over my desk, fixing me with a strange look.

'Guy, how's it going with that spreadsheet you promised us?'

I furrow my eyebrows into what I hope is an efficient look, tapping a brisk staccato on my keyboard. 'I'm onto it Kris. Can I get it to you tomorrow?'

'End of play tomorrow Guy, okay?' He hovers, not convinced.

I produce a warm salute, hoping to convey positivity and a go-ahead attitude. 'Yessir!'

He walks back to his office, frowning slightly.

At the time that this conversation took place, I had been working in the commercial department of *The Scotsman* newspaper in Edinburgh for over five years. I had held a range of jobs at the newspaper, and had some success at coming up with new ways to get money into the company. In 2002, midway through my time at the paper, an indulgent managing director, who seemed as confused about my prospects as I was, decided to see if I might be capable of holding a senior position within the company. I was duly promoted from my position as a lowly sales executive to the grand title of 'Head of Strategic Marketing', and given my own neat little office on the top floor of the building where all the senior executives lurked. For a short period I found myself quite excited about the whole thing, and began to feel that maybe this was the start of something. For weeks I plotted and planned and felt very professional and senior in my new position at the top of the building. I would swivel about in my chair, tap away ostentatiously at my computer and spend inordinate amounts of time drawing complex diagrams in order to illustrate my groundbreaking new approaches. Sadly no-one was able to understand any of these diagrams, as my writing was and remains appalling. Nevertheless there were regular meetings held in my office, and I felt proud to offer people coffee and biscuits as they settled themselves around the faux mahogany meeting table.

As the weeks turned into months the patient and very senior people who held offices on the top floor waited to see what the new lad was going to come up with. Although 'confidential', word had got out that I was planning to launch a new reader loyalty scheme based on subscribing to a gardening club. Having somehow convinced my senior management of the benefits of this scheme, I flung myself into it with gusto. In exchange for subscribing to *The Scotsman*, the gardening club would offer discounts at a range of horticultural retailers, and as an irresistible inducement I planned to offer every signed-up member a free porcelain 'digging dog' with a wind-activated wagging tail.

Each evening I drove home from the office with my head full of readers' incentives and digging dogs, gradually unwinding as I left the city behind me and approached our home in the Scottish Borders. My daily commute added up to a three-hour round trip, but it seemed worth it to live in the country, and to maintain at least the illusion of free choice in our lives. I arrived home just in time to read our two-year-old son, Oscar, a story before he fell away into sleep. Then Juliet and I would cram down a late supper and try hard to feel young and happy and full of life. The next morning I would get up early, slipping out of bed and dressing on tiptoes as my family slept, knowing that they would wake up without me and be half way through their cereals whilst I was still on the road.

The reader promotion launched and was an instant and colourful flop. My office was no longer the stage for a brilliant young protégé on his first step up the dizzying ladder to corporate stardom; instead it became a storeroom for over one thousand boxes marked 'Digging Dog'. My management still clearly saw some benefit in having me around, and shuttled me as unobtrusively as possible back downstairs to the sales floor. From there, I began to dream of escape.

Juliet was shortly due to give birth to our second child, and our mortgage and credit card debt was crippling us. I knew we were not alone – almost all of our friends were in the same situation or worse – but I couldn't accept this was the way we were meant to live. It seemed as though all our pleasures and achievements were propped up on debt, and this debt gave me no choice but to continue my increasingly mournful journey through the corridors of cubicle hell. I was in the prime of my life, yet spending eight hours of each day sitting down in an air-conditioned office, staring into a computer screen. Three further hours each day were spent sitting in my car. I felt trapped, and I was starting to panic.

During my lunch breaks I would visit the health club across the road, and eschewing the rows of machine-tanned perfection jogging in front of their floor-to-ceiling mirrors, set off around Arthur's Seat on a daily five-mile run. Offering an escape from the piped music and egos, including my own, this run was starting to save my soul. I began to smell the seasons as well as see them. I felt pain on the steep sections and cold when the rain and wind numbed my legs and face, and it felt good. Amidst the trivia of daily office life, the run was offering me the chance to reconnect both with my own body and with the outdoors, and it was triggering a rebellion within me. At first whimsically, but then with increasing seriousness, I began to yearn for a wild place, and a way of living that rejected all the trappings of suburban life. No brands, no suppliers, no offices, no company cars or on-target earnings – just trees and space and a chance to rediscover what it is to be a man, as well as a new road to some kind of freedom for my family. As I sat in my car, at my desk, ran in my lunch breaks and sat some more, all I thought about was how to escape, and where.

At home, my wife tried hard to understand what this yearning was about. She also had concerns about our lifestyle, and the fact that despite our company car and nice house we really owned nothing and were simply treading water, detached from all that the world might offer us. Our quality of life as a family was suffering from this way of life – my long hours of work and commuting meant that she was alone for most of the week and was virtually raising the children single-handed. Juliet felt deeply worried about my growing despair, but was understandably anxious at the prospect of my turning my back on my career with nothing else to go to. She was also frustrated at my lack of ability to be happy with what, compared to many people, was a very fortunate life. A nice house, one healthy son and another on the way, a good job – what more did I want? Yet inside she knew that it was not enough for either of us, and that it could only be a matter of time before it all came tumbling down.

Over the next year, from 2003 to 2004, I spent every spare moment at home and at work researching possible places that I might go. Long evenings were spent on the computer, contacting people on the other side of the world who might be able to help me. Early on Alaska emerged as the top contender, as one of the world's last great wildernesses, with an area of 1,477,270 square miles and a population of just 600,000. The far north had long been one of the landmarks of my imagination, given shape by Jack London and the poetry of Robert Service. Through the internet and books I learned more about Alaska, and encountered people who lived there or knew it well. From the confines of my office, I began to discover a vast and wild land, a place where fortunes had been won or lost and where, to this day, few people dared to travel alone. I read lurid accounts of bear attacks and journeys across creaking ice, and of a searing cold that turned men's faces white with frost as they battled with dog teams or toiled to build small cabins before the onslaught of winter. Sometimes the stories of Alaska were simple and stark, object lessons that followed a man or woman as they gradually succumbed to the elements. At other times I would read amazing accounts of journeys by moonlight across glittering expanses of ice and snow, of camp roughly made in the bend of a river, and of watching wood smoke curl into a clear sky while king salmon seared on iron and coffee boiled over charcoal. My heart skipped as I read of the loners who survived and learnt the way of the land, reading the sky and stars and living carefully in the shade of the boreal woods. These men were invariably prospectors or trappers, and many became as adept as the native Alaskans at fending for themselves in the bush, often even surpassing them in their ability to endure great hardship. Some thrived and found their fortunes in those woods, and others lost their minds and lives.

During my journeys on the internet I made contact with an Athabascan Indian woman who worked at the University of Alaska in Fairbanks*. At first she was cautious, believing understandably, that she might be dealing with a maniac, and asked me to send her character references to prove that I was genuine. I did this – to the great surprise of my referees, when they realised what they were referring me for – and she put me in touch with her brother, Charlie. He lived with his family in a small village in the Interior of Alaska on the Yukon river, and made his way by fishing and working as a carpenter†. This was the right area of Alaska – wooded, and very sparsely populated – and he was willing to be my local contact. Now I only had one major obstacle to making my dream a reality: money.

---

* The Athabascan people are native to the Interior of Alaska, and live along the five major river ways: the Yukon, the Tanana, the Susitna, the Kuskokwim, and the Copper rivers. Traditionally they were nomadic people, travelling in small groups to fish, hunt and trap, but today they live throughout Alaska and the USA, returning to their home territories to harvest traditional resources.

† The Alaskan Interior covers a vast area south of the Arctic Circle, north of the Alaska Range, west of Canada and east of 154 degrees west longitude. The mighty Yukon, Alaska's longest river, flows 1,875 miles from Lake Laberge to the Bering Sea, and courses through the middle of the region. The Interior covers 171,200 square miles, with a population of just 50,000 people. Compare this with Scotland, which has an area of 30,414 square miles, with a population of six million.

Without a trust fund behind me, short of re-mortgaging the house (half-jokingly suggested at one point, but Juliet firmly put her foot down) I had to find a source of funding. Juliet had left her job shortly before the birth of our second son, Luke, in May 2003, and so for the time being responsibility for the family's financial security rested firmly on me. With no intention of leaving my family adrift and penniless, I grimly steeled myself for the difficult task ahead. Reminding myself that I was not alone in the need for sponsorship (from Columbus to Shackleton, throughout history expeditions have required commercial support), I put together some letters about my adventure and sent them out to potential sponsors. The reactions of the people I approached ranged from enthusiasm (though usually followed with a regretful shake of the head) to incredulity and outright derision.

By early 2004 most of my potential sources of funding had come to nothing, and only one or two outside possibilities remained. I desperately searched for other solutions. Time was getting short, and I felt instinctively that if I couldn't pull it off this year it would never happen. I also knew that my days were numbered at work, and that the grim spectre of redundancy was lurking in the shadows.

2
ODDBALL MEETS EDITOR

At 5.30 pm I returned to the editor's office. 'Take a seat, Guy', Sonja smiled wearily. 'I'll just see if Iain is free.'

She replaced the handset and raised an eyebrow. 'Well, he's got five minutes. Off you go', and she pointed to the door of his office.

I walked towards the door feeling sick with worry, wondering if I was making a fatal mistake. I was aware that now, for the first time, I was going to let my idea out into the public domain – or more precisely, into the small and very gossipy world of *The Scotsman* newspaper.

Inside, Iain raised a hand to indicate a chair for me whilst holding a phone between chin and shoulder. I immediately liked the intonation of his voice and the look of his shabby desk, which held a mountain of papers, cigarette boxes and books. Behind him an old bookcase stood beautifully askew with a half-drunk bottle of whisky lying on its side on the edge of one of the shelves. A painting of Edinburgh's North Bridge hung on the wall beside the door and it too was off centre. To my right, large sliding doors opened out onto a balcony and a metal balustrade made of steel

stanchions and tight wire. The whole effect was of chaotic movement and Iain Martin resembled a young captain at sea in a storm.
Suddenly his call was at an end. Raising a finger in apology he
tapped into his computer, then swivelled around to look at me.

'Guy – what can I do for you?'

I mustered all of my energy and tried to think clearly. 'Right,
um, okay. Now this might sound odd . . .'

'I am not faint-hearted.' He smiled: 'Try me.'

I brought my fingers together and took the leap. 'Iain – I think I
am losing my mind.'

He laughed. 'So?'

'I have to change my life – I've had a searing vision of the future
and I don't like it.' I heard myself and thought of Billy Graham,
imagining that the editor must be starting to worry about whether
security were still in the building. Yet he was still looking at me
seriously.

'I am sorry to confront you with this – you must be busy, but,
well, I am not sure what I want to ask you except that . . .'

'Guy, don't waffle. What is it?'

I stood up and leaned over his desk like a clichéd character in a
B-movie. 'I'm going to leave my job and go to Alaska to build a
cabin in the wilderness. Then I'm going to live in it through the
winter.'

He blinked and opened his mouth. Just then the phone rang, but
he pushed a red flashing button and there was silence apart from
the muted sounds of the newsroom outside.

'What?'

'I can't live my life sitting down any more. I have to go.' I sat
down again.

'What about your kids – you do have a family, don't you?' He
leaned back in his chair and looked hard at me.

'Yes I do.'

'Well?'

'My wife knows that I have to do this – she supports me. And we
can't carry on living as we are – hopefully this will change our lives
somehow. Nothing belongs to us, our debt is crippling and I hardly

see my family anyway . . .' I opened my hands. 'Sorry – I'm going on a bit.'

He stood up and walked to the glass door, sliding it open. 'Do you smoke, Guy?'

I told him that tonight I would make an exception, and accepted a cigarette.

Standing on the balcony we looked down at the dark wet streets, watching the rush hour traffic circle Arthur's Seat. I felt elated. There was now no reason for nerves or tension – my boats had started to burn and I was enjoying the smell of fire. Iain put out his cigarette, then walked back to his desk.

'Build a cabin you say?'

'Yes.'

'Where in Alaska?'

'The Interior, on the Yukon river.'

'Have you done this sort of thing before?'

'No,' I admitted, managing to force a smile. 'I have done a bit of shooting for the pot, so I'm not too worried about feeding myself. I'm not experienced at building, but I spent a few months working as a labourer, so I know I can work . . .'

He interrupted: 'Have you got a team of people to help you?'

'No.'

He leaned back and looked at the smoke-yellowed ceiling. 'Will you be on your own out there?'

'Yes.'

'What if something goes wrong – if you get hurt. Will you be able to get help?'

I tried to look dependable but failed, and raised my hands in surrender.

'I will be on my own. I can't really say any more than that.'

He chuckled, shaking his head, and my nerves came back in a rush. He thinks I'm insane, I thought. Soon the managing director will know and the axe will fall.

'Why have you come to me about this Guy?'

'I need to earn some money while I'm away, and wondered if I could write a column for you.'

He sat in silence again. 'That Foreign Legion piece you wrote was all right I suppose . . .' He tapped a pencil on the table, then placed the end in his mouth and fixed me with a hard look. 'It's a good story. Okay, I'll take a weekly column from you if you can pull it off. You don't seem like a bullshitter, although God knows what's going to happen to you.'

I stuttered a thank you and stood up feeling dizzy, knowing it was only partly due to the cigarette. Iain walked me to the door and shook my hand, saying 'We'll need about eight hundred words a week from you – you'll have to figure out a way of getting it to us. Good luck.'

I stumbled out of his office in a state of complete disbelief. For the first time someone had taken my idea seriously, and I felt flattered, excited and more than a bit alarmed. The world was calling my bluff and the dream was becoming a reality. The monthly income from the column would help keep my family going while I was away, which was my main concern. I still had to raise the money to finance the adventure itself, but I knew that I had crossed the first hurdle, and there was now a real chance that it might actually happen.

I drove slowly home and arrived just as Juliet was drying Oscar and Luke, our second son who was nearly a year old, beside the fire. 'Well, how did it go?' she asked.

'It went well. He's offered me a weekly column.'

I met my wife's level gaze, and there was a silence between us. Her expression was quietly resigned, a sight that was hard for me to see. The fire flickered behind her, reflecting on the warm wooden floors of our little home. I could smell our supper being kept warm in the oven, and heard the murmur of the radio in the kitchen. Outside it had begun to rain, and I could see the water shining in the outside light.

'Come up and read the boys a story, Guy. Let's get them to bed and then have some supper.'

As we ate and talked quietly about what lay ahead, for the first time it felt as if we were talking about something real. Juliet had already decided that, in the year I was away, she would rent our house out and take the boys to her home community on the Isle of Mull. Having grown up on the island, she had a strong network of family and friends there, and knew they would all be safe and supported. She looked at me searchingly, knowing that I could hide very little from her. 'Guy, are you sure you're prepared for this? I mean, there are the bears, then there's the cold in the winter, and building the cabin . . .'

'I know I can do it.' I held her hand and tried to be as reassuring as I could. 'Somehow I just know it will be okay.' She fixed me with another steady look and I knew just what she was thinking. Only a week before I had spent a whole day wrestling with the assembly of a set of Ikea shelves for the boys' bedroom, and now I was planning to build my own cabin. We washed up together in silence and I thought of my two boys upstairs, fast asleep in their beds. Then I remembered how, when I had tried to join the army in my early twenties, the results of my tests concluded that I was 'uncategorisable' and 'lacking in innate intelligence'. I had no idea whether I could do this. But I was determined to give it a try.

3
THE DREAM BECOMES A PLAN

A few days later I met up again with Iain Martin, and the meeting confirmed that he was serious about giving me a weekly column. I was touched by his belief in my idea, and it gave me the encouragement I needed to push ahead with my preparations. I had a lot to organise: I couldn't leave until I'd found some more money from somewhere, and I had to sort out logistics, including a means of getting the column to the newspaper each week. I trawled through atlases and read through book after book. I contacted Charlie to tell him that I planned to arrive in the next few months. When we spoke I heard in his voice a heavy and understandable note of caution. It was clear that I had absolutely no experience of living and working in the sub-arctic, and he must have thought I was just the kind of man who was heading for disaster.

After this, things began to develop very fast. My gut instinct told me that my days at the office were numbered, and the pressure was on to pull the project together. One night I met up with a good friend who owns Graham Tiso Outdoors, a well-known supplier of outdoor equipment and clothing. Chris is a bluff and wholehearted character, a lover of all things outdoors and of adventure. Over a beer in the Shore Bar in Leith I told him of my plan, and he reacted immediately with enthusiasm.

'Guy, you've got to do this. Tell you what, I'll give you all the equipment you need, and I might come up with some money too if you need it. Do not give up!'

Encouraged by Chris's support, in the knowledge that I had some guaranteed income from the Scotsman column, Juliet and I agreed that there was no going back. There was a crackly atmosphere of anticipation between us, and as we said our goodbyes each morning there was a feeling that our lives were on the brink of great change. Then one day I was called into the assistant managing director's office. He was doing what any good manager would have done, and making me redundant.

I came out of his office feeling oddly calm, knowing that at least here in the office the worst that could happen had happened. I walked past the desks of various friends who, even though it had not yet been announced, must have known that my time was up. I stopped at my line manager's office and found him unusually chirpy and upbeat. No doubt he knew that I was, clerically speaking, a dead man. I wandered over to the sorry pile of paper, books, coffee cups and pens that was my workstation, with vague intentions of clearing my desk. Out of habit, I turned on my computer, and listened for the thousandth time to the irritating start-up jingle that was meant to sound grand and impressive, but instead summed up all that was dull and predictable about office life. I pointed my mouse at 'in-box' and woozily noted that there was an email headed 'Highland Park.' I opened it without any interest, expecting a drinks promotion of some form, and read instead:

Hi Guy,
We have read over the information that you sent us about your Alaskan adventure, and we'd like to be involved. Can you call me?
Best wishes,
Sharon McLaughlin
Highland Park Whisky

I read the message with a thudding heart, and a sense of disbelief. I could not quite believe what I was reading – on this of all days – and looked around to see if someone was smirking. Could this be a cruel joke? Nothing was confirmed in the email, but nevertheless I felt in my heart that this was the moment I had been waiting for.

A few days later I met with Sharon McLaughlin in a department store in Glasgow. We sat at a table overlooking thousands of people shopping during their lunch breaks, and discussed how Highland Park could get involved in my adventure. This was it now – I was definitely going, and as I journeyed back to Edinburgh on the train I felt overwhelmed by a mix of emotions. I wondered what I had got myself into, what lay before me, and whether I might have cause to regret taking this journey into a vast and untamed wild land.

4
THE NUMB DAYS

It was early summer, and our little home on the Rule Water Valley was blooming. The vegetable patch looked like an emerald hidden behind our home, and the strawberries were better than ever before. And yet I felt numb and emotionally displaced, as I came to terms with the fact that in a week's time I would be leaving it all behind. Our children, our home and the gentle country that surrounded us would soon be exchanged for people and a land that I knew nothing about. The warm sunny weather and carefree playfulness of our children only added to my growing sense of doom. Juliet and I tried to maintain a routine and to behave normally, but our impending separation hung over us like a black cloud.

Oscar had been told that I was leaving, and had absorbed the news without protest, though he had little concept of the length of time that I would be away. To celebrate his fourth birthday, on a hot still weekend, we invited a group of friends to come over for a barbecue. The enormity of what I was facing loomed over all of us and conversations seemed oddly stilted. As we stood silently watching our children playing together, I looked at the other fathers around me and felt anxious about the risk that I was taking with my family's security. Amongst our closest friends, I felt my first true touch of loneliness on that soft summer's day. In the eight years that Juliet and I had lived together we had never been apart for more than a week, and now here I was leaving for one whole year. It was an appalling prospect.

My last few days were spent sorting out last-minute arrangements and logistics. I had spent a day at Tiso's the week before, sorting out my clothing and essential survival equipment*. I had figured out how to get my column to the *Scotsman* each week, by sending emails via a laptop plugged into a satellite phone, and dashed down to London to see Inmarsat, who were giving me a satellite phone and free call time, and over to Glasgow to pick up an Apple iBook laptop from Scotsys.

A couple of nights before I was due to leave, a friend who is a local GP came over to show me how to insert an IV drip. She talked me through how to find a good vein, and how to pierce it with Venflon and butterfly needles, then sat worriedly beside me as I clumsily prodded about in my arm. I made the first classic mistake, which was to insert the needle too far into the vein so that it came out the other side into bloodless tissue, but after some practice managed to get it right. It was an uncomfortable and bloody experience, but I emerged an hour later feeling confident that I could, if necessary, administer medication intravenously.

The next morning I drove into Edinbugh and had a hurried meeting in a pub with another friend, a highly respected surgeon. He laid an impressive first-aid kit out on the table and gave me a potted lecture on how to treat everything from dog bite to appendicitis, while I frenziedly took notes. Lost in the urgency of it all, we failed to notice the hard-core boozers at the bar, who were all seated in silence, glancing over occasionally as if afraid that we might practice some first-aid procedures on them. I raised a reassuring hand to the barman who stood staring with open

---

* See notes for list of equipment and medical supplies (p.373).

suspicion, perhaps imagining that we were a couple of supremely confident drug dealers.

On our last night together, when the boys were in bed, Juliet and I walked slowly away from our house, stopping to look at some trees that we had planted the previous summer.

'Well, this is it now I suppose', Juliet said in a quiet voice, as we stood close together looking back at our little house. 'I can't believe we won't see each other for so long.' Her voice tailed away.

'It feels very strange.' I couldn't say anything more, too choked to put my thoughts into words.

The next day I walked with Juliet towards the departure gates at Edinburgh airport. We were surrounded on all sides by people going on holiday, while we stood mute and in pain and about to enter two different worlds. Juliet pulled a manila envelope from her handbag:

'Guy, we forgot this.'

'What is it?' I asked.

'It's your will – you need to sign it.'

We looked around for a witness, and at the same moment our eyes lit upon a pilot, walking towards us on his way to one of the airline desks. I stepped forward.

'I'm sorry to ask you this – could you possibly spare a moment to witness a signature for us?'

'Witness? What for?'

'I'm signing my will.'

He blinked and gave me a confused smile, then glanced at Juliet who was clearly distressed.

'No problem, I can do it . . . But tell me, are you afraid of flying?'

Juliet let out a little cough of amusement and we found ourselves laughing as the ridiculousness of the situation hit us.

When it was time to say goodbye, I held Juliet in my arms and we sobbed beside a dreary shop selling shirts and ties. Hard times were coming for both of us, and Juliet was facing her own challenge of looking after two little boys on her own. I knew that she was going to carry an added daily burden of worry, as I took my first steps in a dangerous and unknown land.

PART 2

It is our nature to be more moved by hope than fear.
FRANCESCO GUICCIARDINI

5
ALASKA ARRIVAL

A tiny passenger plane with a pencil-like fuselage taxied towards the departure hut at Anchorage airport where I sat. Around me were seven other people who I could see were from the Interior. Most of them were indigenous Alaskans, and they were surrounded by boxes and bags packed with everything from tools to fresh fruit and peanut butter. Opposite me a fat woman dressed in a tracksuit sat talking to her dog, which simpered and pawed while delivering a series of wet licks that landed squarely on her lips. Her size and dark clothing made her look like a seal, and I felt for her, as it was hard to avoid the feeling that she was a lonely person. Harder to imagine what her life might be like in the thinly populated Interior.

The co-pilot popped his head around the door: 'Okay y'all – let's saddle up' and sauntered back towards the plane. Everyone stood up, gathering their untidy possessions, and followed him out on to the tarmac. I felt a pang of fear as I entered the tiny plane, made worse by the fact that there was no partition between the passengers and the pilots, and they both looked very young. After a cursory safety announcement we lifted off and circled into the air. I let my head fall back and started a series of mental exercises all aimed at maintaining bladder control: I had been nervously sipping away at a two-litre bottle of water for most of the morning, and had only realised once airborne that the plane was too small to have a toilet. It was cloudy, yet from time to time I would catch a glimpse of a massive and empty land below. I tried to look relaxed and calm in the midst of those seven seasoned bush Alaskans, but from time to time I would catch one of them staring at me. They didn't seem hostile – just curious. Maybe wondering why this tenderfoot was heading for one of the loneliest places on earth.

The cloud grew heavy and I saw nothing for the next two hours until we began our descent into Galena. This tiny village on the Yukon was home to Charlie, whom I had called a month earlier to confirm my arrival. He had sounded somewhat taken aback to hear that I was at last coming – I think he had dismissed me as a crackpot dreamer who needed to be humoured with an occasional phone call, and now perhaps regretted agreeing to help me. The plane lurched and pitched in sudden turbulence as we lost altitude, which did nothing to relieve my bladder misery, and still the thick cloud held the land locked in a grey veil of secrecy. I jammed my head against the window and stared into the void, searching for a glimpse of this land about which I knew nothing.

'Alright everybody, let's think about seatbelts,' the captain announced and we banked steeply. I saw something dark start to take shape as we neared the village landing strip, and then the clouds parted and my eyes widened as a huge river revealed itself in a series of grand meandering curves. I saw brownish water braiding around huge wooded islands, and in places the river showed its bones as banks of sand stood out, exposed high above the stream. I turned to the man seated by my side. 'Excuse me – is that the Yukon?' He met my question with an unsmiling neutral expression before nodding slowly. I looked out of the window for another sight of the massive river, but saw nothing as cloud once again obscured the view. How strange, I thought – so much cloud around still, and yet we're so low.

The plane landed and we clambered down the steps into a hot, humid atmosphere. I took a deep breath and smelt something familiar. The man who had been seated beside me came past, and I said 'Sorry, can I just ask you – are people burning peat here?'

A wide smile opened across his face, revealing gold-capped teeth. 'No, been real big fire.'

'Fire?'

'Oh yeah, and now the ground's burning up too 'cause the trees are gone – burned up long ago.' He smiled and raised his eyebrows, then walked off while I waited for my bags, currently being loaded onto an old tractor beside the plane. I looked up at the sun shining through the cloud, and my heart lurched: it was smoke. I had landed in the middle of a massive forest fire, and now it was burning into the ground, imbuing the air with the wonderful, though at this moment far from welcome, smell of peat smoke. What was this going to mean for me?

I grabbed my heavy bags and turned to walk towards the small log cabin that was the airport for this village. As I drew near, a fit-looking native Alaskan man dressed in a North Face jacket with yellow-shaded glasses stepped forwards. 'Are you Guy?'

I let my bags down. 'Yes. Charlie?'

He smiled and nodded, then held out his hand. 'I'm Charlie and this is my son, Bubba.' He gestured to a young man standing beside him, who slowly raised a hand in greeting. His dark eyes, like Charlie's, scrutinised me, and I knew that I was being assessed.

We walked towards a bashed-up 1960s pickup truck, loaded my bags into the back and clambered in, then turned out of the airfield on to a bumpy dirt road heading for Charlie's home. I cleared my throat. 'I hear there's been a fire here – has it been bad?'

'Yeah, fucking terrible.' Charlie kept his eyes on the road. 'Everything burnt up and very bad around here.'

'Right.' A flutter of panic passed through me.

'I want you to meet my father-in-law, then come and meet my family.'

'Thank you Charlie, I'm truly grateful.'

'Maybe you can stay at my father-in-law's place, maybe not.'

His sentence hung in the air, and my anxiety deepened.

We rattled down the dirt road, occasionally passing another equally beaten-up car. By way of conversation I said: 'These cars all seem to be in quite a rough state.'

'Oh yeah,' Charlie answered. 'Only got one big road and no-one is gonna sell a car here so we don't bother too much.'

'Where does this road go?'

'To the dump.'

'No further?'

'No further.'

I looked up the long dirt road bordered by thickets of willow and alder, and remembered that there were no true roads in the Interior: it was only reachable by river and air. We bumped along for a while, passing an occasional shack, then turned off the road into a wide gravel yard filled with parked river launches and an assortment of odds and ends from welding machines to old storage containers. The end wall of a dark cabin was entirely covered by a range of much-used tools. Charlie pulled to a halt in a cloud of dust. 'This is where Don, my father-in-law, lives.'

I stepped out, and my eyes were immediately drawn to a gracious cabin made of entire trees or round logs, each around thirty-six feet in length. The cabin rested on stilts, and stood on a high bluff that looked out over a giant bend in the wide brown Yukon. I was transfixed by its size and confidence, and it gave me hope that somehow I might manage to build my own little place. The cabin seemed to glow; the logs had caught the light from the sun and shone like gold. As I stared at the house I heard a bark, and a tough black and grey dog trotted lightly towards me, tail and head held high. He stopped a few paces short of me and cocked his head before letting out another playfully aggressive bark. I walked forward to greet him, but he darted away and settled himself in some dusty shade beneath the cabin.

We walked up a flight of wooden stairs to a door at the side of the house before taking off our boots. Inside, a large room opened up before me, the roof held up by entire, huge trees. A wide window looked down on to the steady flow of the mighty river, and beside the door there was a large wood-burning stove.

I stood uncertainly in the doorway, feeling uncomfortable and out of place. Seated at the dining table was a fearsome, wild-looking man, who I guessed was somewhere in his late sixties. He was dressed in rough work cothing with an old pair of braces, dark glasses and a worn welder's cap. He was looking at me, tapping his finger lightly on the table. Close by stood a native Alaskan woman who I took to be his wife. Charlie steered me towards the table, and the man rose to greet me, surprising me with the speed and fluidity of his movements. He shook my hand lightly and got straight down to business: 'Better tell you now – we been having one heck of a fire here lately. Charlie was planning for you to stay in my cabin out in the bush. Pain of it is, my cabin burnt to ashes – just been looking at some pictures.' Like a croupier dealing cards he slid a picture across the table, and I saw an image of complete incineration. A forlorn-looking barrel stood on stilts amidst the ashes. Don read my thoughts. 'That's my barrel stove. And that . . .' he flipped over another picture, '. . . that's my old canoe.' Warped and shrunken by the fierce heat, it looked like a discarded silver banana skin.

'It must have been some fire' I mumbled, struggling to get my head around the consequences of this for my adventure.

'It sure was – three hundred thousand acres up in smoke. Coffee?'

I looked up and saw him more closely, warming to him despite his intimidating looks. His eyes revealed intelligence and a quick sense of humour with a glint of cunning. But good man or not, I was preoccupied with my own problems. I sat down, trying to muster up a feeling of positivity when all I really wanted to do was cry. I felt like a child on his first day at a new school – utterly at sea, and away from everything that was familar. Don introduced his wife and she smiled politely, her eyes giving nothing away. While she went to make coffee, Don and Charlie rooted around for some maps of the area. I sat looking out of the window, lost momentarily in a world of self-loathing. How could I have taken this risk? How could I have left my family and travelled eight thousand miles with absolutely no assurances that this was going to work out? Suddenly all my plans, so confidently made from the safety of my home in

Scotland, seemed unrealistic and stupid. Here I was, just a few hours into it all, and already I had hit a major hitch. I felt sure that Don and Charlie were building up to saying that they couldn't help me, and that shortly they would be offering to drive me back to the airport. They sat down beside me, spreading some maps out on the table. Listening to their commentary did nothing to help raise my spirits:

'Nah – that bit's all been burned, right up to the margins of this lake,' Don pointed at a blue splotch on the map.

Charlie interjected: 'Actually Brownie flew that way yesterday and said it was burned clear up to here.' His hand indicated a vast swathe of land.

They both looked uncomfortable and full of doubt, and a mood of resignation settled upon us. Through the gloom I felt a glimmer of determination: I couldn't give up at the first hurdle. I thought of one of the few things I remembered from my failed attempt to be selected for officer's training in the British army. A swaggering colonel with dazzling white teeth had repeatedly shouted: 'And remember – the first thing that always goes is the plan!' I repeated this internally like a mantra, until almost without knowing it I had said it out loud. My voice cut through Charlie and Don's musings: 'But then again . . . the first thing that always goes is the plan.'

They both stopped talking and looked at me. Charlie's eyes gave little away, but Don slowly shook his head and smiled ruefully, and I could see that the maxim made sense to him. 'Yup, that sure is the case with lots of stuff, and almost always the case with the bush.'

I decided to risk another positive thought: 'Yes and, um, maybe my coming here could be a good thing.'

Charlie sat back and tilted his head to one side, giving me a questioning look. I hesitated, imagining myself at the first stages of digging a deep hole, but continued doggedly. 'Well, maybe it is good that just when you have lost your cabin some oddball from Scotland comes to build another one?'

My words hung on the air for a moment. 'Hang on . . . are you saying you want to build a cabin yourself?' Charlie leaned forward, looking incredulous.

'Yes – that is my plan.' I held his gaze, though I felt far from confident. 'I thought I had made that clear, but maybe . . .' I tailed off.

They looked at each other silently, and I watched as it all sank in. I read their thoughts from the expressions that passed over their faces, and I could see that they were adjusting to a new and alarming reality: I was not just another tourist wanting a trip out into the wilderness, I was on a mission.

A dog barked in the yard, then broke into a long howl. Don folded the maps carefully, then said: 'Well, let's just see what the guy can do. One thing is certain – I ain't got no ideas right now. For the moment you can stay in a little place I got at the end of my yard there.'

I thanked him and asked how much rent he wanted, but he raised a hand to stop me. 'Just hope things work out for you.'

Charlie led me out to the small green shed that stood on its own little bluff overlooking the great slow river. Inside it was painted white, and a small hand-made wooden bed stood pushed up into the corner beside a little window. As he left, over his shoulder Charlie said, 'I'll pick you up for dinner with my family later. You just settle in here.' He jumped into his truck and drove off.

I wandered outside and sat on the edge of the bluff, looking down at a huge tree being dragged like a toothpick in the swirling river. A light breeze drew gently through the needles of a white spruce tree beside me, and I caught my first whiff of the sophisticated scent of its resin. It smelt good, but did nothing to lift my spirits. I looked across the river at the huge expanse of wild country beyond, and thought of all of the Europeans before me who had followed a dream that led them away from the captivity of their lives. I thought of the lines by Robert Service: '*This is the law of the Yukon, and ever she makes it plain: send not your foolish and feeble; send me your strong and your sane*'. I hoped that I was going to prove to be in the latter category.

6

UP THE YUKON WITHOUT A PADDLE

Later that night I walked with Charlie along the dirt road to his house. We passed a few ramshackle wooden houses, and every now and then a beaten-up car would pass, leaving us in a cloud of thick dust. The village was rough and drab and everything seemed to be the colour of dirt, from the roads to the dust-caked scrub, and the great river that flowed sullenly towards the west. The uninspiring surroundings, along with the non-committal looks of everyone who passed by, were making me feeling uneasy and depressed. The conversation didn't help:

'Yeah, I take white men downriver every now and then,' Charlie said. 'We head out into some pretty lonely parts.'

'Oh right – you take them fishing, do you?'

'Yup, I take 'em fishing and make camp.' He fixed me with a complex look. 'Some they say to me: "Charlie, we've had enough now, we want to go home."'

I nodded slowly.

'They get scared and they want to go home pretty quick.'

His fast-moving eyes briefly met mine, and I saw the challenge within them. I realised he was wondering how long I would last.

Ten minutes later we came to a small road that led down towards the river. To my right, a thicket of willow stood dead still in the heavy, humid air, and to my left an open area of ground held stockpiles of raw timber and a battered but effective-looking mobile sawmill. Charlie gestured towards it. 'We pull trees out of the river in spring for firewood, and we cut logs upstream and float 'em down for timber.'

Further on, closer to the river, we approached Charlie's house. It was surrounded by trucks dating back to the 1950s, a few motorbikes and even a snow machine, which appeared out of place on this sultry, humid evening. I looked up at an impressive wooden house, which stood on stilts surrounded by a wooden porch. It was two storeys high, and seemed to teeter like a big woman in high heels. 'Did you build this?' I asked. Charlie nodded and motioned to me to go in.

Inside, I was met by Charlie's wife, Claudette, and their five children who had gathered to greet me. Dark eyes examined me, and I felt swamped once more by the sensation of being eight thousand miles from home, and relegated to the status of stranger. Sensing my discomfort, Claudette stepped quickly forward. She was a tall, good-looking woman and her eyes were warm and welcoming. The three little girls, Bethany, Pearl and Noo Noo, whispered to each other while taking quick, darting peeks at me from behind their hands. Beside Claudette stood Bubba. I guessed he was around seventeen years old, and once again he regarded me with a completely impassive, poker face. A younger boy, Jack, aged around ten, stood beside him, gazing at me in open wonder.

Claudette motioned for us all to sit at a large wooden table that was laid for dinner. The table was pushed up beneath a window that looked out over the great, brown, sluggish river, and everyone bowed their heads as Claudette said a prayer, and then lifted them again to stare at me. I raised a feeble hand in a kind of joke greeting.

Bubba continued to stare, unsmiling, but Jack laughed, and with a note of sophisticated dryness beyond his years came straight to the point: 'So, you have travelled all the way from Scotland to live in the bush?'

I nodded, trying to look confident and decisive. 'Yes, Jack, that's the plan.'

He leaned forward, furrowing his brow. 'Why?'

I straightened my empty plate and fiddled with the cutlery, struggling to find an answer. 'Well, you know, it's difficult to explain . . .' I glanced round the table: the whole family was waiting. '. . . What I mean is, there are many reasons behind what we do, and it would take a long time to answer your question properly.'

Jack sat back in his chair, tilting his head to one side; clearly he was not satisfied by my answer. Claudette broke the silence, ladling a beautiful meat stew on to my plate and sliding over the salad bowl. 'C'mon Jack, give him a chance to settle down – he just got here.'

The stew was wonderful, and I took the opportunity to change the subject. 'This beef is amazing – is it Alaskan?'

A slow smile passed over Bubba's face and I knew he was enjoying my discomfort.

'It's moose,' Charlie said. They all looked at me, waiting for my reaction.

'Where did you buy it?'

Charlie smiled. 'We can't afford to buy meat at the store – it's too expensive. Everything in there has to come by air.'

'Of course,' I nodded, remembering that we were three hundred miles from the nearest road.

'Jack shot this moose.'

I looked over at the bright young boy who had so deftly got to the point with his sharp interrogation. 'Was it your first moose?'

He shook his head matter-of-factly. 'No.'

I waited for him to say more, but he didn't. 'You've shot one before?'

'Yes.'

'He shot his first moose when he was seven,' Charlie said, 'and he has got one for the family each year.'

I regarded Jack with wonder, amazed that a seven-year-old boy could flatten the world's largest deer, which might weigh as much as one thousand five hundred pounds. The family ate in silence, and my mind began hazily to search for any aspect of British life that might amuse or interest my hosts. An image of days spent idling on the cricket pitch came to mind, and I turned to my young inquisitor. He immediately lowered his fork and stopped eating, clearly readying himself for something odd. I didn't disappoint him:

'Jack, have you ever heard of a game called cricket?'

The eyebrow lifted again, and he shook his head slowly from side to side. I looked over to include the rest of the family. 'Well . . . cricket is a bit of an odd game I suppose. Maybe the only game in the world which you can play for five days without either side winning outright.' The family sat in stunned silence as I launched into an oratory on the complex world of modern day cricket – a curious choice for me, as I'm by no means an expert.

Claudette and Charlie had met, so I learnt, when they were young stars of the local basketball team. Many indigenous Americans are now passionate about basketball, and some great teams have had their origins in reservations and homelands throughout the country. As I spoke about cricket, trying to answer various questions that came my way, I thought that the subject was perhaps not ideal for bridging cultural divides – however it certainly was helping to lighten the atmosphere.

'So what position did you play again? What was it called?' Charlie glanced over at his wife as he asked the question, as if saying: 'Just hear him say this again – can you believe it?'

My answer brought a round of gentle laughter to the table. 'Ah yes, my fielding position was usually "silly mid off".'

Jack carefully repeated my words, looking round at his siblings. 'Silly mid off?'

I nodded. 'Yup – it's called that because the position is so near to the batsman that it is actually quite a silly place to be as he can sometimes hit the ball straight at you and very hard.'

They all laughed.

After the meal, I thanked Charlie and Claudette for their welcome. Charlie raised his hand: 'I will do my best to help you. But it's hard out there, and you really know nothing about this land, do you?'

I couldn't deny it. I shook my head.

'Don's cabin is gone, and we don't have another place where you can build one – do you understand?' He spoke quite slowly, as if to a child.

A hot feeling of panic returned and I felt the blood thudding in my veins as, once again, I was forced to contemplate the idea of failure.

Claudette was looking at me too: 'Guy, it is hard on your own here without family, and dangerous too.' I could see the concern in her eyes, and realised that, to them – and particularly to Claudette, as a mother of young children – it must seem strange that I had come all this way, leaving my family behind. They must have been wondering about my motives, and I remembered how, in our early email exchanges, Charlie's sister had pointed out that native Alaskans value family and community above all else, and would never choose to go out into the bush alone. Yet I knew there was a long cultural precedent for white men journeying on their own into wild places, and the ones who succeeded had almost always been those who had strived to forge bonds with indigenous people. Many who came from Britain were escaping the class-bound claustrophobia of the 1800s – a land where, even before birth, people's destiny was fixed. In an oblique way, my reasons for leaving were similar, as I was escaping the ruthlessly structured hierarchy of office life. I looked past Claudette at the big, mean-looking river. On the far bank I could see two large animals that I took to be a moose and its calf, standing dead still on a sand bar. Behind them an expanse of bush and scrub trees stretched to infinity.

'I know what you're saying Claudette,' I said, 'and I feel terrible about being away from my family. But this is important for all of us, and somehow I'm sure I will find a way of making it work.'

Charlie and Claudette stayed silent, and I felt their deep doubt stretching across the plywood floor towards me. I looked at my watch and said, 'Well, I think I should leave you all in peace.' Charlie stood up, ready to offer me a lift over to Don's yard, but I held a hand up: 'Don't worry – I know the way. I can walk along the river.' I indicated the bank beside the house that shelved steeply down to a firm-looking sand beach.

Charlie nodded. 'Yeah, sure you can.' His eyes registered doubt as if he thought that I might get lost. And who could blame him. I had no experience of any kind, and my recounting of my experiences in the game of cricket certainly wouldn't have done anything to reassure him. I felt like an ass: a skill-less, unrealistic, romantic and hopeless ass.

I walked down the flight of creaking stairs out into the warm twilight and down towards the river. A dog shot out of a plywood kennel and barked shrilly at the end of its chain. I stopped to look at him as he strained and jumped, barking and snorting and flashing strong white teeth at me. He was a small, spry-looking dog, with rich blond fur. I walked over and felt his claws grate on my clothing as he raised himself on to strong hind legs and pawed at me. The barking was immediately replaced by eager friendliness, and a frenzy of licking and drooling. I stepped back and the dog dropped again to all fours, resuming his high-pitched barking as I moved away.

I scrambled down the steep incline in front of the house and pushed through a thin screen of willow osiers until I reached the river beach. The water sucked greedily along the firm sand, and occasionally a tree passed swiftly by, carried by a powerful current that reminded me of the more aggressive tidal flows that I had seen off the west coast of Scotland. I could hear the river's power, and it was intimidating – relentless and stronger than any I had ever seen. Behind me the rough little village of log cabins and shacks was settling down for the night. From time to time I heard a dog bark or a shot echo out in the twilight, and I thought of the leap of faith that this family were taking by letting me enter their home. Their cautious welcome reflected the fact that I was being treated as dangerous until proven otherwise, and I couldn't blame them. What did they know about me – except what I told them, and how did they know that was true? I could be anyone, and, in a land that has long attracted stray men and oddballs from every corner of the world, they were right to be cautious.

A lump formed in my throat as I walked along the beach, and I cursed myself for having taken such a terrible gamble with my life and with my family's security. At Don's shed, I drew water from a storage jug and put it on the little camp stove to boil for tea. I saw the word 'London' on the box of tea, and thought of Juliet and her amazing ability to drink tea by the gallon. The memory brought on another bout of sadness, and I decided to forget the tea. I folded sadly into the little wooden bed, feeling more alone and homesick than ever before in my life.

The next morning I woke early and lay very still, slowly taking in the strangeness of my surroundings. My homesickness hit me afresh as I remembered where I was, and I thought of my children, who would normally drag me from sleep, shouting and bouncing painfully on top of me. The fact that I wasn't going to see them for almost a year was something I couldn't even contemplate, and I lay battling with self-pity, trying to summon up some fighting spirit. After a few moments I got up and put on my clothes, then sat back down on the bed. A light tap on the door brought me back to reality. 'Hey, you in there?'

Don stood on the doorstep, looking at me quizzically. Despite the early hour he looked sprightly and alert, and beneath his forbidding exterior I could see that his eyes were perceptive and kind. I sensed that he had seen just about every type of man pass through the great wilderness that was his home.

'How're ya doing?' He raised an eyebrow as he waited for my answer.

'Oh, I'm okay' I replied, hoping that I sounded more positive than I felt. We walked in silence over to the shingle bank and stood looking down at the river. I turned to look downstream, and out of the corner of my eye saw a large brown animal approaching. 'What's that?' I exclaimed.

Don continued to gaze at the river, a faint smirk visible beneath his moustache. 'Don't worry, he ain't mean.'

It was the largest dog I had ever seen. Standing at around four feet at the shoulder, he was covered in brown flowing fur, and must have weighed over one hundred pounds. 'Hey you dummy,' Don called: 'Come here!' The beast tilted its immense head as if to say: 'Sure Boss, but who's the kid?' and lumbered over. He leaned into Don, his great fur-padded paws leaving deep impressions in the sand. I regarded him with amazement: the only time I had seen an animal like this was on the Muppet Show. 'What sort of dog is he?' I asked.

'Called a Mackenzie,' Don patted the dog's head. 'They were freight huskies working in small teams hauling heavy stuff across deep snow, woods and sometimes even mountain terrain.'

'How much weight could they pull?'

'About a thousand pounds per dog – it's them great wide furry feet combined with big shoulders and a desire to pull that does it.'

I looked at the huge dog with respect. 'What's his name?'

'Oh, I call him Shorty.' Don looked down at the adoring beast, then up at me. 'You want a cup of coffee?'

I felt suddenly grateful that fate had led me to this man. Although I felt sure of nothing, he gave me hope. 'That would be great.'

'Son, it's just a cup of coffee,' he said wryly.

I nodded, taking the point, and went on: 'Thank you for letting me stay here.'

He regarded me with a poker face.

'Can I pay rent or something?'

He shook his head. 'Nah. Money does nothing for me.' I felt that if we had known each other better he would have said more, but he was still wary.

As we walked across his yard we saw a group of men standing around a battered old pick-up. One of them was Charlie, and I could see Bubba nearby. Standing beside the driver's door, a wild-eyed man was speaking fast, his deep-set and nervous eyes flitting about beneath his cap. He was pale and dirty, and his monologue was constantly interrupted as he slapped and swatted at flies and mosquitoes, which seemed to be bothering him more than anyone else.

'I really need some help with my place,' he drawled in a rough Southern accent. 'It's gonna fall into the lake and I kinda need to sort out my pilings. Can you help me Charlie?'

'I ain't sure what I can do,' Charlie shrugged. 'I'm just real busy right now . . .'

The man interrupted, a look of desperation in his eyes. 'Can ya just come an' see?'

Charlie gave me an almost imperceptible wink. 'Okay, I'll come and have a look. You come along too Guy.'

We jumped into the back of the old vehicle and rumbled along the dirt road through the village. We reached a jumble of plywood and tin hovels set below a grove of dark spruce trees. The air was heavy with heat, fetid and swarming with biting insects. The man stumbled out of the pickup and led us to his house, which was really a windowless wooden box standing on stilts overlooking a dark, stagnant lake. The stilts on the downward side of the slope were in a state of collapse, and the whole rotting box seemed about to slide into oblivion. The man frantically explained the all-too obvious problem to Charlie, who listened patiently. He then led us up the stairs and into his house, which was dark and smelt bad. I saw a pile of dirty dishes in a bucket, a cracked full-length mirror and papers of every kind lay strewn across the floor. In a corner were stacked boxes of beer. As the man talked to us from the darkness of his hovel, the light from the doorway made him look even more sickly, his unblinking eyes showing pupils shrunk to the size of pinheads. Behind him, wires hung from every part of the room.

Charlie looked around. 'You gonna stay here for the winter?'

The man nodded. 'Yeah, kinda hoping to.'

There was a silence. 'But this place is gonna go into the lake anytime now, you know that?'

'I know, but could you help me Charlie? Maybe we could figure some kinda payment plan?' He looked at Charlie pleadingly. 'See, I ain't got nothing.'

Charlie sighed. 'I'll see if I can get you some pilings.'

We turned and walked back towards Don's yard. 'Another crazy white man' Charlie mumbled, shaking his head.

I felt like asking if he had me in the same category, but said instead: 'What kind of man is that?'

Charlie shook his head again. 'He's the kind that comes here to die. The kind that drinks until he dies, gets lost in the snow or shoots himself, or worse still someone else.'

I thought again of the many people who had come to Alaska, all caught on the tails of some dream or great plan. 'Have many people come unstuck here?'

Charlie smiled. 'Oh yeah, been many people who died out here and things gone wrong. But not just people on their own – we've seen plenty of companies come here to mine this or that, and they fold up pretty quick too.'

I thought of my dream of building a cabin. 'I imagine you must think I'm pretty dumb to want to build a cabin in the bush.' He pursed his lips and kept walking. I kept my gaze fixed on him: 'I'm just another crazy white guy, hey?'

He laughed, then said, 'Can you smell the air?'

'Yes.'

'Well where are you gonna build a cabin if the woods are burning? And who's gonna help you when we are all trying to get ready for winter ourselves? If you head out there on your own you could die very quick.'

His words hit me like an iron bar. I knew he was right.

'Charlie, would you say I'm in trouble?' I said after a few moments.

'No, not trouble,' he smiled again. 'Just deep shit.'

'Yeah, quite literally,' I muttered. 'I'm up the bloody Yukon without a paddle.'

7
LITTLE VILLAGE ON THE RIVER

Diary entry:
Spoke to a man called 'Sand-Bar' Claude today. Found him hauling a net in beside his little boat. He has no arms – just two long bits of metal with some claws for hands. I saw he had a can of beer in his breast pocket with a long straw in it so that he could take a sip from time to time. We spoke for a while. I admire him. Not sure how he lost his arms – didn't want to ask. Yet he handles a boat, fishes and mooches about with a happy look on his face. Spent the rest of the day knocking golf balls about with Bubba, and feeling very depressed and worried. I think I am heading for disaster.

I spent the next week or so wandering around Galena, and found that although it was rough, it had heart. 'Galena' is the chemical name for lead, and the village began life as a supply point for nearby lead ore mines that opened in 1918 and 1919. In 1920, Athabascans living upriver at the settlement of Louden moved to Galena to sell wood to river steamers and to haul freight for the mine. A school was established in the mid-1920s, and during the Second World War an airfield, the Galena Air Force Station, was built. During the 1950s, the US Air Force developed a base around the airfield to use as an outpost during the Cold War, and the construction of these and other facilities caused the village to grow. Today, the village is home to approximately 675 people, mostly Athabascan, and boasts a shop, a post office and a motley selection of self-built houses. The church is a former jailhouse, which was floated fully assembled downriver from Louden. In 1993 the base was moth-balled, and the empty buildings now sit silent and brooding. Part of the base is home to a residential school, set up to offer children from remote regions a chance to get some education. The year before I arrived in Alaska there had been suicides amongst some of the children, and it was terribly sad to think about their lonely deaths, living in the quarters of former airmen so far from home.

I had made no progress on finding a site where I could build my cabin, and as each day came to an end the chances of achieving my goal before winter seemed more and more remote. One morning, looking for distraction, I went in search of Don, and found him outside the old cabin that served as his workshop. He was welding the edge of a battered launch, wearing just a pair of sunglasses for protection. The sparks poured off the metal, ricocheting occasionally off his tough skin and wiry moustache. Behind him the walls of the cabin were festooned with every kind of tool from lengths of chain and rope to axes, blocks, pipes and anchors. When he stopped I pointed to some grappling hooks. 'What are those for?'

He looked, then bent back over his welding. 'For pulling bodies from the river.'

'Do many people drown in the Yukon?'

'Yeah.' He nodded. 'Many, many people drown in that water, and often we don't even find their bodies.' He stood up with a sigh, and I knew he must have lost people he loved. 'The water is so full of silt that their clothing fills up with sand. They sink real fast and don't always come up again.'

At that moment a pick-up truck swerved into the yard, and a jovial but slightly jaded-looking man stepped from the vehicle, raising a hand in greeting to Don who responded with a teasing grin. 'Hey, Mister Mayor, come and say hello!'

The man came forward with a wide smile. 'You the crazy boy from Scotland?'

'Well, I suppose so . . .' I smiled uncertainly.

Don interrupted: 'This mayor is looking tired 'cause he's been out drinking and dancing for three nights solid.'

The mayor shrugged his shoulders, holding his hands out in mock helplessness. 'Well hey, a man's gotta live . . .'

I told them a (true) story about two island policemen's wives who got into a fight in a Hebridean pub, and how the scuffle grew into a bar brawl when their husbands joined in, until eventually the locals had to make a series of citizen's arrests to bring order. They both laughed, and I thought maybe Alaska and the wilder parts of Scotland weren't so far apart after all.

Later that morning Don found me looking out over the river. I was in despair. There seemed to be no way ahead here, and I was facing the prospect of going somewhere else in Alaska and starting all over again, making contact with new people in an unknown place. I dreaded the thought, and knew it would be impossible. Worst of all options would be to return home with my tail between my legs. Don stood beside me in silence for a moment, and then read my mind: 'Time is going on, and you got a lot to do.'

I shrugged helplessly.

He turned to me with measuring eyes. 'Maybe a guy could build a small trapping cabin somewhere away from the fire.'

My heart leapt at the thought. 'Yes of course – and it could be used by your family when I am gone.'

'Whoa there,' Don took a step back, holding up his hands, 'We have native land allotments and don't need nothing.'

My heart sank: I was on my own again.

'Go speak to Glenn,' Don said, 'he might be able to help you. You can borrow the bike.'

Glenn Stout was the Fish and Game biologist for the region, and is responsible for all matters relating to land use on State land.* I had emailed him from time to time during my research about the Interior, and he had always been helpful. With a heart full of hope I leapt onto the old quadbike and charged down the dirt road towards the small wooden shack that served as his office.

When I arrived at the shack, I swung off the road like a seasoned man of the bush, and aimed the bike at a small porch that ran around the little building, planning to pull up beside it in a satisfying half loop. When I pulled at the brake nothing happened, and I was heading straight towards the building at some speed. 'Bloody hell!' I exclaimed, wrestling with the gears in an attempt to slow down. The bike slowed in a series of unprofessional and violent lurches, until I came to a jolting halt in a cloud of dust inches from the porch. I sat for a moment, regaining my composure, and remembered that Don had warned me the bike had no brakes. The dust cleared and I looked up to see a man peering out of the window. He had witnessed the whole sorry episode. I raised a hand, and he did the same.

Inside Glenn's room I was struck by the sense that I was in the presence of a man from another time. He was a big man with a long drooping moustache, and a face which would not have looked out of place in an old sepia print of a miner in a ten-gallon hat. Shaking my hand, he shyly offered me a plastic chair then sat down behind his cluttered desk. 'Gee, I thought you were just gonna be the type that emails from time to time . . . And now here you are.'

* A map of Alaska showing State and Federal land resembles a colourful mid-Western quilt. Federal land belongs to the nation, whereas State land is specifically meant for and run by Alaskans. Added to this there is a third element, which is Tribal land. Large tribal co-operatives were set up in Alaska to enable indigenous Alaskans to maintain their links with the land, and each indigenous Alaskan has a right to a tribal allotment of around eighty acres.

I nodded slowly, remembering the messages I had sent him, how he had patiently tried to answer my many questions, and felt anew the strangeness of being here. 'I know. Life sometimes moves fast, huh?'

Glenn nodded. A silence fell over us, and I looked around a room hung with maps, bookshelves and a vast, mounted elk head. My gaze finally fell on a series of maps pinned on the wall behind him.

'What part of the Interior is this?'

'21d.'

'21d . . . that's a romantic name. And you are the state's man for this region?'

He nodded.

'How big is it?'

He thought for a while. 'About twenty-nine million acres.'

I looked at him in stunned silence, and he raised his eyebrows almost apologetically. I cleared my throat and got to the point: 'Don and Charlie were planning for me to stay in Don's cabin during the winter, but it's been burnt down. Did you know that?'

'Yeah.' He nodded. 'The fire has been pretty bad this year. The snow will be the only thing to put it out.'

I felt the fear return. 'I am thinking that I would like to build a cabin myself. Can you think of anywhere I could do this?'

He shrugged. 'Well, you are not a resident, and homesteading is over, so I am not sure.'

I took a boiled sweet from a bowl on his desk, feeling hopeless and stupid. Our conversation stuttered along with Glenn patiently answering my questions. When I left he shook my hand, wished me luck and said he would think about what could be done.

I drove slowly back to Don's yard, and found him talking to Charlie. They turned and watched me drive into the yard. 'Bike go okay?' Don asked.

'Yup, no problem,' I replied briskly.

'Uh-huh.' He nodded assessingly, his eyes giving nothing away. 'Now come on into the house: we got an idea for you.'

Inside, beside the window that looked out over the great river, the table was covered in maps. I said hello to Carol, Don's wife, who gave me a guarded greeting, then walked over to join Charlie and Don who were examining the green-coloured maps. Don was tracing a route along a wide braid of the Yukon with his finger, counting off the miles as he did so. My eyes eagerly followed his finger along the ribbon of blue, past a river mouth and a mountain, and on in a series of sensuous curves until it stopped, tapped and held firm.

'A guy could maybe build a cabin here.' Don looked at me.

I kept still, scarcely daring to breathe.

He looked down again, and his finger slid gently from the blue to the green. 'It's all forest below this mountain, and a cabin could maybe go up here by this lake. Might be dried up, might be full – this map is old.' His finger moved over red contours and green until it touched on a silver of blue.

I let my breath out, trying not to get too hopeful. 'How far is it from here?'

'Oh it's about three hours by boat.' Don's eyes stayed on the map. 'You would have to cut portage* from the slough to the site, and of course you would have to clear a good space for the cabin. That portage would have to be good enough to get provisions up, and might even become your trail in winter. When winter comes you'd need to break a good trail up the slough to the Yukon, otherwise you'd be cut off completely. You'd have to keep that trail in good shape too or else it would be blown away. For now though you could use the river – that would be your road and you'd just have to hope that ice-up don't come too soon this year.'

I glanced over at Charlie, who raised an eyebrow as if throwing up a challenge, and then sat down, feeling faint with excitement and hope. 'And what then?'

Don threw Charlie a look that was a mixture of frustration and amusement. 'Then you fell trees, cut logs, peel 'em and build a cabin before winter shuts everything down.'

---

* Portage is the name for a working trail cut into trackless land and used to haul goods. Slough is another word for braid, as the river diverts around islands and forms a side channel.

I sat in silence, as the enormity of the task that I had so boldly taken on sank in. Then a thought struck me: 'But will I be allowed to build a cabin here? Do I have to get permission.'

'Well . . .' Don thought for a moment. 'You'll have to talk to Glenn about it, but it should be okay.' He paused, and then continued: 'Now, time ain't on your side. And I got a feeling you ain't got no idea how to build a cabin. Am I right?'

I nodded.

'How about picking the right trees for the job?'

I held up open hands.

There was silence in the room, and behind me Carol let out a cough. Charlie glanced at her, then said directly to Don: 'This is crazy. He's gonna kill himself.'

Don sat down, looking at the map in silence, and I knew he was wrestling with a range of contradictory thoughts. He looked up at me, his wise eyes again seeming to size me up. A fast boat skimmed past the window, leaving a wash that glittered silver in the afternoon sun. Charlie and Don both watched it pass, their eyes registering the engine, the boat and the driver. Then Don looked again at Charlie: 'We'll head down the river tomorrow and see if the woods is good enough for building in that part.'

Charlie nodded slowly, and then looked at me with what I was sure was thinly veiled contempt. Don folded the map and pointed it at me sternly. 'You got very little time,' he said. 'It's gonna make life hard for you, 'cause ice up is not far away and you got no experience. You can never tell how long Mother Nature is gonna give you. A month? Maybe two? I'd say you got two months at the outside.'

'I'm sure I can do it – I have no choice.' I tried to sound confident, rather than desperate. 'I've given up everything at home, and my family and future depend on it.'

'You know,' Don said, 'that is one thing that might just make the difference. When men have built a cabin at this – the wrong time of year – they have only done so 'cause they have no other choice. Sometimes no choice is what you need in the bush. Now you're gonna need to work boy, harder than you might think, and in a place where a small accident or mistake will kill you quick.'

He stopped, and we sat in silence for a moment.

'You better keep it together out there. First thing though is to see if the site will be good enough, and then you gonna have to cut that portage. We will lend you tools and a boat, just as long as you pay for fuel.'

I was lost for words. I felt so grateful that fate had led me to these amazing people, as it was clear that without them I would have very little chance of making it work. Even with their help, the odds seemed to be stacked against me. I stood up, feeling dizzy with relief. I had a long way to go, but at least some kind of path was opening up ahead.

'Don, thank you for this, I cannot say how grateful . . .'

'Hey, don't thank me yet,' he held up a hand, 'we don't even know what it's like on the ground. Let's just hope the place works out, and that you can do it in time, 'cause it gets real cold here.'

'How cold?'

Charlie said, 'A few years back we went to minus eighty before wind-chill.' He seemed to savour the words.

I looked at Don, and he nodded in agreement. 'You can't beat the winter here – ever – and you shouldn't even try. A guy has just gotta pray and work hard and carefully. Even then he might find himself beat.'

A silence descended, and we all stared out the window as a raven landed on Shorty's dog house. My superstitious heart sank at the sight of the big, black, glossy bird, and I imagined a demonic chorus in Latin. Behind us in the kitchen Carol moved about quietly, and I wondered what she must be thinking. Then I remembered Don telling me she had grown up in a rough mining village called Ruby, a place where fortunes were won and lost and hopeful men from all over the world lived and died in almost every way imaginable. She must have seen it all before. Mumbling goodbyes, I stepped out of the cabin and headed towards my shack, just as Don's little dog Pancho charged at the raven, forcing it to lift into the air where it hovered, flapping, as the stocky dog barked and leapt beneath it. The black bird's feathers rippled in the breeze and it fluttered off towards some willow trees beside the river, pursued by Pancho, determined to drive the gurgling black bird from Don's yard. Behind me I heard the cabin door swing open, and Don stepped out on to the porch, raising his arm and motioning for me to come over. I walked back and stood looking up, feeling as if I was receiving orders from the bridge of a warship.

'Guy – you, me and Charlie will head downriver tomorrow and see if the site's suitable.'

'Thanks, Don. You know, I wouldn't be able to do any of this without you.'

He smiled. 'You ain't done nothing yet. And let's see what you think of the bush . . .' he paused: 'Once you're in it.' I said nothing and he kept looking at me, sizing me up as always. Then a thought came to him. 'You know there are plenty bears in the Interior, don't you?'

I nodded, my brain immediately supplying a range of terrifying images of bears and their attacks upon people.

'Are they really that dangerous?'

'Sometimes, sometimes not. They're unpredictable and so you must be ready to look after yourself. In the bush we carry guns, and if you really want to stay out there you're gonna need a gun that can protect you as well as something for hunting.'

'What do you suggest?'

He shrugged. 'We'll just wait and see what comes along, but I can tell you now that a .22 will become a work horse for you – specially for chicken.'

'Chicken?'

'Oh, excuse me,' he laughed, 'what do you limeys call 'em . . . grouse?'

'Grouse – in the bush?'

'Oh, sure. Spruce grouse you find in the tops of trees – they give good meat until fall, and after that taste kinda resiny. Then there's willow grouse that hang about on the sandbars and in birch and willow thickets. We call 'em chicken 'cause they taste good and they're plentiful.'

'Will I be able to hunt these for the pot?'

'Well, sure,' he chuckled. 'Now you be here good and early tomorrow.'

The door shut behind him and I stood quite still for a few moments. I could hardly believe that in the past five minutes I had discussed bears, subsistence hunting and two different kinds of edible bird. This was why I had come, and suddenly it seemed as though my dream was becoming a reality. As I settled down for the night I thought again of my remarkable luck in coming across Don and his family. I realised too that my ideas of venturing out utterly alone and without help into the wilderness, fondly held from the safety of the UK, were artificial, and moreover arrogant and foolhardy. Now more than at any other point in my life I had to practise humility, and try to learn all I could from these people with their vast knowledge and experience. Of the early settlers, prospectors and trappers who travelled into the wild, the ones that did so most successfully relied upon the help and knowledge of those who had lived there previously, as well as the indigenous people of the region. The Lewis and Clark expedition, for example, which ventured throughout the north and west of the USA in the early nineteenth century, relied on beaver trappers as guides through the network of streams and rivers that became their highways.* In the depths of winter I would be on my own for long periods, so I had to soak up every crumb of knowledge while I had the chance. Although there were vast swathes of wilderness that had no name, there was a label for just about every kind of person who lived in or visited the wild, lonely Interior, and mine was 'tenderfoot'. Out of curiosity I looked it up:

> '*A newly arrived immigrant . . . unused to the hardships of pioneer life; a greenhorn. More widely, a raw inexperienced person.*'

I was the living embodiment of the term.

* In 1803 President Thomas Jefferson sent his secretary, Meriwether Lewis, and Lewis's friend, William Clark, on a mission to explore the uncharted land west of the Mississippi River. He called the expeditionary group the Corps of Discovery, and over the next four years they travelled thousands of miles, experiencing lands, rivers and peoples that no Americans ever had before.

8
OLD MAN YUKON

A river without islands is like a woman without hair.
MARK TWAIN

The next morning dawned bright and clear, as if the gods had decided to give the new boy an easy start. I found Don standing outside the golden cabin looking up at the sky. 'Gonna be a good day for looking about.' He pointed to the beach: 'Boat's down there – let's head on down and wait for Charlie.'

We turned and walked through a little grove of birch towards the beach. Behind us, Shorty lollopped along, growling playfully with Pancho, who stank of river mud in which he had been rolling for most of the morning. Don stopped and tightened his belt, where he carried a .44 magnum revolver and extra rounds held in leather loops.

'That looks like quite a cannon,' I said.

He patted the gun. 'Pretty much useless if a bear was actually after me – not much can help in that case, whatever you might have. Them critters move like cats.'

'Lovely.' I nodded sarcastically.

'Can't believe I'm heading downriver with a man that says "lovely",' Don chuckled.

'And I can't believe that a .44 is pretty much useless.'

'Better than a stick.' We both laughed, and I felt the tentative beginnings of friendship.

Don's beach lay in a little indent in the river bank, and water swirled in a deep eddy behind us. After some time Charlie arrived, nodding a curt greeting. He and Don climbed into a sturdy aluminium launch, which I pushed off the beach before scrambling in. Charlie nursed it out into the main stream and then applied the power. The 240 horse power outboard propelled the launch on to a fast plane. We skimmed over the brown water and I looked back as the little riverside village gradually disappeared.

The treacherous nature of the Yukon began to be revealed as we travelled downstream. The river was laced with shoals, and Charlie guided the launch skilfully, taking care to pick a route that would keep us from running aground. He steered the boat close to cut banks, avoiding the parts of the river where beaches ran gently down to the water, where it would be shallow. My nostrils caught the sharp scent of fire, and I looked up to see a treeless and charred landscape. Don shouted something to me, pointing into the woods, and although I could not hear him over the roar of the engine his meaning was clear: the fire was still alive.

As well as watching out for shallows, we had to look out for 'snags', which are the remains of flood-shattered trees that have been thrust deep into the river bed. The strong current pulls the tops of these trees to the surface of the river, where they rise up at a sharp angle, ready to catch the bow of a boat and hold it until the vessel broaches in the swift current and is sucked under. Often snags remain lurking just beneath the fast-flowing surface, ready to sheer off props or overturn a boat. An exposed snag often reveals itself through its movement, wagging in the current, rising up and down as if trying to lure passers by. An experienced river man, which Charlie certainly was, would also keep an eye out for any slight break in the shape of the flow on the route ahead, because this might indicate a submerged snag. During the course of our long journey, Charlie regularly swerved off course when he spotted a danger ahead.

After threading our way past a few large islands in the stream, we turned off the main channel and slipped into a slough that led off to the south. So great was the contrast between the Yukon and its offshoot, it felt as if we had left the ocean and made passage into a river. Yet even the slough – as wide as the Thames in central London – was still formidable, and the same principles of navigation applied. We swerved from cut bank to cut bank, following as best as we could the route of the main current. Now at last I saw trees and scrub that had been untouched by fire, and the higher ground was clothed in great swathes of white spruce trees which stood in rank upon dark green rank. Closer to the water, beds of willow formed a dense undulating curtain of green. Don pointed to what appeared to be an area of stunted growth, shouting: 'Moose been browsing there – them moose sure love willow!' I looked closer and saw the lighter tips of the browsed osiers, white bark showing through where the plants had been neatly pruned.

The slough took us on a sinuous course, deeper and deeper into the wilderness. Every now and then we would pass the mouth of a small creek, and Don would crane his neck to look up the channels. Occasionally he would point, and I would catch sight of an immense moose standing up to its hocks in grey mud, staring as we passed, or a cow and calf lumbering into the bush, their eyes rolling white as the sound of our engine invaded the silence. The slough meandered on and on, and we threaded our way past sand bars and snags and through areas where little tear-shaped islands of willow had formed. It seemed like a lifetime since we had left the village, and I sat in silence, drinking it all in.

Eight miles after leaving the Yukon we rounded a bend, and the slough straightened. Ahead we saw a rounded mountain that glowered over the water, its flanks covered in great stands of white spruce. 'That's Pilot Mountain,' Don shouted. He pointed to the southern bank of the slough, towards a good-sized river mouth: 'That's Bishop Creek – it's gonna be good for fishing and not bad

for water too – see.' He pointed at the two-tone water opposite the
river mouth, where clear, peaty river water met the silty water of
the Yukon. The slough curved around Pilot Mountain and we
passed a large sandbar and beach, before slowing to dodge a series
of treacherous snags that reminded me of giant punji sticks. I
looked ahead and saw that the slough seemed to run on a straighter
course, with cut banks on the south side and a large wooded sand
bar to the north.

Don pointed to the southern bank, and Charlie steered for it,
driving the flat front of the launch onto a black sand shelf. Don
stepped out of the boat, and tied the painter to a tree that lay
submerged in the dark sand. The engine was cut, and there was
silence. I looked upstream, and judged that the slough had a
current of maybe four to five knots, and was clearly almost as
mean as the main channel. Charlie pulled off his windproof jacket
and reached down to lift a heavy calibre rifle onto his back. I
rummaged around in my bag, all the while looking out over the
slough as if hoping for a sight of something familiar. I pulled my
pack on, turned to look up the steep cut bank and saw nothing:
Don and Charlie were gone.

'You bastards!' I thought, suspecting that they were subject-
ing me to a little test. I stepped off the launch and followed
their tracks in the muddy sand until I reached the forested edge
of the bank. The bank edge was at my waist level, and beyond
lay a tangle of thick bush above which tall balsam poplar, or
cottonwood, soared. I felt a jangle of nerves as I realised that I
could not see where they had gone. I looked about, feeling
embarrassed already by the possibility that they might have to
come and get me, until I saw something familiar: a dainty strip
of bright red marker tape, fluttering from the bough of an alder
tree. I pulled myself up on to the ledge and walked in, pushing
through sharp rose bushes and dainty clumps of red berries
which resembled deadly nightshade. So thick was the undergrowth that I could not see more than a few feet in either
direction. But ahead I saw another length of tape, and so, like a
child following a trail of sweets, I moved further into the bush.

The mineral scent of the river was gone, and the air was thick with the smell of bark, rotting vegetation and greenery. I kept pushing through low-lying bush, willow and alder, following the tapes and trying not to think about what I might do if I came face to face with a bear, as I had neither a gun nor a stick. Suddenly I heard a slashing sound followed by a sharp clang. I strained my eyes, and saw a glimpse of Don through the trees, deftly cutting at the vegetal wall with a very useful-looking tool that I had never seen before. He turned to watch as I pushed my way towards him: 'Charlie has gone up ahead. We've found a game trail that'll lead to that lake.' He stood still for a moment, then turned away with his hands on his hips. 'I love these woods – woulda stayed out but for the family.' He held up his cutting tool: 'You better learn to use one of these right – called a Sandvik. When you start cutting your portage you're gonna need one of these.' He turned and slashed through an obstructive branch the size of a man's forearm in a single cut, and then passed the tool to me: 'Now you go.'

I aimed and struck forcefully at another branch, only to hear the blade tinkle theatrically out of its slot and into the leaves as the branch swung away. I dropped to my knees and started searching for the blade. From the undergrowth, I heard Don laughing. 'Guy, you're gonna have a tough time.'

I stood up, holding the recovered blade, and said with some irritation: 'And do you know of many beginners who do everything right?'

He leaned back and gave me a mock-offended look. 'Well, come to think of it, no.'

I fumbled around, trying to slot the blade back into the handle, before two tough old hands took both articles away and deftly put the tool together again. 'This is how you do it – get your angle before you make the slash, and cut low, so that you don't leave a spear at eye level. When you come down this trail in the winter or travel along at night you don't want to get stabbed in the eye.' He passed me the tool and I tried again, this time doing exactly as he said. To my surprise it worked first time. I looked up proudly, expecting approval, but Don's face showed nothing but barely detectable amusement. He was starting to enjoy himself.

A few minutes later we were on our way, following the narrow trail deeper into the woods. Having passed through the bank-side tangle, predominantly made up of willow and alder, I was now standing with bushes up to my armpits beneath the majestic grey trunks of a long strip of cottonwood trees. The trail twisted between the trunks, and above I could see shimmering poplar leaves set against a blue sky. The trees filled the air with the rich scent of balsam, and looked as if they had been planted in an ordered design.

After winding through the trees for a few hundred yards the trail turned south, becoming gradually steeper. As we climbed, the vegetation changed, and we soon found ourselves pushing through a great tangle of alder, willow and every type of birch. The low-lying bushes, mainly roses and high-bush cranberry,* became thick and virtually impenetrable. I stopped at the point where one vegetal regime took over from the other, and Don, reading my thoughts, said: 'Now see – in this country it gets warmer the higher you get. That river down there is where all the cold air flows, so when you step up from that cold sink you get more plants.'

I stared into the impenetrable new layer of plants, and a shiver of fear passed through me. 'There are bears here, aren't there?'

'Well sure,' Don nodded, 'and they'll know you're here, just like all the animals will. They'll see you a long time before you see them – if you see them.'

I looked around, wondering about the odds of being eaten by a bear. 'Not a good way to go is it?'

Don laughed. 'No, them critters take their time over it. Still, no point worrying too much. If you're being hunted by a bear then you ain't got no chance anyway, so just relax. And when you get yourself a gun don't go around all jumpy with it, 'cause you'll kill yourself or worse still someone else.'

I snatched at a mosquito. 'Have you seen people get shot?'

* High-bush cranberry has bright red berries and commonly grows beneath cottonwoods. It is a favourite snack for bears.

'Oh, I seen plenty of dead men.' Don turned and walked on. 'So has Charlie – while back a nervous city boy killed his brother.'

'God, that's terrible – I'm so sorry.'

'Yeah. Kid left a round in the breach and thought his safety could be relied on.'

We walked on in silence until I noticed a large mound of blackened faeces dotted with red berries. 'Don, what's this?'

He didn't turn to look – clearly he'd noticed it already. 'Bear.'

'How old?'

'Yesterday.'

I swallowed, and said nothing.

We had now been walking for around twenty minutes, and the trail had taken us higher, into another change of plants and terrain. The air around us held the deep and complex scent of white spruce. Don stopped and pointed up at a perfect swaying tree: 'Now that is a fine spruce. See how straight the timber is? This is where you'll get the wood to build your cabin.' He turned slowly and looked around. 'Yeah, some good wood here for building and good firewood too.' He pointed to a dead spruce tree with no branches that looked like a large, knotty flagpole. It had been bleached grey by the sun and was perfectly air-dried. 'If you manage to get it together out here you are gonna learn to love standing dead spruce, 'cause it burns better than any wood on earth. Mix it with some green wood like birch, willow or alder, and your stove ain't never gonna let you down.'

I felt excitement at the thought of a stove crackling away in my log home, but then the thought turned to anxiety as I remembered how far I had to go before I reached that point. 'What about those cottonwood trees?' I asked. 'Can you use them for building?'

Don shook his head in humorous contempt: 'Why do you think we call 'em cottonwood?'

'Oh right, yes . . .'

' 'Cause the wood's like cotton, dummy. Sometimes the wood can be good to burn if it's standing and dead and the bark has gone. Wood burns real hot but leaves a lot of ash.'

'Does it have any use for building?'

'Yeah, it grows on land where there ain't no layer of permafrost, so it tells you that the foundations will be okay. And you'll use young cottonwood to catch beaver – that's where the tree comes in handy.'

'Beaver!' I exclaimed, and Davy Crockett strode into my imagination.

'Yup. Makes pretty good eating too.'

'How does it taste?'

'Oh it's just . . . kinda like beaver.'

'Like chicken maybe?' I suggested hopefully.

'Nope, it tastes like beaver. And the meat is good and fat.'

'Oh good,' I mumbled, thinking of my medical kit which was well stocked up with antacid tablets – it looked like I'd be needing them.

We had now left the spruce and passed into another layer of alder, birch and willow as the trail descended again. To my eye it was often barely discernible, but Don seemed to follow it effortlessly. He pointed to a depression in the leaves and grass, and said over his shoulder: 'Bear bed.'

'Oh great – now that's good news,' I muttered.

Don chuckled and strode on. I turned and looked behind me at the thick vegetation, wondering if I'd ever be able to find my way back. I felt like Hansel and Gretel, being led off to be abandoned in the woods, and as each step took me deeper into the unknown I wondered if I should be dropping a trail of stones.

The thin game trail petered out through a thicket of birch and we descended over undulating ground before coming out through an opening in the woods. We entered a sunken open area that was overgrown with thick white grass and isolated stands of willow. To the west it ran as far as I could see, bounded on either side by forest. The contrast between this and the woodland was eerie. 'Grass lake,' Don said. 'Held water once – now it holds grass. He pointed down at some deep prints in the trail: 'Bull moose, maybe thousand pounds in weight or more.'

I knelt and touched the deep print. 'Amazing . . .'

Don gave the print a nudge with his boot. 'Yeah, them moose is great eating, but you know they kill more people than bears in this country – specially in fall when they're in rut.'

I stood up and gave him a twisted smile. 'Is the punchline always "kill" in this place?'

' 'Fraid so.' Don tilted his head sadly. 'There's a lot of death around here. Froze, drowned, got eaten, shot himself . . . there's a lot of ways to die in Alaska.'

We crossed through the strange white grass and gnarled willow of the thin grass lake, and then pushed up a steep hill towards another stand of white spruce. Here we met Charlie, who raised his chin in greeting to me before turning to Don: 'This looks like good wood too.'

Don nodded and looked up, rubbing his grizzled chin. 'Yeah, these trees are good – kinda sheltered here, so they ain't got too much of a bow in them. How far is that lake now? Must be pretty close, huh?'

Charlie nodded. 'Five minute walk.'

They turned and walked on and I stared up at the beautiful trees, mesmerised by their tops swaying in the gentle breeze and the contrast between the rich green of their leaves and the rusty gold of their cones. When I looked down again I had to spend a moment locating the route ahead. My mind was still struggling to find shape, contrast and direction amidst the alien tangle of vegetation. I found the men standing on a little ridge, covered in thick vegetation and a few towering spruce trees. Don pointed a stick ahead: 'Lake'll be through there.'

We pushed through the undergrowth, and then, like free divers surfacing for air, popped out of the woods on to a carpet of luxuriant green grass which ran down to a narrow lake. The lake stood forty yards away, and looked approximately half a mile long with an uneven shore. The far bank was richly carpeted in reddish moss, roses and towering white spruce, and beyond I could see the shoulders of Pilot Mountain. We had been walking for about forty minutes since we left the river, but had probably only travelled around two miles. The blue sky lit the glassy surface of the lake, and the tall trees along the ridge reflected out across the water.

There was something mysterious and timeless about it, and I couldn't believe that this lost world would soon be my home.

I stepped cautiously forward and the grass sagged with my weight, dark water gurgling around my boots. Looking west, my gaze followed the length of the slender lake to where it culminated in a fresh green bed of reeds and what looked like a dam of fallen trees. To the east the lake widened slightly and then seemed to soak away into a low-lying area of scrub and mud interspersed with fallen trees. Don pointed to a substantial mound of mud and branches that stood about halfway up the lake: 'Beaver house and pretty big. Be about ten of them varmints in there.'

I looked at the grey brown mound and was struck by the strangeness of the turn that my life had taken, that I was actually having a serious conversation about beavers. 'Are they really good eating?'

'Oh yeah – you're gonna need to eat beaver.'

I looked back at the woods from which we had emerged. 'So you think the cabin could be built up there?'

'Yup – but that water sure don't look too good. Full of beaver and otter piss and shit.'

I looked at the dark still water and then remembered my water purifier that I had brought all the way from Scotland. 'Oh, I've got something for purifying water.'

'Oh yeah – how much can it do in one go?'

'Um . . .' my mind strained to recall the instructions. 'One litre, I think.'

I could see he wasn't impressed, but he said nothing, perhaps worried about further denting my morale. Instead he changed the subject: 'Okay, so you gotta put your tent up quick as you can and cut a way from the river to here. Then you can clear your site and begin building the cabin.' He paused to watch a gust of wind moving down the lake, rippling the water darkly, before turning back to me: 'And you got very little time.'

I looked over at Charlie, and I could see that he held little belief that the tenderfoot could do it. At that moment I couldn't help agreeing with him. Don looked at the sky: 'We gotta go, it's getting late. We'll talk once we've slept on it.' And with that the old frontiersman turned and slipped back into the woods, with Charlie and I falling into step behind him. As we walked back I looked into the darkening and silent woods, trying to imagine what it would be like to be here on my own. Shadows fell behind me as I walked. I pulled up the zipper on my jacket, shaking myself to dispel the fear.

9

THE TIME IS COMING

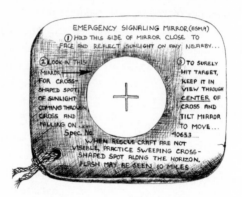

In the half light of the evening we at last pulled the launch up on to Don's beach. Charlie said his goodbyes and I walked with Don towards his cabin. We stopped and looked out over the wide river, Shorty leaning his huge head against Don's waist while Pancho nipped and darted around our feet. I told Don that I was still determined to build the cabin, despite the obstacles that lay ahead. He listened in silence, and then said: 'You gonna come and have dinner with me and Carol tonight – come over in twenty minutes.'

That night we ate a beautiful meal of moose ribs, cornbread and beans. Carol was welcoming, but I sensed she was still wary. We talked about the river, and she told me the tragic story of the night when she lost many members of her family when their boat capsized in the river. Whether in winter or summer, the Yukon was the cause of many deaths – on boats, snow machines, sled dogs or on foot. I thought of the sinister, silty stream, and all the lives it had claimed, and hoped I wouldn't be added to the list. We sat eating in silence for a while, then Don pushed back his chair: 'That place is gonna work out fine for you,' he said. 'It's got everything you need – okay water, wood for building and burning, and it's also close enough for you to get on to the river for travel when the ice comes. You better check in with Glenn tomorrow to see if it's okay, then get in some supplies and get on downriver soon as you can. We'll lend you a boat and tools and let's see how you get on. Now you better get some sleep and get ready to work, 'cause cabins don't build themselves.'

I walked slowly back to my little shack, and sat on the step outside, thinking of the many tests that lay ahead, and feeling singularly ill prepared. The basics of knowledge Charlie and Don took for granted: that I could get the launch down the Yukon myself, avoid the hazards that lay on the way and find the beach where the trail started. They were also confidently expecting me to defend myself against bears and moose and set up camp and find water and food. All this was challenging enough for someone who had never gone beyond basic camping in my own safe country with a nylon tent. This however was just a starting point for the real task of building a cabin – something that called for technical ability and skills which I didn't possess.

After pondering on the sheer impossibility of the task my thoughts turned to home. Juliet and I had agreed before I left that we would try to speak once a week. Even though a week had not passed since our last conversation, I knew I might not get a chance to call for a while. I burrowed about until I found my Inmarsat satellite phone, and hooked the whole thing together on the bluff overlooking the river, waving the dish about in an attempt to get a signal like some kind of 1960s agent. The phone registered nothing and I began to feel very alone, until I heard a little beep that told me that the dish had caught the beam of a satellite hovering above the Pacific. I steadied the dish, sat down, then dialled the number of my parents-in-law's house, where Juliet and the children were staying.

'Hello?' It was early morning in Scotland and Juliet sounded sleepy.

'Julsie, it's me.'

There was a pause as the signal battled to reach me clearly, bending over the earth's shoulder. 'Guy!' I heard tearful joy in her voice, and imagined her sitting up in her warm bed. We spoke for a while, she in the sunlight and me in darkness beside the river, and then I heard Oscar asking to speak to his dad.

'Hello my big boy.'

'Dad?'

'How is everything? Tell me what you've been doing.' I worked hard to hear him above the static beeps and interference, but his voice was so fine and high that I could barely make it out. 'Try to speak a little bit louder Oscar, can you do that?'

He tried, and I managed to follow most of what he was saying about living on the Isle of Mull, going to a new nursery school and making friends. It was painful to hear of this life that I was not a part of, but I was relieved that he sounded happy and well. After a while I looked at the call timer and told him it was time to go. 'Okay biggest boy – I am so glad things are going well for you and Luke and Mummy. It sounds like you are being very brave.'

'Daddy?' I heard a new note enter his voice.

'Yes.'

'What are you going to do now?'

I told him that I was going to make some tea and go to bed.

'Daddy?'

'Yes big boy.' I knew he was prolonging the call, trying to keep me talking just a bit longer, and my heart sank as I realised that my intelligent and sensitive son was missing me in a way that was far deeper than I had allowed myself to predict.

'Have you seen any bears yet?'

'Not yet darling – and I hope I don't.' I tried to sound cheery and positive. 'Now, can I speak to Mummy?'

The line went quiet. 'Oscar? Are you there?'

'Yes Dad.' His voice sounded very small now, and I knew he was wrestling with emotions that were too big for him.

'Big boy, can I speak to Mummy now?'

'Yes Daddy, here she is.'

'I love you Oscar.'

'I love you Daddy.'

Juliet came onto the line. 'Hi Guy.' Her voice sounded flat and sad.

'Is he okay?'

'Not really.'

I heard sobs in the background. 'Is that him? Is he crying?'

'Yes. He's gone to his room now – I'd better go after him. We'll talk later.'

The line went dead.

I replaced the handset and sat in the darkness, swamped by a feeling of powerlessness. When a child is hurting you hug and kiss and reassure, and it was agony for me to be so far away. My relationship with my children had always been close, and I thought of the generations of fathers before me, and how, maybe out of necessity, their relationships with their children were often distant. At one year old Luke was too young to feel his father's absence, but Oscar was really suffering, and seeing him suffer was making it even harder for Juliet. She was fighting conflicting emotions too – although she supported me, I knew she was coping with a lot and must feel resentful. As I watched the phone shut down and saw the little green display fade into black, I felt an all-too familiar welling of sadness and loneliness, mingled with fear. Just then I heard Don's door opening, and his footsteps approaching.

'Hey, you out there?'

'Yeah.' I gave my face a rub and started packing the phone away. 'Just making a call.'

Don pointed at the phone. 'You're gonna have to use that indoors later on, 'cause in the winter it'll just freeze and crack.'

I looked at the phone and its attached dish, wondering whether it was all going to work. As well as contact with home, I was also planning to hook it up to my laptop to send my weekly column to *The Scotsman* by email.

He turned to walk back, then stopped as if remembering the original purpose of his visit. 'Man needs a dog in the bush – it'll keep you company and help you look out for bears. Charlie's got a dog chained up in his yard. Why don't you take him?'

I remembered the yapping dog that I had encountered on my visits to Charlie's yard. I wasn't a big fan of dogs – I had always been more of a cat person – and this dog seemed particularly hopeless, but I couldn't deny the logic of having an animal with a very powerful nose on one's side in the bush. 'Well . . .' I looked up at Don and nodded. 'Do you think Charlie would mind?'

Don shook his head – he was already thinking of other things. 'And you're gonna need two types of gun out there. One for getting food and another for making sure you don't become food. Can you shoot?'

'I've used a shotgun.'

Don nodded. 'Well, if you can point with a shotgun that's good. Before you go we'll think about what you take for protection, 'cause bears are unpredictable and you will be on your own out there just when they're getting ready for winter.' He turned to go.

'Don?'

'Yep?' He turned back towards me.

'Do you . . .' I hesitated, feeling vulnerable. 'Do you think I can do it?'

'Well, if you can't, you may as well find out now as later,' he said shortly. He paused as if he was going to say more, but then decided not to. 'Goodnight.' He disappeared into the darkness with his usual escorts, Shorty and Pancho, by his side.

I folded into my little wooden bed and lay with my eyes open, remembering the deep sobs of my oldest boy. Unable to sleep, I set up the phone again and called Juliet. The boys were playing outside and she was able to talk. 'Yeah he's okay now – he's just missing you like I am.'

'I know – I just felt so powerless there. There was nothing I could do, was there?'

'No.' I heard a sigh. 'You are powerless Guy, that's the sad bit right now.' There was a silence as we both felt the eight thousand miles stretch between us.

'Julsie, I'm heading down river tomorrow.'

'On your own this time?'

'Yes.'

Another pause. 'Guy please, please, be careful – we love you so much and we need you to come home.' I heard the anxiety in her voice.

'I will be, don't worry.'

'Are there bears around there?'

'Yeah – saw lots of what they call "bear sign" today.' I decided not to point out that bears were just one of the risks I would face.

'Get a gun.'

'I will. Don's going to sort me out before I go.'

We spoke for a while, then said goodbye. The time for talking, even with my wife and family, was over. The days of judgement had arrived.

10
INTO THE GREAT SILENCE

Early next morning, in Don's shack, I hurriedly placed my maps, compass, GPS and satellite phone in an unbreakable steel ammunition box, stuffed my hiking bag with my outdoor and camping equipment and loaded my medical supplies into another sturdy container. Outside I gathered the larger items: the petrol generator, which I would use for charging my laptop and satellite phone, a large water container and my stove. The stove had six pieces of stovepipe and was bulky to transport, but essential for both cooking and warmth.* Outside I found a wheelbarrow, piled on as much of my gear as I could and made a couple of runs up and down to the beach. At the end of the second run I found Don beside Charlie's launch, stowing two jerry cans of fuel into the bows of the strong little boat. He pointed to a chainsaw that lay beside him: 'You any good with chainsaws?'

'Well, I did use them occasionally back home for cutting firewood.'

* This was a 'four-dog' baffled stove sent to me by Lehman's, a mail-order company specialising in non-electrical hardware.

Don sighed as he lifted the chainsaw into the boat. 'But I'm assuming you haven't felled trees, cut logs, made portages and built cabins?'

'Sadly, no.'

'Well you better be damn careful in everything you do.' He turned and looked at me very seriously. 'Men who work with chainsaws for a living die every year out here. These saws'll kick back and rip into your face if you don't take great care. Don't ever let this bit touch what you're cutting – ever!' He lifted the chainsaw and touched the top section of the saw tip. 'This is the kick-back zone.'

'Right okay, I see it.'

'You're gonna have to work slowly, don't rush. Take time on everything, and think about how each action is gonna turn out. Always second guess yourself, and if it don't feel good don't do it. Just stop and think about it – even leave it and do something else before coming back to sort it out. You are gonna be on your own out there and ain't no-one gonna know if you get into trouble. Take nothing for granted, and don't ever forget that you're a tenderfoot, and you know nothing.'

I nodded, grateful and yet taken aback by the seriousness of the talk.

He turned and placed some more tools into the boat, saying 'Don't ever forget how big and dangerous this land can be. Respect it, and know that you can't ever beat it, just learn to work with it. And when things start to go right get even more careful, 'cause it's when you're off guard that accidents will happen.' He turned and looked at me with his eyebrows raised: 'Goddit?'

'Sure Don,' I looked down at my feet. 'I understand.'

We said nothing for a while, then Don pointed to the bank side where the morning sunlight glinted dully on blued gun metal. 'Now, you're gonna need some protection out there.' We walked over to the driftwood log against which the guns rested. 'Charlie left these for you – you can choose what you want.'

'Hey Don, I really don't feel comfortable taking these, can't I just buy . . .'

A hand cut me off. 'Now this is a pump shotgun. It holds eight rounds in an extended chamber', he passed the heavy and unwieldy gun to me. 'Loaded with buck or bear slug,* it'll give a very big hit at up to fifty yards. Them solid lead bear slugs is rifled and they weigh about five hundred grains apiece.'

'Sounds like a very heavy round.'

'It is – an AK-47 round weighs one eighty grains or so. This slug is heavier and has more stopping power. With a bear, the most important thing to do is to stop him, and often it'll take more than one shot. It's important to think about shot placement though – many a bear has been felled by a 30/30, which fires a very light bullet, but if well aimed through the eye or behind the ear it will kill. Still . . .' he reached over and tapped the gun: 'you don't wanna take any chances, and this will blow straight through him. And that's only one round – you got seven more in the magazine. Right, let's see how you do – take a shot at that stump.'

Trying to look confident, I lifted the gun, fumblingly pumped a round into the breach and fired one slug. It blew a gaping hole through the half-buried stump.

'And again – jack another one in and fire a couple of shots.'

I fired three rounds and in an instant a mess of shattered wood and splinters lay smoking across the black beach. It was a savage tool.

Don nodded in satisfaction. 'Now, you can get a few lighter rounds in there too and use it for hunting duck.' Before he took the gun from me he said: 'Now check the breach – is it empty? We don't use a safety catch in the bush as it's unreliable, and many a "safe" gun that's been dropped has gone off. So you must ensure that your breach is always empty, and then when you need to shoot you jack one in and fire. Much faster than messing about with a

---

* Buckshot are extra large shot, loaded within a shotgun cartridge. Bear slug is a single slug, also loaded within a standard cartridge, which weighs over five hundred grains, and is 'rifled', or cut into a spiral shape which makes it spin as it comes out of the smooth bore of the shotgun, giving it more impact and range. These lethal loads are heavy enough to break bone, and will stop a large animal such as a bear or moose. See Notes for full description of firearms and ammunition used.

safety catch, and safer. So when you're finished you empty that breach. Understand?'

'Yes,' I said, trying to sound more confident than I felt.

'Now this is a 45/70 lever action rifle, and it fires four rounds.' He picked up a very short rifle about as long as a man's arm. It had steel sights and was compact and rugged in design. 'These are real heavy too – about four thirty grains. This has been shortened for the bush and has no scope, just steel sights, so that you can shoot at very close range. Many a hunter has got into trouble with their scope, 'cause when bears or moose come up close all they see is brown. Open sights is the answer, and lever action is good and quick at getting one in the breach and less likely to jam. This one'll shoot with great stopping power at one hundred to one fifty yards or less. Not very long range for a rifle, but we are talking protection here, not hunting.' He passed me the lethal-looking little rifle and pointed at a paper plate that he had nailed to a tree about a hundred yards away. Squinting, I could just see a black dot in the centre. 'Go on' he said. 'Lie down and take a shot.'

More confident this time, I levered a round in, lay down and took aim. The recoil was immense and the rifle roared as a round tore into the sand behind the untouched plate. I lay still, recovering.

Don took the rifle from me. 'Just want to check something,' he muttered. Then he gave it back: 'Okay, try again.'

I steeled myself for another explosion, aimed and pulled the trigger. Instead of the crash I had expected I was even more shocked by a demure click that I took to be a misfire. I rolled over and looked up at a smiling Don.

'Put nothing in for you.'

'Why?'

'Just wanted to know why you missed that target by well over a mile!'

Feeling like a twelve-year-old again, I stood up and passed him the gun. 'Well, any idea?'

'Yup. You're flinching.'

'Do you blame me?'

He passed me the rifle. 'Now lie down again and aim, and listen to me.'

I lay prone again and aimed at the black dot.

'Centre the mark on all of your sights, breathe gently and take your whole finger off that trigger – just leave the last bit of your finger lightly in place, relax it and keep it light.'

I did as he said.

'When you're ready, hold the rifle good and tight into your shoulder, let your breath gently out and don't think of nothing but that target while your finger starts to squeeze that trigger. Don't expect the shot – be surprised when it happens.'

I fired four rounds, and when we strolled over to the target was happy to see that two had knocked the dot out of the centre. Don didn't comment, but said 'Now you better get going. Keep that 45/70 on your back when you're out there. Put some tape or somethin' over the barrel end so you don't get the thing all plugged up.'

'Thanks Don, I am grateful to you.'

'Forget that – I just wish any man luck who is trying to make a go of it out there. You better get to it.'

I placed my belongings into the boat, along with a number of watertight bags and boxes full of food and other provisions. I put in my wall tent, a heavy mass of folded white canvas that would become my home while I was building the cabin.* Finally I lifted in my stove. Although the boat was sixteen foot long there was very little room left.

Don had disappeared up the bank while I was packing, and he returned with the dog that had been chained up in Charlie's yard, barking and jumping by his side. 'Well, here he is.'

---

* On arrival in Alaska I pretty soon realised that the nylon tent which I had brought from the UK would be inadequate for living in for a long period, so on Don's advice bought a 'wall tent', which is what Alaskans use when setting up temporary home in the bush. The tent uses found wood as its support and is designed to contain a stove, making it possible to live in very cold weather.

My heart sank as I looked at the little dog. He was covered in long hair and didn't look at all practical for the bush. As I watched he galloped excitedly up and down the beach, his golden fur flowing in the places where it was not knotted and in clumps. He looked even more hopeless than I remembered. 'What's his name?'

Don turned to look at him – I could see that he shared my misgivings. 'Well, I think the pant-sniffer is called Fuzzy.'

I thought it seemed a suitably silly name for what looked like a very silly dog: 'What sort of dog is he?'

'Half poodle and half golden retriever.'

As if on cue the golden energy-ball stopped his charging and let out a shrill series of barks.

'Certainly sounds like a poodle,' I muttered. 'Well, I'd better get on with it. Fuzzy!' He raced towards me, then got up on his hind legs and pawed at my shirt with a lolling tongue and an adoring look on his face. I patted the side of the boat and commanded: 'Fuzzy, in!' He dropped down on to all fours, and stood looking at me. 'In!' I repeated, patting the boat more forcefully. He turned in a circle, whimpering and pawing at the ground like a diver trying to persuade himself to leap from a great height. 'Get in!' I shouted, stunned that a dog brought up on the Yukon seemed incapable of carrying out this simple task. Still he cringed, unable or unwilling to do as I asked. I threw Don an exasperated look, then bent and bodily lifted the dog into the boat. 'I meant get in the boat, you idiot!'

I gave Don a wave, pushed the boat out into the water then clambered in. As I did so, Fuzzy jumped out again.

'Fuzzy! No! Come here.'

He swam back to the little beach where Don stood with his hands on his hips, laughing. Swearing quietly I grabbed an oar and poled back into the beach, then jumped out and grabbed the now wet and cringing dog. I dumped him back in the boat, this time tying him so he couldn't escape. He jumped and strained at the rope, barking shrilly. 'Shut up, you pain in the arse' I muttered under my breath. I had taken an immediate dislike to the animal, and yet for fear of offending Charlie and Don felt obliged to bring him with me.

The boat wavered about in an eddy beside the beach while I fiddled with the outboard motor, which soon stuttered into life. I twisted the throttle up and aimed the nose towards the centre of the stream, bringing the boat quickly up on to a plane. The breeze pushed firmly against me, and as I moved swiftly downstream I looked back to see Don still standing immobile on the beach. Above him, on the high bluff beside the house, I saw Carol holding an arm up and waving it slowly from side to side. I felt humbled by the kindness they had shown me, and also profoundly grateful that fate had led me to the doorstep of a family who knew so much about the wilderness. I turned now to look downriver, and as I did so thought of the family that Carol had lost to the Yukon. Looking back, I saw her still standing on the bluff, and wondered what she must be thinking.

Hours of journey time lay ahead, and I pulled a map from my breast pocket so I could keep tabs on where I was. I was cutting through the coffee stained water at a good speed, and soon the little village was long behind me. Fuzzy was sitting awkwardly in the bottom of the boat with this back towards me, showing a complete lack of enjoyment as he stared longingly at the distant riverbank. Occasionally he stole a secret look at me before turning quickly back round, his whole body registering his disgust and resentment at his forced abduction. Beyond him my belongings sat in an immense mound covered by a tarpaulin. 'Well, this is it,' I thought grimly: 'I'm on my own.' Moving away from the centre of the stream, I steered the boat towards the far southern bank. The water grew choppy, and short, sharp waves came at us from every direction, slapping hard against the little boat and spraying us with water. With each splash Fuzzy looked even more unhappy, huddling into a ball and shaking himself every so often over-dramatically. His brown eyes were now trained on me resentfully, and he fixed me with a look of contempt mixed with sadness at his predicament. 'Oh, don't start the blame game with me pal,' I muttered, and he turned away with a wounded look, preferring to look sadly out to sea than at his new and awful owner.

On we travelled, further and further downstream, while I concentrated fiercely on looking out for snags and sandbanks. I passed Four Mile Point, so called because it marked a point four miles downstream from Galena. Rounding a bend, I looked along the wide channel ahead and saw four possible routes where the river was heavily braided. I slowed the motor to idle while I looked at the map, trying to figure out the best course, but the swift current kept us moving downstream at five or six knots. I struggled to remember which way Charlie had gone, and looked from the bank to the map and back again, trying to find a landmark. Fuzzy let out a little whimper of anxiety before slumping down lower in the boat: clearly he had no confidence in my abilities as a boatman, and I couldn't blame him.

I finally worked out the route, and powered the launch towards a narrow, deep channel that passed along a cut bank to the south of a willow-clad island. The sun beat down hard and my throat felt parched and dry, but on I sped past sandbars and eddies and vicious snags which waved and bobbed in the stream like the gnarled fingers of foretellers of doom. Ahead the horizon was flat and featureless, reminding me of the English coast line as I had once seen it from a small boat on the North Sea, but at last I saw the distant top of Pilot Mountain looming ahead, giving me a landmark to steer by.

As I passed through the narrow mouth of Pilot Mountain Slough the force of the river was constricted, and the stream raced through the opening like a Scottish riptide, carrying the little boat along like a bath toy. Despite the force of the river, it felt reassuring to be in a narrower stretch of water, and closer to both banks. Still we had eight miles to go, and as we motored deeper and deeper into wild country the stream meandered and twisted as if trying to ensure that I would never find my way back. I slowed down and the engine purred gently, giving me time to look around. The scent of hot vegetation hung in the air, and everything except the swift stream was still and quiet. I passed through a narrow channel around another willow-covered island, and when I rejoined the main stream a great cloud of duck rose from a sandbar.

With fast flapping wings they flew across the water, rising and wheeling down the mouth of a creek. Fuzzy jumped up at the sight of the birds, letting out a series of little yelps. I glanced at the pump shotgun lying in the bottom of the boat, hoping that I would be able to use this cumbersome cannon to shoot the odd duck before they all cleared off for winter.

We passed the mouth of Bishop Creek and moved through an area of cold shadow beneath Pilot Mountain, which towered over the slough. The water grew choppy here as wind funnelled down the mountainside, and then dropped again as we rounded the wide sandbar that had built up on the bend. A bald eagle sat on a gaunt cottonwood tree, staring down at us with a look of haughty disdain. I steered for the far cut bank and motored slowly round the sandbar, and then saw the long, straight stretch where I had stopped with Don and Charlie opening up ahead. 'So far so good,' I muttered to myself, breathing a long sigh of relief. Just then a movement caught my eye. In the shade of some willows that were growing in a dense belt along the sandbar, I saw a large white wolf stand up to look at me, whilst another lay nearby looking on. Both were panting in the heat, but were otherwise still. I glanced down at Fuzzy who had also spotted them, and was letting out a low, threatening growl. Looking back at the bank, I saw that the wolves had gone. My heart beat with excitement at the privilege of seeing such a rare sight. Wolves are exceptionally wary of people, and it was surprising that they had not disappeared long before I rounded the bend in my slow-moving and noisy craft. In my current state of tension and anticipation everything seemed to be imbued with meaning and portent, and I wondered if the rare sight of the two wolves – on my very first day alone in the wilderness – could be read as a sign of some kind. Perhaps welcoming me to live safely amongst the wild things of the woods, or, more ominously, warning me of the dangers to come.

11
FIRST CAMP

If a thing is worth doing, it is worth doing badly.
G.K. CHESTERTON

I steered the little boat towards the black beach, and climbed out on to the sand. With some difficulty, I heaved the launch up the beach and stood staring down into it. The air was hot and humid, and I was immediately surrounded by a cloud of black flies. The boat was so full of kit that it might as well have been a barge, and I thought with dread of the hours of carrying that lay ahead of me. Fuzzy was still sitting in the boat, regarding me balefully. I untied his tether from the bottom of the boat, and he reluctantly clambered out on to the beach. I tied him to a tree, afraid that he might desert me, and then began unloading the boat.

It was when I was heaving my heavy hiking bag on to my back that I caught sight of the bear tracks deeply imprinted in the sand. They were recent – and huge. This was clearly a very big bear, and I had landed in the middle of his beat. Now I was feeling fear as well as exhaustion, and for the first time facing the fact that I had arrived in a place where I could well be overpowered and eaten. I stood staring, loathe to leave the relative safety of the beach, feeling the deep woods looming above me and aware of darkness approaching. 'Get on with it Guy' I muttered, in an attempt to gee myself up, and began climbing up the bank. I dropped my hiking bag on the lip of the bank and then slithered back down to get another load of stuff, and so on until the boat was finally empty. It had taken more time than I expected, and I was already tired and thirsty. After pulling the boat a bit higher up the beach, I made it fast to a tree trunk, untied Fuzzy, and clambered up to where all my belongings were piled. I pushed into the greenery beyond, and with the Sandvik, carefully cleared a little space into which I began to cache my bags and boxes.

Remembering Don's advice that my priority must always be to set up camp before anything else, I sorted my stuff into two piles. One pile could remain stored by the river until tomorrow, and the other would be needed immediately. On to the 'now' pile went the shotgun and rifle, which I leant against a tree, and a blue plastic barrel holding five gallons of drinking water. Next to this I threw my hiking bag and a smaller bag containing water purification equipment, ammunition, matches, tarpaulin and sleeping bag, as well as my heavy canvas tent and stove pipes that weighed well over fifty pounds. Finally I brought over my food boxes and my boy's axe* and saw. Fuzzy had climbed up the bank to join me, and lay slumped beside the generator, jerry cans of petrol, chainsaw oil and assorted tools that made up the 'later' pile. I looked down at the immense pile of stuff that I had to haul along the tiny game trail to the lake, and my heart sank: it must have amounted to nearly three hundred pounds in weight. I loaded the stove, my small bag, the shotgun and the boxes of food into a little plastic toboggan. Using a light length of rope I tied the kit down, hoping that nothing would fall off on the rough trip up to the lake. I heaved the big hiking bag on to my back and slung the 45/70 over my shoulder. One hand was left free to carry the five-gallon water

* A 'boy's axe' is a multipurpose axe with a twenty-four inch wooden handle and a two pound blade.

barrel, and the other to pull the nylon line that towed the heavy toboggan. My life as a human mule had begun.

I turned and walked heavily into the woods, pushing through sharp rose bushes that scratched and tore at my skin whilst lengths of willow bent and slapped into me. The weight of my load pushed my boots deep into the yielding forest floor, making walking difficult, and my hand was already stinging from the tight nylon cord. Sweat began dripping down my chest in ticklish streams, but I pushed on, concentrating so hard that I almost forgot where I was. Then a thought stopped me in my tracks: I had left my fuel supplies sitting on the forest floor, where they were easily within the reach of bears. Bears are powerfully attracted to all petroleum-based products, and are crazy for petrol above all else. If a bear came across my petrol cans it would destroy them and leave them strewn around the forest. I looked at my watch. It was mid-afternoon, and I was already worryingly late for setting up camp, but there was no way around it: I had to make my fuel safe. I slipped out of my straps and put everything down except the 45/70, which remained clattering about on my back, and swearing profusely walked back down the little trail. Don's first lesson had already proved itself: work slowly, and think about how each action is going to turn out – you'll save time in the end. As we turned back towards the river Fuzzy perked up, perhaps thinking that we were heading for home, and trotted ahead.

Back at the river I cast about, looking for a way of getting the jerry cans out of a bear's reach. I'd left my rope back up the trail, and again cursed myself for not planning things better. I sized up a tall and slender birch tree that looked like a bleached flagpole against the dense greenery all around. A boyhood game came to mind, and I saw a way of hoisting the fuel out of the reach of a bear – or at least out of easy reach. All I needed was a way of tying the cans. I scoured around, until my eye fell upon a single dainty white spruce tree which I had read was a good source of cordage. I took my knife and dug away at the base of the tree, pulling up a few good lengths of root. I tied the withes* to the handles of the two

* A withe is a pliant shoot or bough.

fuel cans, leaving a good long tail, then began shimmying up the birch tree. As I got higher the tree began to arch and bend downward, groaning under my 210-pound weight. Birch is famed for having a superb strength to weight ratio, and was thus often used in the past to make aircraft frames, sleds and snowshoes. At about twenty feet the tree sagged down enough for me to reach the cans, and I timber-hitched the withes around the slender trunk, breaking and bending some thin branches so that I could push the can handles on to them for added hold. I then stepped off the tree, and stood back waiting for it to sail into the air. Instead it rose by about ten feet, and then stayed put.

'Oh, for fuck's sake!' I muttered, pulling the tree down again and untying a can. The tree sailed up high, well out of the reach of a bear. I found another tree, and repeated the whole process with the second can and a few plastic bottles of chainsaw oil. I stood back in satisfaction, but then remembered that I still had a long way to go up the trail. My watch confirmed that there wasn't much time before dark. I trudged back up the trail, heaved on my load and continued on my way. Shortly I reached a place where the trail turned uphill, and bent my back to pull hard. Immediately, the sled hit a hummock and overturned, and my inadequate lashings broke free. I stood very still, looking at the upturned sled and its load, which now lay scattered around the bushes. Not even half way there, I put down my hiking bag once more and considered what to do.

Fuzzy, who had been following me unenthusiastically throughout this whole performance, flopped down beside the upturned sled and yawned ostentatiously. Clearly he thought I was totally incompetent, and he didn't mind showing it. All day, it seemed to me, he had been mocking my efforts, and the yawn was the last straw. My tiredness and frustration boiled over, and I said: 'Oh, you think you're so clever don't you – you little shit!' He stood up, his eyes widening as if in realisation that his new owner was not just hopeless but dangerous too, and slunk away, licking his lips and glancing about as if planning possible escape routes. Everything he did seemed overdramatic and done for effect, but I realized that I was using him as a kind of canine stress ball, and held my hands up in acknowledgement: 'Okay, I'm sorry. I'm sorry.' He gave me a wary look, and then sat down again, half in the bushes and half on the tiny trail. With a heavy sigh, I bent to repack the sled. As I did so, I heard the dog yawning again. I froze for a moment, battling to overcome my irritation, and then heard him doing the same thing again – only louder. I whipped round to catch him in the act, and he snapped his jaws shut, looking away innocently. There was silence between us, nothing stirred except the treetops in the light breeze. I turned slowly back to work, but no sooner had I turned my back than I heard him yawning again, and this time there was no doubt: he was deliberately challenging me. I whipped round again and caught him in mid-yawn, his mouth so wide that it seemed he must dislocate his jaw, letting out a theatrical high-pitched whistling sound at the finish. It was the last straw.

'Right, that's it – go away.' I pointed down the trail towards the river. Fuzzy looked balefully back at me, his face registering disbelief.

'Yes, I mean it. Go away now.' He looked along the tiny line of crushed vegetation, then back at me as if to say, 'Shouldn't we talk about this?' I shook my head and continued to point down the trail. He turned and walked slowly away, stopping to look back occasionally as if waiting for me to change my mind. 'Good riddance', I muttered as he sidled out of sight: 'I don't bloody need you around anyway.' And with that man and dog went their separate ways. The trail seemed interminable this time with my heavy load and the toboggan dragging unwillingly behind. The nylon string bit painfully into my hand, and the 45/70 whacked heavily against my side. I thought about pictures that I had seen of heavily armed Israeli farmers at work, and for the first time experienced the practical difficulty of working with a firearm on my shoulder.

Approximately one hour after leaving the river, I crossed the grass lake, struggled up a steep incline and through the second big stand of white spruce. When I finally reached the lake, I walked with relief on to the grass by the lakeside and stood very still for a moment, taking it all in. There was no time to waste, however, as darkness was coming and I couldn't afford to be without shelter overnight. I walked back into the woods, to the thickly forested site where I would build my cabin, then stacked my kit up beneath a spruce tree and looked around for a place to set up my wall tent*. I needed two trees approximately eighteen feet apart that could support my ridgepole, and soon spotted a large white birch tree and a spruce that would do nicely. I cleared a space between them, and then wandered about until I found a young white spruce whose trunk was about seven inches in diameter, which would make a perfect ridgepole. Before I cut it down I used the handle of my axe to knock the small branches off the trunk, and placed them in a little pile†. I then sawed the bare tree down and knocked off the remaining branches. I threaded the spruce pole through the heavy canvas of the tent, and then pulled the unwieldy lump into position between the trees.

As I worked, great grey clouds rolled over and it began to rain. I thought of Fuzzy and felt a pang of guilt. Where was he? The rain grew steadier and began to run down my neck, further lowering my besieged morale. I made a crude ladder out of alder branches and used the rickety affair to reach high enough to tie up each end of the ridgepole. As I did so I darkly imagined the scenario of falling and breaking both ankles. What on earth would I do if I found myself lying on the forest floor, unable to get up? Once again I remembered Don's maxim about working slowly: even a minor accident alone in the bush could spell the end.

The hard work of getting the ridge up had resulted in what looked like a dirty white sheet hanging on a drying line, and the tent still offered nothing approximating shelter. It was getting dark, and I now needed to cut six long, straight birch poles for the frame. I found these easily, quickly stripping off leaves and branches and

---

* Wall tents can be set up freestanding but this is more time-consuming, and requires nine poles. As there were plenty of trees around I was able to take a shortcut, tying the ridgepole between two trees.
† Using the handle of the axe is a good way of removing small branches from a tree, as that way a miss does not result in a blade in one's leg!

leaning two poles in an 'A' shape against the ridge at either end of the tent. Between them, two more were tied at thigh level to run the length of the tent, and the canvas was pulled out and tied firmly to the poles. I then laid the spruce boughs that I had cut earlier on the floor of the tent, creating a home-made sprung floor and a room that was imbued with the scent of resin.

Still I couldn't rest – I needed to set up my stove, which was vital for cooking and warmth. I heaved the heavy stove into the tent, placing it beneath the pre-made chimney hole in the canvas roof. Then I began to shove the sections of stove pipe together, only to discover I didn't have enough pipe to reach clear out of the roof.* I stared up at the roof, trying to think of a solution. Clearly I couldn't make the pipe longer, so the only answer was to raise the stove up higher. I cut a few lengths of spruce, which I hammered into the soft forest floor. Next I hammered some alder lengths on to the tops of the poles to make a rough cradle into which I placed the barrel stove. The stove was now three feet higher and I was able to push the pipes through the hole and clear of the tent. I stepped outside and looked at the shiny tin chimney protruding reassuringly from the roof.

Back inside I flopped down on to the fresh spruce and lay staring up at the canvas, which was shivering with each raindrop. I lay motionless, feeling cold, damp and exhausted. My brain wrestled with all I had to do, and in so little time, and I wanted nothing more than to close my eyes and escape into sleep. But there were still jobs that had to be done, so I forced myself up again.

Outside the rain had stopped and an insipid setting sun threw very little light into the darkness of my campsite. I poured water from the five-gallon drum into a tin bowl and drank heavily, before turning my mind to the evening's chores. With night falling the air was chilly, and the first job was to find wood for the stove. I felled a good-sized birch tree that stood just outside my tent, and set about sawing it into stove-sized logs. I then split the logs on the birch stump, and having built up a good enough pile for the night, cut

---

* Stove pipes must reach higher than the ridgepole, ideally by two feet.

kindling and larger logs from the dry boughs of a fallen white spruce. While I worked the echoes of my axe rang out through the great woods, and I thought of the animals around me, adjusting to the sounds of their new neighbour. I stacked the logs beside the stove, feeling a little safer and more secure with each one added to the pile. I then set about getting the stove ready to light, starting with some strips of bark, adding some thin, pencil-sized twigs and the resiny white spruce boughs, and then finishing with some sweet-smelling 'green' birch. I filled my coffee pot with water from the drum, and placed it on the flat stove surface. Then I rolled a big log in front of the stove to act as a seat.

I sat for a while looking into the pile of tinder and wood, as another rain squall rattled overhead. The smell of rotting leaves and vegetation hung damply around the tent, and despite the fact that it was only the middle of August, it already felt like autumn. 'Be positive' I told myself, as the worries crowded again. This was the first fire at my camp: it was time for a ceremony. I dug out a match, then closed my eyes and sent out a silent appeal to fate: 'Give me strength and luck. Let me come out of this alive'. I lit the roll of birch and watched as it sparked and sputtered into flame, the fire gathering strength as it reached the kindling and logs. Dense white spoke pulled through the wood, and I closed the door of the stove, latching it tightly with the air vent fully open. It was dark outside now, and I pulled down the canvas door flaps, tying the opening shut. The stove was burning beautifully, and it was immensely cheering to feel its warmth. I lit my kerosene lamp and hung it from the ridgepole, enjoying the warm, swinging light. Sheltered from the rain and dark woods outside, I was experiencing an ancient emotion, the feeling of security that comes from fire. For the first time that day, I was beginning to relax.

The stove sides were now red hot, so I threw some green birch into the furnace to slow it down, closing the air vent to a sliver. I then took my wet clothes off, and hung them on a little line near the stove before changing into some comfortable dry clothes ready for sleeping. The kettle was boiling, and I made my first cup of strong, sweet tea. As the hot brew revived me, I pulled a packet of air-dried king salmon from my bag along with a little box of salt, and sat staring into the fire as I ate. When I had finished, I unrolled my heavy sleeping bag and laid it out on the spruce floor, then climbed inside. I lay back, listening to the occasional crack of wood in the stove, and the wind sighing in the swaying trees all around. With each gust the tent shook and creaked, and I couldn't help wondering whether it was going to collapse on top of me.

Gradually my worries drifted away, and my mind turned to my previous life. I thought of my days in the office, and remembered the terrible feeling that my life was slipping away in that awful grey, clerical world. I imagined what I might have been doing at that moment: in the car on my way to work, perhaps, sitting behind my computer or discussing brands or sales plans with some deadpan sales executive. Instead, here I was: in the Alaskan wilderness, facing the biggest challenge of my life. I lay motionless, filled with joy at my escape. This was tempered with sadness at being away from my family, though in the present circumstances I would scarcely have wished them to be with me. Now I was here, I thought how ludicrous it was that we had ever considered doing this together as a family. Even the simple act of getting up to camp had been hard work, and Juliet and the boys would have hated every moment. No, I thought, this was definitely a job for a single man.*

I was so absorbed with my thoughts that I had almost forgotten where I was, until at the back of my consciousness I became aware of a faint sound carried on the wind. I sat bolt upright, glancing over at my rifle leaning with lethal nonchalance in a dark corner of the tent. The wind had been coming in occasional gusts and I strained to hear the noise again. For several minutes there was nothing, and I was just about to brew another cup of tea when I heard it again: the lonesome, unforgettable call of a timber wolf.

* It should be pointed out, however, that indigenous families think nothing of going out into the bush together, and indeed women play a central role in the traditional Athabascan way of life.

My skin prickled, and I suddenly felt very small and vulnerable in my tent, protected only by flimsy canvas. The wolf sounded close, yet I had already learned that here in this realm of silence sound travels a long way. I stood up, picking up the rifle, and stepped out of the tent. There it was again: another long, lilting call that curled up at the end almost as if it was asking a question.

I looked up at the sky and saw a few faint stars as clouds pulled away from a slim crescent moon. I was remembering a conversation I'd had with Don, as we watched Pancho bounding about his yard. 'Them wolves'll sure suck up a dog,' he'd said, 'so quick and quiet that you'd be lucky to even see it. If it's a sled dog at least he's chained to his run, so the wolf's gotta pull him out and you might get a chance to kill him – if you don't shoot your own dog of course.'

I kept looking up at the cold little stars, the conversation replaying in my mind. I thought of Fuzzy, alone and vulnerable in the woods, and cursed myself for sending him off. I stared into the black woods, wondering where the little dog was, and feeling terrible that I had treated him so badly. I cupped my hands and shouted as loudly as I could: 'Fuzzy!' My voice echoed out into the darkness, then disappeared uselessly. 'Fuzzy!' I cried again: 'Fuzzy!' Now I sounded like Gollum, and I stepped out of the circle of light around my tent, walking a little way into the darkness and calling again. I heard nothing, and turned towards the tent, which shone back through the trees. Again I was struck by how fragile it was, and completely inadequate against bad weather, not to mention bears. Telling myself there was nothing I could do about Fuzzy, I went back inside the tent and stoked the stove. My sponsors, Highland Park, had sent me off with as much top quality whisky as I could carry, and I decided it was time for some medication. I poured a generous measure into my tin mug and stood by the fire. As I did so, I remembered Don's warning about never letting your dog wander. 'If a bear finds him, he's gonna run back to the only thing he knows in them woods,' he'd said, 'and that's you . . . with the bear following on behind.'

I stared at the canvas sides of my tent, remembering how

inviting it looked from the darkness of the woods, and reflecting that, from a bear's point of view, the light from my tent was the equivalent of a neon roadside sign announcing '*Good Food 24 hours!*' I poured another dram, then blew out my lamp and climbed into my sleeping bag, the 45/70 propped within arm's reach. I tried to fall asleep, but guilt and childish fear were making me feel as if I'd had an overdose of caffeine. I kept being wakened by an image of Fuzzy, ducking and sprinting through the undergrowth, pursued by a thousand pounds of enraged, galloping predator while he raced with all his strength towards the only thing that was familiar: me. I sat up and fed another log into the stove, then stared into the crackling heart of the firebox, all positive thoughts gone as I worried about everything from lost dogs to marauding bears and failing to build my cabin before winter. My cabin site, approximately half an acre and thickly wooded, would first have to be cleared – this alone was several weeks' work. Then I had to gather and prepare logs for building, and for that I needed white spruce that grew at least a mile away back down the trail. The logs would weigh hundreds of pounds, and I would have to clear the portage before I could even attempt to get them up to the site. I grimly remembered the words of a well-travelled American hunter, who had told me I was mad to imagine I could live through a winter in the Interior, and even madder to think that I could build a cabin when I was only arriving in summer. 'You're just not gonna have time to do it,' he'd said, going on to tell me that in the deep cold of the Interior trees freeze solid, and are very difficult to harvest for firewood. Now his words echoed in my head, adding to my feeling that I might just have set out on an impossible mission.

Exhausted by worry, I sank back into my sleeping bag and was just on the edge of sleep when I heard a loud sniffing sound coming from outside the tent. My eyes shot open and I froze, straining to hear above the sighing wind. A few moments later it came again: unmistakably a sniff, and this time the animal pushed into the side of the tent slightly. I edged myself up on my elbows, reaching cautiously towards the pump shotgun. I considered whether to shoot through the canvas, but thought better of it, and quietly

pumped a round into the chamber. I listened, but heard nothing –
and then suddenly there it was behind me: a great scratching sound
and clawing at the door of the tent. I whirled round, brought the
gun to my shoulder and aimed at the door. My finger was poised
on the trigger as a black nose came into view, followed by a familiar
golden head. Two almond eyes looked up at me nervously as I
stood rooted to the spot, my heart beating fast. My body was
frozen in the shoot position, and Fuzzy was staring into the barrel
of a gun. Like a police negotiator, he stayed very still, keeping his
eyes firmly on mine as if to say: 'Take it easy, I'm a friend . . . Now
slowly put down the gun'.

I lowered the gun, feeling deeply relieved, and after clearing the
breach knelt down to look at Fuzzy. He didn't move, but continued
to stand half in and half out of the tent, staring at me in shock.
'Good dog Fuzzy – come on.' I motioned inside the tent. He
shrugged under the canvas, then sat just inside the door looking at
me warily. He looked as if he'd been having adventures of his own.
He was soaking, and the leaves caught up in his coat suggested that
he'd been holing up somewhere. We sat for a moment, then I
patted the floor beside the stove and said 'Here.' He cautiously
approached the stove and sat down, looking around as if he
suspected a trap. The firelight played over his coat and I could
see he was actually a fine-looking dog. I had to hand it to him for
finding his way here after being so rudely sent away – clearly he
was tenacious, and could look after himself in the bush. In his eyes,
however, it was obvious that I had some making up to do. He lay
down, one eye half open, watching my every move.

12
A FOOL IN THE FOREST

The next morning I woke up and lay feeling disoriented. Then the memory of where I was returned, accompanied by the familiar waves of worry. Outside it was grey again, and the sight of the damp, forbidding woods did nothing to restore my morale. I stoked the stove, putting in some thin lengths of wood to get a good fire going, then made a jug of strong coffee. I fried some bacon and bread while staring out of the tent at the drab weather and claustrophobic vegetation that surrounded the campsite. Shortly the yellow flames of the fire had banished the morning chill, and the smell of bacon and coffee filled the tent. I wolfed everything down whilst Fuzzy ate sparingly from the little pile of dog food that I had given him, burying the rest with a few deft strokes of his paw. I could learn from him: my food was gone in just a few gulps, but he was making his last.

After clearing up I headed down the trail to collect the rest of my kit from the riverbank, as well as the fuel I had cached in the trees. Up and down the trail I yomped, under a grey sky that produced no rain but plenty of humidity. I noticed a bear bed that had been recently slept in, and stepped over mounds of dark bear drop-pings. I tried to push the many lurid stories of bear attacks that I had heard to the back of my mind. Gradually, a pile of kit built up in the shade of a spruce tree beside my tent, and as the pile got larger, so the level of drinking water in my five-gallon barrel dropped lower and lower.

With everything finally back at camp, I found homes for tools on various handy branches and stored the rest of the kit tidily at the back of my tent. I then stood looking down the path of crushed vegetation that had to be transformed into a useful portage. This was my first task. The portage would have to be wide enough for me to stand in the middle and hold my arms out straight without touching trees on either side, and the ground cleared of all ob-structions. All fallen trees along the route would be removed with no stumps or sharp points left behind. It must be as straight as possible, so that a dog sled could use the route in winter, as well as making it practical for moving timber on one's own. It also had to pass through the two stands of white spruce that Don and Charlie had pointed out as the best source of timber for the cabin. Approximately a mile and a half long, the route down to the river went up and down several steep hills, and passed through some thick vegetation. It would be no easy task. I swung round and looked towards the place where my cabin would be built, currently occupied by my tent. This was the next job: to clear the area ready for building, then I could start to bring logs up my newly cleared portage. More immediately, I had to think about digging a hole for a latrine: Don had warned me of some bears known as 'shit-eaters', who are irresistibly attracted by the scent of human excrement. Better to discover him with his nose in a latrine hole than to have him wandering all over the camp like a pig after truffles.

My mind ranged over the tasks ahead, and once again a feeling of panic rose and threatened to overwhelm me. I looked at Fuzzy, who was tethered by the tent to prevent him bringing back an unwelcome visitor. He was staring at me sadly. It was late after-noon: to start my jobs now would be pointless. Four ducks flew low overhead, heading towards the river. 'That's it,' I thought, 'I'll go and catch something for supper.' It was never too soon to start foraging, and I was keen to try out Fuzzy's potential as a retriever. I grabbed the shotgun, loading four number fives in place of the BB shot* and untied Fuzzy, who stood up on his hind legs and pawed me, tongue lolling. 'God I hate dogs,' I muttered. 'Down!' He dropped to all fours, looking up at me as if disappointed that I hadn't improved overnight.

I heaved the 45/70 on to my shoulder and started to walk down the trail towards the river, feeling silly that I was carrying both a shotgun and a rifle. It seemed like overkill, yet I was mindful of the risk of meeting a bear, and determined never to be caught un-awares. As I walked I stopped to pick the odd high-bush cranberry, growing in profusion along the trail. The beautiful bitter-tasting bright red berries reminded me of the taste of a good gin and tonic. They took some getting used to, but I liked them. Once through the stand of white spruce trees nearest to the river, the trail dropped into a depression filled with thick stands of the berries. All around me lay impenetrable vegetation. A loud buzzing sound took my gaze down to a mass of flies sitting on a large, fresh-looking mound of bear droppings at my feet, peppered with high-bush cranberries. Clearly I wasn't the only one enjoying them. I scanned the undergrowth nervously, and began clapping my hands and singing noisily.

The worst possible thing is to take a bear by surprise, and I had been told always to make as much noise as possible when moving in the bush. Most bears are as anxious to avoid an encounter as we are, and when they detect the presence of a human will move off in the other direction. A surprised bear, however, can be lethal, and may charge. Everything that we know about bears has been won by hard and often fatal experience. In recent times there have been more problems with bear attacks, as people don't so often travel with dogs, and thus have lost their early warning systems. People also often travel unarmed, and so have little chance of defending themselves from an unruly bear. Yet a gun is never a

* See Notes for description of guns and ammunition.

substitute for a woodsman's sense, and can lead to over-confidence, which is even more of a risk than bears in wild country.

Having reached the river safely, I clambered into the launch and called Fuzzy to join me. Just as the day before on the beach at Galena, he turned in circles nervously, reluctant to get into the boat. What was his problem, I wondered: how on earth was he ever going to be useful if he couldn't even jump into a boat? 'Come on,' I shouted: 'Get in!' He steeled himself for the jump, perhaps deciding that it might be his only way out of this hell-hole, then leapt, only to slip on takeoff and fall back on to the muddy beach. He tried again and failed, then moved back up the beach, turning in little circles and barking shrilly. He was clearly physically incapable of getting into the boat unassisted, so I leaned over the bow and lifted him in, smearing myself in mud and hair as he wriggled in my arms. Once in the boat he shook himself violently, then sat back and looked at me in satisfaction. He had had his revenge: I was perfectly covered in millions of specks of sticky river mud, which, in my present circumstances, would be very difficult to get off. I stared at him angrily, rubbing the mud off my face with the back of my hand, and pointed to the bow: 'Stay there!' He turned his back on me and gazed sadly out at the river. I shook my head in exasperation. Far from helping, Fuzzy had been nothing but a hindrance, and constantly seemed to be trying to draw me into some kind of emotional battleground. I had been thinking earlier how difficult it would be to look after my family out here: the last thing I wanted was to be responsible for a neurotic and needy dog.

I started the engine and motored upstream along the slough past the long willow-clad sandbar where I had seen the wolves, and into the shadow of Pilot Mountain. Ahead on the right lay the entrance to Bishop Creek, where the peaty water changed colour as it clashed with the silty slough. I aimed straight for it, and was approaching the creek's mouth when the boat ran aground. The swift slough water raced past, hungrily sucking at the boat's sides, and I knew I couldn't afford to sit there too long. With an oar, I managed to punt the boat off the mud and back into the stream. The engine started and I aimed again for the river mouth, which was now slightly upstream. Again, there was a grinding noise. Fuzzy had turned round to witness this fiasco, and, just as I had watched his attempts to get into the boat earlier, his expression showed frank disbelief at my ineptitude. Clearly he had as little regard for my skills as I had for his.

Finally I figured out a route through the sandbars and slowly puttered into the creek, feeling relieved and reminded yet again of how important it was to be extra careful.

The creek followed a sinuous course, and was bounded to the west by a high forested ridge that led up to Pilot Mountain, and to the east by a long, low bank that led out on to flat country still smoking from the fires burning on in the peat ground. Rounding a bend, I saw four canvas back ducks* lift and fly away, their wings clipping the water as they fought to gain height. I dropped the tiller and fumbled the shotgun on to my shoulder, took aim and shot. To my amazement a duck fell dead in the water while the others banked sharply and flew back over my head. I took a few more shots, but missed them all, and gradually they whirred into the distance. Ahead, the fat duck bobbed in the water. I steered towards it and killed the engine. Fuzzy was standing in the bow, staring intently at the bird. 'Fetch!' I said, pointing in its direction. He continued to stare, not even registering my request. 'Fetch!' I repeated, but Fuzzy did nothing except whine slightly, following the bird with his eyes as it floated past. Then, when it disappeared behind us, he began barking uselessly, as if to tell me 'Quick! Get it – it's floating away!' The stupid dog probably can't swim, I thought, and lost my temper: 'Shut up!' I shouted, but he continued to bark shrilly, frightening other flights of ducks which then flew out of range long before I could take a shot. 'You bloody useless animal!' I shouted, and gave him a sharp clout on his rump.

---

* The canvas back duck is the largest freshwater diving duck in North America.

Immediately the little dog stopped barking and whirled round, giving me a look of pure dislike that stopped me in my tracks. I sat back, knowing that I had again used Fuzzy as a stress outlet, and this time I had overstepped the mark. He continued to stare at me for a moment and then turned away with surprising dignity, staring intently over the side of the boat into the water. Then he leaned back and wriggled his bottom a few times before executing a perfect little jump into the water. He momentarily struggled against the current, and then began swimming power-fully towards the shore. I watched him for a while, then steered downstream to pick up the duck. When I next looked up Fuzzy had made surprisingly fast progress, and was pulling himself out of the water on to the thick mud of the riverbank. I cupped my hands and shouted: 'Fuzzy!' He shook himself and turned to look at me defiantly. Then he let out a single, high-pitched poodle bark, and trotted off into the woods.

I was stunned by the dog's disobedience, yet couldn't help admiring his show of character. I had behaved badly, expecting him to carry out a task for which he hadn't been trained, and clearly for him the smack was the last straw. He obviously thought he'd been treated unjustly, and he'd had enough. Once more I regretted my impatience.

Back at camp I plucked and butchered the duck. I sealed the meat in bacon grease from the morning, and added onion, garlic, dried mushrooms and rice to make an improvised risotto cooked over a fire I had made outside. It was beautiful, and I felt hopeful about my winter menu, though I knew every meal couldn't be as good as this one. As I ate I stopped occasionally to listen to the heavy, sombre call of a great northern owl. His deep hooting echoed mournfully through the black woods.

Suddenly I heard a branch snap in the woods behind me, and slowly put down my plate and lifted my gun, only to see two familiar eyes shining back at me out of the darkness. Fuzzy walked slowly into the circle of flickering light and stood on the other side of the fire. I said nothing, but bent and scraped the remains of my unfinished meal into his battered feed dish. He looked warily up at me, then sniffed at the bowl as if wondering if the food was poisoned. Tentatively he began eating, as usual stopping short of eating it all, then lay down with a sigh between the roots of a large spruce tree and fell deeply asleep. I calculated that he must have travelled through at least eight miles of rough and dangerous country to get back to camp. I thought about his failure to get into the boat earlier that day, and his refusal to retrieve a duck despite being a superb swimmer. I remembered his low whine as he watched the duck float past, and his excited barking as it drifted away, and this gave me hope. Clearly he had been interested in the bird, and felt that something had to be done. Perhaps it was I who had to change my attitude: at least he had shown himself willing. Instead of being signs of neurosis, maybe his whimpering and barking were simply frustration at not knowing what to do.

I thought back to the basic training I had done with my own dog back at home. Only through working together had we bonded, and perhaps the same would apply to Fuzzy. If Fuzzy had a job to do it might lift him from being a hindrance and irritation to a partner and an ally – and perhaps he might also learn to like and respect me. I looked at him again, feeling – if not yet liking – a growing admiration for his character. The owl hooted again and the light of the fire played on the trees above. I poured a dram, thinking wryly that if I was ever going to become an alcoholic this would be the time. I looked at my hands and thought of the task ahead. Tomorrow was the fourteenth day of August, the day that I would start to cut the portage. It was time to see if my body was made well enough to support the whims of my dreaming mind.

13
THE GREEN COAL-FACE

It's the hell served for breakfast that's hard.
ROBERT SERVICE

The next morning I woke feeling ready for anything. It was a clear sunny day and I felt happy and hopeful. After breakfast I tied back the tent flaps and let the stove burn itself out; then I looked around for Fuzzy. I was full of optimism and determined to turn over a new leaf, but he was nowhere to be found. My eyes darted about, expecting another episode of desertion, but then I heard his characteristic yawn and saw that he had settled for the night in the ashes of my fire. I was impressed at his initiative in finding a heated bed for the night; it reminded me of the native Indian practice of making a warm sleeping platform out of spruce boughs over the embers of a long log fire. I clapped my hands and Fuzzy shot over, jumping up and frantically licking me as usual. I pushed him down, saying 'Okay fruitcake, enough', and he dropped to the ground disconsolately. Then he let out another yawn, with the usual high-pitched ending that I found so irritating. 'Fuzzy, no. Please don't do that,' I said, and he stopped in the midst of another yawn. Progress at last, I thought.

I filled my one-litre canteen with drinking water from the barrel, noticing there wasn't much left, and then loaded the saw, the Sandvik and chainsaw onto my little plastic sled. I slung the 45/70 over my shoulder and walked the short distance to the place where the portage would begin, fifty yards or so from my tent. 'Well, here we go,' I muttered, and went to work. With the Sandvik, I began cutting and slashing at the undergrowth, heaving the cut branches out of the way and feeling like a slave labourer on the River Kwai. The bush was putting up a stout defence against this imposter: thorns embedded themselves in my hands and legs, and osiers whipped across my face. As I heaved rotten branches and tree trunks away from the path, I disturbed great clouds of nearly invisible midge-like flies, which added to my pain. On and on I went, cutting and pulling and stacking. I had prepared myself for snow and ice, but not for this sultry, claustrophobic heat. Within minutes of starting I was sweating heavily, and rapidly getting more and more thirsty. Occasionally I would stop and stare at the wall of green ahead, my mouth dry and my eyes blurry, until the clouds of mosquitoes and midges forced me back to work. At times the air was so full of them that I found myself dry retching.

By mid morning I was soaked in sweat and covered in bites, cuts and scratches, yet when I stood back and surveyed my work it seemed as though I had achieved nothing. Beyond the few yards of portage that I had managed to clear, I could see the thin game trail continuing through dense, thick bush leading off as far as the eye could see. I slumped down with my back against a tree, and drained the last few drops of warm water from my canteen.

Occasionally as I slashed and chopped I would remember where I was, and it would bring my work to a halt. I would stand motionless, listening and looking all around me, thinking how bizarre it was that I was alone in the wilderness, when only a few weeks before I had been commuting to and from a desk job in Edinburgh. I would tell myself to work carefully and slowly, and to remember that one mistake could end everything, including my life. These regular sanity checks helped me, and gave me time to think about the enormity of the task ahead, so within a few minutes I would force myself back to work.

By late afternoon I was exhausted and dreaming of tea. I relit the stove, boiled the kettle and filled a big bowl with sweet tea, which I downed as though it were nectar. Afterwards my mind lingered on the subject of water: I had very little left in my five-gallon drum. I looked through the trees at the shimmering lake, and decided to inspect it more closely. The water was completely still, which was not a good sign. My hopes sank: it seemed to be just on the right side of stagnant, and would therefore almost certainly not be good for drinking. I knelt and gazed into the brown water, and then jumped as something whacked the surface. Fuzzy let out a series of barks, and I saw a brown animal swimming determinedly towards me. A large, grumpy, whiskered head broke through the still water, and two outraged eyes fixed on mine, clearly saying 'Get the hell away from my lake, you sonofabitch!'

The beaver swam hard towards us, then ducked fluidly at the last minute, lifting his great flat scaly tail and bringing it down hard on the water. Near the beaver house I saw a large leafy branch moving across the water before it was pulled down into the grog. At least four beavers of varying size were busily swimming to and fro. I lay down in the long grass and waited to see what else might be using the lake, and shortly heard a series of chirping calls. Three otters were swimming swiftly alongside the reeds on the far side of the lake, stopping from time to time to frolic under a series of half-submerged trees. Above me, a squadron of ducks banked and landed on the lake; while at the far end I could hear the honking of geese. Fuzzy went to the edge of the water and drank heavily, reminding me of my own thirst, and reluctantly I pulled myself back to the world of practicalities. If only I had the constitution of a dog, I thought; ironically it was this very abundance of wildlife that made my lake the natural equivalent of a septic tank. I couldn't afford to be fussy, however, and with the help of my water purifier I hoped it would be drinkable. I filled my canteen from the lake and returned to camp. My Miox water purifier* works by mixing a sample of the suspect water with salt, before passing an electrical current through it to make it completely safe for drinking. It is about the size of a torch, and comes with some clever water-testing swabs which all shrieked with hysteria when I dipped them into the lake water. I managed to purify a pint or so of water in the course of an hour, but this simply wasn't enough: carrying out intense physical work in this sultry heat was making me incredibly thirsty, and I couldn't afford to get dehydrated. Another worry to add to my list.

Over the next few days I continued to clear my portage and cabin site, working myself into a state of aching exhaustion. The water shortage was becoming ever more acute, and as an alternative to the lake water, I had experimented with drinking water from the slough. This also had its problems. Collecting water from a source over a mile and a half away was not exactly convenient. The water quality was very poor, and the silty nature of the slough left an unpleasant film of sand at the back of my throat that made me retch.† More than once I had to delve into my medical kit for a sachet of Dioralyte, which brought me back from the brink of dangerous dehydration. Over and over again I marvelled at my predicament: bears, wolves, ice, snow – all that I had been prepared for, but the last thing I had expected was to be battling with thirst. All day long I fantasised about drinking long glasses of pure, ice-cold water, only to return to horrible little portions of a warm, foul-tasting liquid that always left me wanting more.

During those early days of hard labour I settled into a rhythm of working which sustained me. Each morning I would wake early and cook up a good-sized breakfast before getting dressed for

* See notes.
† Later I learned to leave muddy river water overnight, to allow the sediment to settle.

work. I would then walk along my newly cut portage until, like a miner at the coalface, I came to the end of the shaft. Working slowly and carefully, I would then progress through the bush, gradually getting a little closer to the river with each day's work. By early afternoon I would be drenched in sweat and covered in dirt, cuts and insect bites. At this point I would down tools and, bar of soap in my pocket, amble down to the swift, cool slough. I had found a perfect spot for washing, where a large cottonwood had fallen into the water at right angles to the riverbank. Hanging my clothes from its roots, I would walk along the tree until I was right out in the slough, which sucked and flowed under and around it like a pontoon at a rustic yacht club. I would then sink into the water on the downstream side, holding on to a branch while the swift current sluiced and swirled refreshingly around my tired and battered body. After a few minutes I would clamber on to a convenient submerged bough and soap up, enjoying the silly contrast of sandalwood perfume and my muddy wilderness sur-roundings. It was the best possible combination of a shower and bath, and I would return to camp transformed.

About two weeks into my work, I sauntered down to the slough as usual, ready for another joyful wash. It had been a good day: I'd done a great deal of work, Fuzzy had been less irritating than usual and for once I was feeling optimistic about my chances in the race against winter. I slid down the sand bank and walked to the washing tree, where I undressed in a leisurely way and then walked out along the tree, hanging the 45/70 on its usual root. Feeling free in every sense of the word I stood there for a while, watching the water slip by and thinking idly of my friends' reaction if they could see me now, standing naked on a log in the middle of nowhere. On this occasion Fuzzy hadn't joined me for a dip, but was dozing in a cool spot on the riverbank further downstream. I lowered myself in, gasping at the cold, then sat up on the bough and soaped up while the water gurgled seductively in my lap. I jumped in and rinsed off, then clambered back on to the tree and reached for my toothbrush.

I was sitting astride the tree and brushing my teeth when out of the corner of my eye I spotted a movement upstream. I steadied myself on the bough and, looking again, saw a large black bear standing up to its shoulders in the slough one hundred yards or so away. In a scene that could have been directed by Sergio Leone, for several minutes we stared at each other, me frozen in mid-brushing position, him staring as if he'd never seen anything quite like me before. Without moving my head I flicked my eyes across to the rifle, dangling uselessly in the sunshine fifty feet away. If the bear charged, would I have time to get the gun loaded before he reached me? The answer was undoubtedly no; he could easily reach the bank before me, and could then come out along the tree, cutting me off from the gun. Bears are also superb swimmers, and this bruin looked more than a match for the current. I looked back at him, standing motionless in the water, paws hanging by his sides, not taking his eyes off me for a second. Bears do not have good eyesight, and as I was downwind he would have difficulty getting my scent, and therefore probably had no idea what I was. It was important for me to broadcast the fact that I was a human as quickly as possible, in the hope that he might decide to move on. I raised an arm and waved it, shouting 'Hello! Goodbye! Not for lunch!' The bear stiffened but did not move, and a fluttering of fear ran through me, mingled with a sense of the ridiculous as a frothy stream of toothpaste dribbled down my chin. Without standing up or taking my eyes off him, I began very slowly to pull myself back along the tree towards the bank. The bear lifted his head and swung it from side to side, sniffing the air, and I began to move faster, knowing that in the next few moments he would decide whether or not to charge. I glanced over towards Fuzzy, who was now messing about on the riverbank further downstream and hadn't even noticed my predicament. Thanks a lot pal, I thought. I reached the end of the tree, and with deep relief loaded a round quietly into the breach while still keeping a close eye on the bear. As I stood watching, he dropped on to all fours and splashed out of the river, bounding along the bank towards me at consider-able speed. I lifted the gun, ready to shoot, but he dodged off into a patch of brush. I stared at the spot where he had disappeared, but then he suddenly reappeared again, considerably closer to me. I decided to play it cool – I didn't want to shoot him if I could avoid it – and began pulling my clothes on, moving as confidently as I could while chatting loudly. After a pause the bear dropped on to all fours and shuffled away towards the woods.

I sat back heavily on the tree with my long johns halfway up my legs, and breathed a long sigh of relief. Just then the bear stopped and turned back towards me. I stood up again and resumed dressing and chatting. Maybe I should let off a round into the air to scare him, I thought, but then I remembered Don's words: 'No point in shooting to scare a bear,' he'd said: 'better to kill him if he's near enough to frighten you.' The bear mooched about for a while, sniffing and scratching at the ground as if playing for time, and then suddenly darted off into the thick willow. I finished dressing with shaking hands.

I walked back to camp lost in thought, a million miles away from the happy-go-lucky boy who came down the trail an hour ago. Out here it seemed that, just when I began to feel confident, nature had a way of bringing me right back down to earth. This was my first encounter with an Alaskan black bear, and it worried me that he had seemed so curious. Perhaps surprisingly, black bears more commonly stalk and eat humans than their larger grizzly cousins. The bear was now aware of my presence, and might be bolder next time – he might even seek me out. At this time of year, bears are stocking up for winter, and determinedly seeking out all sources of food. I thought of how differently the afternoon's events might have turned out, and imagined the newspaper pictures of my naked and half-eaten body discovered on the riverbank. This adventure was undoubtedly the stupidest and most irresponsible thing I had ever done, and I'd just better make sure it turned out all right.

That night there was a strong wind, and I could hear each gust coming from a long way off, moving closer through the tops of the spruce trees. I felt as though I was at sea as my lashings creaked, the ridgepole bucked and the canvas shivered like a sail under strain. There was a drama about it that would have been enjoyable if I hadn't been in a flimsy and shakily erected tent. I sat huddled beside the stove, looking anxiously up at the ridgepole and hoping it wouldn't fall down – I did not want to be without shelter in this weather. Then I looked at my watch. It was 10pm – early morning in Scotland, and a good time to call home.

I had set up my Inmarsat satellite phone when I first arrived at camp, to check that it was working, and to ensure that I could send through my weekly columns to *The Scotsman*. The signal was a bit dodgy, but by holding it up high in a particular corner of the camp I could hear reasonably well. I charged the phone and my laptop using a petrol generator, and so far the system had not let me down. As always, the technology astounded me: the fact that I could dial up from a phone in the middle of the bush and reach my family on the other side of the world seemed like a miracle, and I was incredibly grateful. That brief weekly phone call made an enormous difference. How much harder it must have been in the days before phones, when the best one could hope for would be a letter, long out of date by the time it arrived. On this occasion I hadn't called home for a couple of weeks, largely because I had nothing to report, and also because I was going through a difficult phase, and hearing my family's voices so far away made it harder. Both Juliet and I had to make it alone this year, and it would be easy to become over-reliant on our phone contact. Now, though, I needed to hear Juliet's voice, and to be reassured that, at home at least, everything was settled and safe.

'Julsie, it's me'. I hear my voice echo and wait for the delay. 'Can you hear me?'

'Guy! Thank God it's you!' Her relief is palpable, and I realise how worried she has been. 'Are you okay? Have you started work on the cabin?'

'Well no, not yet.'

'What do you mean? I mean – then what are you doing?'

My mind runs through the endless list of jobs that lie ahead of me before I can begin building and the immense difficulty of carrying out each task in these circumstances, and I struggle to explain. 'Jules, I don't know if I can do this. Really, I think it might just be impossible. I have so little time . . .'

She interrupts me, her voice clear and strong. 'Tell me what you are doing now Guy.'

'I'm cutting the portage.'

'The portage?'

'Sorry – it means the trail. I have to clear the trail to the river before anything else, so that I can drag logs up from the timber sites.'

'Oh. So how much longer will that take?'

I am about to answer when I hear Oscar in the background, pleading to talk to me. Juliet passes him the phone, and I hear his fresh voice. 'Daddy! Hello daddy!'

I feel a lump in my throat and croak back: 'Biggest boy! How is my biggest boy?'

'I'm okay Daddy. We live on Mull now, do you know that?' He sounds excited and happy.

'I know. Are you having fun?'

He talks to me about the sea, of sailing in his grandfather's boat and cakes and toys and dogs and cats. It is painful to hear and I feel useless again, wishing that I could be with them all in that gentle country. I say my goodbyes to Oscar and Juliet comes on to the line again: 'Guy, Oscar's crying, I've got to go. He wants to talk to you but it's too much for him. You'll have to call when he's asleep – he's got to get on with his life.'

'What do you mean?'

There's a pause. 'Well, he's going to have forget you for the moment and get on with being a little boy again. He's doing fine, but every time you call he's reminded that his dad is gone and it hurts him. I think it would be better if he didn't speak to you for a while until things have settled down.' I hear her voice crack over the line. 'Call later Guy – I love you.'

The phone went dead. I looked around me, feeling strange as I came back to the reality of this world, having for a few minutes been transported to another one. Fuzzy was standing beside the grey circle of the fire outside, staring into the darkening woods as the wind played along his thick fur. I sat and watched him, wondering what he was looking at and at the same time wrestling with the memory of the call. He paced up and down a few times before returning to stare squarely into the trees. 'What now?' I thought. Then the hairs stood up on the back of my neck as the dog began barking and growling, showing white fangs, his lips pulled back in an impressive snarl directed at something in the woods. I picked up the pump shotgun and strained into the darkness. I could see nothing, but Fuzzy carried on barking and I knew there must be something out there. A squall came in, and heavy rain began to fall, forcing me back inside the tent. I tied the door flaps tightly and began heating up a can of soup for supper.

I thought about the conversation with Juliet, the words 'he's going to have to forget you' replaying in my mind. The only thing I felt certain of was that my oldest boy was missing me, my youngest didn't know me and my wife was having to cope with everything on her own. I lay back on the spruce needles and stared at the shivering canvas before letting out a little appeal to the gods of luck and fate: 'Please, please don't let me fail. Please don't let me fail.'

I felt about for a match and lit the pressure lamp, then rummaged for a piece of chocolate to cheer myself up, but was interrupted by another series of high-pitched barks from Fuzzy. Again I stepped outside to stare into the darkness. I patted the dog's head: 'What is it lad?' He didn't turn round but kept looking into the dark, emitting a low growl. I heard a branch crack and froze, but the trees were making so much noise in the wind that I couldn't be sure what had made the sound. I pumped a round into the shotgun and fired it above my head, hoping it would scare whatever it was away. Orange fire and sparks spat from the barrel and my ears sang. Fuzzy didn't flinch, but after a few moments skulked off to his dry spot beneath the spruce and lay down, looking back as if to say: 'Well, that should have done it for now – let's sit back and see what happens.' I stared on into the trees for a few moments, remembering what people had told me about dogs and bear defence. In the past, everyone would have travelled with a dog, but now people were more inclined to go out into the bush alone, and that left them much more vulnerable to being taken by surprise by a bear. I looked over at Fuzzy and felt grateful that I had a partner at camp whose sense of smell and hearing were so much greater than mine. I settled into the tent for the night, glad that the little dog was keeping an eye out for me when all around the world seemed full of menace.

14
HUCKLEBERRY DAYS

It was mid-September before I finally finished clearing my portage. It had taken almost a month of solid work, and I was exhausted. I ached from head to toe at the end of every day. My hands and body were covered with cuts and grazes. I had also run out of provisions, and needed more tools for the next phase of work, so I decided to go back to Galena. Any trip upriver would have to be done quickly, as soon the river would begin to run with ice and I would be cut off for a long time as winter settled on the land. During 'ice-up', travel becomes virtually impossible, as the river is too icy for boats, but the ice is not yet solid enough to bear any weight. I placed the scanty remains of my food in a bag that I hung from a high, thin branch, then strung my fuel up at the opposite end of the camp. The door of my tent I tied up tightly, though bears are renowned tent-shredders, and would be undeterred by a couple of canvas flaps. I walked to the beginning of the portage, then surveyed my camp for a few minutes. Despite all the hard work and problems, over the past few weeks the place had become my home.

I walked down the new portage with Fuzzy at my heels feeling excited at the prospect of seeing people again. At the first stand of swaying spruce I had stopped to admire the fragrant trees when a grating call made me look up. Two immense glossy black ravens sat on a wind-shattered cottonwood, looking darkly down at me with unblinking eyes. One of them let out another dry, sardonic croak, raising its shoulders with the effort like some kind of geriatric demon. Their calls highlighted the stillness and with a little shiver I walked on. If I died, they would be the first to benefit.

The little aluminium launch was waiting at the beach like an obedient dog on a long leash. I pushed it down to the river's edge and jumped in, calling Fuzzy who hopped in after a series of irritating half-jumps. As usual, he clambered clumsily all over me and my bags, covering everything with mud before sitting down defiantly in the bow of the boat, staring me straight in the eye. 'You tosser,' I muttered, and started the engine, pushing off into the stream. The trip would take longer this time as we were heading upriver, against the current. On either side the land was preparing for winter: most of the green had turned to brown, and there was a feeling of everything shutting down.

Out on the main stream of the Yukon we were hit by a stiff easterly wind, and the brown river looked more menacing than ever. The bow of the boat banged against the waves, and Fuzzy rolled into a ball to keep out of the cold spray. The route was hard to define: there were no landmarks, just a low horizon and the river stretching ahead under a cold grey sky. The journey felt endless, but after a few tense and uncomfortable hours the rough little village finally came into view. I strained my eyes to see Don's golden cabin, and when it appeared I aimed the bow of the boat towards it, heading for his deep, eddying beach. As I neared the mud I saw Don walking slowly down towards the beach with the two dogs lolloping behind him. He raised a hand in greeting. 'Still alive, hey?'

'Yup.' I stepped out of the boat and pulled it up the beach.

Don's gaze moved from me to Fuzzy, and I knew that he was lining up a tease of some form. 'Glad to see you haven't flattened the dog under one of them scrub trees . . .' he paused for effect and I smiled back at him wryly. 'So, have you cut the portage?'

In answer I held out my battered hands, and he let out a coughing laugh. 'Ever heard of gloves?'

I fumbled into my pockets and pulled out my shredded gloves, and he laughed again. 'Them gloves'll do for England maybe, but . . .'

I interrupted, 'I think you mean the UK Don.'

'Oh excuse me . . . the *UK*' he said, affecting a fake English accent and looking at me with a mocking glint in his eye. It felt good to have the piss skilfully taken out of me again, and I realised how much I had missed being with people. Don turned and walked away, calling over his shoulder 'Come for supper and we'll talk.' Halfway up the bank he stopped, shouting 'Next time you cut yourself, plug the cut with spruce sap. The sap is like a second skin – waterproof and disinfectant all in one. Pretty damn clever is Mother Nature.' With that he turned and carried on up the hill, having taught me yet another invaluable lesson.

The next few days were spent buying and borrowing equipment and provisions. Winter was coming, and I needed to get started on the building. The heap of kit was growing by the hour: wood, tools, ropes, chains, pulleys, roofing iron, wire and a host of other bits and pieces were added to the pile, and would all have to be hauled laboriously up the portage. There was a limit to how much I could take, and I was faced with a few tough choices: a box of nails, for example, took precedence over an extra supply of flour. Don lent me two chainsaws in addition to the one he'd already given me, and showed me how to correctly sharpen and care for the frightening flying chains. He also gave me some peaveys, which are stout, old-fashioned tools designed for moving big logs by hand. While I had been at camp, a postal delivery had arrived from Lehman's, an American mail order company that specialises in supplying the Amish. The large brown parcel contained a heavy two-bit axe, a Hudson Bay trapping axe and a pair of very solid Canadian snowshoes made of birch and moose gut. The snowshoes were specially designed for working in, and as I opened the parcel and looked at them I felt excitement mixed with apprehension and disbelief. I held the shoes up to Don: 'Do you think I'm going to need these?'

He stopped his work and looked at me with a deadpan expression: 'Nah, it don't snow in the Interior.'

I took the meaning. 'Right, yes. Point taken.' It was easy to forget that I was living just ninety miles south of the Arctic Circle.

Between gathering supplies, I was spending time with Don's family, who seemed keen to find out more about the stranger in their midst. This they did each in their own unique way, and Jack was the first to step over the line of etiquette that normally separates visitor and host. On my second morning back in Galena, at 7 am sharp I heard a knock on the door of my shack, followed ten seconds later by another, and then by a barrage of bangs from an impatient small fist. Outside I could hear Fuzzy jumping up and down, squealing with joy on his tether, and I knew it must be a family member. 'Who is it?' I shouted.

'It's us – we want to show you something!'

I opened the door a crack and saw Jack on the doorstep, accompanied by two other boys.

I shut the door again, shouting 'Hold on!' in mock anger and pulled on a jersey. A few moments later I opened the door wide, and three dark pairs of eyes cased the shack with all the speed and accuracy of Scotland Yard detectives. I watched with amusement, and then affected a stern voice. 'Now Jack, when I got back from downriver I couldn't help but notice that this place had been thoroughly searched. What have you got to say for yourself?'

'Who, me?' Jack gave me an offended look.

I held up a warning finger. 'I'm going to booby trap this shack with dynamite so the next little villain to enter will be blown sky high!'

The boys giggled, then Jack's face turned serious as he got down to business. 'See this?' He held up some thin lengths of pipe that had been fixed together by a complex system of joints and angles.

I raised an eyebrow.

'This is our potato gun and we want to test it.'

I sat down on the front step and examined the menacing gadget, then pointed it at a spruce tree. 'Well, why don't you take a shot at that tree?'

The boys fidgeted and looked at each other, then Jack looked back at me with dark glittering eyes. 'We've done trees.'

'Cans?'

'Done 'em.'

'Bottles?'

'Yup.'

'So what next?'

'Well see . . . we need a live target.' Jack took the gun from my hands and looked at me pleadingly. 'Could we take a shot at you?'

Glad that they had the civility to ask before they assaulted me, I laughingly agreed, naively thinking that a homemade toy shooting little bits of potato couldn't hurt much. A few minutes later the three riverside ruffians were leading me solemnly to the execution ground. Jack stopped the group, then said, 'Okay, walk forward and stop over there by that bush. Keep your back to us – we'll shoot when you're ready.'

Slightly unnerved by their efficiency, I walked obediently to the allotted spot about twenty-five yards from the huddle of ballistics experts. With my back still turned I glanced round, shouting, 'So what size of potato pellet will you be using?'

'This,' shouted Jack. To my horror I saw him hold up an entire, very hard-looking potato.

'Right! Well, um . . .' My brain raced through a range of escape plans but in the end I settled for death and honour, calling out nervously, 'Ready when you are!'

I placed my hands over my neck for protection and waited. Behind me a furious row had broken out as Jack's two sidekicks urged for a high shot at back and head level, but Jack – to his everlasting credit – kept pushing the barrel firmly down. 'No' I heard him hiss emphatically, 'it's safer if we hit him lower!'

All went quiet and I turned slightly to see them filling a chamber with hairspray while Richard fumbled in his pocket for some matches. With a shiver of fear I realised that this was no rubber band operated weapon – I was about to be shot by nothing less than a vegetable rocket propelled grenade. I opened my mouth to protest, but just then heard a kind of pop followed by a whooshing sound as the hairspray exploded and funnelled energy up the tube, propelling the Yukon Gold towards me at a hideous speed. The potato hit hard behind my right knee and I fell to the ground, half in theatrical mode and half in searing pain, and howled for help. The boys jumped up and down yelling with wild joy, before seamlessly switching from their role of gunners to that of stretcher-bearers.

A day or two later Jack presented me with another challenge. He had heard that I liked swimming, and this had planted the germ of an idea in his mischievous mind. One afternoon he sauntered over to where I stood in Don's yard, staring dumbly at a pile of kit and trying to figure out what to bring and what to leave behind.

'Big river isn't it?' he said casually.

I turned and looked at the brown stream, which was probably around two miles wide at that point. 'Oh yeah – biggest I've ever seen.' I turned back to my pile and resumed muttering to myself.

He looked out over the water for a moment, then said 'Why don't you try and swim across?'

I lifted a distracted hand to my chin. 'Has it been done before?'

'Oh yeah, plenty of times. C'mon do it for us!'

By now he had been joined by Bethany, his oldest sister, and they began chanting together. 'C'mon Guy, please, please!'

'Well, I don't know . . .' I searched for a good excuse, thinking that at this rate the children would kill me long before I got a chance to kill myself. 'There's quite a current you know, and I really have a lot to do here.' My protests sounded feeble and were totally ignored. The chanting continued.

'Please! Please!'

Richard and another boy had arrived and joined the begging chorus. Even Fuzzy began to jump and bark, and eventually the cacophony brought Don over. 'Hey you crazy kids,' he said, 'get outa here and don't bug Guy – he's working.'

'But Grandpa, we want him to swim across the river!'

'What?' He looked at me, considering, and all at once I could see where Jack had inherited that mischievous glitter.

'Well I suppose the kids and I could follow in a launch . . .'

I raised my hand in protest, feeling like an Aztec sacrifice being prepared for the inevitable. 'Sorry, could I just say . . .'

'Please! Pleeeeeeease!' The children begged and the dog yowled while Don stood by and grinned.

'Okay.'

They jumped and cheered, skipping off in all directions to find lifejackets and gather more young sadists. 'So mister swimmer,' Don said, 'where do you plan to start from?'

I looked at the swift brown river. 'Over there.' I pointed a short distance upstream.

He turned to look. 'Okay, and where will you land up?'

I pointed a little bit downstream of my start point: 'There.'

'Ha! We'll see about that!'

Before I knew it I was being led down to the beach away from my pile of kit and the gentle job of organisation. The kids piled nimbly into Don's boat, followed by Fuzzy who jumped in with athletic grace. 'You bastard!' I thought. Clearly he was enjoying the prospect of watching me swim like a dog.

The water, although cold, had nothing on the North Atlantic, and I pushed off into the swirling murk. On the way out I caught glimpses of the boat with its load of little scamps, eagerly watching my progress. For the first three hundred yards or so it went well, but as I approached the centre of the river a strong current took hold. Seven knots cannot be argued with, and for every length across the river I was taken five downstream. I could faintly hear the kids calling, no doubt urging me to go faster as they grew bored, but I couldn't hear their words over the suck and swirl of the great river. Treading water for a moment, I strained my eyes to see ahead, but the far bank still looked miles away. On and on I swam, fighting the current and cursing myself with each stroke for undertaking this hazardous swim so casually.

Over an hour later I made it to the other side, and floated

exhausted in the brown water near the shore. As I waited for
Don's boat to reach me a huge fish swam past, rubbing its slick
back along my stomach as if the river was congratulating me for
my achievement. The family heaved me back into the boat
and I felt like an Amazonian pink dolphin surrounded by the
dark-eyed native Alaskan children. Don looked at me with a
deadpan expression. 'So – where did you say you were gonna
land up?'

'Umm . . .' I searched the far bank for my start point, but
realised that the village was long gone.

'I'd say you were five miles out!'

The boat erupted with laughter as I smiled and played the
clown. It was a role that I was only too happy to play at this
moment, faced with months of solitude to come in the bush
through an arctic winter.

Those few days meant a lot to me, as I got to know Don's family
better, and they slowly seemed to accept me as a likeable if perhaps
slightly odd outsider. They included me unquestioningly in family
gatherings, and gently encouraged me in what I was trying to do,
each member of the family offering all sorts of invaluable advice
and practical assistance. Before I left, Don's daughter Jenny gave
me an extremely stout pair of canvas overalls, which she assured
me would take the toughest treatment. I was moved by her gesture,
and, knowing that payment would be refused, looked around for
something to give her in return. With a heavy heart, I dug out an
immense bar of Toblerone that Juliet had sent me, which I had
been hoarding for the darkest moments of winter. Jenny's eyes lit
up with a kind of fanatical zeal, and I realised that this usually calm
and reserved woman had a profound weakness – and I had found
it. As I packed the overalls into my bag I noticed a little green
ribbon attached to the zip, and asked her where it had come from.
She told me that it came from the Stick Dance★ in Nulato, and that

---

★ The Stick Dance is held for one week in March every three to four years,
and is named after the spruce pole that is danced around for an entire
night. The dance is devoted to remembering deceased males, and takes
place in various villages in the Interior.

it would bring me luck. Without knowing it, she had discovered a weakness of mine: an inbuilt and irrational superstitiousness, perhaps inherited from my Neapolitan mother. It felt good to enter the woods with the ribbon zipped up high, close to my heart, as I embarked on my solitary journey towards the long, dark winter.

Jenny works as a biologist for the Federal Fish and Wildlife Service, and is a tall, strong woman with an incisive mind. Her modesty and calm exterior conceal the fact that she shares her father's evil sense of humour, and she and her husband Chris soon became dear friends.

Don gave everything a pet name, and Jenny was known as 'The Kid'. I asked him what had compelled him to give his graceful daughter such a name, and he said, 'Well, I don't know. She is one tough girl though.' He was right – I later learned that she taught new Fish and Wildlife employees how to handle a pump shotgun when dealing with menacing bears.

'So why do you call Claudette "The Grump"?'

Don gave me an irritated look, as I was distracting him from an important thought. 'Call her that 'cause she's always smiling and happy.'

Clearly Don seemed to go for opposites when it came to pet names. I wondered idly what he might one day call me – 'Genius' perhaps?

I felt privileged to get to know Don's daughters, who both became almost like sisters, and despite their often savage teasing, their friendship lifted my morale. Don's support and the gradual acceptance that came from his family combined to somehow blunt the knife edge of sadness that cut into me each time I thought of my own little family.

When it came to time for me to leave Galena, Jenny's husband Chris volunteered to take me back downriver. Down on the beach, he helped me to load my pile of kit – if anything even larger than the last time – into his boat. It was a cold steely day, and as we motored away from the warmth and friendship of Don and his family, all my worries began to return. I sat in silence, rubbing Fuzzy's ears and looking out across the grey brown river that flashed a smoker's smile from time to time as the waves broke in a growing breeze. The water level had dropped since I had come upriver, as if nature was huddling up in readiness for the cold, and Chris had to steer the boat with great care. We passed banks of grey mud that held pinpricks of gold where willow and alder leaves had fallen from the forest edge to stick like postage stamps. Chris pointed as we passed Pilot Mountain, and I saw a large black bear look up at us, then bound up the beach into the spruce. As we rounded the sandbar he shouted, 'Sure hope those bears haven't ripped your tent up!'

'Yeah, me too,' I replied, and fell back into gloomy silence. Fuzzy licked my hand and I resumed the job of rubbing his ears. We finally reached my familiar little beach, and pushed the boat on to the yielding bank that ran steeply up towards the forest edge. I stepped out on to the mud, stacking my kit on the edge of the bank until a great mound stood behind me.

'I better get going,' Chris said. 'Weather looks bad, and the river will be choppy. Good luck.'

'Thanks.' I tried to make my voice sound calm, 'I hope I won't need it.'

I pushed the boat into the current and Chris turned upstream and powered away. He looked back once and waved, and then he was gone.

I stood for a while on that mean shelf of bank, listening as the sound of the engine faded away. The silence was overwhelming, and I could hear nothing but the wind in the trees, which were losing their leaves with each gust. I looked at my immense pile of kit lying on the bank and wondered how long it would take to get it up the portage. The feeling of loneliness on that windy spot was greater than anything I had ever experienced before in my life. I now had no way of getting upriver, and to walk back would be impossible. When I last arrived at this spot I had been bolstered by the excitement of the unknown, but this time I knew exactly what lay ahead of me: spartan living in a tent, interspersed with long days of hard work. With each day winter was coming closer, bringing with it temperatures that I did not even have the experience to imagine. On a normal winter day in the Interior the temperature would be somewhere between minus twenty-five and minus fifty degrees farenheit, but I could regularly expect it to be much colder, and had even heard of it dropping as low as minus eighty degrees before wind-chill*. I stood thinking and looking out over a landscape that seemed to have lost its sense of humour, when a series of haunting calls made me look up. What I saw depressed me still further: hundreds of cranes were flying south, filling the cold air with their cries. Everything that could move was getting out, and here I was just moving in.

Forcing myself into action, I climbed up the bank and began collecting my stuff, telling myself that nothing was going to happen at all if I continued to mope. I pulled the .357 magnum out of my bag and strapped it around my waist, feeling comforted by its lethal weight. This was an extension to my bear defences, the logic being that should I find myself pounced on by a bear and unable to use my rifle, then the .357 by my side could be offloaded into a bear's ear/eye/mouth/shoulder, or into myself if it was all getting hopeless. I started to talk to myself in a stiff upper lip, terribly British sort of way, like a character in some jingoistic film, and discovered that the tactic worked. My rock bottom morale began to laugh back, at first out of politeness like a commuter humouring a drunk on the last bus home, but then gradually beginning to warm up, until a kind of manic banter ensued as I slipped and heaved my gear along the sinuous, rising portage. 'C'mon Grieve! Look lively! Chop chop – there's a boy!' My voice – like John Cleese on acid – echoed out across the woods, making a bizarre contrast with the silence and solemnity of my surroundings. If any person – or indeed any bear – had seen me, they surely would have slunk away to hide as I must have looked completely insane. This made me laugh even harder. Friends and colleagues would now

* Unless otherwise specified all temperatures are given in farenheit.

be padding across carpeted offices or tapping away on their computers, while here I was, homeless, heavily armed and engaged in a series of hectoring conversations with myself in the depths of Alaska's Interior. All afternoon I trudged up and down the portage, lumping and heaving and dragging, until by nightfall the job was complete. I had expected to find my campsite in ruins, with my stuff strewn everywhere and my tent torn down, but to my relief it seemed to be undisturbed. I set about sorting my kit beneath two spruce trees, and hoisted a fifty pound moose leg up a spruce a little way from my tent. I lit a small, slow-burning fire beneath it to keep the flies away, though the growing cold made me relatively confident that insects would be kept at bay.

It grew dark earlier than I had expected, and a mean wind brought spits of rain that I knew would soon turn into a downpour. Grateful that I had left a good store of wood, I lit a roaring fire and warmed myself beside it, whilst looking through a box of books that had been sent to me by family and friends. I reached for a slim paperback and smiled: *Heart of Darkness* by Joseph Conrad.

15

A GENTLEMAN OF THE OLD SCHOOL

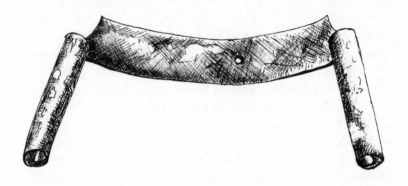

Do not protect yourself by a fence, but rather by your friends.
CZECH PROVERB

The nights were getting colder, and when I looked up from my lake to the side of the mountain I no longer saw a dense canopy of green. Every day I saw thousands more birds flying south, which heightened my sense of isolation. At night the tent billowed and swayed in the cold wind and rain, and sometimes I would lie awake as eerie sounds stretched through the woods towards my little camp. At sunset, the long, lingering calls of the loon birds would float and hang in the trees like wood smoke, sometimes joined by the cries of the great northern owl.* The loon birds fascinated me. They are the oldest and most primitive water birds in the world, with legs flattened to allow ease of movement in the water and set too far back for walking. It is this characteristic that gave them their name, as loon is derived from

* The great northern owl is a huge bird, around twenty-two inches in height, which is known for its ferocity.

'lum' which is a Scandinavian word meaning clumsy. They are reputed to have seventeen separate calls, each of which has a meaning, and their cries are wreathed in legend and superstition. Many indigenous people believed that the loon carried messages from the other side, and I could understand why. Their cries echoed as they looped up into the cold sky, sounding as if they were calling: 'Who are you? Who are you?' and making me feel even more alone.

Each day I worked hard on clearing the site for the cabin, but living in a tent and carrying out hard physical labour at the same time was proving a difficult combination. This work would have been challenging enough back at home, with a square meal and a hot bath at the end of the day. As it was, before I could even begin to relax I had to cut wood for the stove and collect water. As ever, my drinking water supply was not good, and I had now resorted to boiling it all and treating it with iodine. This yielded a greater quantity than the purifier, but still it was always in short supply, and I felt permanently on the edge of dehydration.

Gradually the site began to clear, and as the dark, looming forest gave way to light and air my spirits lifted. I was also looking forward to a visit from Don who was coming down to see how things were going. He arrived one cold, dry afternoon, having been dropped off at the slough by Charlie, and stepped lightly into the clearing with a dry, 'Well, hullo'. He proceeded to unashamedly inspect my camp, looking inside my tent and checking over my gear with an inscrutable expression. He picked up a piece of firewood, then said 'You need to cut your green birch thinner – your stove'll be too cool to burn big chunks. Come winter you'll have the stove on all day, so you can burn bigger green stuff.' Then he picked up a chunk of bone-dry spruce, and a far-away look came over his face. 'Love this wood – don't it burn damn well?' He peered into the tent again, then pointed at the five-gallon water barrel. 'Why's that water jug empty?'

'Well . . .' I considered flannelling, but decided to be truthful. 'I just can't seem to clean up enough water for drinking.'

'Oh really?' Don shook his head. 'Been raining quite a bit every night. Rig up your tarpaulin on some poles in the clearing, and angle it so the rain runs down into your dixie tin.'

It was so obvious I could have kicked myself. 'Okay, I'll do that. But won't it fill with leaves and bits and pieces?'

'Get a clean t-shirt and tie it over the mouth of the tin – that'll be your filter.' He looked up at the sky. 'Gonna rain again soon – how much water can you store?'

'Fifteen gallons.'

'Oh you'll get that in no time, and no need to mess with cleanin' it 'cause it's come from heaven. Where's your chopping stump?' I pointed and he walked over to it, gently lifting the axe from its place and dropping it on to a large, knotty log of spruce. With the blade biting in he lifted the thick log onto the block, then held the axe up for me. 'Come and split this.'

Feeling uncomfortably under the spotlight, I took the axe and raised it high before bringing it hurtling down on to the log. The blade stuck in hard, hit a knot and went no further. Feeling like a latter day King Arthur, I tried with all my might to free the axe, heaving and grunting and all the time aware of how completely inept I must look. Don stood watching, saying nothing. When at last I managed to free the axe, almost falling over backwards with the effort, he took it from me. 'Now, you're gonna need to learn how to cut wood properly, 'cause it'll be your only fuel. You gotta work slowly so you don't waste energy, and so you don't sweat.'

'How can I work without sweating?'

'We wear layers out here, so when you think it's gonna be hard work you take a layer off before you get hot, and when the work's done you put it back on.'

'Even at minus fifty?'

'Especially at minus fifty. When it's that cold, sweat will freeze into your gear, and then when you stop working you start to freeze. You got to avoid sweating at all costs.' He gave me a sardonic look. 'Moisture is the nemesis of the North.' He raised the axe and brought it down lightly, tilting the blade so that it struck the wood at a forty-five degree angle. The axe bit into the wood, and wedged out a neat little chunk from the block. He then pulled the wood round and struck again, working his way round in the same manner until a neat little circle of offcuts lay around the block ready for stacking. He picked a thick knotty block from the pile and chopped, and the axe stuck. I cleared my throat in anticipation of some kind of humiliation. Don fixed me with a wry look, then flipped the axe and jammed log into the air, spinning the handle deftly and bringing it down so that the back of the axe head came down first with the wood still on top of the blade. With a 'clink' the log split obediently in two.

'See – that way you don't sweat hammering away at it,' Don said. 'You're gonna use this time to practice working like you will when it's cold. That way you'll be in the swing of things.'

With that he turned and walked down towards the brown lake, moving easily over the hummocky ground. He stopped to look at the beaver house, and then, to my horror, bent and drank from the lake before wiping his mouth and walking on, clearly totally unaffected. I started up the stove and got the kettle going, and when Don returned he resumed his lesson. 'Now, let me show you a trick if you're gonna be living for a while under canvas,' he said, stepping inside the tent. 'Now you can stand up straight when you're right in the middle of the tent under the ridgepole, but look at this . . .' He held his arms out to touch the sloping sides of the tent, '. . . you lose space at the sides. Now come with me.' I followed obediently as he lifted the Sandvik from the tool tree, then walked along the portage until we came to a belt of willow where he deftly cut some stout but springy osiers, each about eight feet in length. Back in the tent he pushed the osiers up over the ridgepole, letting them flex naturally so that they held the sides of the tent out. Instead of crouching beneath a mean slanting roof, I now had a wonderful light domed space above my head.

It felt good to have company, and although Don couldn't stay long because ice-up was coming, I knew he was going to teach me some fundamentals. Already, within the space of a few hours, he'd taught me several life-saving lessons. And he could cook too: next he grabbed a pot and set about making a classic standby, 'Bacon and Beans'. This is an archetypal frontier dish – bacon is easy to store if canned or salted, and beans are a great source of energy, thus it has long been a favourite meal for trappers and prospectors in their lonely camps. The bacon becomes even more vital as a food source in the winter, when a fatty diet is essential. Even with plentiful sources of food, people have died through lack of fat in their diets.*

When the dish was cooked we sat on logs outside, eating off tin plates. Before he started his meal, Don took an innocent-looking bottle of sauce from his bag and applied it liberally to his food. 'What's that?' I asked.

'Oh, just a little spicy stuff – want a taste?'

'Sure.'

I put my finger over the opening of the bottle and up-ended it, leaving a little red circle on my index finger. I sniffed it – it smelt of nothing – and then popped it into my mouth. The reaction was instantaneous: I felt a wave of stinging on my tongue, followed by a vicious prickling and burning on the inside of my cheeks. I made the mistake of swallowing, which sent a toxic bolus down my throat, burning all the way down like molten lava. My eyes filled with tears and I went into spasms of coughing, almost retching as my body tried to get rid of the stuff. Finally I stood up, my mouth and throat numb and my voice hoarse: 'This stuff is awful, Don, horrific. How can you eat it? It's insanity.'

Don couldn't hide his sadistic joy. 'You're right!' he cried, 'It is Insanity – here, look again!' He held up the bottle, and on the faded label I read 'Dave's Insanity Sauce: the hottest sauce in the world!'

I stared at the evil substance; amazed that pure torture could exist in a bottle. 'But why Don? How can you taste anything?' He

---

* During the 1800s an isolated Hudson's Bay Company outpost was suffering from starvation. It was mid-winter, and the men were harvesting rabbits from a plentiful supply, yet they were still dying of malnutrition. This was because rabbit meat has virtually no fat, and the body uses up more energy than it gains in digesting the lean meat.

laughed and returned to his beans with renewed gusto as I looked on in disbelief. That night I tasted very little.

Later on I offered Don some of my precious supply of Highland Park whisky, but he held up his hands. 'Ah, I just love whisky . . .' he said, 'but them days is over. I'll just have a little sip to be polite.' I lifted a mug and was about to pour a dainty snifter, but before I could do so a rough old hand grabbed the bottle and Don drank straight from it before carefully returning it to me. 'Yup, it's pretty good stuff you got over there in Scotland' he said. 'I used to smoke a fair bit too, but had to kick it. Them days are over.'

I could see that the subjects of whisky and tobacco were close to Don's heart, and started to describe in detail a particular tobacco shop in Piccadilly: the smell, the range of tobacco, the pipes, cigars, cigarettes and snuff that they sold. A dreamy look came over Don's eyes, and as the wind swirled around the tent, catching the smoke from my stove and whipping it into the clear night air, we talked of wine, whisky, women, tobacco and food.

Later that night it began to rain, and from a corner of the tent I heard Don mumble, 'There's your water, dummy.' I smiled to myself, thinking how strange it was that my hopes for the future had somehow become entwined with the life of this sixty-eight year old backwoodsman, who had decided against all reason to help me get a foothold in his wild country.

The next morning, like a child running to the Christmas tree, I headed straight for my rainwater traps and found them full to the brim with clear, clean water. I poured some into a tin and drank, but instead of the invigorating taste I expected it was flat and dull. Don strolled over with one of my large dixie tins and said, 'That water'll taste real stale – you gotta put some air back in it'. He took a collecting drum and held it high up above the dixie, poured some water into it from a height, then back into the drum and so on. After he'd repeated the process several times, he said 'Try it now.' I poured a cupful and found that the water was transformed from tasting like a glass of stale bedside water to a sample taken from a highland spring. Obviously in a survival situation over a short time this kind of 'extra' is not required, but when living for a prolonged period in the bush any little increase in comfort or taste is vastly important to morale.

After a few days, Don was nearing the end of his visit, and the weather had grown much colder. Winter was coming in unseasonably early, and temperatures were already dropping to the minus twenties and thirties at night. All the waterfowl had gone, and the woods had become even more silent and forbidding. I had finished clearing the campsite, and was eager to lay the foundations of the cabin before Don left – after that the long, hard job of collecting and preparing logs for building would begin. We had felled some nearby spruce trees to make three twenty-four foot logs which would be the 'sill logs',* each around two feet in diameter. We worked companionably together, rolling the heavy logs using peaveys† along lengths of cottonwood that acted as tracks, allowing us to slide the great lengths into position. Once the three sill logs were in place Don stood looking at them for a moment, his hands on his hips, then looked over at me and smiled.

'Now you're gonna have to find a way to handle your cabin logs without help. They gonna be green logs and heavy, but once you get the centre of balance right you'll be able to move 'em about with a little finger.'

I leaned on my peavey and looked at him. 'How will I do that?'

He looked around, thinking, then pointed to a space in the clearing about ten yards from the ends of the sill logs. 'That's where you should stack up your cabin logs once you've got 'em here – then you roll 'em over to the cabin site with your peavey.'

I saw the logic. 'Okay.'

'Then you gotta be able to lift 'em up on to your floor, so that you can notch 'em and pin 'em in place for each round.'

We talked on about the logistics of building the cabin, my heart sinking all the while as I was already panicking about felling the trees, processing the logs correctly and getting them to camp – I

---

* The sill logs make up the foundations of the cabin, holding up the floor platform.
† A peavey is a tool about four and a half feet long, with a cant hook and spike for levering and manoeuvering timber by hand.

hadn't dared even think about reaching the building stage. I was also beginning to worry about the danger of working with these great trees, alone and completely cut off from help of any kind.

'This is going to be dangerous, isn't it? I could kill myself here.'

'You know that – I don't need to say it.' Don was looking at me with complete seriousness. 'Fact is, quite a few pros manage to kill themselves every year doin' just what you're gonna have to do.'

I did what I usually do when feeling tense, which was to swear. 'Oh shit.'

Don gave me a severe look. 'Now you just use your head and let's figure this out, 'cause you ain't got no choice but to get this house built.' He looked up at two majestic spruce trees that stood on either side of the cabin site, then over to where the logs would be parked. 'You any good at tree climbing?'

'Umm . . . yes.'

'Good, 'cause you're gonna climb these trees and string up a high line over this cabin.'

I looked up at the trees. 'Good idea.'

'Then we attach a coffin hoist to the centre, and fix the come-along on to that. So when it comes to liftin' the logs, you roll the log over to the cabin, hook up the come-along* onto the centre of the log, and ratchet it up. If you lift it dead in the centre it'll come up straight and safe.'

'Brilliant idea!' I said, as always dazzled by his ingenuity, and his seeming ability to find a solution to everything.

I shimmied up one of the spruce trees and looped the wire around it at about forty feet, then gingerly lowered myself via a series of brittle branches. Then I climbed the tree opposite, carrying the other end of the wire over my shoulder. When I reached the required spot I wrapped my legs around the tree and rested like a koala bear. Don worked at ratcheting the cable tight, and I then cable-clamped my end, so that after a little work we had an almost tight cable passing high above the cabin site. The only

---

* A come-along is a highly portable hand-winched chain lever, essential for moving logs and other heavy objects by hand. A coffin hoist is used for lifting heavy objects and uses a 'never-ending' chain.

obstacle that remained was a scraggly little cottonwood that stood between the two trees, and its branches had got caught up with the cable, preventing us from pulling it tight. We flicked and rattled and swung the cable from both ends in a series of attempts to clear the obstacle, but to no avail. From my tree top position I watched as Don strode to and fro below, muttering to himself and gradually getting more and more frustrated. For the first time I saw signs of him losing his temper, and felt thoroughly glad that we were friends.

'Goddamn sonofabitch!' I looked down and saw his moustaches quivering with rage, his beady eyes staring with personal affront at the offending branches. A cold wind was blowing, and I held on tightly as the tree swayed and creaked, enjoying the scent of spruce that surrounded me. Another expletive drew my attention back to Don, who was pacing about again, seemingly lost in thought. He stopped and looked up at me: 'Hey!' he shouted. 'You still got that pump shotgun?'

'Yeah,' I shouted back.

'And it's loaded with buck?'

'Yup – it's in the tent.'

'Good.' He turned and marched into the tent, then came out with gun in hand. 'Tuck yourself away on the other side of that tree!'

I shuffled around to the lake-ward side of the thick trunk and tucked in as tightly as possible to the timber. A series of shots echoed out over the lake, which, from my bird's eye position, I noticed now held a thin layer of ice. The sound died away. 'Safe to come out?' I called.

'Yup,' he replied.

Like a nervous squirrel, I peeped round the trunk, and saw all that remained of the cottonwood branch was a fluffy stump. Above it hung the cable, swinging free at last. Don looked up in triumph and shouted, 'Don't forget how useful a shotgun can be for building. Now tighten that fuckin' wire!'

By evening the coffin hoist and come-along had been secured on to the high line, and they hung dead centre above the sill logs, ready for use. That night Don told me a little bit about his life, from his boyhood in the Sierra Nevadas to the wild parts of the western United States where he lived a range of lives from prospecting to being a member of the POBOBs. The 'Pissed Off Bastards Of Bloomington' were a group of men in California who found their freedom on motorbikes, and Don had ridden with them for years while earning his living as a heavy equipment driver. After a while heavy drinking and fighting progressed to drugs for the POBOBs, who later became the Hell's Angels, and Don lost interest and moved north, looking for wilder and freer ways of living. He fished for some time in the Aleutian Islands in south-western Alaska, before moving into the Interior where he worked in construction during the summer and as a trapper in the winter months. Over time he became respected by the many native Alaskans who trapped, fished and hunted alongside him, as well as by the few white men in the region.

In the village of Ruby, once a thriving mining town, Don met and married Carol, and when they had children they moved down the Yukon to Galena. Physically powerful and clever, Don soon earned a reputation as a man who should not be crossed, and throughout his life there had been fights with everything from fists to guns, knives and broken chairs. He had taken and given many a beating, yet I knew that he was a good man, and that when his wrath fell it normally landed on the head of a man who deserved it. As I sat sipping from a tin mug of whisky, listening to Don's many stories of life in the bush, I formed a picture of a life in the Interior that was even rougher than it is today – and given the stories I had heard, that made it very rough indeed. One of Don's stories featured an old saloon called Hobo's, which had nothing more than a small wood stove and human warmth for heating. The rickety log building had a rota hanging above the bar, listing whose turn it was next to empty the 'Piss Barrel'. The toilet was unheated, of course, and patrons would relieve themselves into a barrel that eventually filled to the brim with frozen excreta. When his turn came up on the rota, the man on duty would enter the toilet and roll the barrel and its frozen contents out through the bar to the front porch, where the lump of brown ice could be neatly knocked out and rolled off to an out of the way spot. The rota was usually observed, but sometimes a particular shift would be waylaid on his way through the bar by the promise of a drink or a shot at the pool table, and on these occasions the barrel would be forgotten; at least until it began to thaw, at which point the noxious semi-frozen sludge would slowly seep from the barrel.

As we spoke in our little circle of tented light, winter was slowly creeping closer all around, and occasionally we heard the lake 'sing' in a series of lilting, rolling tinkles that came from the thickening layer of ice. We sat in silence listening to the sounds, and when I stepped outside the sky was clear and studded with the cold light of the stars. Don emerged from the tent behind me and tied the canvas flaps closed tight. A great northern owl hooted deeply in the woods, and I looked over the open clearing towards the lake, where I could hear the occasional splash as the beavers dragged fresh sticks to their pile through a narrowing channel of water that remained clear of ice. Ice took time to form over this shipping lane as the busy rodents worked ceaselessly, swimming backwards and forwards from house to shore where they clambered up the steep slope to gnaw away at various deciduous trees. Once felled, they would cut up the trees and drag them into the water and over to their stick pile, where they would store them up for winter feeding under the ice. As each day passed the pile grew bigger, and soon, when the ice sealed the beavers in, they would rely on it as their winter larder, swimming from their house and re-supplying whenever they needed food.

Through the cold night air I heard a tree yawn and fall with a swishing sound into the lake. 'Seems I could learn a thing or two from beavers when it comes to timber work,' I said.

Don laughed. 'Hell, I've come across a few of them critters trapped and dead under a tree that went wrong for 'em.'

I turned to him in astonishment. 'Really?'

'Nature ain't perfect.' He shrugged his shoulders. 'Mistakes are a natural part of what makes the world go round. One animal makes a mistake and another finds an easy meal.'

We stood a bit longer in silence, and then I asked Don about the people who lived wild in the Interior. I was curious because I'd been told that very few people chose to live alone out in the bush through the winter. Those that did so in the past were usually either trappers or prospectors, but today were mostly people who were opting out of life, and for that reason were seen as odd or lacking. Don told me about a day when he found a man who had been murdered: 'I found him on the floor in his shack all covered in deep cuts and stabs. He was alive but the blood was running out of him.' Fuzzy had come over to greet us, and Don patted him absent-mindedly. 'Yeah, he was in a bad way and trying to plug them cuts with his t-shirt which was soaked red with it all. He knew he was gonna die but we could do nothing.'

'Who did it?' I felt a tingle of fear as I pictured the savage scene.

'A wild man with a crazy mind. I found him and held a shotgun at him till he dropped the knife. His family took him away.'

I stood in silence, lifting my head to catch the incense of burning birch wafting towards me on the breeze. 'There's been a lot of death and killing in this place. Have you seen many dead men?'

'Yeah. We have to do everything for ourselves out here. When a man dies there is no ambulance or police van to go get him – his family have to do it.'

'Have you ever had to do such a thing Don?'

'Yeah.' He drew air into his lungs and let it out again. 'Three years ago my son died.'

He went on to tell me about his son's death, and of his funeral. 'I'm sorry,' I mumbled when he had finished his sad story, thinking of Don and Carol and their children and feeling the weight of their tragedy. I also realised afresh the extent of the favour they were doing for me – a stranger from a different country and culture. What had started out as an adventure from the safety of the UK, I now saw was an ill-timed and very dangerous indulgence. Standing there on that dark night with winter hiding in the woods, I fully understood how lucky I had been to find such friends.

Death is all around in bush Alaska, and I had noticed people's matter-of-fact attitude to it, in contrast to my world where denial of death has almost become an art form. In Galena I had seen people drinking out of mugs with a person's picture printed on them, with their name and dates inscribed below. A mug hanging in Carol's kitchen read: 'Jimmy Malemute, one great dog musher and violin player', and I also saw people wearing t-shirts with similar images. It is a way of celebrating the lives of deceased friends and relatives, keeping them amongst you, and also perhaps remembering what killed them. The traditional Indian burial is also a very intimate way of celebrating a life. The dead person is dressed in their best, warmest clothes and laid out in the village hall. For several days they lie there, never alone, surrounded by family and friends playing cards, cooking or just sitting, until they are taken to be buried.

'Don . . .' I began, searching for words to express my thoughts, 'I hope you know how grateful I am for your help. I am out here alone . . . I don't know what I'd be doing if I hadn't run into you guys.'

'Well, not many prospectors and such went out alone on the first year. They often had a partner or worked in little co-operatives to get their cabins built. Them that did go out alone were usually already seasoned woodsmen from places like Sweden and Finland and such.'

'Then I suppose my idea of being one man on his own against the elements was somewhat artificial?'

'Here more than anywhere else you need friends. Make no mistake – you're gonna be on your own for a long time, but while I can I'm gonna show you the way from time to time, or else you're gonna learn nothing and this cabin ain't gonna happen.'

'But why are you helping me like this?'

'God only knows.' He chuckled wryly. 'Maybe 'cause everyone's saying you can't do it. I kinda like a challenge, and besides, you're a family man. If you was on your own I wouldn't give a damn.'

The lonely cries of a wolf pack started up in the distance, and we stood in silence for a few minutes, listening. I looked up in the direction of Pilot Mountain, from where the sound seemed to be coming, though I could see nothing in the darkness. 'There's a big family of wolves that have their den on that mountain,' Don said. 'They've been there for generations. When you hear 'em you know that they're hunting in this area and they'll be around for a few weeks more – then they'll head off to hunt in another territory and come back again, chasing moose ahead of them all the while.'

'How many in the pack?' I asked.

'Oh, about fourteen or so. Brownie flew over 'em a while back.'

As we settled in that night, Don told me that he would have to leave the next day, as ice was beginning to form on the river. He couldn't risk getting stuck with me for the time it would take for the ice to become solid enough to travel on, so Charlie was coming back out to pick him up. Don hoped that, while he was here, Charlie would help us get the floor down on the sill logs. He was a skilled joiner and would do the job much faster and better than either of us.

That night I lay awake, listening to the sound of the lake singing with the wolves howling their eerie chorus in the background. The days with Don had given me a temporary reprieve from my anxiety about building the cabin, and it had been a great relief to work under the eyes of a veteran woodsman. Soon I was going to be on my own again, and dealing with the onset of winter at the same time as starting the building – a process that I knew next to nothing about. Every action would be made much more dangerous by the cold weather, and I would have to work extra slowly and carefully.

16
THE FLOOR THEN NOTHING

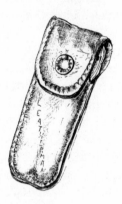

Charlie arrived looking unhappy, and the atmosphere at camp plummeted with the cold. The river level had lowered due to ice forming further upstream, so Charlie had had to leave the boat further down the slough and travel the rest of the way on foot. While Don and I went down the portage to collect the tools and food, Charlie sprang into action laying down the flooring for the cabin with amazing skill. By midday the job was done, and we all stopped for coffee. Sitting on a tree stump with a steaming mug in his hand, Charlie said 'We gotta go Don – there's ice in the main channel.'

'Shit,' Don said, glancing at the newly laid floor platform lying on the sill logs. Then he looked at me. 'You better get working, 'cause ice-up is coming and it ain't good news.'

'Sure Don, I know.' I stood up and paced around nervously. 'Trouble is, I just have very little idea about what to do next, I mean . . .'

He held up a finger to silence me. 'Get your logs cut and up to camp. Use the chainsaw hoist to drag 'em in, then practice your notches with some finger-sized willow and build the cabin in small scale. When you're happy with it, do the same with the house.'

I swallowed. 'Okay, um . . .'

Again he interrupted, pointing at a huge log I had cut and left at the side of the camp. 'Now we're gonna cut that big log in half, and place one half at each end of the floor platform to make the start of the cabin. Then you'll notch and fit your logs from there. D'you follow me?'

'Yes . . .' I said uncertainly, 'but . . .'

'Don't worry – it'll make sense once you get goin'. Tip then butt, then tip then butt, till you got seven rounds up per wall. Now, we gotta get goin'. C'mon Charlie!'

I stood back and watched as the two of them set about halving the log. Having made a chalk line along its length, Don started cutting while Charlie held the end of the chainsaw with a G-clamp to keep it straight. It was precarious but it worked, and the first log was ready to put on the floor. Between us all we carried the heavy timbers on our shoulders up to the floor platform, and placed them as Don had said, one at the north-facing end of the floor and the other at the south. All the time the day was growing darker, and by the time the job was finished the men were in a hurry to get away. The four of us walked together down my portage till we reached the slough, which was still navigable, but had ice edging in from the sides. 'It's coming,' Don muttered, looking up at the iron-grey sky. 'It sure is coming.' We walked a few miles further along the slough, fighting our way through the uncut trees and undergrowth, until we reached the place where Charlie had left the boat. After saying a brief goodbye, they pulled the boat down the beach, clambered in and started the engine. I stood watching as they disappeared into the grey half-light.

A very cold wind had come in from the north west, and it ripped at my clothing, deepening my dark mood. Fuzzy whined and cringed against me to keep out of the wind as we walked slowly back through the woods. Charlie had brought me a little parcel from home, and I tucked it safely into my breast pocket, feeling vulnerable and very small. As I neared the grass lake I heard a familiar fluttering and a few little tweeting calls. 'Pheasant?' I thought, 'surely not.' I took a step forward and a large, grouse-like bird lifted up from no more than five feet away, flew along the portage and up and over the trees. I stepped forward again, and this time a whole covey lifted and whirred away – seven large birds had appeared and disappeared before me in the space of five minutes. These could only be what Don called 'chicken',* which was good news for me, as it seemed that every other edible bird had long since left the woods. I walked on with a new spring in my step, thinking that even if I didn't have a home, at least I would have a chance of some fresh meat through the winter.

By the time I reached camp it was nearly dark, and I was grateful to be back inside the tent. I poured some whisky into a tin mug and topped it up with some rainwater, then stoked the fire and sat back, feeling restless. As always at the day's end, when all my jobs were done, my thoughts turned to home. I needed to write my next batch of columns for the newspaper – I'd been sending them in every fortnight or so. I switched on my laptop and waited while it started up, then carefully set up the satellite phone and plugged the laptop into it. First I checked my emails, and saw there were several from Juliet. She had been sending me regular messages that I would download all at once when I logged on to send my columns. They were full of reassuring news of the children and what they'd all been doing and they brought a bit of normality into my strange world. These three were titled 'Important!', 'Very Important!' and 'F******Important!!' With a prickle of worry I opened the most recent one, and read:

> Guy,
> Are you okay? I haven't heard from you for ages and my imagination is running riot. Please, please phone me IMME-DIATELY!!

'Shit' I said aloud. I was so wrapped up in my problems here that I was forgetting what really mattered, and I felt guilty that Juliet had

* In Alaska 'chicken' is the name used for willow or 'ruffed' grouse.

been so worried. I unplugged the phone from the computer and then dialled the familiar number, imagining the phone ringing in the chaotic but homely kitchen of my in-laws.

'Hello?'

'Julsie, it's me! I just got your email – I'm so sorry, Don's been here and we've been so busy . . . But how are you?' I stop and wait for the delay.

'Guy!' Her voice is strong and clear. 'We're fine – but how are you? We've been really worried.'

'I know, I'm sorry. I'm all in one piece – but I met a bear when I was having a bath a week or so ago.'

'A bear?' Her voice is incredulous, 'When you were having a bath?'

'Well, trying to.' I laugh, thinking what a bizarre picture it must make. 'It was a big black bear.'

'But hang on – aren't they supposed to be hibernating?'

'No, not yet. They make a bolt for their holes when the first proper snows come in. Just now they're still wandering around – and they're not in the best of moods.'

I hear her sigh – she must be wondering what on earth has happened to her life. 'And what about grizzly bears?'

'Well, they're around, but they'll all be asleep soon. The brown bears are more wakeful than the black bears though – sometimes they wander about in winter, and Don told me that they drag the black bears out of their holes from time to time.'

'Why?'

I laugh. 'To eat them.'

'Very funny Guy, really reassuring, thanks.'

'I'm sorry Jules, I don't mean to sound like a twat, but this place is hard – so much harder than I thought it would be. I'm getting kind of lost in it. But I'm being careful though, don't worry.'

'How's it going with the cabin?'

'Well . . .' My heart sank as I searched for the words – I was longing to give her good news, but I couldn't. 'It's going slowly. I've got a floor, but so far that's it. Don and Charlie were helping me, but they've had to go because ice-up is coming.' I hesitated, trying to sound positive because I knew that unlike the bear stories, which I could joke about, here she would pick up my real fear. 'So I've got to just get on with it on my own. It's hard work though . . .' My voice tailed off – I never could hide my feelings from Juliet: 'It's so much harder than I thought it would be Jules, and dangerous too. Even just cutting down the trees is going to be deadly.'

The response was silence, and I regretted my words immediately.

'Don't worry – I'm not going to kill myself, but to be honest I don't know if I'm going to be able to build this cabin. Ice-up is coming in early this year – that's why Don and Charlie had to go. The main channel on the river is still open, but Charlie couldn't even get up the slough. And there's still so much to do.'

'Oh God, Guy. Why are you doing this?'

'I'm not sure actually.'

There was silence for a moment, then Juliet spoke in the clear, practical tone which I knew so well. 'Well you're there now – there's no point in regretting it. We need to make a plan. What are you going to do if you can't build the cabin?'

'Don said it is possible to live through a winter in a wall tent . . .' I looked around at the dark tent, lit poorly by my hurricane lamp. 'I'll just put a tarp over it as a second layer and pile snow up the sides.'

My voice sounded uncertain, even to me, and I knew that my wife was wrestling with a horrible image of the father of her children living out the winter in a tent in temperatures that regularly dropped to the minus sixties. A note of steel entered her voice: 'Guy, just get that bloody cabin built, because I do not like the idea of you being in a tent all winter – it just doesn't sound possible.'

'I'll try Jules, I really will.'

'Look, you've always been pretty good at doing stuff at home, as long as you had the instructions . . .' She said it seriously, but we both found ourselves laughing as we remembered my notoriously poor efforts at DIY. Now here I was, attempting to build a house from scratch when the only thing I had ever made before was a chicken coop – and that hadn't worked out very well either. The laughter ended the call on a good note, but there was a note of desperation in both our voices as we said goodbye.

As I replaced the handset I did an internal reality check to make sure I was not overreacting or exaggerating things. I stood up and peeked through the canvas flaps at the forlorn-looking floor standing exposed on the sill logs. It had begun to rain, and I noticed with a pang that the raindrops were freezing as they fell. The lake was white with ice, a patch of light amidst the sombre dark of the trees all around. It was all too depressing, and I knew that if anything I was understating the growing horror of my situation: winter was on the verge of smothering everything, and I had not even felled a tree, never mind moved any logs on site. As I retied the tent flaps and settled down for the night, I thought about my wife and children and my duties as a father. There were no jokes now to lighten my mood. I looked at the guns that hung glinting from the ridgepole support, and remembered some lines from a poem by Robert Service:

> *Gnawing the black crust of failure, searching the pit of despair,*
> *Crooking the toe in the trigger, trying to patter a prayer.**

---

* Robert Service, *The Law of the Yukon*, from *The Spell of the Yukon*.

17

THE SORROWFUL BUSINESS
OF FELLING TREES

The next morning I headed down my portage to the first stand of spruce trees, pulling my sled which contained the two chainsaws, fuel and my two-bit axe. My mission was to cut fifty-two logs and get them up to the cabin site as soon as possible. I approached the first suitable-looking tree and sized it up as Don had instructed. The first thing was its height: I needed to get at least one eighteen-and-a-half foot log out of the trunk, and maybe two if I was lucky. The logs had to be between nine-and-a-half and ten inches in diameter at the tip, and the trunk as straight as possible. Having made sure of all these points, I had to think about how the tree stood. In which direction did it want to fall? I stood staring up at the colossus, weighing up all of these factors, knowing that once I had made the first cut I would be vulnerable, particularly as I was alone. Satisfied on all fronts, I stepped forward and cleared all the sharp, dry branches from the trunk with my axe.*

* Later I deliberately sought out spruce trees for fire-starting, as I could use their very useful dry and resinous twigs, known locally as 'squaw wood', for kindling. The driest are found lowest down.

When the trunk was clear I made a note of the direction that the tree would be taking when it fell, and positioned myself at ninety degrees to that deadly zone. I looked up for any large dead branches, known as 'widow-makers', which might fall on to my head when the cutting began, and then glanced behind me into the 'safe zone', looking for fallen wood that might trip me up, or bushes that could delay escape just long enough to ensure that I was crushed if the tree fell the wrong way. Once satisfied that my escape route was clear, I fired up the saw, said a prayer and began cutting.

My first two cuts were on the side of the tree that faced the direction in which I wanted it to fall, about three feet from its base. I made first one, and then a second diagonal cut about six inches deep, the incisions meeting in a triangle so that a woody wedge fell from the trunk like a slice of watermelon. I then stood back and checked all was in order, before moving round to the other side of the tree to make the final, 'felling' cut. Standing as firm as possible, I began cutting a straight line exactly opposite the wedge and a little above it. The idea was that, finding itself under attack, the tree would lean away from the cut, only to discover that there was an open chink on its other side. This chink would then act as a hinge over which the tree would fall. When I had cut about four inches I stopped for a moment and heard a woody creak, then saw the cut opening a little as the tree leaned away. I pulled the chainsaw blade out of the cut, and replaced it with the wedge of my boy's axe, thus ensuring that the wounded tree could not lean back. The creaks increased and echoed through the silent woods, until with a final woody yawn the hinge gave way. The tree plummeted to the ground, its branches crashing through the surrounding foliage and the ground vibrating with the impact as it fell. I stood beside the round white stump with its sharp tuft of splinters, observing a moment's silence for the giant which I had betrayed. I had felled the first tree for building my cabin, and it had gone well, but mingled with the sense of achievement there was also a feeling of sadness. Nobody with any heart could ever truly savour the death of a good, straight, healthy tree.

Using the axe to save fuel, I chopped the boughs off the trunk, and then hooked my logging tape to its base and walked along until I had measured exactly eighteen-and-a-half feet. I marked this spot on the bark, and then used the chainsaw to cut through the thick trunk, leaving the rest of the tree to fall away. Freed from the weight of its top, the trunk jumped up on its remaining boughs, and I kicked it over and cut them off. At last, dressed only in a tight suit of bark, my log lay at my feet: heavy, green and seemingly immovable. I glanced at my watch: it had all taken far too long. 'One down, fifty-one to go' I muttered, reflecting that, at this rate, it would take me almost a month just to cut the logs, never mind get them up to the site and start building.

For the first few days I worked slowly and only managed a few logs each day, but as I became more confident I worked faster, until I was cutting around ten to fourteen logs per day. The work was intense and dangerous, and demanded full concentration, yet constantly at the back of my mind was the pressure to work as quickly as possible. I would return to my tent tired and dirty, yet I couldn't rest until I had prepared firewood, built a fire and cooked a meal to keep myself strong and ready for the next day of work. Cuts, bruises and splinters became so numerous that I ceased to notice them, and I used Don's trick of plugging cuts up with spruce sap, which stopped the bleeding and made a sterile seal over the wound that would remain in place for days. Each morning as I put on my working clothes I noticed my trousers were a little looser – my weight was steadily dropping, as hard work and gradual dwindling of food supplies took their toll.

For nine days I worked ceaselessly, marking the number of logs cut each night in my diary. A warm spell came, and for this I was grateful, as the still days made the felling easier. Even the slightest breeze across the top of the canopy could have a great effect on where a tree fell, and sometimes, after I had made my last cut, the giant timber would pivot and teeter in a state of deadly limbo, laying all my careful plans to waste and causing a cold sweat to gather on my forehead. When this happened I would stand back, look up at the top of the tree and mutter a silent prayer. When the gust had passed, I would rush in and hammer a wedge in the cut to make it fall in the right direction before the next treacherous zephyr. Two or three times I got my last cut wrong, and was not fast enough at getting my saw clear before the tree sat back and trapped the blade under its immense weight. My only option then was to take the engine off the blade, and store it in a safe place before starting the whole process again with my second chainsaw, cutting a foot or so above the trapped blade. This was a tense business, as it meant working up close to a tree that was fundamentally unstable, and ignoring all my instincts to get out of harm's way. It felt as though I was diffusing a bomb, and when the tree fell safely away the relief was profound. Only then would I chop into the wood and free the saw.

I also learned to trust my instincts, as in one instance when I had felled a perfectly straight seventy-foot tree, which would give me two logs. I felled it badly, and in such a way that it caught a third of the way down on another tree, where it stuck fast. I stared at the deadly conundrum for some time, and then crept over and cut a wedge in the supporting tree. Nothing moved, and all seemed well, so I began on the final hinge cut. But then something stopped me. Looking up, I realised that, looming behind and above me, the timber leviathan was not only placing great strain on the supporting tree, but was also teetering directly above me. Moving very slowly, I pulled out the chainsaw and stepped gingerly away from the dead fall trap, pushing my way back through the bush to the portage where I could look at it from a distance. My gut instinct told me to leave it alone for today, and I began walking wearily back to camp. I heated up a great jug of water on the outside fire and had a joyful wash, first soaping myself down with a sponge and then pouring the wonderful – albeit somewhat brown – hot water over myself. As I stood by the fire drying I heard a series of strong gusts coming in from the north east, and midway through one I distinctly heard the leaning tree and its support fall heavily. Patience had proved its point.

By mid-September I had felled fifty-three trees – wasting only one, which was not bad for a first-time tree feller – and thankfully had come out intact. It felt like a minor miracle, and I was jubilant. I set up the satellite phone and called Don, trying to sound casual about what for me was a major achievement.

'Well, you done good' he said. 'Now, you know that draw knife I made for you?'

He had fashioned a sharp draw knife* from the leaf spring of an old car.

'Yup.'

'Well, you better get to peeling them logs.'

'Okay . . .' Don had talked me through log peeling when he gave me the draw knife, so I knew the basics. 'Any idea how long it will take me?'

'Hell no,' he chuckled. 'but the sooner you start the sooner you'll finish.'

'Well I do know that Don, thanks a lot.' I heard Carol talking in the background.

'Oh, and Mom sends her best,' Don said.

'Tell her thanks. I'd better go – I'm low on fuel.'

'Just remember, keep an eye out for bears, be careful and work slow.'

'Thanks, I will.'

'And Charlie says there might be a chance that we could get down again if this warm spell lasts – the river has got some ice but not a whole lot yet. We'll try for you.'

His words gave me new hope – I knew that the three of us could achieve as much work in one or two days as I could do in a week. 'Well if you could that'd be great Don, but don't take any risks on my account.'

He chuckled. 'Don't you worry about that, we'll be just fine. Goodbye now.'

I sat back and thought about peeling logs, wishing that I could just build with the bark on. Logs must be peeled because the bark holds many little lives, such as the bark beetle, and if it is left on the

* A drawknife is a heavy curved blade set between two handles. The user pulls it down and towards him along the surface of the log, peeling off the bark as it goes.

cabin will soon be crawling with insects – people have been kept awake by the sound of beetles boring away at the wood. The peeling process has to penetrate deep through the bark and the cambium layer, leaving behind clean, bare wood. The cambium is a whitish, gut-like layer that lies beneath the bark and holds snugly to the wood. It is full of sugars, and if left on the wood it will mildew and rot, making the logs turn slowly black. In spring it would take a man roughly half an hour to peel a tree, as a thick, lubricating layer of viscous sap would lie between the wood and bark. At this time of year, however, the sap has gone, and the bark and cambium are stuck hard to the wood, making the job much more difficult.

I decided to take a day off to work on the camp, which had been neglected during my intensive tree-felling phase. Some essential maintenance was needed, as well as some preparations for the bad weather that was inevitably coming, and which I was determined would not catch me unawares. First I began reinforcing my wall tent, setting up a second stout ridgepole of spruce above the roof, slinging a tarpaulin over it and pinning it down outside the canvas, leaving an insulating space in between. The arrangement looked promising, and I was comforted, although I knew it was still woefully inadequate. I then set up a smaller tent and stored in it all the remaining tools lent to me by Charlie, along with rolls of insulation ready for the cabin roof. I watched as Fuzzy strolled off through the dry leaves, lifting his leg against a favourite tree, and this turned my mind to my own toilet arrangements. I still hadn't found myself a proper toilet site, and up till now had been making do with digging small latrines every few days. What I needed was a proper khazi, I thought: somewhere I could sit and reflect for as long as required in simple comfort and safety. I scrambled down the ridge behind the cabin site and found a flat area of ground where a belt of willow grew. Clearing the leaves and fallen wood, I discovered that the ground was firm and sandy, and set about digging.

An hour later I was standing in a decent-sized hole, and this spurred me to dig even deeper, until eventually I could no longer see out of the hole, and was flinging the earth high above my head to get it over the sides. I stopped. Fuzzy had walked to the lip of the shaft and was gazing down with a look of bewilderment. I glanced up towards the darkening grey sky, and then at the dank walls that surrounded me. A flutter of panic passed through me: had I dug the hole so deep that I could not get out? 'Oh God – please no,' I said aloud, and turned in a small circle, feeling like a prisoner in a mediaeval oubliette. I wondered if the sides might collapse in on me. I could not think of a more ignominious and dreadful end than to be found buried at the bottom of my own latrine hole. As always when playing out the many potential disasters that might befall me, a headline came to mind: *Alaskan Adventurer Digs His Own Grave.* The sheer stupidity of it amazed me – how could I have let myself get into this situation? 'Be calm,' I said to myself: 'Think.' I tried to stand on the handle of my propped-up spade, reaching up to catch hold of the edge of the hole, but the spade fell over and I only succeeded in dislodging a good bit of earth.

For a while I could think of nothing, except the image of a large bear arriving at the edge of the hole, unable to believe its luck. I imagined it reaching down into the hole with its great paws – or jumping down into the hole with me. The vision was all too believable, and shook me into action. I pulled my thicker knife from its sheath and cut foot holes in the crumbly soil all the way up one side of the bank. Slowly I began to climb, the foot holes giving way under my weight but providing just enough leverage to enable me to scrabble up the sides. I grabbed hold of the edge, pulled myself out and lay face down on the ground, savouring my freedom. Fuzzy nudged a wet nose into the palm of my hand, as if to say, 'Get up – don't be so overdramatic.'

Back in the tent, my thoughts turned to food. I was running seriously low on provisions. Thanks to the cold I at least had plenty of water: I had been chipping ice from the lake and melting it on the stove, yielding about two and a half gallons a day. But my food stores were low: I only had a couple of bags of rice and flour, some potatoes and dried beans. On the positive side, I had hundreds of tea bags and plenty of coffee, as well as ample supplies of cooking oil. I also had, bizarrely, three small portions of honey in bear-shaped bottles (why did I buy them?), one tin of condensed milk and a carton containing the juice of eight Sicilian lemons. This last was sent to me by my mother, who was worried about me contracting scurvy. My oil lake was good news, as it meant that I could cook anything I managed to catch, but nevertheless my staples were very low. On my last provisioning trip I had had to sacrifice food for tools, and had been unable to do what old timers traditionally did, which was to place orders for their 'winter outfit'. All the staples needed for 'wintering out' would arrive on the last barge* in a solid nailed box, which would be carried off to stoutly made winter camps.

I sat looking at my pathetic pile of provisions, and thanked luck that I had been taught to cook from a young age, and could thus make the most of the meagre rations. It would be some time before I could make a provision run to Galena, as I had to wait until after ice-up. One thing was certain – I needed to do more hunting to bolster the contents of my food store, or I would soon run into trouble.

Night was coming on when I headed off along the portage with my .22 rifle, Fuzzy by my side. Contrary to the Western way of looking at things I scanned the trees and undergrowth from right to left for grouse as this way it's easier to pick up any movement. Nothing stirred, and the woods seemed totally empty. Where were they? My mouth watered as I imagined a large grouse and some chopped potatoes roasting with black pepper and a pinch of sage and rosemary in my heavy iron pot. Suddenly a loud aggressive chattering stopped me in my tracks. A little red squirrel sat on a spruce bough above me. Quietly I loaded the rifle, leant against a tree and waited, and when the squirrel settled I fired. A heavy thud on the soft forest floor told me he had died quickly. 'Fetch!' I said to Fuzzy, and he looked at me uncomprehendingly. I trudged into the undergrowth and picked up the tiny creature, relieved that it

---

* A large barge plies skillfully up and down the Yukon during the months when there is no ice. Normally the last barge comes in September, before the ice floes set up in earnest.

had died instantly but disappointed by the size of the meal to come. Back at camp, I gutted and skinned the squirrel – a similar job to preparing a rabbit except in miniature – and then chopped the haunches away and fed the rest to Fuzzy, who skulked off to eat it under a tree. I then removed the meat from the bone and fried it in olive oil with some garlic. I ate it with boiled rice, and tried to convince myself that it was delicious, but had to admit that it was a drab and rather sinister repast. Perhaps my next hunting trip would be more successful, as the meal had involved much effort for very little enjoyment.

The next day dawned still and mild again, and I set off early after a sturdy meal of porridge and sweet black coffee. It was time to start peeling. Arriving at the nearest logging site, I cast my eye around the logs that lay waiting in the thick bush. They would be difficult to extract, but I had no choice but to get started. I straddled a log nearest to the portage, leaned forward with the draw knife and dug the blade through the bark until it touched the wood. I tilted the blade towards me and pulled hard, and a thin strip of bark and cambium curled up from the black steel edge, revealing the beautiful white wood beneath. A residue of thick, glutinous sap clung to my hands and clothes, turning black as it dried, and the air filled with the intoxicating scent of spruce. I could only peel off a strip about a foot wide before I had to reposition the log, and my hands and wrists took the strain as the blade repeatedly stuck on knots. Day after day I peeled, until I was bug-eyed and my hands were raw. The work was tedious and painfully slow, and I grew increasingly morose. Sometimes the silence of the woods seemed to grow to a point where I could not ignore it, and I would stop and sit very still. During those solitary days my moods altered wildly, and although occasionally happy, the tension and self-inflicted pain of my situation would often overcome me. The woods were dark and lonely, and I would imagine a great brown bear silently edging its way across the thick moss towards my vulnerable back.

18

WHEN BLACK BEARS LOOK LIKE MEN

After each day's work my spirits rose as the pile of peeled logs slowly grew. They lay in the dark undergrowth, standing out from their unpeeled cousins like British holiday-makers on a Spanish beach. But the endless work was taking its toll: I was getting thinner, and one morning noticed that my hand was behaving oddly. My fingers felt numb, and when I made a fist and then opened it again two fingers remained clenched. During the following days I got used to straightening the digits out with the other hand before starting work.

One morning after breakfast I was sitting in my tent, sipping coffee and staring out at nothing in particular, when I heard a thud, followed a split second later by the retort of a powerful rifle. The sound rang out in the silence of my little camp, and I leapt to my feet, startled. I strained my ears for more shots, but heard nothing, and began preparing for another working day. Pocketing four extra rounds for the rifle, I ambled down the portage, passing through the nearest logging site, where twelve peeled logs now lay. At my second logging site, a dense stand of spruce stood darkly over rich, mossy ground. I had named this 'the enchanted wood', because of its serene quality and deep silence, which was due to the particularly thick forest that had grown there. All around me logs lay ready to be peeled, and I picked one nearest to the portage and started work. After some minutes I became aware of an unfamiliar sound, and realised it was the sound of voices. I looked up to see two Indian men approaching, their sleeves rolled up and hands and arms red with dried blood. I stopped work and raised a hand in greeting, and the larger of the two men asked, 'Who cut the portage?' His voice was neutral, and I was uncertain where my answer would lead.

'Well, um . . . I did,' I replied.

He spat contentedly, showing teeth blackened by chewing tobacco. 'Well hey, you done pretty good job there.'

'Thanks' I said, waiting for whatever was coming next. I had grown used to these conversations with Indians, which seldom contained unnecessary information. There was a silence, during which both men openly scrutinised the stranger before them, and then the smaller one spoke:

'Your portage sure helped us get a moose.' He raised his chin towards the river: 'we can take him down to the river better.'

'Oh that's good – I'm glad.' I remembered the shot. 'So you got him this morning did you?'

'Yeah, shot him way down at the grass lake. Gonna be good meat, and we're happy 'cause the season ends in two days.'

The big man took out a tin. 'You chew?' he asked.

'I wish I did,' I said. 'I've got whisky if you boys would like a drop.'

They both held up their hands. 'Shit, no!' the big one said. 'We Indians go crazy on that stuff!'

We laughed, although the history on that subject is truly grim, and not a subject for humour except in the company of Indians.

After another pause, he spoke again: 'What are you doing here?'

I stood up stiffly from my position on the log, feeling like a bow-legged rodeo rider. 'I'm building a cabin up at the end of this portage.'

They looked at each other and nodded: 'You living in the woods?'

'Yes. A man named Don Lowe up at Galena has been helping me – you know him?'

'Oh yeah, now he's one real good woodsman – you're lucky. Are you staying when the cabin is done?'

'Well, for the winter – then I have to get back to my family.'

'Family?' The little one whistled. 'Hmm, that's tough.'

Another silence, then the big man nodded at the logs. 'You peeled these logs?' he asked.

'Yes' I admitted, feeling a little sheepish as I felt they probably didn't look very professional.

'Look good,' he said. 'How you gonna get 'em up to camp?'

I shrugged. 'I'm not sure yet.'

They looked at each other and laughed. Then the big man said: 'We need more white men like you here!'

'Why?' I asked.

' 'Cause you come and make portage, build house and go home!'

We all laughed, and I turned back to my work. As they left, the bigger man called, 'Hey, you seen the bear sign around?'

I looked up. 'No.'

'Well you better be real careful, 'cause we seen lots of it on the portage down towards the river. When you been down at the river?'

I thought for a moment. 'Not for about three weeks now.'

'Three weeks?' He shook his head. 'Well, them bears is using your portage too, so watch out. We've cached a moose in a tree up there by the grass lake – tomorrow we'll come back with a four wheeler to collect it.'

As they walked off, talking quietly, I raised a hand to say goodbye. When it grew too dark to work I hung up my drawknife. I reckoned I had just a few more days of peeling to go.

The Indians' warning about bears weighed on my mind as I walked back to camp, and I scanned the undergrowth warily on both sides of the trail. Suddenly Fuzzy stopped and stood dead still, a blood-curdling growl playing out from behind bared teeth.

My blood froze, and I stealthily unshouldered my rifle and chambered a heavy round. Fuzzy sneaked slowly forwards, sniffing the path as he went until he stopped at a great black mound of bear droppings lying in the middle of the portage, steaming in the chill air. I stared down at it, alarmed by the thought of a large predator passing along my portage, and defecating where I had just walked. Had it watched as I passed by? Was it watching me now? I carried on slowly up the trail, shouting and clapping my hands to ensure that it heard me, and would perhaps move away.

I arrived at camp exhausted and deeply relieved to be home. It was fully dark now, and black clouds rolled overhead, bringing heavy drops of rain. I set up the tarpaulin for collecting water, and loaded BB shot and lead slug into the pump shotgun before settling into my usual night-time routine. It rained heavily all night, and I kept the stove burning until morning as much for comfort as necessity. Before going to bed I called Don on the satellite phone to ask his advice about a technical point, and he passed me a message from his daughter, Jenny. She had been flying over the area with a colleague, surveying for moose, and had seen a big brown bear mooching about not far from my camp. I found it hard to sleep that night, feeling jumpy and anxious. Although well armed, there was no way I could defend myself if a bear burst into my tent while I was sleeping. Every noise outside was exaggerated, and in my mind became the sound of a bear, nosing around the camp.

The bears of the Interior of Alaska are renowned for being particularly aggressive. This can be largely attributed to their limited supply of food in comparison with the coastal bears, which have rich shorelines on which to forage, unhindered by the cold of the Interior. Stories of bear attacks abound, including a particu-larly nasty one about a young couple who were visiting a family who owned a cabin on a lake in the Interior. They had rowed across the lake with some provisions, and came across a large black bear loitering in the bushes near the cabin. Far from being perturbed by their presence, the bear seemed interested and began to approach. The couple clambered on to the roof of the cabin to get out of the bear's reach, whereupon it came over and stood on its hind legs, sniffing above the gutter line to try to reach them. The woman began to panic, and the bear started to climb up the roof, intent now on pulling one of them down. Somehow they managed to keep the animal at bay for several hours, until it gave up and ambled off into the woods. In the respite the couple decided to take a risk: he would run for the canoe and strike out across the lake to fetch help, whilst she would remain on the roof just in case the bear caught him on his way to the boat. He made it to the canoe without incident. When he returned, however, he found that the black bear had pulled the woman from the roof. He found her mangled and half eaten body nearby.

The advice regarding bear attack is well tested, and over the years there have been certain revisions in approach. Although there are many things that one can do to reduce the chances of coming face-to-face with a bear, sometimes an encounter is unavoidable. The accepted approach with a brown or grizzly bear is to stay very calm and still, while keeping up some kind of dialogue with the animal to try to communicate that you don't mean it any harm. The Hollywood version of a bear attack would have us believe that bears stand up when they're about to attack. This is wrong – the standing bear is simply using his height to get a better view and scent. If the bear is upwind of the person it will usually manoeuvre itself into a position where it is downwind, and can get a better scent. This is a critical point, and more often than not it will drop on to all fours and move away fast. Sometimes, however, it will decide to move in, and if you are lucky enough to have a gun, this is the time to get ready to use it. Hopefully the bear will opt for a stalking approach, thus giving you a chance to shoot it. However if the bear charges then God help you, as bears move with the speed and fluidity of cats. Men have been found mangled and dead beside rifles with barrels bent by the attacking grasp of a bear. Examination has shown that more often than not a round has been chambered, but too late to be fired. The advice is to visually fix a point between yourself and the bear such as a tree, stone or branch, and determine that if the bear crosses that point he must be shot. In this close up, unplanned meeting with a dangerous bear, the best thing a tenderfoot can do is get as many bullets into the bear's chest as possible, in the hope of stopping it in mid-charge.

For the unarmed the advice is never to attempt to fight a brown bear, although some incredible stories are told of men who have fought and survived despite terrible injuries. One involved an Indian hunter who was cornered when he was out of reach of his rifle. He drew his bowie knife and waited. Having been around bears all his life, he knew that they were often right handed, so he waited for the first scything blow from the bear's right paw. After each swipe, he darted in and stabbed the bear, until finally, half dead himself, he managed to kill it. For most unarmed mortals, however, the only hope is to 'play dead', and lie face down with elbows and legs spreadeagled to brace oneself with hands joined over the back of the neck. The idea is to try to avoid being 'flipped' by the animal. In the past the advice was to tuck into a ball, but this led to bears rolling their victims playfully about in the under-growth. Climbing trees is not recommended, as bears are excep-tional climbers. There have been instances of people managing to shoot bears while up a tree, but most trees are not that good for climbing, and more often than not the bear would catch the person long before they even got to a branch. At all costs, one must try not to stimulate the bear's chase instinct, and running is the worst idea of all, as bears can reach thirty-five miles per hour. More often than not, with a brown bear, the playing dead approach will do the trick, and once the bear has reassured itself that the human is no threat, it will move peacefully away.

With a black bear, however, the tactic is completely different. Playing dead is as good as serving yourself on a plate; meeting with no resistance it will happily settle down and start eating. Here there is no choice but to fight for your life, and unlike a brown bear, which can weigh over one thousand pounds, a black bear is usually half the size, so there is some hope. Bears of all kinds, however, are unpredictable, and will often act totally out of character. What they all have in common are bouts of bad temper – particularly when they are going into or coming out of hibernation, protecting a food cache or accompanied by young cubs – and incredible agility and strength. My approach was firstly to take every measure possible to avoid an encounter, and second, if by bad luck I did find myself face-to-face with a bear, to be at all times well armed and able to defend myself. This is the approach of most native Alaskans, and for this reason very few are killed by bears.

A well-documented case of a bear attack took place recently in Katmai National Park on the Alaskan Peninsula, and involved a man named Timothy Treadwell.* He had spent thirteen summers living amongst and filming grizzly bears, and had become a self-taught expert in bear behaviour. He refused to accept the danger of getting too close to these immense animals, and swam and moved freely among them, touching and whispering messages to them. In October 2003 he was staying with his girlfriend in a remote cabin when a brown bear came into camp. He stepped out in order to communicate, and his girlfriend filmed as the bear approached, dropping the camera when it pushed him down and – unexpectedly – began to eat him. She too was killed, and the camera's audio recorded their terrible last moments. It takes a long time to be killed by a bear, as they start on the lower limbs, buttocks and soft tissue. Bears are also keen on our glands, and seek these out with relish. Timothy Treadwell was heard crying out in desperate pain, trapped and begging to die. His death lasted for over an hour.

As I walked down the portage to peel more logs the next morning I still felt nervous, and the sight of that great mound of bear scat did little to calm my increasingly over-active imagination. I returned to the purgatory of log peeling with the heavy 45/70 strapped across my back, and despite the discomfort felt safer with it near at hand. I, like all the animals around me, was getting panicky about the coming cold, and I knew that the bears would be unhappy and

* Timothy Treadwell's story was documented in the film *Grizzly Man* (directed by Werner Herzog, 2005).

tense, trying to cram in as much food as possible before the snow gave them the signal to hibernate.

Around mid-morning the two Indian hunters passed by again, this time riding an ancient Honda Fourtrax quad bike. They both carried light calibre (.223) semi-automatic rifles, which were nevertheless effective due to their high output of around thirty rounds from a curved magazine clip. I took a break and we sat chewing dried fish and talking about moose and bears before they headed off to the grass lake where they had cached their moose kill in a tree.

Half an hour after they had gone I heard a long volley of shots echo through the woods. I put down the draw knife and sat still, listening. Another series of shots rang out, the sound dying away in the silence. Assuming that the hunters were being attacked by a bear, I ran as fast as I could along the twisting portage, through the darkening woods and down on to the grass lake where I set out along the parted grass where the Honda had passed. Out of the corner of my eye I spotted a large pair of black shoulders in the bushes. Thinking it was the black fleece of one of the hunters I stopped and called out: 'Hey! Are you okay?' In response a large black bear turned around and fixed me with her small eyes, and then, to my further horror, two large cubs trundled up. I had committed the cardinal offence: I had surprised a bear. Worse still, it was a mother and two cubs – the worst of all possible bear encounters. I stopped dead in my tracks, chambered a round into the rifle and rested my finger on the trigger just as the bear dropped and pushed through the bushes towards me. She stood up on her back legs and sniffed loudly, staring at me myopically. For a few seconds she stayed still, and my thoughts floated in molasses as I readied myself for the worst. Then she suddenly dropped again and charged away through the bushes, followed by the two cubs. I remained frozen where I stood, still pointing the rifle and feeling weak with relief. With trembling hands I levered the round out of my breach to clear the chamber, but failed to catch the shiny brass cartridge, which fell at my feet. I stood staring in vain down at the ground, astonished that such a shiny piece of brass could disappear so completely.

I was still moving the grass about with my boot when the two hunters appeared, driving slowly towards me with the moose meat tied to the front and back of the bike. They switched off the engine and sat looking at me respectfully. After a moment's silence I realised they thought I was analysing the tracks of the troublesome bear. I raised a hand, deciding not to disillusion them by telling them I had simply lost a bullet. They stepped off the bike and walked slowly towards me. 'You seen anything?' the smaller of the two men asked.

I kept looking down, not wanting to reveal that I had been stupid enough to call out to the bear, mistaking it for a person. 'Well . . .' I paused for effect and the two men waited in silence: 'One female over there.' I nodded towards the bushes in a sage, grizzled sort of way. 'Got two cubs'.

The two men nodded slowly, clearly impressed. 'Yeah, you right,' the bigger one said: 'Them was big cubs too. That big black bear was after the moose kill – they got a good bit of our meat, the fuckers, and they did not want to go.'

'Did you shoot at them?' I asked.

He stuffed some tobacco under his lip. 'Nah – we don't need no bear meat. Too much to carry, and we gotta go three hundred miles downriver.'

I nodded. 'So . . . I better keep an eye out for bears.'

They both looked serious. 'Yeah, you better.'

As they turned to go the bigger man's gaze fixed on something on the ground. 'This yours?' he asked.

'Oh yeah – actually it is,' I mumbled, 'Thanks.'

He looked on as I loaded the bullet into my rifle, and a knowing smile spread across his face. He'd rumbled me, but thankfully he was merciful. 'Hey – thanks for coming to see if you could help.'

'Don't mention it.' I smiled sheepishly and shrugged. 'Don't quite know what I could have done, but I thought you might be in trouble.'

'So how you gonna get them logs up the trail?' he asked.

'Planning to use the chainsaw winch.'

'Shit, that's pretty slow, ain't it?'

'I know' I answered, 'But unfortunately I don't have a choice.'

He looked down and thought for a moment. 'We'll leave this bike for you,' he said. 'You got rope?'

'Yes.'

'You got fuel?'

'Well, I've got a bit . . .'

'You can use this bike then. We don't need it 'cause soon it will snow and then we'll be using snow machines. Won't need the bike again till summer.'

'Are you sure?' I asked. I knew that the battered old four-trax would make a huge difference to the laborious job of dragging the peeled logs up my portage, and could hardly believe my luck.

'Hell yeah – we don't need it. You take it.'

They climbed back on the bike and puttered down the portage with their load of moose meat, somewhat depleted by the scavenging bear. I walked behind them down to the slough's edge and helped them load their boat. It was very cold with a heartless easterly breeze, and I looked on jealousy as the men stepped into the heated wheelhouse cabin and started the engine. Fuzzy leaned against my leg as though pushed there by the wind, and we must have looked a sorry sight. I noticed the two men rummaging about in the boat for something, and then the big one emerged with a box.

'Candy, beer, .22 ammo, fish-sticks,' he said, passing it over the bow.

'Hey, thanks – that's great.' I accepted the box without protest. Any boost to my provisions was welcome, and the time for polite refusals was over.

He stood back and looked at me. 'You want a wife?'

I widened my eyes in amused surprise, and then held up my hand. 'Um . . . no thanks, I've got one.'

He tilted his head, raising an eyebrow. 'So?'

'So . . . Ah . . . Well thanks, but I'll be okay.'

He smiled and raised a finger, then turned and disappeared into the wheelhouse before re-emerging with a copy of *Playboy* magazine. 'Here – you might run out of toilet paper . . .' He gave me a knowing look: '. . . course you could use moss and save the magazine!' He jumped nimbly on to the beach and pushed the boat off into the frigid brown stream before jumping back in.

I placed the box down on the frozen sand. 'Thanks!' I shouted, and waved the lurid magazine above my head. 'Especially for this – it'll make perfect fire starter!'

They laughed and clapped before aiming the boat downstream and opening the engines out to power away.

I watched the silty water turn creamy-coloured in their wake, and didn't take my eyes off them until they had disappeared. With a shiver I felt the return of my old companions: loneliness and fear. Everything looked cold and hard: the slough had shrunk and flowed now between dark frozen beaches of black silt; the willows and alder had lost their leaves and the cottonwoods above were bare except for a few washed-out blotches of foliage in their canopy. Fuzzy sat staring up at me with a worried expression as the wind parted and then flattened his thickening coat like the hands of a ghostly judge at a dog show. I turned and looked up at the steep cut-bank, realising I would have to cut a siding into it to ensure I could reach the bottom of my portage when everything froze over. I pummelled the silt with the heel of my boot and the frozen top layer broke away, showing that I still had time to dig it out before the ground became too hard. 'More bloody work' I mumbled, edging up the bank towards the woods.

I ambled slowly along my portage, thinking of the two hunters and reflecting on the fact that instead of the white man handing out his charity, here was I, alone and on the edge of a river, gratefully accepting a box of goodies from two native Alaskans. I glanced into the precious box, catching a glimpse of a tanned thigh on the cover of the magazine, and let my mind wander on to the subject of women. For months now I had been separated not only from a woman's body, and all the comforts and joy that came with it, but also from the civilising influence of women. I was living in a relentlessly macho world, where blood, guns, fear and brutality were everyday companions, and I badly missed my wife's gentle and reasonable take on things. The Indian hunter's offer of a wife came back to me, and I smiled at the thought, wondering what he would have come up with had I accepted. If I'd been single I might have been tempted, as I knew that many dark, lonely months lay ahead.* Instead I looked at my gold wedding ring, which seemed especially bright against my cold, battered hand. It felt good to wear it, a spiritual beacon – a reminder of what I had waiting for me at home, in case I ever got lonely enough to forget.

---

* In reality this is just a practical solution to the problem of finding a mate in one of the most deserted places on earth. Generally speaking, the frozen expanses of the sub-arctic do not make an ideal meeting place, and courtship could never be subtle in a place where the cold turns words to ice. Thus a kind of informal match-making is often practiced, and brothers keep a weather eye out for suitable men for their bored sisters, and vice versa.

19
SADDLE NOTCH SORE

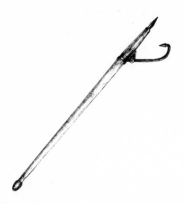

The hunters had left me an extra twenty gallons of fuel, which I cached thirty feet up a slim tree, and by early October, after five days of dangerous improvising, I had managed to drag all the heavy green logs up to camp. The logs weighed much more than the Honda, yet somehow the battered old quad bike did it for me time after time. Some mornings the starter button had frozen, and I had to take my gloves off and hold my hand over the mechanism or blow on to it through a cupped hand until it unstuck.

Each log had first to be dragged laboriously out of the thick undergrowth and on to the portage, using a rope attached by the endlessly dependable timber hitch, which is quick to tie and holds firm while pulling, yet still slips off easily when the job is done. Once the log was on the portage I would charge up to camp at full speed, somehow gathering sufficient momentum to heave it over the peaks, troughs and obstructions. Sometimes I would make it up to the brow of a hill, then the bike would lose power as the great log joined forces with gravity to pull me back down again. Just before I felt the backward slide begin, I would grab a wooden wedge, cut specially for the purpose, and shove it under one of the front wheels. Then, moving as softly as a cat-burglar in the Louvre, I would ease myself off the creaking bike and attach the hook from my come-along to the bumper. I would then harness the winch mechanism to a tree, so that I could hand-winch the bike and its load up and over the brow of the hill. When all was steady, I would continue the charge for camp. Once in camp I would hand-lever the log up on to cottonwood rollers using a peavey. At the end of each day's work I would stand and count the logs, slowly but surely drawing closer to the magic fifty-two I needed to begin building.

On the night following my last log run I sat on my bedroll, trying to read a collection of poetry given to me by a friend. After a short while I threw it aside, too preoccupied to concentrate on anything that didn't relate to building my cabin. I lay back and stared at the canvas above my head, mentally rehearsing the work that had to be done in the last few weeks before winter started in earnest. Tomorrow would be my first day of building, and although Don had given me basic instructions as to how to get started, I felt far from confident.

The world outside my tent seemed quieter than normal, which I put down to imagination until I noticed that when the wood in my stove cracked I couldn't hear the usual corresponding echo in the woods. I parted the tent flaps. It was snowing: great fat flakes were falling, and had already covered my camp in a thick, white carpet. I crouched in the door of my tent, watching the snow silently fall.

My thoughts were interrupted by the soft padding noise of footsteps on snow, and I saw Fuzzy approaching. He had a thick layer of snow on his back, and as I looked at him he made a friendly growling sound. 'What's up fruitcake?' I asked. He pawed at the tent, and I saw his meaning. I lifted the canvas and pointed to a spot by the stove: 'There.' With a great show of respect and understatement he picked his way over to the stove, turned three times and settled down with a contented grumble. I wrote in my diary: 'Must build house for dog . . . Maybe I can live in it too.' Fuzzy was making a soft growling sound, and I looked up to see two great loving brown eyes fixed on me. 'Good lad Fuzz' I said, and carried on writing. A few minutes later the friendly growling returned and I looked up again. He had not taken his eyes off me, and now his tongue was slurping in and out in time with his passionate growling. I half stood up from my log and leaned over to give him a pat. This was a mistake, as the display of canine passion went up a gear, and he began to make a distracting thumping noise with his tail. I gritted my teeth and tried to carry on writing, thinking that if I ignored him he would go to sleep, but the noises continued: Growl, slurp, thump . . . Growl, slurp, thump . . . Growl, slurp, thump, thump, THUMP!

Finally I couldn't stand it any more, and said, 'Fuzzy! Shut up!' His eyes darted about – clearly he was embarrassed and he rolled up demurely, pushing his nose down on to his tail and gazing up at me sadly. I turned back to my diary to continue my account of hopeless despair, and then, just as I found my rhythm again, from the corner of my eye saw that Fuzzy was creeping slowly towards me. I quickly looked up and he froze like a prisoner caught by a searchlight. 'There!' I said firmly, pointing back to the warm spot by the stove. He slunk back and lay down again, only to renew covert operations the moment I attempted to get back to work. The charade continued for some time until I gave up and sat staring at him in bewilderment. He looked steadily, almost defiantly, back at me, and I couldn't help admiring his determination. Don was right: having a dog around – however annoying – was good for one's morale. There is something so irrepressibly positive about a dog's spirit. After a while some of it has to rub off on the owner, no matter how depressed he might be. I closed my diary and made myself some tea, then sat staring into the fire with my hands sunk deep in Fuzzy's rich fur. I thought of those past adventurers and ex-plorers who had found themselves in the horrible situation of having to kill and eat their dogs – the great Antarctic explorer Ernest Shackleton, for example, had to order his men to kill their beloved sled dogs shortly after they abandoned their boat to the crushing ice. It must have been a terrible day for morale.

The snow continued to fall heavily all night, and the next morning I woke up with a deep sense of foreboding, half wondering if I should just call it quits. In fact, I knew full well that getting anywhere would be impossible until after ice-up, so there was nothing for it but to get up and get on with it. I put off opening the tent flaps, wanting to delay reality for as long as possible, and stoked up the stove ready for breakfast. I brewed a large jug of coffee, then made a pot of porridge which I ate as if it was a last meal. I looked at my satellite phone, considering making a call home, but then realised that it was the middle of the night at home. I also knew that it was not a good time to make a call: everyone was already worried, and a call from me in this mood would be unfair on Juliet. I looked down at Fuzzy, who gave my hand a firm nudge with his nose as if to say 'C'mon! Get on with it!' 'Okay boy' I sighed, 'I'm coming.' I drained the dregs of my coffee and opened the tent flaps.

I stepped out into a world that had changed. Everything had turned white, with all the mud and chaos of my camp rendered picturesque by its soft covering of snow. I stopped to look at my thermometer, which read minus twenty, then ducked back into the tent to pull on my rabbit fur hat and thick jacket. I wandered across to the cabin site, stopping to stare at the exposed cabin floor, covered in about four inches of snow. 'How am I going to do this?' I thought. 'Oh God help me . . .' I swept the layer of snow off the pile of peeled logs with a spare bough, and then moved over to clear the floor platform. Then I stood back for a moment, looking around at the picture-postcard scene that in other circumstances would have been enjoyable. 'Growl and go,' I muttered to myself, remembering that it was one of Shackleton's favourite phrases.*

Starting at the log pile, I began to peavey the first log along the cottonwood rollers towards the floor platform so that it came to rest alongside the ends of the sill logs. As I levered and shoved the heavy log over, I wished that there had been time to get a mobile

* *Shackleton's Boat Journey*, Frank Arthur Worsley

sawmill down to the site, as this would have enabled me to 'three-side' my logs. This would have vastly reduced the work involved in building the cabin – I would simply have placed one flat side flush with another, then hammered through a steel pin to hold them together. The side of the log that was left round and uncut would have been on the outside, leaving a nice smooth interior with no gaps. Instead, I now had the more difficult job of having to fit round logs to round logs, which meant that I would have to do much more cutting using the chainsaw and axe, which was particularly danger-ous in snowy conditions. The logs would also be much heavier and more difficult to work with. Round logs require far more skill from the builder, as each log has to be notched at either end in order to fit over the log beneath. To cut the saddle notches I would have to use a log scribe* to trace the contour of the bottom log onto the uncut log above, then using chainsaw and axe I would cut out the round or 'saddle' notch. Once notched, the theory was that you would flip the log over so that it fitted snugly over the bottom log as though you were slinging a saddle on to a horse.

All this took quite a bit of doing, but before I could even begin to cut notches I had to raise the logs into position. First I had to get the log as near to the cabin as possible, and then I would drag my pulleys to the centre of the highline, and pull the come-along and coffin hoist chains to their maximum extension. I would hook the come-along chain around the centre of the log, and then crank it up above the level of the floor platform, dodging the heavy log as it hung suspended from the highline like some kind of mythical battering ram. I would then push it gently along until it was above a round of logs, and when happy with its position would gradually let out the come-along chain until the log came to rest. Then, using little 'log dogs',[†] I would begin to peavey and man-handle the timber into position over the supporting logs below, where it would rest precariously

---

* A log scribe is used to trace the shape of the lower log onto the log above, thus giving a guide as to the shape of the notch, so that they will fit snugly together.
† Log-dogs are simple gadgets that are hammered in place to hold a log while it is eased into position, or while cutting notches.

while I jumped down to stare along its length. This 'sighting' of the log was important, as it allowed me to make minor adjustments to the log's position, and to ensure that the natural 'bow' of the log faced out. I soon discovered that 'minor' adjustments to heavy green logs invariably involved a sledgehammer and a lot of brute force, but it was vital that, before starting to cut a notch, the log was in exactly the right position. Once I had one end where I wanted it, I would hammer the log dogs in place to keep it there while I wrestled with the other end. Magically, if I could get the chain precisely at the log's centre of balance, I found I could indeed move it with one finger as Don had said. But once the log was down, with its full weight resting on the timber below, then I had to be very careful that it didn't roll off the cabin and on to the ground, or – more worryingly – me.

The laborious process of getting each log into position took about one hour, if all went to plan. If things didn't go to plan, however, it could take much longer, and tides of panic would well up in me as the hours slipped past while I wrestled with a huge slippery log. Once the log was in place over its supporting round, with its tip resting on a butt and vice versa,* I would step back and take a breath. Now it was time to cut the two saddle notches, and to start the job of fitting it flat on to the log below, resting snugly over the two perpendicular logs at either end. Cutting a good notch was not easy – an extract from my diary on the first day reads:

'Managed the first log then winched another new one up. Practice log went well, so decided to try round notch. Completely failed – such a mistake. Led to the total waste of a log.'

The loss of a single log was a disaster, as it meant going back into the woods to fell a new tree. With each day that passed, as more snow fell, this would become increasingly difficult, and I knew that pretty soon it would be impossible. On this particular occasion, I stood staring down at the mutilated tree, knowing that it would have to be discarded and feeling waves of self-loathing and self-pity. I didn't have many thick logs, and those I had were vital for

* The butt of a log is the thick end and the tip is the thin end.

my first rounds so that I could leave the lightest logs until last. I thought of the tree's one hundred and fifty years of life, wasted by my incompetence, and of the effort in cutting it, peeling it and getting it up to camp. I looked around at all the tools Charlie and Don had lent me, waiting for an experienced hand to use them, and wished fervently that I had more practical skills. They had helped me all they could – and yet still I was failing. Bleak thought added to bleak thought, until I could stand it no longer and walked over to the tent to brew some coffee.

It was midday and it was getting dark already. Inside the tent, I looked at my sleeping bag, rolled up over the dried-out spruce boughs, then at my clothing and kit piled chaotically in one corner. The air smelled of stale coffee, and everything looked grey and grimy in the weak light. To make matters worse, a large shrew ran across my shoe heading in the direction of my meagre food stores. This wasn't the first time I'd noticed one of these invaders, and the prospect of being overrun by rodents made me snap into action. It was time to improve my living conditions, I thought – this grimy existence was demoralising, and it couldn't go on. I decided that I would make myself a bed, as I was tired of sleeping on the floor, and a chair with a backrest so that I would no longer have to spend all my time perching on a log.

I set out for a little stand of birch that lay on the other side of my lake, where I knew I could cut suitable wood for my furniture-making project. Outside the snow had stopped, and as I walked towards the frozen lake, with Fuzzy following loyally behind me, it felt quite warm. I walked out gingerly across the ice, using my axe to test the strength of the surface before taking each new step. It was some time before I raised my head, but when I did I saw something that made my hair stand on end. It was a large grey timber wolf. He had stopped dead in his tracks about fifty yards away, and was standing motionless. He had been about to cross the lake as well, and was heading in the same direction except that he had got a little further out. We both stood for a long time, simply staring at each other, and then after a while he must have remembered his errand, and trotted on down the lake in a wonderfully loose-limbed manner, turning from time to time to look back at me. My eyes followed his every step, until after a bit he darted to the right and bounded effortlessly up the far bank, disappearing into the deep stand of white spruce. He must have weighed well over one hundred pounds, and was a magnificent sight. All the guidebooks said that it was very unusual to even hear a timber wolf, never mind see one, so I knew how privileged I was to have encountered one of these shy animals so close at hand.

I looked down at Fuzzy, who gazed back at me with a blasé expression, seemingly completely unfazed by the encounter. I carried on my way, gingerly testing the ice with my axe as I walked, thinking about that incredible animal. The snow was not deep, and using young birch and alder trees I was able to pull myself up the far bank and up onto the spruce-topped ridge. I found a game trail and followed it along the ridge, down across a little grass lake and up on to another ridge, where I found myself surrounded by paper birch and white birch trees. Their delicate white trunks swaying sedately in a light breeze reminded me of the motion of yacht masts on a lumpy swell, and I watched them idly for a moment, wondering what the weather was up to. I pulled a length of bark from a large, flaky paper birch, and a wide, thick strip obligingly unravelled, revealing a sensuous orangey-yellow underside that contrasted beautifully with the white of the outer layer. Deprived of colour in the growing darkness of my black and white world, I savoured the sight, and stuffed the bark into my pocket to save it for stove tinder. Nearby I found a few delicate young trees that stood as straight as flagpoles, which were perfect for my furniture. I felled them easily, stripped them of their light branches and carried them home.

Back at camp I made a simple, surprisingly comfortable bed and armchair, as well as a long shelf to keep my clothes and food off the floor. When the chair was finished I sat down warily to try it out, worried that it might collapse under my weight. It gave a long creak and then held, putting an end to my days of perching like a parrot. The bed too was a great new luxury, and that night I slept in comfort, away from the freezing floor and the sooty-coloured shrews, who were prone to late-night arguments, and had even on occasion run rudely across my face. As I gently stretched myself out on the stout birch bed, I banished all tension relating to failed cabin projects, and watched the firelight flickering across the birch armchair. I remembered a worn-out book of Victorian stories that my father occasionally read me as a child. It is one of the few memories I have of him, and although he lived on the seventh floor of a concrete tower block in Johannesburg, those stories carried me far away from that dreary African city into other, more exciting worlds. One story in particular stuck in my mind, illustrated by a glossy colour plate depicting a man dressed in goatskins with two pistols sticking out of his wide leather belt. His blue eyes shone out with nineteenth century fervour over ruddy cheeks, and behind him there was a rough shelter complete with homemade furniture. His name was Robinson Crusoe.

Another memory I have of my father is of him teaching me to dream. When I went for occasional overnight stays in his little flat, he would tuck me into bed on the sofa and sit down beside me. 'Now Gaetano,' he would say, 'You know that when you are asleep, you can travel anywhere in your dreams – anywhere at all.' I would nod my head earnestly, eager to please my father and excited about the mysterious prospect of travelling in my dreams. 'Will you try to go far away tonight, to the other side of the world? Maybe I will do the same and we'll meet up somewhere. We'll talk about it in the morning.'

I noticed that the canvas above my head had begun to buck a bit: more snow was falling outside. I closed my eyes and decided to try to go home. I imagined my two little boys, their blonde heads and small, capable hands, and thought of Juliet alone in her bed, reading as she always did before turning out the light. I thought of her laugh and her green eyes, her serenity and intelligence, and the long, lonely journey that she too was undertaking, despite being surrounded by childhood friends and family. I pictured the Island of Mull, and the ferry cutting a white path across the blue Sound of Mull as it passed Lismore Lighthouse. I imagined myself on that ship, sitting with my family and drinking tea. As I fell asleep, the thoughts turned to dreams, and I was transported eight thousand miles back home.

20

THE ATHABASCAN CHARLES BRONSON

Sour, sweet, bitter, pungent, all must be tasted.
CHINESE PROVERB

The weather stayed warm over the next few days and the snow began to melt, turning my camp to a quagmire of slush. Freezing rain began to fall, covering the logs in a layer of ice and making them even more treacherous to work with. Despite this, the respite in the weather was giving me precious extra building time, and I was grateful. In the back of my mind was a faint hope that Don might make it out to check on my progress, and I called him on the satellite phone:

'Yeah, we been thinking of you out there.' His gruff tone was reassuringly familiar. 'You winning?'

'No, I'm losing.'

'You got them logs in camp?'

'Yes.'

'And you're making them notches?'

'Yeah. But badly – in fact I'm worried I might waste every log here.'

A silence, then, 'I'm gonna talk to Charlie. You call tomorrow, and be careful.'

I replaced the handset and prayed for the warmth to hold.

The next day I was busy hauling logs when I heard a rifle shot. The shot had come from the direction of the river, and I knew it was Don. My heart leapt, and I called Fuzzy, who had been chasing shrews. Together we charged down the portage to the slough. I sat huddled on the edge of the black beach, straining my eyes downstream until I saw two men walking slowly towards me. I lifted my 45/70 and shot into the air, and the men stopped and waved. I could have cried with joy: it was Don and Charlie, my guardian angels. As we greeted each other I had to restrain myself from hugging them, it felt so good to be with them again.

'Well, you've lost some weight,' Don observed dryly, his eyes glittering above his wild moustache. Charlie stood behind him, his dark eyes framed by a hat made of marten fur.

Charlie followed my eyes. 'So what fur is your hat?'

'Well, um . . .' I took it off and looked at it: 'It's rabbit actually.'

They laughed. 'Well, you could do better than rabbit . . .' Don looked at Charlie and shook his head: 'Comes to the Interior with rabbit fur on his head.'

'Well, what do you suggest?' I asked.

'Oh, you gotta get a beaver hat or marten maybe. You need fur that has guard hairs.'

We walked up the portage together, the men gently but persistently teasing me, hoping with each wise crack to get a good reaction.

When we reached camp Don inspected my work with the critical eye of a government inspector. 'Yup, you was heading in the right direction,' he said, 'but piss poor slow.' He looked at Charlie: 'You gonna be able to stay long?'

Charlie shook his head. 'Nah, few days at the most.' He looked at me: 'That river is running bad with ice you know – it's no time for travelling.'

I nodded seriously – I knew they had taken a risk in coming out here, and I was profoundly grateful. I mumbled something about paying for their time, but they simply waved the subject away, making me feel embarrassed at the suggestion. Don inspected my notches: 'Not too bad, but you been fucking up 'cause you haven't used a plumb line. You need to be able to adjust your log scribe so it gives a level reading.' Within minutes he had us organised and working efficiently as a team, achieving in a few hours what would have taken me the best part of a week.

That night Charlie headed back to the boat, and Don cooked up a great meal of eggs, bacon, beans and bread. I accepted my plate gratefully – it felt good to have a variation on my own cooking, but when he offered me the bottle of Insanity Sauce I firmly declined. He rustled about in his bag, then pulled out another bottle: 'You gonna need Tabasco,' he said, and scattered the sauce liberally all over my eggs. 'A man needs a hot sauce.'

I demolished the meal, hot sauce and all. Afterwards he carefully placed my bedroll on the spruce, and then lay back on my birch bed. He bent down to inspect the bed underneath before looking up with a grin. 'Yup, you're trying. Bed is badly made, but it works.' He leapt up and flew out of the tent, returning with a hammer and nails to 'make it better'.

I watched him, stunned by the man's energy and zest for life. He read my thoughts: 'See I'm just like a beaver' he said. 'My best time is when the sun goes down.'

After he'd finished he glanced around my tent, looking for something else to criticise. His eye lit upon some clothes that I had washed, and was now attempting to dry by the stove. 'Don't hang them clothes over the goddamn stove,' he said. 'One day a sock is gonna fall and you'll burn the place down.'

I got up wearily to move the clothes as instructed, and heard the bed creak as Don lay back. 'Now this bed'll do me,' he said. 'Where are you gonna sleep?'

'Oh, don't worry about me,' I said with just a touch of sarcasm. 'I'll sleep on the floor with the shrews.'

He sat bolt upright. 'Shrews! Did you say shrews?'

I stared at him in surprise. 'Yes, shrews.'

He cast about wildly. 'Gimme that bowl and get some peanut butter – there's some in my bag over there!'

I scurried about, responding to his instructions and watching as he put some peanut butter in the bowl, then placed it carefully in a corner of the tent with a little wood ramp leading up to its rim.

That night, when Don was finally satisfied with my living conditions and the lamp was off, we talked further, and I felt more relaxed than I had since coming out into the bush. Help had arrived, and I felt that at last I had a chance of completing the cabin. I was also keenly aware that these men, between them responsible for two households and five children, had made a dangerous and ill-advised journey down the river to help me. I thought of the pain that the river had inflicted on that family, and yet here they were, risking everything to reach me. I knew that I could never even come close to repaying the growing debt.

A thought suddenly occurred to me, and I asked Don: 'Hey, how's that other guy doing? The one who came out when I did?' A lone American man had arrived in Galena around the same time as me, intent on living out the winter in the wilderness. Local people had been worried about his safety, as he was clearly ill-prepared, but he had refused all advice and gone his own way.

'Oh, you mean the strange guy?' Don replied, at last sounding sleepy. 'Yeah, last time I heard he was still walking up the Koyukuk.'

'I wonder if he'll make it?'

Don shifted in his snug bed above my frozen floor. 'Don't care,' he mumbled. 'He's got no family.'

'Family . . .' I repeated to myself, thinking what a magic word it was, and knowing that my family – even though Don had never met them – were at the core of why he had agreed to help me. Since my arrival in Alaska, Don's daughter Claudette and Juliet had been emailing each other, and an enduring connection had been established between the families.

'What's that?' Don asked.

I hunched down into my bag. 'Nothing. Good night.'

The next morning we woke up to a bowl full of shrews, which I took off into the woods. The day was clear and sunny, but Don looked unhappy. He stood by the thermometer that I had hung on a birch tree, and tapped it intermittently while casting worried glances up at the sky. He came back into the tent, and I topped up his tin mug of coffee.

'Yeah, this is not the weather we need,' he said. 'We need snow, 'cause then it'll stay warm. This weather'll be making a lot of ice.'

We heard a shot echo in the woods.

'That'll be Charlie,' Don said, throwing his coffee out of the door. 'Let's get to work.'

I set about moving logs and notching, and Don moved off briskly to sort through the logs. I could see he was ordering them for me, and it worried me to see him doing this as he must have known he wasn't going to be able to stick around for very long. He bustled about, stopping from time to time to inspect my work or answer my inane questions. As I wrestled with various problems he would listen with a wry look that registered a mix of impatience, humour and disbelief. Yet we worked well together, and with Charlie on site were making good progress.

The next day again dawned cold and clear, and I knew that the dramatically falling temperatures meant that the men would have to go. By midday Charlie had arrived, and was clearly worried about the state of the river. He got to work nevertheless, and the woods were soon resounding with the sound of hammering. Beneath the positivity, however, I could feel something brewing. There was a tension emanating from Charlie, and as the day wore on I became aware that it was aimed at me. Throughout the day the atmosphere between us grew worse, and although often sugared with jocularity, every remark seemed to be barbed. At one point, when we were discussing the way a log was lying, I stepped forward to say something only to be cut off by Charlie, who said: 'Shut up or I'll kick you in the balls!'

I was momentarily stunned, but managed to laugh it off, and mooched off to peavey some logs. Later, we were both sitting on a log round cutting out a notch when Charlie dropped his chisel. It clanged on to the frozen plywood floor, and without looking at me he said: 'Get that now.' I hesitated, then dropped to the floor platform and picked up the chisel, which he took without comment. He carried on working and I went back to my notch. After a while he said: 'You go get me a pin from the tree.'

This was too much, I decided. I may be in his debt, but I wasn't going to be so rudely ordered around. 'No – you get it,' I said.

He stopped working and stared down at the log, blinking like a short-sighted man trying to read a traffic sign. I kept still, watching as his jaw muscles moved beneath his dark skin, one hand clenching and unclenching whilst the other, holding a mash hammer, began to shiver. He slowly raised his head, and as I met his eyes I saw a different man staring at me, his entire body quivering with an uncontrollable fury. His eyes were bloodshot with rage, and for a moment we stared at each other until he exploded. 'Get off this fucking log!'

'What?' I said.

He lifted himself up on his forearms, like a rider about to jump a fence. 'You get away from me! Get off this fucking log! You get off this fucking log!'

The contrast of his violent, pure white rage and the silent darkness of the surrounding trees was surreal. 'Anything could happen here,' I thought, and out of the corner of my eye saw Don looking up from his work.

'Charlie, what is wrong with you?' I said, my voice purposely quiet and calm. 'Don't order me around like your dog.'

I watched his clenched hand raise the mash hammer slightly, and saw his mouth opening and shutting as a torrent of abuse was unleashed. I heard nothing that he was saying, but watched in an abstract way as the white spittle gathered in the corners of his mouth, wondering when he was going to launch himself at me. Suddenly Don appeared between us. He had climbed up the ladder on the outside of the log wall, and was saying 'Hey, Charlie, calm down goddamn it! Whoa there now. Easy!'

He glanced at me coolly. 'Guy, you come on and help me pull them logs over. You stay here Charlie.'

'Just leave me alone,' Charlie responded coldly. 'I don't want to work with him.'

I climbed down the ladder feeling jittery and shocked. Charlie's burning attack had bitten deeply into my already fragile morale. I worked in silence, feeling upset and angry. Without Don's intervention we would have come to blows: Charlie would have attacked me and I would have had to defend myself. I brooded over this as I worked on, grateful that it had not come to a fight, but feeling that at least that might have offered some kind of release for both of us. On the other hand, in this wild part of the world anything could happen. There were guns everywhere, and fights could easily escalate until one or both protagonists was fatally injured. Don was all too aware of this, having been shot and stabbed a number of times, and no doubt having himself dished out some strong justice on luckless attackers.

A few hours passed, during which my anger ebbed away. I could understand Charlie's point of view: here he was, spending time away from his family helping some stranger from Scotland who, as far as he was concerned, was wasting his time. On the other hand, I hoped the cabin was going to be for their use after I left, so his work wasn't all for nothing, and he had been aggressive. I rehearsed both sides of the argument for a while, then decided it was time to try and build bridges. I put down my tools and walked over to where he was still working up on the cabin wall.

'Charlie, whatever happened between us there . . . I'm sorry.'

He looked up slowly.

'Maybe we were both to blame,' I said. 'Perhaps I should not . . .'

He cut me off: 'BOTH to blame?!'

'Yeah, well . . .' I paused, realising he was still very angry. 'I'll happily get stuff for you, but I just won't be treated like a dog with it.'

He sat upright and stared down at me, his expression a mixture of rage and disbelief. 'Who do you think gave you all these fucking tools to use?' He gestured around at the camp at all the kit. 'I gave you everything you fucking need to build this cabin, so don't say I've been treating you badly.'

I swallowed hard, feeling miserable and ashamed, and cursing myself for not just doing what he had asked me. Again it came home to me what a massive favour he was doing, and I knew that I had no right to expect any kind of special treatment in return. 'Charlie, I am sorry,' I said. 'I owe you an apology.'

'Oh fuck that,' he said and climbed down from the log. 'Let's leave him,' he said to Don. 'I've had enough of this – I'm going.'

As I heard those dreaded words I looked up towards the two towering spruce trees and then out across the white lake. I felt surprisingly calm, like a man in the dock receiving his life sentence, happy that at least now he could rest as the months of tension and uncertainty were over. Don's voice brought me back to the present:

'C'mon Charlie,' he was saying, 'Let's just give it one more day. C'mon!'

Charlie stood still, saying nothing.

'No-one in this family lets a man down once we say we're gonna help – that's final,' Don said. I felt for Charlie then, and clearly saw his predicament for the first time. The fact was that he did not like me, for a number of understandable reasons, and now he was caught between his perfectly human desire to see me fall flat on my face, and his duty to help and obey Don, his wife's father and a man he greatly respected. It was an awful place to be.

Persuaded by Don, he reluctantly agreed to stay on, but after a short time he left, saying he was going back to the boat.

'You better come back and pick me up,' Don said, ' 'Cause we're running outa time here.'

'Yeah, I'll be back.' He turned and walked away.

That night I kept going over the day's events, trying to fathom why Charlie's explosion had been so powerful. I began to remember all the occasions when he had predicted my failure: that I would kill myself felling trees, that I wouldn't be able to handle the isolation and hard work and so on. I then thought about his wonderful family, and the fact that in the beginning he had agreed to help me willingly. I knew that at heart he was a decent and generous man, and a good father and husband, but also – like many people out here – someone who was quite primal in his reactions. That night I called home, and as I spoke to Juliet wished with all my heart that I could be home. I felt isolated and vulnerable – in this lawless land it was not comforting to feel that I had an enemy. Don said nothing, and I knew that he was purposely keeping out of it. I didn't blame him – I felt he was probably sympathetic to both parties, but as his daughter's husband, his loyalty had to lie with Charlie.

After we had eaten, we sat by the stove. 'Guy, we're gonna have to ship out tomorrow, you know that?' Don said.

'Yes I do.' I nodded, staring into the fire. 'I think I'll be able to finish off this cabin by myself . . .' I tried to sound confident, but knew I was failing.

'Damn right you will,' he said firmly. 'Now, how are you for food?'

'Oh, I'm okay,' I lied.

He looked at me in silence for a moment. 'Well, I've cached some bacon and fish for you in the equipment tent,' he said finally. 'Not much, but a bit.'

'Thanks so much for all of this.' I looked at the ground. 'I hope I haven't caused a lot of trouble . . .'

'Nah – it'll be fine.' His tone let me know that he didn't want to discuss it, and he pulled himself closer to the fire. 'Now, you should think about killing a beaver and getting him hung up for meat – also them grouse'll be easier to spot now the leaves are gone. Shoot them at night, and if you come across a lot get as many as you can, then hang 'em on your game pole. Soon you're gonna have a freezer that never breaks down.' He stood up. 'You got any chocolate?'

'No' I said gloomily. 'All gone I'm afraid.'

'Ha!' he said with satisfaction. 'I see you're the type that can't hoard a treat.' He stood up, pulling his braces out from his chest. 'Well here's one man who knows how to hold on to 'em.'

'Hang on . . .' I said. 'Have you been saving up your chocolate bars while I've been scoffing mine all at once?'

'Yup,' he said triumphantly, rubbing his hands together in anticipation. 'And now I'm gonna eat 'em up real slow, right here in front of you.'

I shook my head ruefully. 'Don, you're a bad man.'

'No,' he chuckled, 'just a man who's been around quite a bit longer than you.'

'So where did you stash them?' I asked.

'Oh, in a little corner of that equipment tent of yours.' He opened the canvas and stepped briskly outside.

I waited, wondering if he would give me a share. A few minutes later I heard him swearing loudly. He came back into the tent bristling with rage.

'Where's the chocolate?' I asked.

He threw me an empty Snickers wrapper, gnawed almost beyond recognition and slippery with frozen rodent spittle.

'SHREWS!' we both shouted at once, and as Don sank on to the chair, shaking his head in disgust, I laughed and laughed and laughed.

The next day I walked down the portage to meet Charlie, and found him walking up through the poplars. He gave me a curt nod: 'Hey, we gotta go today – that river is full of ice floes and if we don't go we'll be stuck.'

'I know,' I said. 'And thanks so much for coming out here. I know you took a risk.'

I fell into step beside him. 'Listen Charlie, I don't expect you to say anything, but I'm really sorry about yesterday.'

'Me too,' he said, glancing quickly at me and then back at the ground.

'I want you to know that I've got a huge amount of respect for you, and without your help I would have been totally fucked out here – I know that.'

He nodded silently, still walking.

'I've been feeling under a lot of pressure out here on my own,' I said, 'and maybe I forgot my manners. So can we be friends?'

I stopped and held my hand out, and he took it immediately, a great wide smile passing across his face.

'You know, I think you're the Athabascan equivalent of Charles Bronson,' I said.

'Athabascan Charles Bronson . . .' he laughed. 'I like that!'

We walked on in companionable silence for a while, and I felt deeply relieved that we had made peace.

At camp, we stared at the half-finished cabin. I was striving to seem relaxed, but Don as always read my mind: 'Worst comes to it, you just pitch your tent up on that floor off the freezing ground,' he said. 'Plenty guys have done that when they got beat by time.'

'Okay . . .' I stared at the two massive twenty-four foot purlins* and ridgepole. 'Now just remind me: how am I going to get those into place?'

Don stared at me in mock surprise. 'Just hoist 'em up like the cabin logs, dummy.'

'But won't they smash into the cabin and knock it to pieces?'

'Yeah they will. So tie 'em off against one of the spruce trees, and just belay 'em out as you go up real slow. Once they're up you can put the roof on – you've got some tin cached down at the river, haven't you?'

'Yes I do.' I remembered a fly-filled August day, unloading tin from the boat and stacking it on the riverbank.

We stood in silence for a moment, then Don took his glove off and shook my hand. 'You'll be okay. Just work slow, and be real careful, 'cause it's gonna be a while before anyone can get to you now. No boats can come downriver 'cause of the ice, and no planes can land as there's no clear water for floats, and no ice yet for skis.'

'How long will it be?' I asked, and they shook their heads. It was clear that no-one could predict the workings of Mother Nature. 'Any chance of another break in the weather?' I asked hopefully.

'Nope – cold's coming now,' Don said. 'Better get ready.' Charlie looked on as he gathered his things, calling out nuggets

---

* Purlins are notched in on either side of and below the ridgepole, and support the roof.

of last-minute advice. Neither of them was smiling, and I felt the seriousness of my situation.

We walked together down the portage, moving with a sense of urgency as it was clear there was no time to lose. We walked across the snow-bound slough towards a narrow stream of open water that had remained unfrozen. As the men pulled on their waders, Charlie gave me a parcel and some letters from family and friends. 'Good luck and be careful,' he said gruffly, stuffing a bar of chocolate into my pocket.

'Thanks Charlie.' I shook his hand: 'Now maybe you will see me die.'

He smiled. 'No – you're gonna make it.' And they turned to walk across the icy, fast-flowing water.

I watched as they moved off towards the main river where the boat waited. Soon they were gone, and I turned and looked up the massive white slough. The familiar silence descended upon me, accompanied by the equally familiar loneliness and anxiety. I looked at the parcels and letters with their British stamps, and the sight of Juliet's clear writing brought on a wave of homesickness. Fuzzy looked up at me and barked, wagging his tail. I took my glove off and stroked his deep fur. 'Well Fuzzy,' I murmured, 'I think I can say that now we really are up the creek.'

We walked slowly along the slough, towards the high poplar trees on the bank that had become my landmark, and then up along the cold, silent portage to my camp. I stood looking at the half-built cabin, which now had four walls made up of seven rounds of logs each. I felt a new kind of calm settle over me: suddenly it seemed immaterial whether the cabin got built or not, whether I failed or succeeded, or what people back at home might think of me. I was in the hands of fate, and the stakes were much higher now than mere pride or opinion. Now all that mattered was that I came home alive.

View of the Yukon from the little shack that Don lent me in Galena. The far "bank" is really just an island.

From the start, even though he drove me crazy, I knew Fuzzy was a dog of character. He was half poodle and half golden retriever, which gave him brains and a fighting heart tempered by the loyalty of a retriever.

Heading downriver to the cabin site alone for the first time. The far bank is a long way off, and winds often went against the flow, creating rough water. Don threw in an inner tube before I left—a somber moment. Fuzzy was not happy.

Rose hips are a favorite snack for bears. Advice is to avoid thick bush—low visibility makes it easy to surprise a bear. Bears hate surprises.

The mouth of Bishop Creek, with the shoulder of Pilot Mountain on the right. I was entering the great silence.

A sad sight. Just the sill logs and floor, and winter has arrived.

Plenty of chainsaw, axe, and winch work. It's a miracle I didn't kill myself.

I would peavey the logs over to the floor and hoist them up on the highline. It was a cold, ominous time: see the wind flattening the smoke from the stove.

Don and Charlie made it out for a few days to help, and I was getting hopeful. Note the practice notch on the log in the foreground, and my birch armchair in the tent, which I was very pleased with.

Somehow it was up. Note the planks hammered up to keep the gables from wobbling about.

There it was: a picture-book log cabin in the Alaskan Interior. How strange to see a dream become a reality.

The prettier the day, the deadlier it was. This is my camp at –60, and that's not wood smoke coming from the stove-pipe, it's heat showing in the frigid air. To breathe without a veil was to risk frostbite of the lungs.

Bacon 'n' beans: The classic frontier dish. Protein aplenty and fat to keep you warm.

The months of hard work and low food stocks had begun to take their toll—I dropped three stone.

The spring sunshine plays tricks on the frozen Yukon. A mirage hangs like a curtain made of mercury.

This picture was taken towards the end of my stay. My skin prickles at the memory of those sled rides, and the exhilaration of this ancient—and hair raising—means of travel.

Towards the end Fuzzy and I were inseparable. He had a maturity that I have rarely seen in any dog. Note his superbly warm winter coat, which meant he could live out even in those incredibly cold winters. He hated to be indoors, and even when it was –50 could only stand so long inside before he'd start whining to go back out.

It was all over. Sad days of saying goodbye and traveling on a melting river.

PART 3

A sad tale's best for winter

WILLIAM SHAKESPEARE, THE WINTER'S TALE

21
THE TENDERFOOT'S CABIN IS HIS CASTLE

The weather was closing in, and I knew that I had just a matter of days to finish off the cabin. The conditions were horrendous, with freezing rain one moment, thick snow the next. My mood was as dark as each short day, and I thought enviously of the bears, snug within deep burrows, and of the beavers safe in their solid house on the lake. My tent offered little comfort because it billowed in the cold, mean wind, making any idea of living in it through the winter seem ludicrous. Thoughts of failure haunted me, but each day I carried doggedly on, working as fast as I could, though I was all too aware of the danger of working in these slippery, dark, icy conditions.

My first task was to complete the gable ends, which involved hoisting six logs on top of the walls, decreasing in length as they went up to form a triangle shape that would support the roof. It was precarious work, because the logs could not be notched and held firmly in place at each end as the wall logs had been, and had nothing but two pins each to keep them in place. For extra security I nailed a baton at each end of the gables and secured it to the walls, and this more or less kept them in place. Then it was time to begin the roof. I had dreamed of reaching this stage, but any self-congratulation was cut short when I faced the difficulty of getting the roofing materials up to camp. Twenty sixteen foot lengths of galvanised tin, weighing fifty pounds apiece, were buried deep in the snow beside the slough where I had cached them back in the summer. It took a day to dig them out and stack them, then a further day to heave the wet, icy tin up to camp through the soft, deep snow of the portage. No time to pause and reflect, however: the next job was to raise the purlins and ridge-pole, which would support the roof.

These three logs – each twenty-four feet long – were the longest and heaviest in the cabin, and their combined weight would push down on the cabin walls, solidifying the whole structure. This would be the most challenging job yet, and frightening, as the logs were so heavy. I knew that as I raised each great timber on the high-line it would want to swing to the centre, as every log before had done, only this time there was a partially built cabin in the way. Given free rein, the log would become a battering ram, and could knock the logs from their notches or damage the pins that had been hammered into each round to keep them in place. To prevent this, before lifting each purlin, I timber-hitched a ship's warp around its centre and tied it securely to a spruce tree beside the cabin. I then stood on the log, using one hand to ratchet it slowly into the air, and the other to gradually feed the rope out from the tree that was anchoring the whole operation. Once each purlin was in place on the shaky gables, I cut two hurried notches, but in reverse, as this time I had to cut into the log below. When I had finished, the purlins sat snug and round within their cup-shaped notches in the top of the gables, and the whole structure looked distinctly more solid.

Now I was facing the last hurdle – raising the ridgepole. I repeated the whole process, holding the log carefully away from the cabin as I raised it, until it dangled exactly above the highest point on the gables. I slowly lowered it into place, fully expecting the whole structure to tumble under the weight of the great log, but to my relief, after giving one long creak, it held. Instead of cutting a notch at each end, I jammed a chock of wood on either side of it, then hammered a pin through each to keep them, and their captive, in place. I climbed down and took a good look – not perfect, but it would hold.

Now the gables no longer shook, thanks to the many tons of weight that rested on top of them, and all that remained was to trim off the uneven ends of the gable logs, making a nice neat triangle shape for the roof. To do this I used a monstrous chainsaw with a thirty-three inch long bar and ripping chain. The great saw was heavy and cumbersome, but had runners that allowed me to slot it on to a length of plank that I had tacked onto the gables to act as a cutting guide. It ripped through the logs as if they were marzipan, and I tried not to imagine what it would do to my head if it kicked back. Working carefully, I managed to cut the gable edges away, and when it grew too dark to work retreated to the tent, now sagging under a thick covering of snow. My body ached, and I climbed straight into bed, too tired to even make a cup of tea. I reached for my grandfather's copy of *Henry V*, which he had carried through the First World War, and which I had brought with me for moments when I needed courage. A line leapt out at me from the page: '*Hold hard the breath, and bend up every spirit to his full height!*'

The next day I put the tin roof up, hammering it roughly straight on to the purlins and ridgepole, and then slinging the tarpaulin from my tent over the top for extra protection. I had planned to build the roof properly, putting up a plywood ceiling first, and then a layer of insulation between this and the tin, but time was running out, and a tin only roof was better than no roof at all. I tacked up some planks for a doorframe, and then made a crude door from a length of plywood, with a rope handle fastened by two empty shotgun rounds. I began shovelling the snow out of the cabin, which lay about three feet deep, but found the wood was covered in a thick layer of ice which was impossible to get rid of. I looked around the dark cabin, now as ready as it would ever be. The prospect of moving into the dark, frozen space was not at all inviting, yet as I returned for my last night in the tent, I knew it was a lot better than the alternative.

Diary, October 27th

A triumphant day! After 3 long months, I am finally in my cabin. I have completed stage one of this difficult journey: I have built a home from the woods, using logs I cut, peeled and notched myself, and it's a great feeling. Got up at 5am to let the stove go out so that I could move it across to the cabin. The tent was billowing in the wind and it was dark and ominous. Threw the charcoals on to the snow and then with gloves lifted the stove outside. Waited for the stove to cool down, and watched the steam rising as its hot sides melted the snow. It felt very, very cold, and made me realise how much I depend on that stove. When it was cool enough to touch, I moved the stove into the cabin and it fitted easily, but then panicked as I'd forgotten to make a hole in the roof for the stovepipe. Tried to hammer axe through the galvanised tin, but couldn't. Had a bright idea to use shotgun, so loaded it with buck and slug and lay down and shot at the ceiling. Bit brutal, but it worked – after 8 rounds I had a perfect six-inch diameter hole! Hammered the sharp bits up and fed the stove pipe sections through, then got the stove going straight away to start warming things. Strange and exciting to bring fire into this cold, dark space. Spent ages moving all my stuff across, until finally all my worldly goods are in my new home. Cooked my first meal in the cabin, and am now tucked up in bed with the stove burning red hot. Dripping wet as the ice melts, but I don't care. The wind has picked up outside, but I am enjoying hearing snow thudding against my new solid walls made of whole trees a foot thick. After all these months of worry and hard work, at last I feel safe.

The first few days in the cabin were bliss, despite the dripping dampness as the logs thawed out. It felt wonderful to be protected and enclosed, when for months the only thing that had lain between me and millions of acres of wilderness was a flimsy canvas sheet. Whereas the tent had seemed to magnify everything, from the weather to the wild animals, my cabin felt safe and solid, and at last I could afford to relax. A word formed in my head – one that was unfamiliar, and sounded out of place in this empty wilderness. Home. 'Home', I said to myself aloud as I sat in the cabin that first night. Against all the odds, I had managed to make a home in one of the world's coldest regions, and it was a great feeling. Where would it have all gone without Don and his family? I thought, also, of the native Alaskan hunters and that tough old Honda that they lent me. It was so unexpected to have found such friends. With a shameful sense of smugness I looked around at the solid timbers that surrounded me, and listened to the storm thudding impotently against the bulwarks of fifty-two entire trees. Nothing moved or wobbled, and I knew that the box I had built was as stout as a battleship.

The stove was burning like a jet engine, and the firelight flickered and played across the sensuous curves of the woody walls. Beside it there stood a tidy pile of logs, ready for burning during the night, and in the corner a lamp hissed warmly on a tree stump beside my new bed, made from a sheet of plywood standing on four slender birch logs. At last my months of living on the ground were over, and it was a joy to be able to impose some order on my existence. I had put up some rough shelves to hold my food and other essentials, and between the purlins had fashioned a crude loft space from some straight lengths of birch, where I slung up my extra gear. I unzipped my sleeping bag and hung it up to dry in the warm air, realising that at last I would have good space for hanging up washed clothes.

It felt luxurious to move around the new home, which had miraculously come out at exactly sixteen feet square as I had intended, and to have a proper floor, albeit still covered in a dirty layer of ice. The crackling sound of wood in the stove merged beautifully with a deep scent of pine that emanated from the drying logs, and I felt as though I was enclosed within a pine cone. The only thing that diminished my joy was the lack of a companion with which to share it. I was alone – smug and happy, but alone. I wanted to celebrate: to shout and laugh and pop champagne corks, but there was no-one to do it with. I opened the plywood door and called to Fuzzy, who padded quickly across the snow towards me. He looked up at me questioningly, and I gestured for him to come in. He glanced back towards his rustic hovel, and then, less than enthusiastically, stepped daintily inside and settled with a sigh beside the stove. I emptied the precious dregs of my last bottle of whisky into a tin cup and sat down beside the furnace, savouring each sip whilst looking down at my odd companion. After a while he got up and sat by the door, clearly feeling overheated, so I let him out. I watched him scurry into the snow-filled darkness, then pulled the door tight shut and climbed into bed. I turned the lamp fuel off and watched the flame shrink, then turn blue before disappearing with a pop, and lay listening to the sounds of my new home. Outside the wind howled above several feet of freshly fallen snow, and I knew that in the morning there would be no sign of where my tent had stood for nearly three months. Wind and snow would conspire to remove all trace of me, and I shuddered to imagine what might have happened if I'd tried to live out the winter in that tent. I lay awake for some time, lost in the sheer surging weirdness of it all, and wondering, in an oddly detached way, how it was all going to end.

22
THE WINTER'S TALE

Fire is winter's fruit.
ARAB PROVERB

After one week of burning the stove at full blast, the cabin at last dried out. During this period, the joy of living above the frozen ground and surrounded by solid log walls had been somewhat diminished by the fact that everything was wet. The log walls ran with water as the ice thawed, and all of my clothes were damp, although thankfully my bedroll was within a solid canvas outer bag so it had remained dry. My rushed job on the roof meant that I had to work doubly hard to keep the cabin warm. If the roof had been insulated as intended, the snow falling on it would have warmed the cabin further. Instead, the warmth of the cabin melted the snow on the roof, leaving nothing but a dramatic curtain of icicles hanging along the sides of the house.

My labour hadn't ended with the completion of the cabin, and I now found I was having to work hard just to stay alive. The stove had to be kept burning constantly, and gathering wood was an ongoing chore. At times I felt like the stoker on a steam engine's crew, as I pulled neat round logs from my woodpile and stuffed them into the raging firebox. Before I came out to Alaska I had been warned by various 'experts' about the difficulty of gathering and cutting wood for burning when all the trees were frozen solid. The warning had hung around in the worried corners of my mind during the endless toil of cutting the portage, and then during the cabin-building period, but Don had quickly dispelled it. He pointed out that standing dead trees, of which there were plenty within easy reach, did not freeze, as there was no moisture left inside them. Standing dead spruce were perfect for starting fires, and would help to light my green wood, such as birch, which would burn for longer. Contrary to what I'd been told, the frozen green wood was not difficult to work with, in fact in many ways it was easier, as the ice in it created less resistance than water, and the brittle logs split effortlessly. Still, the job of collecting wood was constant, and took up most of my time. When I had envisaged the winter months I had imagined long, dark hours in my cabin, reading books or writing in my diary. A good friend had even given me a squeeze-box as a parting gift, as I had imagined I could use the long, lonely hours to learn a musical instrument, but little did I know how hard I would have to work. With the short daylight and atrocious weather conditions, it took all my time just to survive, with nothing left for enjoyment. With entertainment in short supply, however, it was probably just as well.

Another daily chore was collecting water for drinking, and each morning I would trek out along the lake searching for a berm of compacted, wind-blown snow. This firm, clean snow would be pummelled into my biggest pot and left on the stove, which I had banked up to burn slowly during the day. Once melted, I would use Don's trick of pouring it into a jug and out again several times, to aerate it and make it tastier to drink.

A week or so after I moved into my cabin, I was lingering over breakfast one morning, drinking tea and putting off the endless toil of collecting wood. The temperature outside had not risen above minus thirty-five for days, except when the snow was falling, when it was always warmer.* When I pulled the blanket away from the door, I was concerned to see that the plywood door was white with ice. I scraped it away and pushed the door out just enough for me to take a peek. It was snowing again, and where there had been bushes there were now just comical white mounds. I stepped gingerly out of the cabin and closed the door behind me.

Outside, the world was silent, so quiet and still that I could hear nothing except my own breathing behind my scarf. I looked over to my snowshoes which hung on a spruce tree, but decided that my portage would still be navigable without them. I turned to pick up my rifle, taking off my glove to lever open the breach and see if it was empty. The lever didn't budge: it was frozen shut, and worse still my hand had stuck to the frigid steel. It was a schoolboy error, followed immediately by another one; I pulled my hand away and ripped the skin from my fingers. 'You fucker!' I exclaimed, noticing that my voice didn't echo as usual, but disappeared in an instant, as if a white-gloved assassin had placed a hand over my mouth. I pulled my wool glove back on, watching as the blood seeped through the light-coloured wool and then froze, becoming a hardened red disc in the material. Don's advice regarding frozen guns came to mind. I walked over to the fuel tree and washed the gun through with petrol, pouring the precious fuel through the working parts and down the barrel, before drying it with a cloth. I called for Fuzzy, who appeared at the end of a tunnel of snow that he had dug into the mound that now covered the little log kennel I had made for him. His home was lined with thick, dry grass that I had cut from beside the lake, and was probably better insulated than mine.

We left the camp muffled in fresh snow, and walked along the pure white portage. My boots sank into the snow with a satisfying sound, while behind me I heard Fuzzy's little paws marking out

* Contrary to what we are used to in more temperate zones, where we see snow as a sign of extreme cold, in Alaska when it is snowing it means the weather is warm. Snow comes during periods of depression, when low lying clouds act as insulation. In high pressure, what little warmth there is disappears fast into the cold, clear sky.

their own arctic tattoo. When I stopped he stopped, and in these moments we both stood very still, just listening and watching. The portage appeared as a pure, unbroken line of white that meandered ahead of us through the black and white of the snowy woods. Light saplings of alder, birch and willow were bent across the portage, and I had to duck to avoid being dumped with their loads of snow. Some young trees had been bent beyond the point of no return, and I cut them carefully and laid them aside. The portage must be kept clear so that I could travel along it without breaking my neck or blinding myself.

We walked down to the slough, and peered down at it, as it had now sunk about thirty feet below the bank. It had stopped snowing, but a strong wind was blowing fallen snow along the slough, whipping it up into a cruel, swirling ground blizzard. It seemed to me that nothing could live in these conditions, and I felt as if Fuzzy and I were being given a rare glimpse of an impossible world.

I walked back to the cabin slowly, taking care not to sweat, as Don had taught me. But as I walked I felt my feet getting cold: my boots were too tight for these conditions, and gave no space for movement. I felt a twinge of anxiety until I remembered my mukluks, a very special present which had been given to me by the women of Don's family. They were made out of canvas with moose-hide soles, stuffed with felt and tied with lengths of moose hide. I was greatly moved by the gift, but as I looked at the beautiful blue canvas with its bright gold stitching along the top, secretly wondered if they would ever be of any practical use. They looked more suitable for a pantomime production of Aladdin than for the backwoods of Alaska, but later they were to prove their worth.

By the time I got back to my cabin it was almost dark, even though it was only midday. I fed Fuzzy from a dwindling bag of dog feed, then watched as he scurried into his cosy lair. Inside the cabin the air temperature was warm, but the floor was so cold that I couldn't stand on it my socks. The dregs in my coffee cup, which I had left on the floor, were frozen solid. When I closed the door I could see nothing, as the cabin had no window and I couldn't benefit from what little light there was outside. I fumbled about on the icy floor feeling for matches, and then lit a candle that gave me enough light to find the pressure lamp, which I pumped and then lit. The lamp's hissing light filled the wooden room, giving it a cosy glow and helping to warm it as well. I took off my socks and started to rub the toes of one foot, which had taken on a sinister, white waxy look that I knew was the beginning of frost nip. Frost nip can quickly develop into frostbite, and I cursed myself as my toes began to burn with pain. In the Interior it is seen as shaming to suffer from frost nip or frost bite. No respect is ever afforded to anyone suffering from these self-inflicted and completely avoidable complaints. As my toe came back to normal I compared this approach to the machismo that seems to surround the subject in temperate lands, as grizzled adventurers return with bits of their extremities missing, like some kind of token of bravery. Out here, it is more of a badge of stupidity.

I ate a plate of beans with olive oil, and lay back on my bed above the frozen floor, thinking about my children and Juliet. She had been absolutely right: my dream would have been her nightmare, and I could now see how utterly foolish and irresponsible it would have been to bring the family out here. I was a complete beginner, and though I was learning new things every day, each lesson seemed simply to underline my lack of experience. Today had been my first proper encounter with winter, and I had been shocked by the severity of the conditions, which I knew would get much worse. A short walk to the end of my portage had resulted in frostnip, and all my worries about bears now seemed trivial in comparison to the much more sinister, powerful threat of the cold. Now I was truly cut off, and if I fell, got hurt or made a mistake I would very quickly die. The seriousness of Don's words as he said goodbye came back to me: he had known what I didn't, the true power of an Alaskan winter.

23
TRACKS, TREES AND ANIMAL TANKS

It was early November, the days were dark and my food supply was getting leaner. The snow was four feet deep and still falling, and I was working very hard to keep the stove going around the clock. It was now impossible to walk without snowshoes, so I set out one morning to try them out. I strapped them on over my mukluks, and strode out of my cabin with big, comical steps down to the latrine hole. I had covered it with a tarpaulin so that it didn't fill with snow, and stared at it for a long time, trying to figure out what adjustments it needed to make it comfortable in this new, hostile world. Putting the problem to one side, I decided to go in search of new wood for burning, and snowshoed off towards the lake. I enjoyed walking easily on the surface of the fresh snow, now and then seeing deep holes where I had struggled to walk just the day before. The snowshoes felt like a magic carpet, taking me anywhere across frozen white clouds. Like a child with new shoes I stared down at them, lost in the old-fashioned sight of the bright blue mukluks inside the creaking birch snowshoes moving across the dry, powdery snow. It reminded me of a time when we bought Oscar some new shoes with lights that flashed each time he put his foot down – he was so entranced that we had to remind him to look ahead while he ran, fearing he might trip or run into something. I thought of his delicate blonde head, his neatly arranged nose and ears and big, green eyes. Tears welled up in my eyes, straining to fall but then subsiding as if afraid of freezing. I was missing my family more than ever, but couldn't afford to give full vent to my emotions, which given the chance would rise up and overwhelm me.

I walked on until I reached the steep, snow-covered bank on the other side of the lake, where I experienced for the first time the unique sensation of falling uphill. I placed one snowshoe on the incline ahead, and then, as I lifted the other leg, it slid back down the hill, creating a small avalanche which resulted in me falling flat on my face in the snowy bank. I lay there for a moment before pushing my hands into the snow to lift myself up, only to find my arms sunk up to the armpits, and I was left lying like a stranded whale. Finally I rolled on to my back and used gravity to get myself upright, brushing all the snow off my body before it began to melt. Clearly in this new world everything had to be relearned, including walking.

I walked up the bank at an angle, using the tops of small trees for leverage. Fuzzy walked behind me, cleverly using the compressed footprints of my snowshoes like stepping-stones. I came across a few standing dead spruce, perfect for burning, and then passed through a belt of dark spruce trees into a glowing stand of paper and white birch which stretched as far as the eye could see. I looked around in satisfaction: here I would find good-sized green logs to mix with my spruce, enough to keep me going for a long time to come. I looked down at the ground and saw the marks of a small animal in the snow. Then I realised something new and exciting: all around my camp, and especially on my portage, which was the only road in the woods, I would be able to follow animal tracks in the snow. I now had the equivalent of closed circuit television, and no man or animal would be able to enter my snowy domain without my knowledge.

Later on Fuzzy and I walked along the portage, and came across a set of large wolf prints that led right down the portage from my camp. The prints followed the clumsy trail that I had left on my first trip down to the slough, and behind the deep paw prints there were mysterious slices in the snow made by the forward flick of its paws. I followed the prints until I came to the grass lake, where they left my trail. I stood looking at the tracks, snaking off in the deep snow around the willow trees, and then stepped off the portage to follow. Fuzzy let out a concerned yelp that seemed to say 'Woah there – let's think about this'. Patting his head for reassurance, I pulled a stick of dried fish from my pocket and divided it between us. Then we walked on, following the tracks that led me for the first time down the long, snowy avenue that was the grass lake.

I was discovering new country, and with each step my little map was expanding. I followed the tracks as they led up from the lake through some willow, alder and a stand of birch and poplar. The going was harder now, and I was snowshoeing through thick, snow-covered bush and fallen trees. Remembering Don's advice about not allowing myself to sweat, I stopped just before a stand of spruce, and cut some branches to sit on. I reached into my outside pocket for my water bottle, and found it was frozen solid. 'Idiot!' I said aloud, resolving next time to carry the water under a few layers of clothing. I considered eating some snow, but knew this would make me cold, and offset any benefit the water might have done me. I sat chewing on a fish stick instead, feeling relaxed as I knew that the trail had taken me round in a rough circle, and I wasn't far from camp. Fuzzy settled on a bough that I had cut for him, chewing out ice balls that gathered between his toes. A light breeze sighed through the tops of the spruce trees, and for the first time in months I realised I felt happy. I thought back to my life in the office, and felt enormously privileged to have escaped from that hidebound environment to such a magical, unspoiled world.

I was shaken from my reverie by a great crashing and crunching noise coming from the woods ahead. I stood up quickly and whipped the 45/70 into my hands, then leaned against a tree trunk and stared into the woods, waiting to see what would emerge. Beside me, Fuzzy was growling, his lips curling and hair standing on end. I peered into the murky light beneath the trees.

The sun had gone down and night would very soon be upon us. I strained my ears, but there was nothing but silence. 'Okay,' I said after a moment, patting Fuzzy's head to reassure myself as much as the dog. 'It's okay – must have been a tree falling.' Fuzzy clearly was not reassured, however, and raised his nose to sniff the air. Then the sounds came again: CRASH, BANG, RRIIP, THWWAAAACK! It was clearly a very big animal, and was not bothering to walk around obstacles but instead crashing straight through them. I kept straining my eyes to see into the spruce forest, feeling very frightened as the sound grew louder and louder. How could there be such a sound of breaking vegetation, I wondered: there was relatively little growth beneath the dark spruce trees apart from the odd sickly looking birch or alder. Suddenly I became aware that the animal was coming from the other direction, from the birch, willow and cottonwood belt I had just passed through, and I whipped round to face the other way. 'Be calm' I muttered, as I levered a 500 grain round into the breach. The crashing and breaking continued as the animal came steadily closer, and I saw snow falling off the tops of the trees as it approached.

'This is no wolf,' I muttered to Fuzzy, who was now engaged in a series of bloodcurdling snarls. And then, suddenly, an immense, dark brown, shaggy bull moose broke through the screen of trees thirty yards away. It was a stirring sight. The animal was huge, and I felt like a hapless infantryman surprised by a tank suddenly thundering into a narrow street. A brown eye rolled in a pool of vivid white as the bull raised its huge head, topped by immense antlers, to sniff the air. The beast raised a leg and thumped it down, and I remembered Don telling me that moose killed more men in Alaska than bears, and that if ever I found myself in the unlucky situation of being chased by a moose which I didn't want to shoot, I should run round a tree. The theory was that you ran round until the animal got tired, bored and disoriented. It sounded easy, but if you slipped or if it caught up with you, the moose would kill you quickly by pummelling you into the ground with its great piston-like legs. At least I was near a tree. I looked closely at the animal's huge flank, judging that he must have weighed well over one thousand pounds, and his rack of horns looked at least four feet wide. Dog, man and moose all stood very still, until finally the leviathan engaged his reverse gear, and crashed back into the woods.

I stood in the same spot for a few minutes, feeling utterly drained by the experience but also incredibly excited at having met the world's largest species of deer. It was dark, but the snow gave off some light, and I called Fuzzy, who trotted ahead, showing me the way home. I walked through the woods, occasionally looking up as the night sky advanced towards the paler, lemony light in the west. Above me, a beautiful shape caught my eye. A willow grouse was seated high on a branch, looking down at me. The bird looked plump, and I imagined it roasting gently in my heavy iron pot. A series of worried chirps came from a nearby tree, and the bird lifted and whirred off over the twilight canopy. Then another whirred up, followed by another and another. Fuzzy stood on his hind legs, whining and pawing the snow, as nearly twenty plump birds flew off to land in nearby trees.

I walked on, marvelling at the abundance of this seemingly empty land. Visitors to Alaska are not permitted to shoot moose unless they shell out thousands of dollars for a guide, but in the past I could have shot that huge bull, and his meat would have guaranteed me sustenance through the winter. Storage was easy now, as bears were generally out of the way and the air outside was many times colder than a freezer. My hungry imagination lingered on the possibilities: steaks, ribs, roasts, stews and jerky for travelling. I consoled myself with the thought that at least I was able to hunt grouse, and now it seemed I had stumbled upon a colony.

When I got back to my cabin the woods were utterly silent and the first pale stars were alight. The stove had burnt low, and it was cold inside. I split some birch logs, and placed light lengths of spruce on the fire to get the blaze going. The thermometer read minus forty, my coldest night yet. The cabin gradually began to tick with warmth, and even the floor had lost its icy chill. Earlier that day I had piled up snow to a depth of four feet all around the cabin, and this had stopped the cold air getting in around the bottom. I bolted the door tight shut and hung the thick blanket over it, then lay back on my bed staring at the hissing lamp. My body ached, and I knew that I was thinner than I had ever been. Although I enjoyed wearing my snowshoes, carrying out any task with the equivalent of a pair of tennis racquets stuck on one's feet was not easy. Yet I was comfortable and warm, and felt an immense sense of satisfaction at having this safe haven after all the months of work.

I reflected on the sheer vastness of it all, and how strange it was to be lying in comfort while outside a Sub Arctic cold was sinking across the land. I reached over to turn off the lamp, and the flame died down, the mantle flickering from white to orange before letting out a blue tongue which quivered and spluttered before going out. I blinked in the pure blackness of the cabin, listening to the stove gently tapping with heat. Outside it was utterly still, and I could hear nothing. My eyes gently closed and I fell sweetly asleep.

Through my slumber I heard a loud noise outside, and jerked suddenly awake. What was it? The stove? I lay very still, listening. Then there it was again – another loud cracking sound – and it seemed to come from the cabin walls. I leapt up, still half asleep and prepared to be buried in logs. I could see nothing in the pitch darkness, and stood still, uncertain what to do. Another loud crack resounded from a corner of the cabin, then another that sounded more like a high-pitched creak. It seemed as if an entire log had creaked and shifted, and I imagined the massive ridgepole coming loose, or one of the purlins rolling off whilst sheets of frigid tin sliced down on top of me. I fumbled about for a match and lit my candle, and then stood in the middle of the floor looking around me. The cabin walls were making contracting and tightening noises like a ship caught in pack ice. Then I realised what was happening: the intense cold of the clear night air was freezing the logs, and the cabin walls were contracting. After a while it stopped, but I could see my breath in front of me, and knew that the fire needed to burn hotter. I needed more wood, so I pulled on my mukluks and popped on my hat, feeling grateful that I had a good stack of logs beside the door. I lifted the blanket aside, noticing that the door was thick with ice, and quickly stepped outside.

Outside the snow glowed blue-white under a full moon. The sky was studded with stars, and I saw my white breath fall away, ice instantly forming on my eyelashes. I was now very, very cold but I had to stay for a moment to look around me. It was a wonderland: a place of exquisite cruelty, and the intense cold added to the sense that this was a world in which I was not really allowed. Yet this cold menace was beautiful, like the honed blade of a razor sharp sword. I opened the door of the cabin quickly and grabbed my heavy jacket, then walked along my frozen path down to the white lake that glittered and glinted in the moonlight. I looked up, and saw to my amazement a ghostly curtain of brilliant, lime-coloured light shimmering in the eastern sky. 'The Northern Lights' I whispered, watching entranced as the hazy cloud teased its way out across the empty sky, then retreated quickly as if responding to some heavenly rebuke before flickering out again. My head hung back until my neck ached, and I tried to ignore my legs, which ached with cold as I was wearing nothing but my long johns. Still I stood, enraptured by this awesome natural spectacle, until across the lake, out of the complete silence, a shot rang out. I jumped and stood staring at the dark, spruce-clad bank. Another shot resounded, and I saw snow falling from a tree as if it had been shaken. The trees were contracting in the cold just as my cabin logs had done, and as the cold deepened I heard the sound of woody cracks ringing out all over the forest.

I was breathing through my zipped-up jacket, my eyelashes were heavy with ice and when I sniffed my nostrils stuck together as the moisture within them froze. It was time to get warm again, and I walked back towards the cabin where the scent of birch smoke hung like incense in the clear air. Once in the cabin the warmth coated me, and my nerves tingled with the contrast. Outside it was minus fifty, yet those lights in the sky had been so beautiful that I had barely noticed the cold. My stove devoured the frozen logs of birch and bone dry spruce, and soon gently purred like a contented, well-fed lion.

24

DOYON

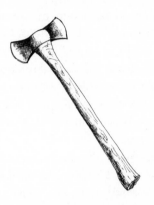

As the light faded and the cold increased I settled into a simple rhythm of existence. Each day I worked hard cutting wood and melting snow, gradually learning tricks to make my work more efficient. Before felling a tree I first cut the tops of little saplings and bushes that stuck out above the snow, then laid them out in a line where the tree would fall. The brush acted like a snowshoe, holding the tree up and preventing it from falling too deep into the snow, and making it much easier to work with. As the days passed I grew more confident, and began to feel that I was learning the ways of the wild white land of the Interior. The Interior is not easily accessible to the newcomer – there are no majestic peaks or crystal clear rivers, just thick bush and forest, dark sandy beaches and silty rivers that soon sink away as the cold winds of winter bear down from the north. The newcomer has to work hard to find its beauty, cutting through bush to reach the ridges and hills and snowshoeing for miles to discover the gentle balance of lake, river, forest and sky. My life had been pared down to its barest essentials – the cold had long since stopped my watch, and I was keeping time by daylight and the slow, clockwise movement of the plough around the pole star. The days passed slowly, mostly without event, and I savoured their simplicity.

Don had told me that I must work to maintain my trails, as they would become increasingly vital as more snow fell. So each day I walked down the portage to the slough, my snowshoes packing the newly fallen snow on to the hard, previously compressed snow. Overnight the trail would freeze, and become harder as the depth of compacted snow increased with each day's progress. My wood-gathering and hunting trails which had once led me across ex-haustingly deep, powdery snow had also begun to freeze and harden down, and thus became increasingly useful. As the snow continued to fall it rose up on either side of my trails like English hedgerows, and increasingly the animals used my trails to get around. I had become the equivalent of a local government roads contractor, and as I passed along the trails each day I would observe what had passed before me.

The trees resounded with the shrill call of red squirrels, and their scampering footprints criss-crossed my trail. I followed the progress of the odd lone wolf or fox which used my trail as a short cut to the grass lake. There they hunted for arctic hare or willow grouse, which rested during the day on the sunny side of the lake. The grouse left beautiful patterns, the stiff feathers at the ends of their wings slashing delicate lines into the snow as they whirred into the air. I would stop whenever I saw these marks, and Fuzzy and I would hungrily search the nearby trees in the hope of catching the birds unawares. The arctic hare population was going through a temporary dip in my region, and so I rarely saw their tracks. When I did, I would also sometimes see the wide indents of a lynx, which live almost exclusively on hare. The lynx, which is a large cat, is famed for the delicate and light flavour of its meat, which is white like chicken, rather than dark and stringy as I had imagined. Throughout my time in the woods I never saw one; in common with all cats they are masters of silent movement and camouflage.

In forested parts I often came across the neat and agile prints of a marten. This voracious weasel is also known as sable, and feeds mainly on shrews, making it an ally of mine. Its rich, dark brown fur is light but also very warm, and thus the perfect fur for making hats. Occasionally I would come across a moose track, and the great weight of the animal would leave irritating potholes in my trails. Like a grumpy contractor I would fill them in, cursing the great brown lump and wishing I had a means of imposing a weight restriction. As the snow got deeper through the course of the winter and food grew scarce, the moose became increasingly dangerous. There was a very real danger of meeting one face-to-face on one of my trails, and if that happened I had been told to give way and get myself behind the nearest tree. Don had once come across a grumpy moose on his portage. He grabbed a tree and the moose charged, but it couldn't quite manage to gore or trample him without wrapping itself around the tree. The little struggle went on for some time, until the moose lost patience and gave up. A few days later Don was passing along the portage when out popped the monster again, intent on continuing the battle. Don jumped for the nearest tree, and just like the last time the battle continued, until the bull eventually gave up. Don was now starting to feel victimised, and shouldered his rifle before heading along the portage the next day. Sure enough, the moose was in position, pawing at the ground and defensive of 'his' trail. This time Don leaned calmly against the tree and shot the animal, storing the meat for eating through the winter.

Sometimes I made one-off, short-term trails, scouting for wood in new places, or hunting for grouse. To anyone who had seen them, these winding, seemingly pointless little tracks would probably have left the impression that I was either drunk or crazy, but over a number of days I realised that someone was following my every move. Some sort of animal was tracking me, not only along my established trails, but also on every one of my forays. The creature left a deep, regular print with one defining feature: each imprint in the snow seemed to be kicked up at the front, as if the animal were flicking the snow as it moved along. It was fascinating, and I couldn't figure it out. I called Don to ask him about it.

'You say he's been following all your trails?'

'Yup. And kind of kicking up his feet.'

'On all your trails, long way from camp too?'

I thought about it. 'Actually, yes. On the ridges away to the south.'

I heard him draw his breath in. 'That's Doyon!' he said excitedly.

'Doyon? Isn't that the name of the Tribal Foundation?'*

'Yes,' he said impatiently. 'Doyon means Chief, and it's also another name for a wolverine. He's the biggest weasel in the world – real tough sonofabitch – and he's been following your trails.'

'Amazing,' I said. 'Do you think I'll get a look at him?'

'Nah – he's very secretive. You'll never see him. His pelt makes the best ruff for a parka you can get: it's tough stuff and it holds less frost. Have you seen his tracks near the beaver house?'

'Yes,' I replied, remembering that the distinctive prints had circled the beaver mound.

'All the animals are hoping to catch a beaver. Them critters are full of fat and good meat.'

'I suppose I should think about trying to catch one.'

'Yeah, you'll need to.' There was a pause. 'You eating good?'

'Well . . .' I hesitated slightly: 'Beans, beans and more beans, with fried bread and grouse when I've got it.'

'Where's all the hot cake mix, bacon and fish gone?'

'It's, aah . . . Gone.'

'Okay. You getting plenty of grouse?'

'Yeah I am, now that I've figured out how to see them. I'm also trying to snare some hare.'

'They make fine eating, but still not enough fat in them. What does their sign look like?'

I described it in great detail, telling him that it seemed as if the hare were jumping through my snares.

* All tribal lands are run by multi-million dollar tribal foundations which try to reinvest and manage the lands to the benefit of their indigenous communities.

He said something to Carol that I didn't hear, then said: 'You finding any bits of spruce cone along those hare trails?'

'Yes actually, quite a lot. I didn't know that hare eat cones. Do they dig them up? They can't climb, surely?'

There was a silence, and then laughter erupted on the other end of the phone. 'It's a squirrel, dummy – you've been trying to snare squirrel!' He roared with laughter, and I waited patiently until the tide of mirth had settled.

'Well thank you Don,' I said finally, 'glad I gave you a good laugh anyway. Got to go now – need to save my battery.'

'Well okay – okay now.' His tone was suddenly serious. 'You be careful.'

I was smiling as I packed the phone away, knowing that I had supplied the man with another amusing tidbit that would keep him going for days. And I was certain that Carol would be getting the first laugh, letting out an evil chuckle as she sat beside the fire with her knitting on her lap. I had long since given up hope of maintaining any kind of pride where Don was concerned – I knew that the bargain between us meant giving him full access to my mistakes and humiliations in return for his sage advice. But from that moment on, I never again confused a hare with a squirrel.

25

THE GREAT ALASKAN POTATO FAMINE

Over a month had passed since Don and Charlie had left, and I was feeling seriously deprived of human company. The combination of hard work, limited food and the shock of acclimatising to the cold had affected my body badly, and it was also beginning to affect my mind. I was losing six minutes of light each day, and now had just one hour of daylight before the sun slipped out of sight far to the south. To make matters worse, I had run out of fuel for my pressure lamp, and was having to rely on the feeble, acrid kerosene lamp and candles, because all of my hopeless battery-operated gadgets had run down in the cold. I tried to make the most of the short period of strange, lemony sunlight, but often found myself working in the feeble light provided by the moon and the stars. Thanks to my stove, however, I was always warm, and as I slogged back to the cabin through a blizzard or a cold snap I would strain my eyes towards the stovepipe, hoping to see smoke. Once inside I would stand in the ticking darkness for a while, the warmth and darkness feeling like a return to the womb.

I had been giving some thought to improving my toilet arrangements, and in a moment of inspiration had decided to build myself an 'ig-loo'. The idea was to use the principles of igloo-building to create a comfortable, enclosed space in which I could perform my toilet, which was currently rushed to say the least. Igloos are not normally built in this part of Alaska as the snow is too dry and powdery, but I got round this by spending a few days mounding up snow with my shovel, so that the snow would lose some of its air content and become firmer. One morning I set about energetically cutting igloo blocks from the mound, giving them a slightly beveled shape so that they would lean inwards, and placed them in my hand sled. I pulled it over to the latrine hole and began construction.

The basics of building an igloo are gradually to taper the blocks up in a spiral, working round and round so that each spiral gets progressively smaller. Finally a 'king' block is laid on the top. After several hours of labour my rather shaky igloo had reached a height of about six feet, and I finally placed the last block. I cut two holes on either side, through which I slid two wood slats on either side of the latrine hole. On to these poles I placed a portable loo seat that I had been hoarding in a tree for just this opportunity, and inside I cut a cubby for a candle, and stuck a stick into the snow to form a kind of improvised toilet roll holder. The structure held perfectly, protecting me from the wind and giving me a sense of privacy, which was absurd given the circumstances. The whole thing seemed ludicrously civilised, and I laughed every time I sat within its hygienic walls. Indeed, having a place to relieve oneself in safety and comfort is one of the essentials of keeping up morale, and that khazi became a beacon of joy.

Thankfully the extreme cold ensured that, although unsightly, the noxious mess nine feet below my exposed bottom never had a chance to stink, because it froze solid almost at the point of delivery. This in itself could have been a problem, however, had it not been for Don's advice, which extended even to this most sensitive aspect of wilderness living. He had warned me of the danger of building up something known as a 'shitsicle', which results from lazy management of the outhouse. Unless the wilderness-dweller takes due precautions, shit piles upon shit each day, freezing as it rises, until soon an evil brown frozen stalagmite rises proudly from the bottom of the latrine. Try as he might, he will not be able to push the column over, and pretty soon will realise that his only option is to descend into the hole armed with a chainsaw. As he works to fell the noxious stump, his chain will pepper him with minute specks of frozen waste, just as a tree covers the lumberman in sawdust. Once out of the hole he may try to brush the chips of brown ice from his clothes, but will never manage to remove every speck, and when he enters his warm cabin the brown ice will thaw into his clothing, imbuing clothes, hair and skin with the most awful stench.

With this horrific possibility in mind, I became obsessed with spotting the early start of a shitsicle, and would quickly topple a suspicious looking column with a stout pole before things got out of hand. Each time I did this I thanked my lucky stars that I had learned from local people, whose advice was based not just on visiting, but on truly living in the sub-arctic. No guidebook or survival manual that I had ever seen offered advice on how to manage one's poo-hole, perhaps understandably as the subject does lack a certain glamour. Yet to anyone living in the boreal woods for a prolonged period, these little nuggets of knowledge make a huge difference, and, in my case, went a long way towards keeping me sane.

The success of the 'ig-loo' momentarily lifted my spirits, but the next day things took a turn for the worse. I dropped my kerosene lamp and broke the glass, which meant that I had even less light than before, and was unable to read – a terrible blow as I was midway through *The Magus* by John Fowles. His writing, along with my multivitamins, had become an essential antidote to the increasing darkness of my world, and each night I would eagerly look forward to being transported to the Greek island of Spetses, where the novel is set. I had visited this island as a boy, and John Fowles perfectly conjured up the dry, searching sunshine of that ancient and mysterious place. As the blizzards pounded against my cabin, swaddling it in snow, I would be thousands of miles away, lost in descriptions of azure seas lapping gently on hidden beaches, the whirring of cicadas at dusk and the scent of thyme rising from sun-soaked land. I was devastated when the light situation deteriorated to the point where I could no longer read, and bitterly resented having to give up my fantasy land.

I was spending as much time as possible hunting grouse to supplement my ever-dwindling food stocks. Gathering shot birds from the deep snow presented a serious problem, but to my joy I discovered that Fuzzy was an instinctive retriever. With just the minimum of training he had become a wonderful hunting dog, and our partnership strengthened in our shared mission to find food. We would set out each day just after sun down, when there was still a little light, and snowshoe down to the grass lake, then off the trail and into the woods, searching with ears and eyes strained for grouse. Once I had spotted a bird, I would keep my eye fixed on it while stalking up to a suitable tree and steadying myself for the shot. I did not use a shotgun, as the noise would have flushed every bird for miles around and could also have wounded birds. Instead I used a battered old .22 rifle called a 'Nylon 66', which was very accurate and virtually indestructible. I aimed for the head of the bird, knowing that if I hit I would kill it immediately, and if I missed it would be a clean miss. If I was lucky there would be more than one grouse around, and so with a few shots I would have a bounty. The bird would drop heavily in an instant, and I would hear it thud into the snow. Fuzzy would be waiting close by my side, sitting tensely like a spring until the command 'Fetch!' set him loose, and he would bound, crawl, sink and then swim across the deep snow towards the hole left by the fallen bird. Like a diver, he would launch himself head-first into the hole, retrieving the bird and then scrambling back out again. Then he would power back towards me, breathing noisily through his nostrils, and place the warm bird into my hand.

Despite this glut of grouse, the benefits of my hunting forays were dubious, as I had to snowshoe for miles to find a quarry, and this effort, combined with the cold, meant that I was using more calories than I gained. People living in these extremely cold conditions need forty percent more body fat to keep warm, and I had used up all my fat reserves long ago. Gradually I was beginning to starve. I was feeling lethargic, and my brain was working slowly; each day it was harder to force myself to get up and on with it, especially as there was no prompt from a bright and cheery sun. I had to get up every four hours through the night to feed the stove, as I couldn't allow it to burn low, and it was agony to have to pull myself out of my warm bag to creep across the icy floor. One night, following a hard day of heaving firewood, I fell into a deep sleep and failed to wake up to bank the stove. Cold seeped rapidly through the log house, and at some point I must have sniffed in my sleep because my nostrils clung together, feeling as though two icy fingers had closed a grip over my nose. I spluttered awake, and found that I could barely see the stove through a heavy cloud of cold air that had been pouring silently in from outside as if it had been waiting for this chance to smother me. I lit my candle and watched as the flame struggled to open into a full shape against the dense, frozen air. As I walked to the stove the white cloud swirled ominously around my legs, making me feel as if I was in an old horror movie. I knelt shivering by the stove, desperately blowing the feeble coals until at last the thin strips of spruce caught light and I was able to shove some good-sized logs into the firebox. I clambered back into my bag, and lay trembling with cold as the cabin warmed up, gradually dispelling the deathly mist. Once again, I had been given a stern reminder that any laziness or short cuts would be severely punished.

One morning after breakfast I checked my store of potatoes, which I kept in a warm place beside the stove to stop them from freezing. My heart sank as I saw that I had just three remaining potatoes, which were sprouting and distinctly green. I placed them in a pot containing a whole grouse, which thankfully had a little layer of yellow fat. I added some beans and covered the whole thing with grouse stock that I had saved from my last meal. It looked delicious to my starved eyes, all the more so because I knew that it might be my last decent meal for some time.

Outside it was a whiteout, with snow thick in the air. At least it would be warmer, I thought, although the new snow also meant more work on my trails. I decided to have a wash for morale's sake. I had plenty of wood, so warmed about two gallons of water and poured it into my wide tin washing bowl, and then undressed and stepped in. The door of the stove was open, and it felt good to feel the heat of the fire against my bare skin, which I imagined as the sun. I sponged myself over with water, then soaped up and sponged the suds off again. Then I knelt beside the bowl and washed my hair, before towelling off and standing up to warm beside the fire. It felt wonderful to be clean and naked, after months of being enclosed in the same, sour clothes. The smell of soap brought back memories of bathtime at home, and the two boys' chubby little arms and legs splashing about in the soapy water. I hung the heliograph* from a nail and shaved, and for the first time in many months caught sight of my body in the mirror. The sight scared me. I had arrived in the bush weighing sixteen stone, and I could see that I was nowhere near that now. I was pale, and could see the bones showing through my skin. I took a better look at my face, and saw that it was emaciated, my skin grey with deep hollows under my eyes. For the first time, I truly took on board the severity of my situation. How long would it be before ice-up, I wondered. What would I do once my provisions had run out altogether?

I lay back on my bed feeling suddenly weak, the shock at my appearance having cancelled out my lift in spirits brought about by having a wash. I gazed at my candle and the darkness around me, and thought again about all the people who died quietly in this great frozen land, and of the unreal sensation of being profoundly hungry. I had no cultural memory of starvation, having been lucky enough to be born into a Western, middle class world, and now for

---

* A heliograph is a device for signalling by means of a movable mirror which reflects flashes of sunlight – very useful in the midst of a dark Alaskan winter!

the first time was experiencing what it felt like to run out of food. To my surprise I didn't feel particularly panicky or urgent; rather I felt resigned, and had almost a sick curiosity as to how things would progress from here.

After a while I forced myself to get up, knowing that my passive state of mind could spell the beginning of disaster. I knew that my diminished physical state had begun to weaken my judgement, and would seriously affect my ability to keep safe, but nevertheless I strapped on my snowshoes and forced myself to go about my chores as usual. Where before I had taken some pleasure in these tasks, now I did them out of necessity, feeling light-headed and weak, and having to work hard to keep focused. A kind of unreality was settling over my life, poisoning the air like gas, and my cabin had become a womb-like pocket of retreat, where the images and dreams I had of my family seemed increasingly more real than my circumstances. Despite my wooly mental state, I was still clear-headed enough to know that I was endangering my life by venturing out in this physical and mental condition, and decided to stay in my cabin for the next few days. Fortunately I had stockpiled a week's worth of wood for an emergency, and I had a couple of grouse hanging outside which would keep me going.

In the cabin that evening I tried to focus my mind on writing a column for the newspaper. I set the satellite phone up to send the article, knowing that I could only keep it on for a few minutes as I was low on fuel for my generator. After I had sent it I wrote an e-mail to Juliet:

> I can't wait to be with you again and our little boys who are so precious to me. I am missing being a father badly. I keep telling myself that this whole thing will be good for us, and that we'll find a way ahead. I just hope I can make it.

PART 4

'We are alone, absolutely alone on this chance planet: and, amid all the forms of life that surround us, not one, excepting the dog has made an alliance with us.'

MAURICE MAETERLINCK

26
POETRY AND FILM

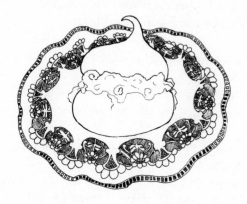

There is poetry in a pork chop to a hungry man.
PHILIP GIBBS

'Guy! Are you okay? I hear you've finished your cabin – that's great news.'

The urbane voice of Tom Roberts was at the other end of my satellite phone, winging its way halfway across the world from the comfortable offices of his film production company in London. He had sent two film-makers out to visit me back in the summer, and they'd taken some footage with a view to perhaps making a documentary at some point in the future. As we spoke I thought of the beautiful, clean world that surrounded him, and wondered what he'd be having for lunch. I had begun to fantasise about food now, eating having long ago taken over from sex as my main area of deprivation. As Tom talked my mind ranged over pies, chips, beer and pub lunches, and then on to silly, pointless food, with no use other than pure pleasure: meringues, Danish pastries and ice cream floated through my mind, until his voice brought me back to the present:

'Hello? Can you hear me?'

'Yes, sorry Tom.' I cleared my throat. 'What were you saying?'

'Just saying that we're hoping to come out and do some more filming. We're looking at flights for Matt and Ashley – they want to come out in about a week.'

The meringues were haunting me again: big ones, sitting demurely in patterned paper cases and full of whipped cream. 'Tom, have you ever eaten home-made meringues?'

'What?'

'You know, meringues – crisp on the outside and just slightly chewy in the centre.'

'Yeah . . .' he sounded confused. '. . . they're good. As I was saying, Matt and Ashley are planning to come out next week – is that okay?'

'I suppose so, but you'd better warn them it's pretty grim out here, and very cold.'

'Sure, they know that,' he said. 'That's why they want to come now – to catch some of the winter. Now they can get as far as Galena, but what I want to know is how will they get out to you?'

'Well . . .' I thought hard, as it had suddenly occurred to me that if Matt and Ashley were coming out they could bring food – perhaps even meringues would be a possibility. 'They might be able to fly in and land on the lake,' I said, sounding much more enthusiastic, 'but it would be tricky.'

'Is the ice solid enough?'

'I'm not sure, but I can check it out.'

'Okay. Call me back tomorrow and let me know.'

I replaced the handset with mixed feelings. Half of me felt excited at the prospect of seeing the two intrepid documentary makers again – I liked Matt and Ashley, and relished the thought of spending some time with people from home. Yet mingled with my anticipation was a strange reluctance to give up my solitary existence, and my well-established, albeit uncomfortable, routine. There was also a kernel of discomfort at the thought of being filmed again, as they made me feel like one of Dian Fossey's apes. Back in the summer, they had arrived with the camera running, and then had barely switched it off during the whole time they were with me, making me feel sometimes uncomfortably exposed. I pondered this for a while until my social side, and more importantly the lure of food, won out. I called Don on the satellite phone to ask whether he thought a bush pilot might be able to land on the lake.

'Yeah, maybe. I'll get Brownie to take a look. Now if it's just them two, you could think about hitching a ride back when they go, 'cause the ice is still not good on the river. Brownie will land on the strip here in the village.'

I put down the phone with mixed feelings. It seemed that all my problems might have been solved at once, but still I felt a strange reluctance to give up my solitude.

Over the next few days I was unable to feed Fuzzy more than just a handful of dog feed and the odd scrap of grouse, and one night when I called him he didn't come. I stood outside the door of my cabin, listening for the sound of his paws on the snow, but heard nothing except the wind. I gathered some logs and passed them into the cabin, then shut myself back inside and sat worrying about the little dog. Where was he? My mind raced, and then settled morbidly on the wolf pack. I recalled something I had read about the Vlach shepherds in Northern Greece, and how they used to place fearsome spiked collars on their dogs to protect them from marauding wolves. That was it, I thought: he probably went further than he should have in search of food, and was ambushed by wolves. Guilt descended: I should have given him a spiky collar, and I should have packed more dog food. I spent the rest of the night straining my ears for the sound of his footsteps, and miserably wondering if I would ever see him again.

The next morning I woke and lay still for a moment, staring at the stove. I feared something bad had happened, but what was it? Just then I heard the unmistakeable sound of Fuzzy's steps in the snow outside, and my heart leapt with joy. He was back! I could hear that he had stopped outside the door, and must be waiting for me. I hurriedly pulled on my clothes and stepped outside. It was very cold, and even in the murky half-light I could see the thick, white, heavy air, hanging like fog about a foot above the ground and tumbling over itself as it rolled and swept into the cabin. Fuzzy barked, and I looked around for him, peering through the dim light. When I saw him, I knew immediately that something special had happened, because his whole body radiated pride. He was sitting side on to me, his back very straight and his nose pointing up towards the sky, like a seal sunning itself on a rock. One friendly, almond-coloured eye was fixed upon me, and as I watched him he glanced down at something lying in the snow before him, then back at me. Clearly he was waiting for my reaction, and I walked closer and bent down to see the object of his pride. When I saw it I drew in my breath in amazement, for what he had brought back to camp was an entire moose leg. It was three feet long, and the biggest dog bone I had ever seen. He sat with one paw resting proprietarily on the bone, looking up at me as if to say: 'See? I can bring back food too. I am indeed a great dog of the North!'

I stood back, laughing in admiration at the little dog's bravery and ingenuity. The scene reminded me of one of those pictures of a puny colonial type standing proudly beside some gunned-down leviathan of the savannah, and I had to capture it. I went back inside my cabin and rummaged around for my camera, and then returned to Fuzzy, who was still frozen in position as if waiting for his photograph. I examined the bone more closely and my admiration increased still further. It was truly enormous, with a good amount of fresh meat and skin still attached, and looked like it had been stolen from a dinosaur exhibit at a museum. By this time Fuzzy had clearly decided that the viewing was over, and I followed him around the cabin to watch as he tried to get the bone into his snug. It took a few attempts for him to drag the great prize inside, but finally he managed it, leaving just the end poking out of the door. I walked back to the cabin, still laughing and shaking my head in disbelief. Far from being helpless and in trouble last night, Fuzzy had taken matters into his own paws, and had embarked on a brave mission to find food. I wished that I could have followed him, and imagined him creeping through the dark, snowbound woods. The moose leg must have been the remnant of a kill by our local pack of timberwolves, and Fuzzy would have known that he was risking his life as he sneaked up to the site and dug up that leg. He then had to negotiate the long, hard journey back to camp, dragging the heavy load and pushing through the trees and deep snow until he reached the portage. What terrors had he faced, I wondered. Had he lain in wait for his chance, or had he walked boldly into the arena, as if unconcerned that fourteen massive timberwolves were nearby?

After a barren breakfast I strapped on my snowshoes and moved off across the lake, then up the ridge and over the next grass lake, scouting for standing dead spruce. The lemony sun had come up, and although outrageously far away down towards the south it was still beautiful. I stopped within a thick belt of birch, and saw ahead of me a small frozen pond which lay deep in untouched snow. Its banks were fringed with rushes and low bushes, and it was surrounded by spruce trees that looked very correct and ordered, almost as if they had been planted by hand. The scene had an intimacy and gentleness to it that reminded me of home. It could almost have been a pond in a village green, such was its sweetness, and I stood looking down at it for a long time before turning round to gaze to the south. Here the view was utterly different, bleak and windswept with mile after mile of black spruce trees stretching far into the distance. Black spruce are small trees which are often hundreds of years old, but unlike their towering cousins they can't reach a great height, because they grow over permafrost regions where the annual thaw is low and the soil stays frigid. Thus their roots can only dig so far in search of nutrients before they touch ice, and the trees become knotty and small, almost like bonsai.

The sun was very low now, and I watched in wonder as its yellow light seeped through the endless plain of black spruce. The sky above was a pure, pre-Raphaelite blue, gradually lightening to purple, and then yellow, and finally to a glistening white as it touched the frosty tops of the trees. There was a ferocity to the view that fascinated me, and the frozen tops of the trees looked like the points of a thousand scimitars held up by a mythical army. The cold was growing as the sun went down, freezing my breath to my eyelashes so that occasionally I had to pull off a glove and brush the frost from my face. When the sun had gone a cold wind began to move through the tops of the birch trees, and I heard their frozen hearts creaking as they swayed gently in the breeze. I walked back slowly, stopping to watch as the slender birch branches rubbed and clinked together in the cold wind, sounding like bamboo chimes in a temple garden. That night I went to sleep hungry, yet I was happy as my heart was full. The days of hunger and isolation had been hard, but I knew that they had been special, and perhaps I would not experience my wilderness in the same way again. I still had not touched the book of poetry given to me as a parting gift from a friend, and I saw now that it was not needed. Man's art at its best can only hope to come close to nature, but it can never surpass it. Maybe for the simple reason that we exist only for a second, and our eyes are too young to fully capture the depth of it all.

27
GOING BUSHY

I was on the ridge loading birch logs into my sled when I heard the distant sound of a small plane. Fuzzy trotted over, and we both stood staring up at the grey sky, listening as the whirring sound of the engine grew gradually louder. 'This must be him, Fuzz!' I shouted, and he let out an excited yelp. Brownie, a local bush pilot, had promised to come out and check whether my lake was safe for landing. He buzzed the cabin before banking to the north, beginning a wide arc that would bring him in to land at the western end of the lake. I snowshoed fast towards the edge of the lake, relishing the positive, capable sound of the little plane. Then I saw him coming in over the tree tops, lining up over the middle of the lake and descending rapidly until his skis touched the surface just beyond the beaver house. To my surprise, like a man flying off a ski jump, he lifted back up again, and seemed to just make it over the tall spruce trees. I felt a twinge of anxiety that perhaps he had decided not to land, but then saw that he was making another arching turn, and flying back along the lake. This time he stayed high, and I wondered what he was doing until I saw him tilting over at an angle and peering down at the lines of his skis. 'Of course! He's checking to see that the lake ice will hold,' I shouted to Fuzzy, who by now was jumping up and down with excitement and almost walking on his hind legs. I waved as the plane banked round for a third time, then watched as it skied along the surface, banging alarmingly on the ice. Just before the beaver house it hit a large lump of snow, and the plane catapaulted into the air again, before coming down thirty feet later and finally skidding to a halt. The pilot gunned the engine and the prop whirred, sending out a great blizzard of snow as he taxied towards me. The excitement had proved too much for Fuzzy, who was now standing on his rear legs with his forelegs wrapped around my waist. We must have looked like a very odd married couple.

At last the engine stopped, and there was silence. I stepped forward in anticipation, looking forward to meeting my first Alaskan bush pilot. I was expecting a grizzled Vietnam veteran to step out of the plane, but instead the door opened to reveal a middle-aged, bespectacled man who looked more like a family GP than an intrepid pilot. 'Hi, I'm Brownie,' he said, his legs still dangling out of the door of the plane. 'Is your trail good, or do I need snowshoes?'

'No, the trail's fine,' I replied, glancing towards the fine-looking pair of snowshoes that he had strapped to the wing supports. 'That was quite a landing!'

He grinned. 'Yeah, snowy landings in a new place are hard, 'cause there's no contrast from the air. All looks flat from up there 'till you come in to land, and then it's kinda late.' He leaned down and patted Fuzzy, who had stood up on his back legs to look into the plane. 'Yup, that windblown snow was fun. Must've jumped quite some way there.'

'Well, can I offer you some coffee?'

'Sure thing.'

He hopped lightly down from the plane, and we walked to the cabin. He cast a critical eye over the house: 'Imagine that roof is pretty good at holding the heat in,' he said dryly, and then bent his head to duck through the door. I rolled over a stump for him to sit on, and we sat by the stove with our coffee. Brownie listened as I talked, nodding patiently every so often.

'How long since you seen anyone?' he asked in a soft voice, when I finally stopped to draw breath.

'Oh, maybe six weeks or so – I've lost track.'

'See, I do a lot for folks in the woods, and some are even more remote than you here.' He smiled. 'Now first off, like you, they get real chatty and kinda have to tell you everything. It all kinda comes out at once.'

I blushed as I realised I'd been talking non-stop since his arrival, and he hadn't been able to get a word in edgeways. He saw my embarrassment and raised a hand: 'Hey, I don't mind one bit – the chatty ones are fine.'

'What do you mean?' I asked, consciously trying to speak slowly.

'Well, after too long they stop talking.'

'Completely?'

'No – but they only talk when they need to. They get like animals: more inclined to listen and watch than to speak. You really have to coax it out of them until they get into the way of being with people again. Out here we say they've gone "bushy".'

He placed his tin mug down and looked at his watch, then said he would have to go. We walked together back to the plane, and lifted the cover off the engine. 'I remember once picking up a couple to bring 'em back in mid-winter,' he said. 'She started crying when we got into the plane – said nothing all the way, just kept on crying and crying until we landed.'

'What was wrong with her?' I asked.

He looked up at the sky, then out across the lake. 'She just kinda seemed to have lost her mind.' He smiled and patted my shoulder. 'But you look okay to me!'

I raised my eyebrows. 'Well, just get me out of here if you think I'm going bushy too, will you?'

We laughed, but I knew I had already skated dangerously close to the edges of insanity.

As he climbed into the plane he seemed to remember the point of coming out here: 'Oh yeah, two guys in Galena want me to bring them out tomorrow. That okay?'

I appreciated being asked – allowing me space to say no could have lost him some valuable business, yet it was part of the etiquette here in the bush that you never broke in on a person's solitude unless asked.

'Sure Brownie,' I replied, 'it'll be good to see them. Have they got much stuff?'

He nodded. 'Yeah. Boxes of food, and I believe a case of whisky.'

'They've got whisky!' I had long since run out.

He looked at me quizically for a moment. 'I think the food'll do you more good than the firewater . . . You look like you could do with a square meal.'

I nodded sheepishly, remembering that he didn't know me, and might think I was an alcoholic. 'Yes, some grub would certainly be welcome.'

'You been living on beans and flour?'

I smiled weakly. 'How did you guess?'

He laughed. ''Cause that's what every cheechako lives on when he starts out in the bush!'

'Cheechako? Is that the same as tenderfoot?'

'Yup! Now after I've gone you flatten down that windblown snow and cut some spruce to mark out the runway. See you tomorrow.'

With that he shut the door, then turned the plane and charged at the far bank of trees, before heading off in the direction of Galena.

I walked back to the cabin feeling happy: the prospect of seeing people, and more to the point food, was growing on me. As Don had suggested, when the film-makers left I planned to hitch a lift back to Galena to re-supply. I also wanted to see Glenn Stout, who had a dog yard and had offered back in the summer to help me get a dog team together – I wanted to be able to travel through the winter, and other than a snowmachine, this was the only way to do it. That night I put on my snowshoes, and in the light of the full moon flattened the hummocks on the lake and marked out

Brownie's runway with Christmas trees. This seemed curiously appropriate, because I was looking forward to Matt and Ashley's arrival as eagerly as a child waiting for Christmas. Later I stared into the bottom of my tin mug of coffee, thinking with joy that tomorrow I would be able to add whisky again. At my feet, Fuzzy had rolled onto his back and lay stretched out beside the stove. I looked down at him: 'Hey Fuzzy, we're going to have company tomorrow.'

He lifted his head and looked at me backwards.

'And you will have food again.'

A tail thumped on the plywood floor.

28
MR KURTZ, WE PRESUME?

I have a great deal of company in my house;
especially in the morning when nobody calls.
HENRY DAVID THOREAU

Brownie buzzed the cabin the next morning at ten o'clock, the
bush equivalent of ringing the doorbell. I stoked up the fire and put
the kettle on a cool spot of the stove, then snowshoed out to stand
by the lake. He circled round in the grey sky, then landed neatly
between my Christmas trees. He slewed to a halt, then taxied over
and stopped the engine. Inside, two smiling faces peered out at me,
and I saw Ashley digging for his camera, ready from the first
moment to start filming. I stepped forward to shake hands, but
instead was treated to a series of North London-style hugs before
they stood back and scrutinised me.

Ashley was the first to speak. 'Shit! You've lost some weight!' he
said, looking suddenly serious. Behind us Brownie was beginning
his take-off.

'Yeah, I know.' I felt rather vulnerable, remembering my image in the mirror, and knew they were shocked by my appearance. 'I haven't been able to make it back to the village to resupply, because the ice on the river is still bad.'

Matt looked at me closely, and I heard that film-maker's zeal in his voice as he asked, 'How's the mental state?'

'Oh, it's fine' I said casually, loading their bags into my sled.

Of course I knew this was not music to their ears. For the sake of their film, they would have been delighted to find me in the grip of cabin fever, huddled in a dark corner of the cabin muttering 'The horror! The horror!'* Yet they would never know what it felt like to be utterly alone, and how close to the edge I had come.

When Matt and Ashley had visited me back in the summer I hadn't even begun work on the cabin, and as we approached the little building they stopped and stared in disbelief. 'We never thought that you would do it,' Matt said, stepping forward and touching a log.

'Well, it was a nightmare' I replied, feeling somehow guilty, 'There were some awful times, and without Don's help I wouldn't have pulled it off.'

'Yeah, I can imagine.' Matt glanced at Ashley, 'So glad it's worked out for you.'

I couldn't help a smile. 'Sorry – I know it would make a much better film for you if everything went wrong.'

They had the good grace to smile back, and as we packed their gear into the snug cabin I thought of the months of darkness and hardship they had missed, when winter began in earnest and I was still living in my tent. Once in the cabin I poured them some coffee, and Ashley produced a box. 'Hey, we brought you some stuff from home.'

I took the box eagerly, seeing Juliet's handwriting across the top. Inside I found a bounty of chocolate, biscuits, honey and coffee, and from my mother there were some beautiful Southern Italian staples, including olive oil, sugared almonds and pine nuts. I was overwhelmed by the gifts with their luxurious, scented

* *Heart of Darkness*, Joseph Conrad (1902)

packaging, and had to resist ripping them open immediately. The boys looked on as I explored the box – I must have looked like a wild man on a desert island, having my first contact for years with civilisation. Then Ashley pulled a little parcel from his bag.

'Here,' he said, passing it to me.

It was another packet from Juliet, with postcards showing pictures of the Isle of Mull, Juliet's childhood home and her haven during this long and difficult year. The pictures were incomprehensibly green and gentle, and brought back treasured memories of times we had spent there together when we first met. In between some cardboard there was a drawing by Oscar – he was trying to show what his daddy was doing, and I could make out something that looked like a bear and then some squiggles which could be a house. At the top he had written his name in big, wobbly letters with a felt pen. My eyes filled with tears, and my throat was so swollen with sadness that for several minutes I couldn't speak. I bowed my head, and we sat in silence on our stumps around the stove. Two men from North London, sensitive and kind, and one undernourished mongrel.

After a few minutes Ashley slipped a bottle of Highland Park whisky into my hands. 'I think we could all do with some of this,' he said, 'especially Matt, who hates flying.'

Matt leaned forward in mock anger. 'No I don't!'

We all laughed, and I was relieved to move away from the painful subject of my family, whom I was missing deeply. The only way I had coped with this pain was to try to put it out of my mind, and somehow seeing friends from my own country highlighted their absence. I sat back and looked at the two men, admiring them for taking the risk of coming out here to film. I poured a healthy measure of whisky into a tin mug for each of us, then added a drop of water to each.

'Is this snowmelt?' Matt asked.

'Yes.'

He raised his tin mug: 'Well here's to Yukon snow-melt!'

We raised our mugs, and I savoured the taste of the whisky as it burned comfortably through me.

Later that night they told me they'd brought a film which Juliet had been making for me, showing snippets of her and the boys' lives back on Mull. I lay on my bed and watched it on one of their cameras, seeing the boys playing with buckets and spades on the beach, with Juliet's voice occasionally calling out to one of the little scamps. Images that would have filled a parent with joy under normal circumstances now filled me with almost unbearable pain. I lay there totally absorbed, my eyes often clouding with tears and occasionally smiling at something one of the boys did or said. At the end of the film I couldn't speak, but instead got up and left the cabin, walking out into the snowy night with Fuzzy pattering behind me. I was in turmoil. The arrival of these two men had been wonderful, but had also brought forth a great mix of emotions, from reassurance at still being missed and loved to heartache at missing out on this vital chunk of my childrens' lives. I felt as though they had opened the floodgates of my guilty heart, which I had worked so hard to keep under control. I just hoped that I would be able to close them again when they had gone.

The next few days were full of laughter and discussion, yet still lurking within me there was a feeling that they had invaded my icy world, and I could not help but subject them to the occasional bit of torture. Parts of the cabin were susceptible to dripping after I had stoked the fire at night, when our breath would rise and freeze to the tin roof, clinging there in a blanket of white frost until the stoked stove warmed the cabin sufficiently for the frost to melt. Then the dripping would start. Like an evil schoolboy, I would grin darkly to myself when I heard the boys muttering in anger as their sleeping bags were assaulted by a series of heavy drips. Yet when I enquired after their health the next morning they always smiled cheerily and said they had never slept better. They filmed on determinedly, dogging my every move as I worked like some kind of Cossack babooshka, cutting firewood and melting snow round the clock to keep up with their fanatical washing and consumption. They even set up the camera while I was sleeping, so that when I reached over to light my candle one morning there they were: two cinematic ghouls waiting to capture my every moment.

The arrival of new food stocks had transformed my quality of life, and I eagerly looked forward to each meal. Ashley was a fine cook, and soon seduced me completely with delicious stacks of pancakes drizzled in maple syrup. I returned the compliment, cooking up seared grouse breast on noodles flavoured with oregano and lemon juice. Matt's attempts at cooking, however, threw me into fits of unreasonable rage, because I had become fanatical about making good use of ingredients and not wasting a morsel. Whenever he bravely offered to cook I would subject him to close and often aggressive scrutiny, poring over his shoulder and muttering darkly. He soldiered on nevertheless, grinning blithely throughout the awful barracking, and I grew to respect his understated form of endurance. I heard later that he had been held hostage in Haiti during a film shoot, and have no doubt that he is built of stern stuff.

Soon it was time for them to go, and we all prepared for our trip back to the village. It was snowing heavily on the day of departure, and there was a strong, blustery wind. Brownie set off with Matt and the film equipment on the first trip, and I watched the little plane as it took off shakily and disappeared into the snowy sky. I imagined a plane crash, and the futility of dying just because I wanted a free ride to the village. I turned to Ashley: 'You know, I don't think I'm coming on this one.'

He looked up from his bags. 'Why?'

'Because it's too risky – I just don't like the look of this weather.'

He stared at me, perplexed, and I thought that it must seem bizarre that someone who was living out a winter alone in the wilderness could be afraid of flying. I searched for excuses: 'My wife and children – I'm taking enough risks out here. They wouldn't want me to do it.'

'Well I'm going, whatever the weather,' he said, and I could hear in his tone that he'd had more than enough rough living.

We sat in silence for a few minutes, watching the snow falling. 'Well, I'll come and help you load up at least,' I said finally.

An hour later Brownie returned, and we struggled over to him through the snow.

'Okay guys, let's move it along here,' Brownie said, when we'd finished loading up the plane. 'This snow storm is getting worse, and Matt and I almost did a barrel roll 'cause of that down draught from the mountain.'

'Well, travel carefully,' I said.

Brownie stopped and looked at me. 'You not coming?'

'Sorry Brownie, but no. Don't like the weather. Things are risky enough for me without adding to the list.'

He rubbed his chin and looked at me with an expression of wonder mixed with irritation. 'Do you think I would risk anything to come and get you all?'

'Ah . . . No.'

'Well just get in then, 'cause let me tell you – Brownie does not take risks.'

'I'm sure that's true Brownie, but I have a family to live for here.' I tried to sound firm, but instead my voice came out high-pitched and defensive.

'Guy, I don't give a damn about my family or anyone else when I fly. All I care about is me. Now, I aim to get me back to the village, and I'm giving you a free flight. Get in!'

I stared at the tiny plane for a moment, then swallowed and got in. Fuzzy was stuffed into a locker in the tail compartment, where he immediately packed himself into a tight, worried-looking fur ball. I looked sadly towards my still smoking stovepipe, wondering if I'd ever see my cabin again. Brownie ran through his checks, then said 'Okay Guy, put your arm around my shoulders.'

I raised my hand: 'Thanks, Brownie, but don't worry – I'm fine, really.'

He looked at me wryly. 'No, you need to do that during take-off to keep the plane balanced.'

'Oh right – okay.' I obligingly put my arm around him.

'You all right in the back there?'

Ashley looked up from where he was tinkering with a camera. 'Fine.'

Brownie turned to me. 'Now brace yourself by holding on to that handle as we go, and don't touch that stick between your legs.'

With that we charged off at full tilt into the snow. After a series of bone-shaking jumps off the icy ridges, the skis were in the air, and we were aiming for a gap in the trees. The plane shuddered as the wind hit it, and as we passed Pilot Mountain we bucked violently. I looked down, wishing I had brought a sick bag, and saw nothing beneath us but mile upon mile of bleak, black and white land. The cabin was long gone, hidden beneath the swirling snow, and as we bumped and jolted along I marvelled at how harsh and barren the landscape looked. I had never been able to look down on the wilderness that surrounded me – instead I had always been consumed by it, living low like an animal and dwarfed by it all. It seemed unbelievable that within that dark wilderness there was a cosy home with four walls, a stove and a bed. Flying high above the land, the cabin seemed like a miracle to me, because it had become my home, safe and warm just ninety miles south of the Arctic Circle.

Gradually I began to relax and even to enjoy the flight, and as we flew over the wide, ice-covered Yukon I wondered whether I would ever be able to travel along it by dog. Half an hour after take-off the lights of the little village came into view, and we landed on the grass lake beside Brownie's house. I stepped out, deeply relieved that the journey was over. Brownie pulled the earphones from his head and looked at me with a smile. 'Well, you look like you're alive, and this . . .' he indicated the village around him. 'This sure don't look like heaven to me!'

29
GOING TO THE DOGS

Later that evening I walked through the snow-covered village to Chris and Jenny's house, where I was invited to a meal with the whole family. It felt wonderful to be surrounded by people, and to come into a warm, well-lit house. I was particularly enjoying the electric lights, and resolved never to run out of lamp oil again, as the past few weeks had been grim. Chris and Jenny's four-year old daughter, Tirzah, met me at the top of the stairs. 'Hey – what you doing back here?' She stared at me in mock-seriousness with her clever dark eyes.

'Well, I couldn't miss out on the cooking,' I replied with a smile, and just as she was thinking up a stern reply her little brother Asa appeared and started to flump down the stairs towards me on his bottom.

'Guy! Guy!' he shouted, giving me a big hug, and then Tirzah ran to hug me as well. Tears welled up in my eyes, and for a moment I felt unable to go through with this gathering of children and their loving parents. Upstairs I found Chris and Jenny cooking and getting things ready. Chris greeted me with a warm smile, and shoved a bottle of beer into my hand.

'Please don't hug me. Just have a beer instead.'

'I wouldn't dream of hugging you,' I said.

'Good, 'cause you smell like a bonfire,' he answered, and ambled back into the kitchen.

I demolished the beer in a split second, and was given another as a beautiful table was laid. Soon Claudette and Charlie arrived with their family, and the noise of happy children filled the room. I sat quietly watching, wondering what my own children were up to, and not enjoying the experience of being a lone man in a family setting. Yet I was also happy to be there, comfortable and warm and surrounded by a family that I loved. The table sagged with the best cooking I had seen in a long time: moose ribs, pumpkin pie, salads, potatoes, grouse and corn bread. I stared at it, my mouth literally watering. The two sisters stood back and looked at me critically.

'Hey – you're looking thin,' Jenny said.

Charlie cut in: 'Yeah, and you smell of camp, that's for sure!'

The room filled with laughter, and it felt good to fall back into my familiar role. We sat down to eat, and I was halfway through an immense moose rib when Don and Carol arrived.

'Well, look what the cat brought in,' Don said, looking at me with his familiar expression of wry amusement. Carol stood beside him with a poker face although her eyes were smiling.

I slowly lowered the rib, feeling like a caveman. 'Hello Don, hello Carol.'

'The woodsman is back in town,' Don grinned, 'skinny but alive!'

I smiled. 'It's really good to be back.'

'So what are you up to?'

'Well, I'm here to get some supplies, and I'm planning to learn to mush,* so that I can get together a dog team.'

There was a sudden silence, and I looked around, wondering what I had said. Don shook his head. 'Kid gets the cabin built, and now he wants to get going with a team of pant-sniffers!' He raised

---

* French trappers, explorers and travelers in the North were some of the earliest white men to use dog sleds, and the word 'mush' comes from the French command 'marche!' which they used to get their dogs going.

his hands: 'Now don't you come asking me to help you with them! No way. I ran my trapline with a team of dogs, and was pretty happy when them snow-machines came along, I can tell you.'

Everybody laughed, and now Carol was grinning. Clearly this was going to be another subject of great amusement.

Before he headed home, Don said, 'You can shack up in my little cabin again while you're here, and hell, you can even come over for scraps round dinner time.'

I could have hugged him – he just never seemed to let me down. 'Thanks, Don. I'm really grateful.'

'Yeah, yeah.' He waved me to silence. 'I got an old snow machine which might come in handy when you get sick of dogs. It's called a Tundra II – real light and easy to move when you get stuck. You any good on a snow machine?'

I shrugged. 'Never been on one.'

He smiled. 'Well there's a surprise. See you for coffee tomorrow morning.'

That night I settled back into the warm little cabin in Don's yard, and sank into the homemade bed and fell into a very deep sleep. It felt good to be safe and surrounded by people, but after months of solitude I was exhausted by the effort of talking. I was also missing my family more than ever, and I was learning that in many ways being apart from them was even harder when I was with other people. When I was alone I could put children and families out of my mind, but being with Don's family that evening had reminded me of what I was missing.

The next morning I walked into Glenn Stout's office. He looked up when I came in, a broad smile crossing his long, morose face. 'Well, you're still alive, hey?'

'Just about – lost a bit of weight.'

'Nah.' He looked me up and down. 'You just lost the stuff you don't need.'

I saw a bowl of boiled sweets on the table, and he followed my gaze. 'Have a bit of candy – go ahead.'

I grabbed the bowl like a starved Dickensian orphan.

'So, you ready to learn to mush?'

'Yes!' I had worried that he might have forgotten his offer to teach me, but clearly Glenn's promise held good.

'Come to my dog yard at midday and we'll get started.'

Later on, I walked over to the far corner of the settlement where Glenn's house stood. It had been an air force home in the days when the village was a Cold War base, and stood not far from the old perimeter wire. The house was small and unpresuming, but as warm as freshly baked bread. He fired up his snow machine, and we drove together over to his dog yard.

'I got twenty-one huskies here,' he announced when we arrived, 'and I can give you six for your team.'

'Six!' I said in amazement. 'Didn't we say three?'

He looked at the dogs, which were running incessantly around the pegs to which they were tethered. Their eyes flashed white and blue, and the noise of barking and howling was alarming. 'Nah, you'll be okay,' he said. 'Sure I started with three dogs, but I had no one to help me, so I just had to start small and work up. It's best if you start with six.'

'Right,' I nodded, 'I see the logic.' As I said it I wondered why I had ever thought this was going to be easy. The dogs looked half wild, and their energy and power was intimidating. Children are regularly eaten when they stumble inadvertently into these dog yards, and it has even been known in mushing legend for huskies to eat their handlers. This was a particular problem in the past, when some handlers bred their huskies with wolves to give them extra strength and endurance. The results were virtually untamable, vicious dogs, which, although they could pull a sled almost indefinitely, would think nothing of attacking people. I remembered the reaction of the family last night, when I had said that I was going to learn dog mushing, and wondered whether what I was doing was wise.

Glenn was watching me closely, as if reading my thoughts. 'Now, I've got your dogs from a whole bunch of mushers,' he said slowly, 'so we don't know much yet about their characters. Let's go ahead and hook up your six for a start, just for the practice.'

He brought out a small birch sled, and unravelled the gangline ahead of it, which is what attaches the huskies to the sled. He then carefully separated out the necklines, which keep the dogs pointing forward and in position, and the tuglines, which are attached to the harnesses for each dog. 'First dog on is the lead dog,' he told me. 'He keeps the gangline straight, and if he turns and wanders back you make sure he straightens out.'

'How do I do that?'

'Better to watch and learn – you'll see.'

We walked into the swirling midst of the dog yard, where the animals were jumping and yowling and tearing around their tethers. 'These dogs are Alaskan Huskies,' Glenn shouted over the canine cacophony. 'They can pull about two hundred pounds per dog when good and fit.' He grabbed a wiry, dark-haired dog, which immediately jumped on to its hind legs. Its eyes were filled with fanatical zeal, and it looked as though it was engaged in some kind of infernal foxtrot as it dragged Glenn towards the sled. 'This is Bubbles – she's a good lead dog,' Glenn yelled, moving through the other dogs who barked and growled jealously as he passed. At the head of the gangline, Glenn held the dog between his knees while he slipped the harness over her head, then pulled her legs through and let her go. She fizzed out of his hands like a fish from an angler, coming to an abrupt halt as her tugline lifted and went taught, pulling the whole gangline up tight behind her. She kept straining forwards, leaning into her harness, and everything in her body said 'Let me run!' The birch sled was held fast by a claw-like steel anchor that had been stamped deep into the snow. As a further precaution, a rope stretched from the gangline to a cargo crate that doubled as a store-room. We walked back to get more dogs.

'You get that one there,' Glenn said, pointing to a small but wiry-looking black and white bitch that was barking at me furiously, its mouth white with spittle.

'What if I let go?'

'Don't do that,' he said over his shoulder. 'Dog'll just keep running.'

I steeled myself and walked over to collect her. She ran shyly into her kennel, then re-emerged, jumping up and down with excitement. I unclipped her from the tether, and was immediately taken aback by her strength as she pulled towards the sled, hopping on her hind legs and wheezing against her collar. It was incredible to hold an Alaskan husky, and to feel for myself the legendary pulling power of a working sled dog. I reached the gangline and asked Glenn where he wanted her. 'Just put her anywhere for now,' he said. 'We'll be moving them around until we find the place that best suits each dog.'

I walked over to a harness and tried to hold her still while I yoked her up, but she was so excited that I couldn't get the confusing thing on.

'Stand with her between your legs,' Glenn called, 'and hold her with your knees. Then fit the harness without letting go of the collar.'

In the end I managed to get the dog yoked up, but it had felt like trying to lasso mercury with a length of wet spaghetti. It didn't help that my fingers were freezing – I couldn't use big gloves, as I needed to be able to fiddle about with the collars and clips, but working with bare hands at minus thirty-five is no joke. The frigid metal clips kept sticking painfully to my exposed skin. I noticed that Glenn used woollen gloves for detailed work, then in between times sunk his hands into big beaver mitts which he wore strung around his back. Four dogs were now attached to the line and Bubbles held it tight, straining forwards despite the excited jangling and jumping from the rest of the team. Once she let the tension go, and looked back as if she was about to turn round, but Glenn came down on her quickly, pulling her forwards and saying: 'Line out!'

Next Glenn brought me two big dogs, saying, 'Stand between these two and hold them for a moment.' I took a firm hold of the dogs' collars, looking down at them as I did so. My right hand was attached to a thin, mean-looking red dog with a scarred face, which looked more like a dingo than anything else. He bucked violently in all directions, straining against my grip, and there was an unhinged quality to his howling and barking that I found spooky. My left hand held a very big brown dog, whose luminous eyes had immediately caught my attention. He also jumped up and down, yowling and barking with a deep voice that reminded me of an adolescent boy whose voice was breaking. I held on to the dogs for dear life, watching Glenn, who was examining the feet of one of the dogs, and hoping that he wouldn't be too long. Out of the corner of my eye I could see Matt and Ashley, who had appeared from nowhere to do some last-minute filming, and were sitting a discreet distance away. Just then I heard a sinister growling, and realised it was coming from the dingo, who was staring fixedly at the dog on my left. His lips were wrinkled back over a jagged line of teeth, and he was drooling saliva. The brown dog tried to pull away but I held on to him, knowing that if I let him go even worse chaos would ensue. 'Glenn,' I called softly, trying to keep my voice low as I felt that to shout would crank up the tension still further: 'Ah . . . Glenn!' He didn't hear me, and it was too late anyway, as the dingo suddenly launched himself at the brown dog and tore into its shoulder. I saw his flashing teeth open and crunch shut on the brown dog's fur, and noted with a degree of concern that those teeth had come together remarkably close to my groin. 'Glenn!' I yelled, abandoning all hope of keeping things calm, but he still couldn't hear me above the din of the excited dog team, which was now jumping around me like a charm bracelet from hell.

I tried to pull the dogs apart, but was finding it difficult to avoid their slashing teeth. I knew I mustn't let go, however, and struggled to hold them as rough claws ripped into the fabric of my im-maculate North Face jacket and frozen saliva flew. I felt like a UN peacekeeper caught in the crossfire between two warring tribes. I pulled with all of my strength, but the dogs were like two bits of steel colliding, and sparks of frozen blood were hitting the snow. I kicked the red dog, and my foot bounced off his rock hard flanks. 'Oh shit! Glenn!' I shouted, and then in desperation committed a musher's schoolboy error. I put my hand between the two dogs, and in an instant the red dog had sunk his teeth straight through my thick glove and deep into my left wrist. The sensation was not of pain, but of massive and concentrated weight, and I looked on in a distracted way as my own blood began to join that of the dogs' in the snow. To my relief Glenn appeared, bringing another dog to the gangline. He sprang into action and, still holding the other dog by its collar, launched his whole body on top of the dingo, pushing it down hard into the snow. It let go of the brown dog, who stood shaking by my side, still bleeding copiously. Glenn dragged first the dingo and then the brown dog back to their tethers, before returning to examine my hand. 'You better go and get that dealt with at the clinic,' he said, concern showing in his eyes, 'I'll sort things out here.'

As I walked away from the crime scene Ashley and Matt ran over to ask if they could help. I could see from their expressions that they had been treated to a filmic bonanza, capturing me almost being digested by my future means of transport. I called back a goodbye to Glenn, who sadly raised a hand to me as we headed off to get help. We went first to Don's cabin, where we found most of the family, who all examined my bleeding wrist with concern. Chris had parked his ancient pickup outside and we clambered into it, followed by Don, who was muttering and shaking his head. When we arrived at the pre-fab clinic Chris pointed out its name, *Edgar Nollner Senior Clinic*, which was printed on a wooden plaque above the door. 'See that?' he said.

'Yeah,' I mumbled, 'So?'

'He was my grandfather. He was one of the mushers on the Great Serum Run to Nome,* and went from Galena to Kuyukuk.'

'Great,' I muttered, 'Salt in the wounds. Did he ever get shredded by his team?'

'Nah,' Chris shook his head.

I said nothing. It was all getting to be a bit too depressing. My first day learning to mush and I was already heading for a doctor.

---

* In 1925 the Alaskan town of Nome suffered a diptheria outbreak. Countless children had been exposed, and there were only five units of serum. Twenty mushers carried 300,000 units of anti-toxin 674 miles across the frozen Interior from Nenana, passing through hard country in bitter cold.

The clinic was staffed by a couple of medics who worked on a shift basis. I walked into a little room, where I was met by an attractive, intelligent-looking woman who examined my hand. 'Oh yeah, that dog got you good,' she said. 'You must have felt that on the bone.'

I admitted that I had felt a grating sensation, and she let out a little laugh. 'Yeah, these sled dogs can be rough.' She rolled up her sleeve to reveal a livid scar. 'See this?'

'Yes,' I replied, knowing what was coming.

'That was one of my dogs.'

'Oh dear. Was it a sled dog by any chance?'

'Yup.'

I sighed. 'Thought so.'

Just then there was a knock on the door, and in came Don, Chris, Matt and Ashley.

'Mind if we watch Guy?' They stood sheepishly in the doorway.

I shrugged my shoulders, resigning myself to yet more humiliation.

'Okay,' the nurse said. 'We're going to irrigate the wound now.' She held up an immense syringe filled with saline. 'This might sting a bit.'

Using the full strength of her shoulders, she proceeded to squirt saline into the wound until it felt like my arm was going to explode. I bit my sleeve theatrically for the benefit of the audience, then found that I really did need to bite something, as it hurt like hell. Don's mouth was twitching at the corners as he watched and soon he held a hand over his mouth to try to disguise the fact that he was starting to laugh. I looked around and saw that the others were trying to hold back from laughing too, and I cynically nodded my head. 'Thanks a lot friends. So glad you're enjoying yourselves.'

The whole room erupted with laughter – including, most disturbingly, the nurse.

I left the clinic with a dramatically bandaged hand, and when I arrived back at Don's place found Carol laying the table for supper. She too was darkly laughing about something, and I watched her quizzically without saying anything. Don saw my look: 'Yeah, she's kinda enjoying your stay I think,' he said. 'And your learning to mush is of interest to her – she ran her first team of dogs when she was seven years old. How many did you run, Mom?'

'Eight.' Carol was taking a baking dish out of the oven, and straightened up with a big smile on her face.

'Eight?' I repeated, clenching my teeth.

'Mm hm'.

'Do you remember what it was like to learn?'

'Nah – we just got on and went,' she replied, making me feel even worse about my disastrous first day.

Ashley and Matt ate with us that night, as they were leaving the next morning. We sat and talked for a long time, and despite my throbbing hand it felt good to sit around a table with friends. Towards the end of the meal, Don noticed Matt toying with a last piece of moose on his plate. 'Hey – you should have a drop of sauce on that. How 'bout it Matt?'

'That would be perfect,' Matt said, demonstrating his good English table manners. 'Thanks very much.'

I knew exactly what was coming. Don handed over the little red bottle of Dave's Insanity Sauce and Matt read the label, looking slightly nervous.

'It's not very hot, is it Don?'

'I don't find it too bad,' Don replied with a poker face.

'Great,' Matt said, 'I love a hot sauce.' And he sprinkled the sauce liberally on the piece of meat.

I kept my face impassive as he popped the morsel into his mouth cheerfully, then chewed and swallowed whilst looking around at us as if wondering why we were staring. Then it hit him. He froze, still holding his knife and fork above his plate. Then he choked, and his face went an amazing bright red before he broke out in a sweat and began to hiccup profusely. He was clearly in agony, yet he said nothing, and kept smiling bravely throughout it all. Don bent double with silent laughter, and placed the bottle back in the cupboard, ready for his next unsuspecting victim. We all joined in the laughter, and as we did so I marvelled at Don's uniquely sadistic character. He had a wild, dangerous streak of humour that had grown in the construction camps and bucking bars of unruly, out of the way places – places where the humour was harsh, and often involved near-death escapes. Today his prediction had been borne out, and the tenderfoot had been savaged by a pack of dogs. He had also witnessed him being surgically tortured, and now he had tricked another innocent with his Insanity Sauce. Yes, it had certainly been a perfect day for Don. Unfortunately it had been less perfect for me, and I slept badly that night, knowing that I would now lose a few days waiting for my hand to heal before I could continue learning to mush. Perhaps Don was right – maybe the last thing I needed was a team of dogs. Back in my cabin I lay staring at the ceiling, filled with worry and trying to ignore the intense throbbing of my hand.

30
LIFTING THE SNOW ANCHOR

A few days later I went back to see Glenn, and found him sitting in his snug little sitting room. He looked up at me over his morose looking cowboy's moustache, his eyes passing from my face to my bandaged hand. 'How's that hand of yours?' he asked, and I smiled sheepishly.

'Oh it's okay thanks,' I said. 'Looks far worse than it is.'

'I sure am sorry Guy.' He shifted in his seat. 'Kinda feel that red dog was not right.'

'Well it wasn't your fault,' I said. 'What happened with the dog?'

'I shot it.'

There was a silence. 'Not all because of that bite surely?' I asked.

'No, he'd been biting other dogs as well. I can't have dogs that bite in the yard – I bred many of them myself and I can't risk one coming in and causing problems.'

I could see his point. 'So what now Glenn?' Part of me was hoping that, as I was one dog down, we would have to go back to the plan of using just three dogs.

He stood up. 'Spoke to a guy out near Tanana. Think he might have a dog that he could sell or maybe give you.'

My heart sank. 'So we stick to six dogs?'

'Yes we do.'

'Why would he give me a dog?'

'He's got around five hundred dogs, and some of 'em ain't fast, but would be just fine for getting about.'

The thought of a yard with five hundred dogs appalled me – twenty-one had been bad enough. I gave my hand a squeeze: 'I think I'll be okay for more training if you can bear it.'

'Sure I can,' he smiled. 'I'm real happy to see you ain't giving up. Come back here around five and we'll get going.'

It was dark when I returned, and very cold. We walked over to a fifty-five gallon drum that had been converted into a makeshift stove. Glenn quickly lit a fire underneath it, and then lifted a tarpaulin from a massive pile of fish. 'Caught about twelve hundred green fish★ in the summer,' he said. 'Now I cook 'em in the dog-pot every night.'

'What else is in it?'

'I chop in about half a fish per dog, then mix in some dog feed, rice and snow for water.'

As we talked, the leftover chowder from the previous night began to thaw, and soon an acrid cloud of smoke hung around us in the frigid air. We scooped in more snow, and chopped the mix of pike, grayling and perch with an axe before adding the fishy bits to the steaming cauldron. Glenn stirred the pot with a long stick. 'We leave this to cook up while we're out,' he said. 'That way by the time we get back it'll be ready. Great grub for warming a dog. Now we give 'em some fishy water.' He ladled some of the odious brew into a bucket, and then carried it into the howling yard to scoop into each animal's dish. I stood in the middle of the yard, watching the dogs leap and bark, their eyes glinting in the light from my head torch. Above me, a great white fishy cloud was rising

---

★ Green fish are simply the fish species that are not routinely eaten by people, and thus usually feed dog teams. They are called 'green' because it is not necessary to store them in prime condition and so they are usually mildly, and sometimes profoundly, rotten.

into a black sky lit by thousands of stars. Glenn walked over to his snow machine, gesturing for me to sit behind him. 'Gonna show you the route that you'll learn on,' he shouted over the noise of the engine.

The wind chill had picked up now and the temperature must have been around minus fifty, but I was well wrapped up and hidden behind Glenn. We passed out of his yard and along an icy gravel road towards the brightly lit watchtower of the sinister Cold War base, then turned towards a high dyke that had been built to safeguard the village against flooding. We leapt over this, and then followed a snowy portage that passed through willow and alder woods before crossing an open, hummocky area that led on towards the great frozen Yukon. We drove on until we reached the steep river embankment, which we passed over and down before turning sharp right. Now the claustrophobia of the woods was replaced by an immense open vista, as the narrow sled trail ran along the river for a mile or so before turning to the right, back up the bank and into the woods. There it snaked along, meandering and dipping down into hollows and up over wooded ridges, before finally returning to the dyke in a loop.

We drove back into the yard and readied the team, which I managed more easily, despite the difficulty of working with a heavily bandaged hand. I was feeling nervous and ill prepared, and the thought of travelling along that dark, snowy portage pulled by these alien creatures filled me with worry. The dogs barked and yowled as we hitched them up, their breath forming a white cloud that rose above them, then froze and fell on their backs as frost.

'Okay Guy,' Glenn said when we were ready, 'I'm gonna be tied on behind you on the snow machine to slow 'em down as you go out. Put these on Bubbles feet – she needs the protection.'

He handed me four material 'booties', and I walked to the head of the gangline to secure them on the lead dog's feet. As I pulled them on she licked my cheek, and on that cold hard night, feeling anxious and vulnerable, her show of affection meant a lot to me. I gave her a pat and she looked at me briefly with intelligent and determined eyes, silent while behind her the whole team was at a fever pitch of barking excitement. I walked back to the sled and stood in position on the runners. 'How do I stop this thing Glenn?' I asked, thinking that I should at least know this if nothing else.

'That metal pedal there is the snow brake,' he replied. 'You see it?'

I saw a piece of metal held between the runners by a thick piece of black rubber. On the underside there were three stout steel studs.

'You shout "Whoa", and push your foot down hard on the brake. On an icy trail it'll only slow the dogs down, but on snow it'll hold 'em good – just don't let it off.'

I looked ahead at the jumping dogs, the occasional eye reflecting back at me as they turned impatiently to see what the delay was about.

'Any other way of stopping them?' I asked.

'No, but you can slow 'em down by standing with your feet astride the runners and digging your heels in.'

'Okay.' I hoped I sounded more confident than I felt. 'And how do I steer?'

'You shout "gee" if you want to go right, "ha" if you want to go left. "Hike" means go, and "whoa" means stop.'

'And they'll stop just on voice command?'

'No – never. That command has to be backed up with the footbrake, then when they've stopped you stamp in the anchor.'

He showed me how to use the anchor, and to hold the team on the footbrake while throwing the anchor into a suitable spot and stamping it into the snow. Once the anchor was in I would gently release the footbrake, with the idea that the team would strain forward, pulling the anchor in deep. Sometimes the anchor does not hold, and many a careless musher has been horrifically injured by the heavy steel hook dragging along at high speed behind the team before sinking itself into a leg or worse.

He walked back to the snow machine and started the engine, and I did up my jacket and braced myself. 'Okay,' he shouted over his shoulder. 'Pull the anchor!' I did so, and as it squeaked out of the snow the dogs immediately stopped barking and went silent, leaning into their harnesses and heaving the sled, which was being held back by the snow machine. Nevertheless, they still managed a fair speed, and we clattered out along the frozen road, then up past the tower and on towards the dyke, which seemed like an impossible obstacle when looked at from a little birch sled. Like a team of seasoned trench raiders carrying a stretcher, the dogs streamed over the lip of ice, and we pulled along the snowy portage until we reached a straight section, where Glenn stopped and shouted for me to stamp in the anchor. I did so, and the dogs came to a reluctant halt.

'You sure you got that anchor in good?' he shouted.

'Yes, I hope so,' I answered over my shoulder.

'Good, 'cause I'm gonna unhook you from the Tundra, so they'll just be held by the anchor and footbrake. That okay?'

I raised a hand, although all my instincts told me I wasn't ready, and only pride was preventing me from saying so. Glenn unhitched the snow machine and the sled jerked forward. I watched the anchor line tighten as the claw bit deep into the snow. The dogs strained and leapt impatiently, their harness jangling as they barked and yowled up at the stars. Before me the dark snowy trail loomed ominously, lit only by the dim beam of my head torch.

Glenn's voice came from behind me in the darkness. 'You go when you're ready, and remember: you're sending commands to the lead dog and not the others. Don't say too much, but when you do shout commands you need to sound like you mean it. If they're going too fast shout "easy", and push the brake down for a bit to back that order up, or else stick your feet down into the snow.'

'Okay Glenn,' I replied in a feeble voice. 'Just give me a minute.' With shaking hands, I put on my neoprene mask and goggles, and then pulled my hat down firmly against the cold. I paused for a moment and took a deep breath, then pushed the brake down with my left foot while I leaned over and pulled up the anchor. The dogs immediately responded to the sound of it squeaking up through the snow, and began jumping into their harnesses and falling back again, reminding me of salmon leaping against a waterfall. The front of the sled lifted with their pulling, and all that now held them was my little footbrake. They yowled and jerked and pulled, looking back at me as if to say 'C'mon tenderfoot! Let us run!'

I let the brake go and jumped on to the runners, and in an instant we were off, tearing at full speed into the darkness. The dogs were completely silent now, and for the first time I experienced their immense pulling power. The only sounds were the creaking and straining of the sled, and the swishing noise of the runners on the snow. It reminded me of sailing, and that joyful moment when the engine is turned off and the boat becomes part of the elements, the only sounds the wind and water and straining cordage as the vessel responds to the breeze. We tore along the trail beneath a glittering arch of frosted trees, and although I felt utterly out of my depth I was captivated by the elemental power of it all. The dogs ran and ran, and my left hand ached as I gripped hard on the wooden bar of the sled. I glanced behind me and saw the light of Glenn's snow machine following at a distance, then I realised that we were charging straight for a series of hummocks before the descent into the river basin, and going much too fast. It was too late to do anything about it, and I held on for dear life. The dogs flew across the obstacles, sending the sled flying up into the sky. I just managed to hang on, and then ahead of me saw the river bank approaching. 'Whoa!' I shouted, and jammed the brake down hard. We skidded to a halt, and I held the pedal down while I gathered my breath. The dogs didn't seem in the least tired, and looked back at me impatiently, eager to be off.

A few minutes later I let the brake off again, but this time more carefully, holding it half down as we neared the embankment. The three studs plowed deep furrows into the trail as we descended, such was the force of the dogs' pulling, and at the turn I let the brake off fully. They shot off again, following the trail as it turned sharply to the right, one runner lifting off the snow completely. I held on desperately, and then relaxed a little as the trail straightened out along the river, standing tall on the runners and trying to clear my mind of everything except getting back in one piece. Just before the trail re-entered the woods Glenn came abreast of me and waved for me to stop. 'You're going too fast,' he shouted. 'Try

to hold 'em back a bit more at tricky points, and when you make a
turn, lean back on the sled and be very firm about your direction.
Set your runners hard on the turn – don't try to muddle through.
Do you follow me?'

'Yes,' I said, though in fact I didn't.

He looked at me for a moment, then asked, 'You ever skied
before?'

'No.'

'Water-skied?'

'No.'

'Kind of a shame.' He shook his head. 'I was gonna say that
driving a sled was just the same. Never mind,' he clapped me on
the back, 'you'll get there.' He started the engine. 'Oh, when you go
up that steep bank get off and run behind the sled just to help 'em
up the hill. When you get to the top jump on again. When you're
going downhill put the brake on, otherwise you'll run into the dogs.
Always keep the gangline tight.'

We set off again, surging forwards at great speed, and before I
knew it we were approaching the steep bank Glenn had men-
tioned, which was about ten feet high. The dogs now showed their
superb traction, and bent low in their harnesses. I jumped off as
Glenn had instructed, and stumbled along between the runners,
holding tightly on to the sled. When the front of the team was at the
top of the bank the speed picked up dramatically, and I just leapt
on in time before we shot off again. We swerved through the forest,
each turn almost finishing me, but by some miracle I hung on. At
each corner I started leaning on the outside runner, while the inside
runner lifted off the snow and sent the whole sled into a dangerous
wobble. To correct this I would throw my weight on to the airborne
runner, so that at the last minute it straightened out again and
made contact with the snow. We flew over hidden dips, where it
felt as if the sled had fallen away from me, and sudden ridges,
where I was momentarily suspended in mid-air. Just when I
thought I could take no more, we reached the end of the forest,
pulling up the embankment before descending on to the road. I
held the brake down hard as we went downhill, remembering

Glenn's maxim about always keeping the gangline tight, and a cloud of white sprayed up behind us as the studs bit into the icy road. We barrelled into the cul-de-sac in front of the dog yard and came to a stop.

I braked and stamped in the anchor, deeply relieved to be in one piece. Glenn shook my hand: 'You made it,' he said, 'well done.'

'Thanks.' I shook my head, feeling a mixture of shock and exhilaration. 'That was quite an experience.'

'Now we keep practising that trail, and when the dogs can pull you up that embankment at the end we'll know they're fit enough to take you home.'

'What, you mean they're unfit?'

'Oh yeah, they're running real slow now – you'll see the difference when they're fit. Then you'll really feel the power.'

'I can't wait,' I said.

'Oh yeah, that's some feeling.' Glenn's face was lit with excitement. 'And when the trail gets frozen the sled runs even faster too – you'll see.'

I looked over at the six dogs, panting in their harnesses, and wondered how I, a confirmed cat person, had found myself in this position. We unhitched the dogs and put them back on their tethers, then ladled out their reviving chowder. Silence descended over the yard, and it felt good to see them putting away a warming meal. I walked around the yard with a bucket and spade, lifting frozen turds and urine from the compacted snow of each dog's run.

When the dogs were settled and all the kit had been put away, Glenn invited me to come over for some tea. I sat in his warm kitchen, watching with a mixture of guilt and sadness as he cradled his beautiful youngest son. My hand throbbed, and my body ached from the jolts and bumps it had suffered on the sled. Outside the snow was falling, again.

31
AN ARCTIC KNEECAPPING

If the pleasures that an age offers are insipid,
passionate souls will seek pain.
BRENDAN FRANCIS

Days and nights of training were gradually leading somewhere, and Glenn was a patient and determined teacher. I was learning not just how to mush, but also how to run a dog yard, and under Glenn's instruction stretched the dogs' legs, checked their feet carefully and learned to spot and treat common problems. We took the team out for a practice run each day, increasing from five miles to ten as their fitness improved, and they were rapidly growing stronger and faster. At the same time the cold weather was hardening the trail, which was closer to ice than snow in some places, making the runs faster still. Dangerously, running in tandem with this gradual upping of the stakes was my own confidence, which was growing with each run survived.

One night I was harnessing the dogs up as usual in Glenn's yard. It was a very cold night, but I worked without my hat and jacket to

ensure that I didn't build up a sweat. We moved out of the yard
with the snow machine attached to the sled as usual, then stopped
at the straight line of trail outside the village. I dug in the anchor
and began pulling on my extra layers of clothing.

'Coldest night yet,' Glenn said. 'Trail is gonna be slick and fast.'

I nodded coolly, like a boxer taking advice from his trainer in the
corner of the ring.

'Keep it under control and don't let go whatever happens. The
team'll keep running – they'll never stop if they get away from
you.'

'Okay,' I said, and then pulled the anchor and held the dogs on
the footbrake for a moment, enjoying the feeling of their coiled
power in the moment before they were unleashed into the night. I
lifted my foot and we blasted off along the trail. I looked up and
saw a great citrus-white moon, which lit the snow around me so
brightly that everything glowed. I gave the dogs full rein, whooping
with excitement as we fizzed like a comet through the cold air. We
were going too fast, but I was hooked by the speed, the ethereal joy
of shooting at full tilt along a trail that was so icy that the runners
barely held. The glittering, frost-rimmed canopy flashed and
sparkled in the moonlight, and the dogs ran as if possessed by
some infernal spirit, their backs arching and stretching with each
galloping stride. A voice in my head was telling me to slow down,
but the fifteen-year-old boy in me had taken over, and all caution
and common sense was lost. Suddenly I saw the river embankment
ahead of me, and slammed too late at the brake pedal. It skipped
away from me, unable to grip on the ice, and we flew down on to
the river at great speed. The dogs whirred to the right, making the
sled the equivalent of the end of a cracking whip. I needed to show
strength and commitment in the turn, and should have jammed
my right runner in hard and leaned back with a steely attitude that
said: 'Now make this turn!' Instead I panicked and leaned on my
left runner. In an instant the sled flipped into a barrel roll, and I hit
the ice hard. All my weight smashed down on my right knee, and I
screamed with pain. I held on grimly to the upturned sled as the
dogs hurtled along, dragging me like a rag doll across the ice. A

moment later Glenn shot past and grabbed hold of the team, then pulled the sled from my grip. I lay back and stared at the cold moon, hoping darkly that I had broken my leg – at least that would give me a honourable way out.

'Hey, you okay?' Glenn's face loomed above me. 'You must've been doing about twenty-eight miles an hour there – way too fast!'

I knew I had to get up – I had hurt myself badly, but I wasn't about to admit it. I stood up, wincing in agony, and hobbled over to the sled. 'Okay Glenn, I'll take it,' I said. 'Thanks.'

'You sure?' He continued to hold the sled, not convinced.

'Yeah.' I stood on the runners, feeling nothing now in my right knee beyond a jelly-like quivering.

I lifted the anchor. Soon we were up in the woods again and swerving through the trees. Each jolt was sending shockwaves of pain through me, and on the tightest turn I lost my grip and fell off again. This time I let go of the sled, and landed face first in soft snow. The sled shot off along the moonlit trail, looking like some kind of arctic ghost train. Behind me I heard Glenn approaching and rolled out of the way. He came alongside the running dogs, and then, like a highwayman hijacking a coach team, grabbed the gangline and pulled with all his strength. Eventually the dogs came to a stop, and he jammed in the anchor and waited as I limped over to him. Without saying anything I stood on the runners and set off back to the yard.

I limped about feeding the dogs and putting them away, then went to say goodbye to Glenn. I was deeply humbled by my accident, which was entirely my own fault. 'Take a day or two off,' Glenn said, giving me a whack on the shoulder.

'Thanks Glenn,' I mumbled. 'I'm sorry about all of that.'

'Don't be,' he smiled. 'We've all had a smash up in our time. The important thing is to get back on those runners, which you did.'

Back at Don's yard lights were shining warmly from the windows of his house and smoke curled up from the stovepipe. I knocked on the door. 'C'mon in!' I heard. Carol was knitting socks by the stove, and Don was sitting beside the window, looking out over the moonlit river. Both of them fixed me with their sharp eyes, and Carol lowered her knitting. 'Oh man!' she said. 'You just got back from mushing?'

I nodded miserably.

'First smash up?' Don asked.

I nodded again, and he walked over, looking me up and down. 'Done your knee?'

'Yeah.' I bent down to feel it and winced.

He shook his head, laughing quietly. 'Well, I did warn you about them pant-sniffers!'

'I know,' I sighed.

Carol let out a few of her characteristic dark chuckles, and then stood up to make tea.

Later I hobbled back to my temporary home in Don's yard, and on the way stopped to see how Fuzzy was doing in his snug wooden kennel. He padded out to greet me, rubbing his nose against my leg and growling affectionately. I scratched him absent-mindedly, staring along the shining white river and wondering whether I would ever make it back to my camp by dogsled. What if tonight's episode had happened when I was alone in the bush? It had been a timely reminder. Overconfidence in the wilderness could only mean one thing: death.

32
THE SOLO MUSH

The shortest answer is doing.
ENGLISH PROVERB

My knee was in bad shape and throbbed constantly, yet I couldn't afford to hang around. I needed to get to grips with mushing so that I could get back to my cabin, and Glenn never let me down. We went out in all weather, from deepest cold to blizzards, and as I became more adept I began to relish some of the perks of travelling by dog. The best of these was being able to move in silence, and instead of the relentless drone of a snow machine's engine the only sound was the beautiful swish of wooden runners on snow. This meant that I saw much more wildlife on my travels, and because I was not moving at the high speed of a snow machine could look closely at the land I was passing through. I also knew I wouldn't break down, and as long as the dogs were fed and watered we would make it back home. As an added bonus, if I were caught in a blizzard they would find the way for me. At night when the moon was out I would turn my head torch off, enjoying the feeling of dogs and man floating like ghosts across the moony landscape, a method of transport that was thousands of years old.

One morning I stopped in to see Glenn at work. 'You're ready to take them dogs out on your own now,' he said. 'Go round to the yard and hook 'em up.'

I froze with excitement and fear, feeling like a young pilot taking the Sopworth Camel for his first solo. 'Well, if you think I'm ready . . .'

'You're ready, and you'll need to start thinking about making trails down the river to your camp.'

'How do I do that? I can't run the dogs across virgin snow, can I?'

He laughed. It is a common misconception that sled dogs can run anywhere they want in the sub arctic. They can't, as the snow is usually too deep and dry, and trails have to be made for dogs just as they are for humans. Above the tree line the windblown arctic provides a firmer surface, allowing dogsleds to range more freely. Dogs further north also run in a different formation, and each have their own long ganglines which fan out from the sled. In the sub arctic they have to run close together, to allow them to traverse the many obstacles and narrow portages that typify the terrain.

'What do you suggest?'

'Take a snow machine down to camp to break trail. It'll be tough, as there's been a lot of snow, but once that trail is there it'll freeze and you'll be able to get the dogs down.'

'Right.' I sat down, thinking about the miles of river, slough and woodland between here and my cabin. 'What did people do before snow machines?'

'They snowshoed ahead to break trail, and then walked back for the team. Hard work, and took a long time. When the trail was done they'd make sure to keep it, and each time it snowed they'd walk along it again or ride it with the dogs. You'll be doing the same.' He cleared his throat. 'Now, where you planning to keep the dogs?'

'I'm going to cut a dog yard in the woods by my cabin.'

Glenn nodded. 'Make sure you cut it close to the cabin so wolves don't vacuum up your entire team. Put your most valuable dog nearest to the cabin and your least effective dogs nearer to the perimeter – that way if wolves come they'll hopefully not eat your lead dog first.'

I nodded, struck anew by the savagery of arctic life. My time in the village had begun to soften me, and I had to get back while the scar tissue was still in place. 'Won't the dogs kick up a fuss if wolves come?'

'Yes, and this'll give you a chance to do something about it. They'll bark at everything that comes into camp except a brown bear.'

'What do they do then?'

'They go quiet and sneak back into their boxes – you won't hear a thing.'

I thought about the horror of being visited in midwinter by a brown bear. Brown bears, unlike their black cousins, have sometimes been known to wander around the woods at the wrong time of the year.

'What else should I watch out for?'

He stood up and stretched. 'Well, moose'll be getting meaner as the winter goes on, and because a dog sled moves quietly you could surprise one on your portage.'

'What should I do then?' I asked, thinking that Don's advice of running round a tree would be a bit tricky with a team of dogs.

'Well that's when you need a gun, 'cause sometimes a moose'll stamp on a team of dogs, smashing 'em all to pieces.'

I looked closely at his face, wondering if he was trying to scare me, but then realised he was merely being practical. A memory of my dark, winding portage came back to me and I felt a trickle of fear.

'So when can I head out on my own?'

'Any time I guess.' He looked out the window. 'Though if you're goin' today better go quick while there's still some light.'

Back at Don's yard I found him talking to Chris and Charlie.

'Glenn says I can take the dogs out on my own today,' I said, keeping my voice deliberately casual. 'Thinks I'm at that stage.'

'Uh huh.' Don raised his eyebrows. 'Going now?'

'Why not? Might as well get on with it.'

Charlie raised his chin. 'You want me to follow along?' he asked, glancing at Chris as if to say, 'the kid's trying to kill himself again.'

'Thanks Charlie, but I'll give it a go alone.'

Don looked at his watch. 'What time you going?'

'Oh, in thirty minutes or so.'

He gave me serious look. 'Just 'cause this is happening near the village don't mean it's safe, d'you hear me? You be careful.'

'Thanks Don.' I glanced over at Charlie, 'And thanks again for the offer.' I was touched by their concern, particularly from Charlie, who hadn't been entirely easy with me since our confrontation. I went back to the little cabin and packed my day bag with a thermos, an emergency fire lighting kit, change of clothes and rations. Then I set off for Glenn's yard.

It felt odd setting up the team without Glenn around. I set the dogs out on the gangline, working slowly to ensure that I didn't forget anything. The yard was full of barking excitement as usual, and my ears rung with the noise. I untied the line that I had secured to the crate, feeling the sled inch forward and then hold as the anchor gripped. The dogs strained against their harnesses, barking and whining as they looked back at me with eyes that pleaded to be let loose. I lifted the anchor and they rose like sprinters to the mark, and then let go of the brake. A split second's pause and we were off, hurtling along the hard icy road, and just a few seconds later we reached the turn that led uphill to the embankment. I braked, but the studs couldn't grip on the ice, and as we turned the sled simply slipped sideways across the slick surface. I relaxed and let it happen, and just before the sled hit the piled snow on the far side of the road the dogs' upward course straightened things out. Somehow I kept the gangline tight as they vaulted the embankment, and soon we were skimming through the woods towards the river. The sun was going down, and the western sky was lit by a cold, yellow light. I passed over kneecap ridge without incident, and down on to the river where I looked out across four miles of frozen white water towards the distant tree-lined bank. I held the sled tight as the trail straightened out, leaning back and staring up into the darkening blue of the sub arctic night. I wished that I could rip off my neoprene face covering and suck in a great gulp of the clear night air, but knew that to do so would risk frostbite of the lungs. Instead I contented myself with drinking the scene in with my eyes, and as I looked up caught the flash of a comet, spitting a bright little trajectory towards the northwest.

We rounded a sandbar covered in snow, and I noticed the dogs suddenly upping the pace while looking off to their right. In a stand of willow I saw a dark brown shape, which I could dimly make out was a moose calf standing up to its armpits in the deep snow. My eyes scanned through the willows, looking for more, and I noticed deep footprints leading from the sandbar to the trail. A split second later my eyes widened in horror as a great dark brown lump rose up from the snow just thirty yards ahead. It was a moose – a great big cow, and she was standing right in the middle of the trail.

'Oh shit,' I said desperately. 'Not a moose – please no!' The dogs barked furiously and sped up, and I imagined a scene of utter destruction beneath the animal's great pounding hooves. I pushed the brake down hard, but the dogs were pulling so hard that it did nothing at first, only ploughing a deep furrow along the trail. I jumped on it again with both feet, and managed to hold it down just long enough to stop the dogs. Then I quickly let a foot off to stamp in the snow anchor. The anchor also pulled through the snow, and only by stamping repeatedly on it was I able to make it hold. My heart pounded. The six dogs had completely lost their minds with excitement. They jumped, barked and whined, looking back at me and then at the moose which stood stock still, staring at us. I had no rifle, and felt very small and vulnerable on the wide-open plain of snow. The moose dropped her ears and lowered her head in a threatening manner – then she stepped forwards and swung her great head over towards the other moose in the willows. 'Stalemate,' I thought, and knew that I had to take action of some kind. Thinking of face-offs with Highland cattle back in Scotland, I ripped the mask away and started to shout. 'Fuck off you arsehole!

Fuck off!' The cow raised her head and looked at me in a shocked way, clearly appalled by my bad manners. For a few minutes I continued to swear at her, heaping insult upon insult, until eventually, holding her head high in disgust, she stepped haughtily off the trail.

As she waded away towards the willows I thanked my lucky stars that I had met that great beast in an open place, where she had not felt cornered. What on earth would have happened on a tight portage through the woods? Feeling jittery, I waited until she was well out of the way, then pulled up the anchor and moved off fast. I had been warned that another danger on encountering moose is that the dog team will give chase, ripping the hapless musher and his sled through whatever lies in their way. Sharp willow osiers become spears that can blind, wound or worse, and sleds can be shattered, leaving the musher alone and without provisions.

Without further incident, we entered the forest, passing along the narrow, twisting trail. Having survived the close encounter with the moose I was feeling wonderfully calm, and enjoyed our meandering journey through the icy, silent woods. I saw a fox trot out of the willows, and the dogs turned their heads to look at him as we moved swiftly past. Closer to the village the trees were full of the round silhouettes of grouse roosting for the night. At last I could see the lights of the watchtower, and soon we surged up the bank and then down on to the road. I braked hard, and we skittered back to the yard where I stopped the dogs, calling 'whoa' to Bubbles who looked back at me trustingly. They were all panting, their faces covered with frost, and I felt the beginnings of a partnership with the desperate half dozen. As I stepped off the runners I felt a powerful sense of satisfaction: I had travelled ten miles on my own in the darkness, run into a moose and come home in one piece. I thought of the comet and my superstitious mind told me that it was an omen of good fortune. It was time to head back to camp.

33

CHRISTMAS AT THE GOLDEN CABIN

Without a family, man, alone in the world, trembles with the cold.
RUSSIAN PROVERB

'Hello, hello, hello – can you hear me?' I was calling home and having trouble getting a signal.

'Yes I can hear you,' Juliet's faint voice replies. 'Are you okay?'

'Yes, but I'm missing everyone badly. It's harder being in the village – it makes me miss you all even more. I need to get back to camp.'

There's a pause, and I can hear her saying, 'I'm talking to Daddy. Oscar, do you want to say hello?' I wait to hear his little voice, but instead Juliet comes back on.

'He's busy with a puzzle – he says he'll speak to you later,' she says, and sadness wells up inside me. So this is what it feels like to lose touch with your children, I think, feeling guilty and angry at the same time.

'That's fine,' I say. 'It's normal for him to start being a bit distant, isn't it?'

'Well, he still loves you Guy, but he's got to get on with it. If he'd kept missing you like he did in the beginning he couldn't have coped.'

'Do you think he'll be okay? I was really worried that I might be causing permanent damage.'

'I'm sure he will, but right now you are in the background and that is good. If you were in his every waking thought God knows what kind of state he would be in.' She changes the subject. 'You haven't forgotten that it's Christmas next week have you? What are you going to do?'

'I'm going back to my cabin – then I'm going to run naked into the snow and shoot myself.' In fact I had been planning to forget about Christmas altogether, as I knew it would be a difficult time.

She laughs. 'No seriously, I had an email from Claudette saying she'd like you to be with them.'

'How could I do that?'

'Well why not?'

'It would feel wrong to be with another family while my own is without me. Better to be on my own.'

'No it's not. This isn't just any family – they've helped you so much, and they really want you to be there.'

'Yes I know that, and I love them but . . .'

'Suffering alone in your cabin won't help us have a better Christmas – I really think you should stay.' She pauses. 'Besides, at least if you're in the village we can all relax and enjoy Christmas, knowing that you're safe for another week or so.' Juliet is blessed with a clear and accurate mind, and when she puts an argument together you can never really win.

'Okay, let me think about it', I say, 'but you have got a point.'

I packed away the little phone, then sat for a minute considering the two options: Christmas alone in my cabin, or in the midst of Don's wonderful family. There was no contest. I wondered what beautiful food the family was planning to prepare, and made a solemn prayer for pumpkin pie.

As the days wound closer to Christmas, I began to struggle. Every time I played with one of the children, or saw them folding into the arms of a loving mother or father, my heart ached. I remembered last year's Christmas tree at our home in the Scottish Borders, and how I had lifted Oscar up to put the star on the top. This year he would be old enough to decorate it himself, I thought, realising how much he would have changed since I last saw him. I remembered their excitement last Christmas morning, and little Luke gurgling at the sight of the baby-sized stocking that hung from his cot. We had given Oscar a new bike, and he spent the whole day solemnly cycling round the room on his stabilisers. I felt deep sadness at these memories and at the thought of what I would be missing, but then reminded myself that it had not all been sweetness and light. In the run-up to Christmas I had been worried and unhappy, as heads were rolling at *The Scotsman* and I knew my time must be nearly up. Some good friends had been laid off that year, and worst of all I remembered the day that my former manager had been made redundant. We watched him clear away his desk, and he showed his good West Coast spirit by laughing and joking as he did it, yet it must have cast a deep shadow over his Christmas. Beneath all the merriment last Christmas was the knowledge that I had been lucky to have made it that far, and that it couldn't last.

Still, I felt bereft without my family, and Don and Carol seemed to sense what I was feeling. They included me in everything, and I was so often with them that I was nicknamed 'Grandpa and Grandma's Big Boy' by Jenny and Chris's daughter, Tirzah. My relationship with Carol was growing, and she happily joined Don in teasing me whenever there was an opportunity. She had an unrivalled line in mean looks, which she tested on me from time to time. Whenever I walked into the cabin she would fix me with a steely look that said: 'You make sure not one flake of snow comes past that doorway – if it does, you die.' She was a remarkable woman, and hearing stories of her childhood gave me an insight into where she had gained her strength of character. One morning we were sitting drinking coffee when she told me the story of her first encounter with a bear.

'One spring we were at camp by the river,' she started. 'I went to collect water for Mom, and on the way saw that one of the dogs was running round his tether – just running and running, and real quiet too.'

As she spoke Claudette came in and stood quietly by the door, and I knew that I was being granted a rare privilege. 'So I told Mom when I got back to the tent, and she said "Girls – get to the back of the tent and keep your fingers in your ears, you hear?" ' Carol took a sip of coffee, and outside I saw wind whipping snow off Shorty's box. 'Well Dad and the men went out with their guns, 'cause there was a grizzly in the camp – no dog ever barks at a grizzly, that's how they knew. They shot him, and as he fell he cried out like a man – sounded just like a man crying. I heard it 'cause I didn't listen to Mom, I kept my ears open and heard it all.' She smiled, and I glimpsed the rebellious girl she must have been.

A day or so later the family gathered for the Christmas meal. The table groaned with delicious food, and children milled about, wide-eyed and happy and excited about the presents to come. Watching them I began to feel my carefully constructed defenses, which were already very shaky, crumble altogether. It was agony being part of family life yet so abstracted from it, and increasingly I yearned for home, or failing that at least the seclusion of the woods where I could forget that children and families existed. Juliet had sent a box of presents for the family, and the children ripped into the wrapping paper with true Alaskan ferocity. Jack had been given a science kit, and I saw his clever eyes glitter as he read the word 'Explosions' on the box. I grabbed it from him and said jokingly, 'Hold on – it must say somewhere that this is not for Alaskan kids, surely?'

'It does not!' he shouted indignantly, grabbing it back.

I looked at him, wondering what my own boys would be like when they got to Jack's age. The sadness welled up again, but I kept it hidden, not wanting to spoil everyone's day. Next little Asa jumped on to my lap. 'Look guy, look!' he said, tensing his muscles and shivering with effort as he showed off two biceps the size of sugar lumps. I squeezed his arm admiringly, saying 'Wow! That's massive!' before he popped off my lap and sauntered away like a proud little jungle beast, whereupon he was promptly run over by Tirzah on her little red scooter. Screams rang out as she stopped in front of me, fixing me with her wide, wickedly clever eyes. I braced myself, getting ready for the piercing question that I knew from experience would be coming. She had a way of cutting straight to the heart of the matter, and her questions often hit uncomfortably close to the bone.

'Where are your kids?' she asked.

An arrow straight through me. She'd done it again.

'Well, they are at home in Scotland,' I said, 'and I'm going home in the spring.'

She inspected me narrowly. 'That's a long time.'

'Yes it is,' I nodded slowly, feeling miserable.

She stared at me as if about to go on, but then decided to abandon the subject, perhaps realising it was too sensitive even for her. She darted off under her grandpa's legs, which he had made into an arch for her. Around the tree Jack's older sister Bethany sat carefully folding paper, looking over to her two little sisters Pearl and Noo Noo who were rolling about in a ball playing like two little kittens. Beside Charlie sat Bubba, quiet and loyal as usual, and when I looked over he smiled gently and raised his chin. Looking over them all proudly were Claudette and Jenny, Don's two wonderful daughters. In these past weeks I had got closer to them too, and they had become almost like sisters, full of concern, compassion and wise advice. Jenny's husband Chris too had become a good friend, and I knew Juliet would get on well with all of them. I hoped that a bond would be formed between our families, even though our worlds were so very different.

Later I gave the adults some modest gifts that I had bought in the village, including a doll for Carol which she placed carefully inside a glass cabinet where she and Don kept their most precious possessions. That cabinet represented their simple and unmaterialistic approach to life. They didn't have much, but what they did have they cherished in a way that puts our throw-away culture to shame. For Don and his family, less definitely meant more.

When the Christmas meal was all over, I walked alone back to the little cabin in Don's yard. I called home, and spoke first to Oscar, who was full of excitement and happiness. Then I talked to Juliet, who was quietly hopeful, feeling that at least we were on the home run. All too soon it was time to end the call, and I lay back on the bed and closed my eyes. I felt lower than I had ever been in my life. It is hard being a loner, but even worse being a loner in a family setting. I cursed myself, feeling like a hopeless father, husband and man. Worse still it was snowing heavily, which meant that the weather was warm, and the trails would be unreliable. I knew my salvation lay in getting back to camp, but it looked as if that would be impossible for some time.

It snowed more over the next few days, and to take my mind of things one night I decided to go and have a beer. I hopped onto Don's old snow machine and made my way to the log building that houses the saloon. I knew that bars in Bush Alaska were a far cry from British country pubs, but still I was shocked. The atmosphere was appalling, yet I recognised a few people and soon found to my surprise that I was enjoying myself. There were a dozen or so people in the bar, and in the corner a band was playing badly, though it didn't matter as most of the audience were too pissed to notice. After a while I went outside for a breather, and sat in the shadows by the door on a wide plank that ran along the porch. A few other people were sitting smoking, when the saloon door flew open against the wall. A man staggered out backwards, and a voice from inside shouted 'Get the fuck outta here you fucker! Don't you behave like that!'

The man held up his hands and started to plead. 'Oh c'mon, I'm real sorry. Please let me in again!'

He spoke with a deep Southern accent, and I could see that he had a good-looking but rotten face. The pleading continued but to no avail, and the door was slammed shut. I looked the other way, sensing that he was the type who would become your best friend fast, and that he was dangerous. A moment later I heard him say 'Hey you! Want a beer?'

My heart sank. I leaned back against the wall and looked at him.

'No thanks, I'm heading off. Why don't you go in through the back door?'

He looked at me menacingly, and I felt the people beside me edge away. He stepped forwards. 'I said, come and have a fucking drink!'

I said nothing, realising that after the humiliation of being thrown out of the bar he was asserting his manhood. He knew that I had seen him begging to get back into the flea-pit, and that made me an obvious target. I turned my head to look at the couple sitting nervously next to me on the bench, and before I knew it he was behind me, and had me in a tight headlock. He pulled me on to my feet, and I stood there for a moment overwhelmed by disbelief. I've survived six months in the wilderness, I thought, only to get killed by a guy in a bar. I studied the homemade tattoo on his arm in front of me, which said 'Cathy' in blurry blue ink. And then I decided that enough was enough, and I wasn't going to be pushed around by this overgrown schoolyard bully. I pulled my head sharply out of his grip, and grabbed him tightly from behind. Then I wrapped my arms around him, pinning his arms to his sides like a zoo-keeper restraining a run-away primate. He became very still, and I took the opportunity to talk to him. 'Hey, let's forget all this stuff,' I said in what I hoped was a soothing tone. 'I'm a visitor from Scotland, I'm not here for trouble, just relax . . .'

I thought it was working for a moment but then he started to swear and struggle, and I knew he would attack me if I let him go. I considered throwing him down the frozen wooden stairs, but realised it would hurt him badly, which I didn't want, no matter how much he deserved it. We stumbled about a bit and I was beginning to wonder how it would end, when one of the people who had been sitting outside opened the saloon door and pointed inside. I nodded my head in thanks, then frog-marched the poor sod towards the door and threw him, with all my strength, back into the saloon. I caught a glimpse of him as he tripped on a chair and went flying head-over-heels, then lay looking around as if wondering what had happened. The saloon door swung shut and I looked at the person next to me. 'What now?' I asked.

'Run?' he suggested.

'Good idea!' I turned and ran for the snow machine. As I started the engine I saw the saloon door fly open again, and a triangle of yellow light hit the snow.

The primate stood framed in the sickly light, shouting, 'Hey, come back here you Scottish chicken!' I waved cheerfully and drove away.

The next morning I discussed it with Don, who took a keen interest in such matters. 'Did he have a drink in him?' he asked.

'Yes, but he was still sober enough to fight.'

He nodded like a doctor considering a course of medication. 'Yeah, you wanna hit a drunk man square in the stomach – always gets 'em I find.'

I smiled. 'Good advice, thanks.'

'It also means that you don't break your knuckles, and you leave no sign on the man.'

'Yup, sounds sensible.'

'So how did you deal with him?'

'Well . . . He got me in a headlock.'

Don raised an eyebrow. 'And?'

'I pulled out of that, then held his arms tightly so he couldn't use them.'

'That's good. Then did you slam him into the floor from there, or up against the wall or somethin'?'

'Ah, no . . . I did think about throwing him down the stairs.'

'But you didn't, did you?' He looked disappointed.

'No.' I felt apologetic. 'I just threw him back into the saloon.'

He perked up again. 'Okay. So did you run in after him? Maybe pick up a chair or a pool cue or something?'

'No. Actually I ran away.'

'Gee . . .' he sighed, shaking his head. 'Oh never mind.' Clearly the old bar brawling biker in him was not happy. 'Hey, you never opened your present,' he said. 'It's under the tree – better get it before you go.'

There I found a heavy bundle with my name on it. Inside was a huge pair of thickly padded overalls, made of indestructible canvas. 'We hope they fit,' Carol said. 'They'll save your stuff from being shredded by them dogs.'

She was right: the outdoor gear that I had brought from the UK was superb, but was not designed for the daily rough and tumble of living and working in the bush over a long period. 'Hey, what's this?' I pulled some wire snares from the pocket.

'You gotta catch some beavers out there,' Carol smiled. 'They're full of fat and will give lots of meat for you and the dogs.'

The thought of hauling one of those prosperous rodents out of the stagnant lake didn't seem particularly appealing at that moment, when I felt safe and well-fed. Nevertheless, I knew that when I hit lean times back in my cabin those snares would come in handy.

34

OVERFLOW

I stood beside Don, looking out over the frozen river with my hands sunk deep into Shorty's shaggy coat. It was snowing lightly, and I could see from the darkening sky that more snow was on its way.

'How difficult is it going to be making the trail back to camp?' I asked.

'Lot of snow this year.' Don looked downriver. 'Might take a bit of work. We'll come with you as the more men you got breaking a trail the better.' He pointed to the old Tundra: 'You can drive that one. If the weather's not too white we'll head off tomorrow.'

When travelling in snowy country it is always best, if possible, to choose a day that has enough light to give some contrast. Without this it can be very difficult to judge accurately the route ahead, as the sky merges with the snow and ice like driving into a bowl of milk. Often the best visibility comes when the sun is long gone, and the snow machine's headlights shine the way ahead, creating shadows and contrast across the white wilderness.

That night Don showed me how to keep the Tundra in good order, and how to change a drive belt. People get themselves into terrible trouble with snow machines, which cause many deaths in the sub-arctic. Snow machines can travel at speeds well in excess of 120mph, and drivers get caught out by travelling great distances and then breaking down. Thirty minutes on a snow machine can equal more than one day's walking. Many drivers set out woefully unprepared, and younger people and visitors particularly fall into the trap of being overconfident in their machines, going out without snowshoes for example, or not packing gloves, preferring to rely entirely on the machine's heated handle-grips. Needless to say, if the engine breaks down they are in trouble, and I could only imagine the fear of feeling your machine die out beneath you, and slowing to a halt miles from anywhere. The silence and cold would flood in, and you would quickly freeze to death.

Luckily my teacher was old school, the message was simple: always prepare for the worst. I packed enough food, clothing and kit for five days, and also carried my snowshoes everywhere. I was obsessive about carrying every possible means of starting a fire, and always had lighters, matches, flints and birch bark, as well as some squeezy bottles of anti-freeze, which is highly flammable and a superb fire starter in any conditions.

The next morning Charlie and Chris arrived on their powerful machines. We dressed warmly, as the wind chill at the speeds we were travelling would cause the temperature to plunge. Unlike on the dog sled, where I would constantly be making small movements, on the snow machines we sat still. On my feet I wore hiking boots, as I had left my mukluks at the cabin. We set off in a little convoy, with Charlie leading followed by Don, then Chris and me at the back. We swooped down from Don's yard on to the river, following a trail made by people travelling between villages or out to their winter camps. Once on the trail we stopped, and everyone went though last-minute checks of their clothing. Then Charlie looked back, raised his hand and blasted off along the jagged ice, followed shortly by Don and Chris. I gunned my engine and followed, but couldn't see how they were able to go so fast. I wobbled and whacked and bumped along in their wake, falling so far behind that more than once they had to stop and wait for me to catch up. On and on we travelled, the trail leading up and down steep hummocks of ice and windblown snow, rattling my bones on the jagged, rutted surface. As I struggled along I thought back grimly to my first journey downriver by boat, and the hazards lurking beneath the surface. Whether under ice or not, the Yukon never made life easy for the traveller.

When we reached Four Mile Point the trail dipped sharply down, and the river stretched away for miles, a great cruel expanse of white leading off as far as the eye could see. It grew much colder now, as we were in the lowest part of the river basin.* I pulled on my mitts, and we continued to travel mile after bone shuddering mile. Still we had not even come near to the mouth of the slough, and I wondered how on earth I would make the journey by dogsled. Finally we came to a stop and Don pointed across the river towards a snowy opening. 'That's the slough!' he shouted, 'Lot of snow there. Gonna be some overflow.'

I sat still and said nothing. I was worried, as even the established trail had severely tested me, and now we were going to be breaking trail, which would be much harder. Don turned and scanned the bank behind us and I saw him focus on a large fallen tree. I looked at it, making a mental note of its position. A good landmark is vital, as it offers a hope of return if you lose the trail. Don set off first, and immediately sank into deep snow. He stood on one leg and leaned his other knee on the seat, and I saw the old Hell's Angel come to the fore as he powered out of the hole, then stood astride the snow machine and pulled ahead. The rest of us followed one by one, and even though I was at the back and had the benefit of the others' trails, the going was difficult. The snow was deep, and we had to go fast enough to stop the machines from sinking, yet slow enough to maintain control as we negotiated round blue pinnacles of rough ice that rose from the snow like icebergs.† Several times I

---

* The lower the land in Alaska the colder it gets, and the Interior, being low-lying and set between high country, is really just one great cold-sink. Rivers particularly hold on to the cold, as it sinks down from the high ground on either side.
† Rough ice is formed as ice floes pile up against each other during ice-up.

got it wrong, and sank into the snow, whereupon the Tundra's belt clogged and stopped. Then I had to get off the machine and start compacting a snowy platform beside it, so that I could heave the machine on to the platform and gingerly climb back on. The idea then was to accelerate out of the hole and back on to plane across the surface of the snow, but often the Tundra simply dug a deeper hole, into which the machine and I both slid backwards. More than once Chris noticed my predicament, and came back to help me out.

Eventually we reached the mouth of the slough, and stopped on a snowy hummock to look back at the trail behind us. Don rubbed the frost from his moustache – unlike the rest of us he didn't seem to need a face mask, and would simply hold a fur mitt up to his face from time to time when it felt cold. 'That'll do,' he said. 'When we come back we'll widen the trail some more, then it'll freeze up overnight.' From here we knew there were eight miles to travel before we reached my portage, and Don threw me a look, as if to say, 'See how much trouble you're causing?' 'Okay,' he said decisively, 'let's go', and the four of us shot off across the deep snow that had blown thickly down into the slough basin.

When breaking trail on a river, you employ a set of criteria that are exactly opposite to those used on a journey by boat. Whereas by boat you would steer purposely towards cut banks, knowing there will be deep water below, in snow you veer well away from them, aiming instead to make trail across sandbanks or areas where there is likely to be little or no water. Falling through ice is the Arctic's greatest hazard, and whenever we were forced to cross an area of deep water we would do so as quickly as possible. The ice at the edge of the river is also likely to be thin, so you stay away from the bank, though it can be quite difficult to make out where the bank ends and the river begins beneath the deep snow. There is also a phenomenon known as 'drum' or 'hollow' ice, which has been responsible for many deaths. These pockets are formed as a direct result of the amazing drop in water levels that occur as winter sets in. Early on during ice-up, when the river is still relatively high, the surface freezes, forming a layer of ice. As winter progresses the water level drops as ice thickens upriver, and soon that first ice surface is left high and dry. Unsupported by water, it becomes brittle and breaks easily, and the unsuspecting musher or snow machinist plunges through to find himself trapped many feet below, either on frozen gravel or another layer of ice. Not a good place to be with a broken leg. Old timers named it 'drum ice' because of the drumming sound it made as their sled's birch runners rattled across its thin, vibrating skin. This would be a terrifying moment, alerting the musher to the danger but too late, like a drum roll before the fall of the guillotine. Some mushers have been saved by their dog team, which remained on the surface, and managed to pull both man and sled free of the hole. A snow machine will drop through drum ice like a stone, unless it can get across fast enough. Some men have been able to climb out of the icy pockets by cutting steps in the ice, but others have been less lucky and died entombed in ice.

On we travelled, me still trailing behind but gradually mastering the snow machine over the difficult terrain. About three miles into the slough, I was looking down, concentrating fiercely, when I heard a shout. I looked up to see that the three men had stopped about two hundred yards ahead, and were standing on their machines and signalling for me to stop. I slewed to a halt and watched them for a moment, wondering what was up. Then my eyes fell on the trail they had left behind them, and I saw a terrible sight. The trail was steaming, and a long slender cloud followed its course for about fifty metres ahead. I strained my eyes to look closer, and saw that where there should have been white, compacted snow, instead the trail was covered by a long streak of putrid water. There is something appalling about the sight of water when all around the terrain is frozen, and it steamed gently like an outside Jacuzzi, emitting a sinister, stagnant smell. That's river water, I thought, and realised I was about to have my first encounter with overflow.

Overflow is a dangerous winter phenomenon, and this year it was particularly bad due to the heavier than usual snowfall. It occurs when the weight of the snow forces down the river ice, and water comes up over the edges and lies on top. There it remains liquid, insulated by the heavy snow that caused it, lying deep and invisible to the traveller. Those who do not go through fast enough may find their machines stuck to the river ice as the exposed water freezes around them. Rescue is very tricky, and can only be done by cutting poles and winching the machine out, and the driver will invariably get wet. As always, wherever there is water there's a greatly increased danger of frostbite, and the driver will get rapidly colder as he works. Then he must restart the engine.

I looked across at the men and saw them beckoning energetically – their message was clear: 'Charge!' Taking a deep breath, I gunned the throttle and charged along the trail. The machine hit the stinking, stagnant water, and immediately floundered, sinking backwards. I felt the steerage fail as the skis slewed about in the water. 'Come on!' I shouted, and threw my weight forwards to lift the belt from fast freezing water. The Tundra struggled for a moment, then shot forwards and planed across the rest of the water to safety.

'Tip it over and knock the ice away from the engine,' Don said, when I rejoined the men. I did as he instructed, using my axe handle to knock the heavy chunks of ice out of the belt housing, and then without saying anything got back on the machine. We travelled up on to higher ground above the river, where the snow was deep on the hillside. Here we had to balance on the upward edge of the machines, leaning in to avoid rolling down a slope that culminated in thin ice and deep water. After a while we came to a point where we had to cross the river to the long sandbar at the foot of Pilot Mountain. We stood on a high section of trail and looked down in the half-light to the wide slough below, where the water beneath the ice ran fast and deep.

'I'll go first,' Charlie said. It made sense, because he had the most powerful machine.

'And Guy goes last,' Don said, nodding at me.

Charlie charged down the slope and out across the river, and before he was even half way across we saw his machine sink back and send up a cockerel's tail of hideous brown water. He powered hard and made it to the other side, then waved us on. Don came next, followed by Chris, and then it was my turn. The overflow was so deep that for a moment I seemed to be losing the battle, until I managed to swerve in such a way that the snow machine got up and going again.

At length we reached the little river beach at the end of my portage, and I was thankful that I had cut a siding through the embankment for my winter trail. We charged up it and then on up the portage, where the snow lay in deep drifts. I felt relieved to be back in the woods, and to have the four heavy snow machines compressing my trail. When we reached the cabin, we found it was almost buried in snow, and everything inside was frozen solid. It would take a long time for the place to warm up again. We took a break for a few minutes, then got back on our snow machines and set off back to the village.

It was dark now, and the lights of the snow machines lit up the portage as we made our way back down to the slough. Being last wasn't such a good position on the return journey, as by the time I reached patches of overflow the others had already broken the newly formed ice, meaning that I had to cross water again. I stopped before the longest stretch, watching as the others crossed and then turned to wait for me. It took a new kind of courage to hurtle myself into that sour fog, which looked even worse in the headlights, and I had to overrule all my instincts to go slowly. I knew there was no other option however, so I swallowed my fear and charged. The crossing was the worst yet, and twice the machine almost tipped over sideways. It was also harder to balance in the dark, as there was nothing ahead to fix on, and at one point I stuck out my right leg and to my horror felt water enter my boot. By some miracle I managed to reach the other side, and as I did so I could feel the icy water seeping down through my sock. I felt foolish and didn't mention it to the others to begin with. But there were still many miles to travel, and as we journeyed on I felt my foot growing colder and colder until I couldn't feel it at all.

The next time we stopped I told Don about my foot, and he immediately told me to get the boot off, and to start rubbing my foot while they dried my sock on the carburettor of the snow machine. Ice dropped out of my boot when I took it off, and frost-nip had attacked one toe. I rubbed my foot while the men stood around me, and wondered whether I would lose my toe. A rust-coloured moon had risen above the vegetation, eerily illuminating the steam that rose all around us. My foot wasn't responding, and suddenly losing a toe seemed a good outcome, compared to the prospect of losing the whole foot. Charlie took off his gloves and knelt down, massaging and rubbing my clammy foot between his warm hands. Taking off your gloves in these temperatures is not recommended, and I was moved by what he had done. 'Thanks Charlie,' I said from my prone position, 'although my book says you should hold the foot against your bare stomach.'

'Hey, fuck you!' he said, flashing me a grin.

'The Athabascan Charles Bronson is back,' I said, and we all laughed.

Once we reached the Yukon we were able to move much faster, and the trail that had seemed so difficult when we first set out now felt easy. Throughout the rest of the journey I tried to keep my foot moving, stopping and running up and down the trail occasionally to get the circulation going. Like boats approaching a tiny harbour, we at last saw the distant lights of Galena, and half an hour later I was warming my frost-nipped toes by Don's fire. This had been my closest brush with disaster yet, and I knew I had been lucky.

35
ATHABASCAN TEMPTATION

It was now a couple of weeks since Christmas, and each day that I passed in the village seemed to stack up on my shoulders, weighing me down with worry. I was being seduced by the lure of human company, and knew that if I was going to be able to cope on my own again I had to get back to my cabin fast. I hadn't come out to Alaska to hang around the village, and the longer I stayed there the guiltier I felt, as it defeated the point of the separation from my family. However there was no way that I could take my dog team out to the cabin with the overflow situation, which was getting worse as the warm weather continued. Reports from travellers coming up the Yukon trail were grim, and if that well-worn trail was bad I knew that the slough would be much worse.

I blurted out all my worries to Jenny one morning, and she patiently listened, then thought for a moment. 'Well, maybe Brad could help out,' she said. 'He's a good flyer and he goes all over in that little plane of his.' Bradley Scotton was a colleague of Jenny's at the Alaska Fish and Wildlife Service.

A spark of hope flickered. 'What kind of plane does he have?' I asked.

'He flies a Cub – made in 1940 I think.'

'Right, um . . . Maybe not then.'

'Scared of flying are we?' Fear of flying is regarded as extraordinary in the Interior of Alaska where people jump in and out of bush planes as casually as taxis.

'No. Did I say I was?'

She laughed. Jenny is a skilled biologist, and her keen observation of my behaviour made me feel at times like one of the native animals on which she is such an expert. 'Brad's upstairs,' she said, 'go on up and ask him.'

I ran up the wooden stairs to Bradley's office two at a time and knocked on his door.

'C'mon in!' a voice answered.

I found Bradley Scotton sitting at his desk, regarding me with a dry, quizzical expression that I soon discovered summed up his whole take on life. In his mid-thirties, he was light and agile, with sparkling blue eyes and a bushy beard that gave him a rebellious look. He looked every bit the bush flyer.

'Hello – are you Bradley?' I took my hat off and smiled. 'My name's Guy.'

'Ah, yes, the cheechako from Scotland.' He nodded and leaned back in his chair, looking me up and down with intelligent, humorous eyes. Clearly my reputation had gone before me, and I predicted that another person was going to be added to the evergrowing ranks of people who were getting a laugh at my expense. 'I heard you were in the village. Enjoying them dogs?'

'Oh yeah. The dogs are doing fine, and no disasters so far, bar a smashed knee.'

'Yeah, I heard about that.'

'Well, let me see, how can I say this?' There was a pause, and I walked over to the window and looked out at the snow.

'Let me say it for you – you need a flight back to your camp, right?'

I nodded, wondering how he knew. 'It's the overflow – I can't take the dogs out till it hardens up, but I was thinking that if it was possible to get to the slough opposite my portage I would be able to walk across it and on up to camp. Does it sound possible?'

'Well, we could give it a try, but overflow's no fun in a plane either. Possibly we could land on the sand-banked bits of the slough, then you could walk across from there.'

'How much will it cost?'

'Nothin' at all. I'll give you a call when this snow stops and we'll see what can be done.'

'Thank you so much Brad – I'm really grateful.' I gazed at him as if he was some kind of guardian angel.

I returned to the snow machine feeling suddenly full of hope. I just wished I did not have to go by air.

Overnight the weather cleared, and over coffee Don told me that Brad was planning to fly me out later that morning. I stared into my mug in silence. 'I hate flying in small planes,' I confessed. 'It's not fear of dying, just of vomiting all over the place.'

'D'you hear that Mom!' Don laughed and looked over at Carol, 'The kid's gonna mess up Brad's plane!' He chuckled and shook his head, then a thought occurred to him. 'So what about the pant-sniffers?'

'I'll come back for them once the overflow settles.'

He looked out over the river, then at the clock beside the stove. 'You better get goin'. And be careful.'

I called to Fuzzy who was urinating copiously as if to pass the time.

I said my goodbyes, then ran back to the shack and loaded up my bag with provisions. At the last minute I remembered that I desperately needed .22 ammunition and some sugar. I ran back up to Don's house. 'Hey Don, is the Mayor's store open?' I asked breathlessly.

'Yeah, should be, if he's not sleepin' in.'

The Mayor's store was one of the most costly shops I had ever been to, as everything in the place had to be brought in by air, but I always enjoyed my visits. The Mayor was always smiling, genuinely and simply happy with his life, and we always had a good chat. On this occasion I was in a rush, and was making my way towards the checkout, clutching a bag of sugar and a box of bullets, when a good-looking native Alaskan woman stepped out in front of me. She looked me up and down with open and unashamed interest and asked, 'Hey – who are you?'

I felt vulnerable immediately, and suddenly worried that my many months of abstinence were going to lead me into trouble, despite the fact that when I left home I had resigned myself to living like a monk for a long time.

She scrutinised me with dark eyes. 'You speak English?'

'Yes I do – I mean, hullo. My name's Guy – I'm from Scotland.'

'Scotland, huh?' She leaned against a flimsy shelf. 'What you doing here?'

'I'm living in the bush.'

She raised both eyebrows. 'You got a camp here?'

'Yes.'

'How long you stayin'?' She tilted her head winningly.

'Well . . .' I fiddled with my provisions. 'Quite a few months left to go.'

'Months!' She gave me one of those flirtatious, knowing looks that women deliver so well. 'So where's your camp then?' She waited with a teasing smile playing across her face.

This was the moment of truth for me – my true test. It was time to shine with virtue, and to overcome my natural instincts, which understandably were by now somewhat pent up. Abstinence had been easy when I was out in the bush, but now here I was faced with an attractive woman who was making her intentions clear. I raised my left hand and brought it to my chin, thinking that my wedding ring would give her the message, but her gaze didn't waver. 'You know . . .' I tapped my finger against my nose: 'I can't tell you where my camp is.' I felt a bit rude, but like a shining paragon of virtue at the same time.

She gave me another alluring look, as if giving me a second chance, then said, 'Hey, no problem,' and continued her shopping as if we had just been discussing the price of eggs.

I was not feeling so cool, however, and I walked to the checkout feeling like a basket case. I had passed the test with honour, but as I walked over to Brad's house my heart yearned sadly for my wife. I had been tested on all fronts now: physical, by the man in the bar, emotional, by Don's family and the children, and now Biblical. It was all getting to be too much. Chris drove by on his snow machine and slurred to a stop, interrupting my tortured thoughts.

'Hey, Guy,' he said. 'You gonna fly out?'

'Yeah.' I walked on distractedly.

'Something on your mind?' he called after me.

I stopped and turned. 'Well, I've just turned down a proposition from a good-looking Indian girl. I've got to get out of this place or I'll either get shot in the saloon or land up with a small family – which Juliet would not be happy with.'

Chris laughed. 'So who was she?'

I described the girl.

'Oh yeah, I know her – she's a nice woman,' he said.

'I didn't tell her where my camp was.'

'Just as well – she would have wrapped up and gunned down there on her snow machine at 120 miles an hour.'

'Would she really travel that far through this kind of country?'

He gave me an incredulous look. 'Hey – she's one of us. You know we go all over the place.' He was right. I remembered Don laughing as we heard a news report about some hardened adventurer preparing to be the first man to walk across the Bering Sea. 'Them Eskimos been crossing the Bering to see family for years,' he said. 'Heck, not even the Cold War stopped 'em. First time for a white man, maybe.'

'Funny thing is,' I said to Chris, 'I showed her my wedding ring, so she knew I was off limits, but it didn't seem to put her off at all.'

'Off limits?' Chris laughed. 'Guy, you see that ring?' He mimed a crazed animal savagely devouring a morsel. 'That's what that girl would do with your ring!'

We said goodbye and I walked on to Brad's place, knowing that I couldn't hang around a moment longer. People were dangerous for this vulnerable tenderfoot, and plane or no plane, it was time to get back to the woods.

36

BRADLEY SCOTTON AND HIS MAGNIFICENT FLYING MACHINE

I found Brad behind his snug house, standing at the top of a flight of stairs that led down to a frozen lake on which I could see his plane, ready for the flight. I thought of my last flight in Brownie's plane, and remembered vomiting copiously as a child on endless flights to and from South Africa. Brad saw my expression and looked concerned. 'Not the sick type are you?' he asked, 'Cause there ain't much room in there.'

'No! Not at all,' I said briskly, 'Ready to go. Anything I can do?'

He gave me a quizzical look, then his eye wandered up to my hat. 'Yeah – you can get rid of that crappy rabbit fur hat. It's useless.'

'Oh,' I grinned ruefully. 'I've been wanting to get a new one, but I don't know where.'

'My wife Sandy will make you up a beaver hat no problem. I got lots of beaver last year and the fur is good and warm.'

'Really? Are you sure? Do you trap quite a bit?'

'A bit – I use the plane for that.'

'The plane?' A nasty thought occurred to me. 'So . . . you use the plane to move carcasses about?'

'Yup.' He looked at the sky distractedly for a moment. 'Now let's go.'

My legs felt weak as we walked towards the plane. I felt like a man being led to a torture cell – and worse still I now knew it was going to smell of dead animals.

The plane was a 1940 J-3 Cub, a superb machine, made of birch and canvas with a 125 hp engine, and perfect for the bush because it only weighs around a thousand pounds.

'You go there.' Brad pushed the front seat forward and I stuffed myself into the tiny space in the back of the plane. It felt like crawling back into the womb, and I wished I had two sturdy midwives to assist. Somehow I managed to get in and turn around, and found that my shoulders filled the width of the plane entirely and my knees were around my chin. The plane did have an animally smell, and felt distinctly claustrophobic. Behind me in a fetid cubby I had stuffed my bag, rifle and Fuzzy, who seemed far too casual about the whole thing. He'd wrapped himself into a ball and appeared to be asleep, although I suspected he was playing mind games with me, and was secretly wide awake and shit scared. I looked around desperately, wondering where I could vomit if the worst happened, and came to the conclusion that the only place would be the back of Brad's neck.

Brad walked over to the propeller and began to crank the plane's engine in the time-honoured manner that I had seen in countless vintage films. After two impotent spins the engine turned over and spat deafeningly into life, sending out a white puff of exhaust as it did so. He passed me a headset and pulled his flimsy door shut, and before I knew it we were charging for the trees, then up into the great blue sky.

As we banked over the village I caught a glimpse of the saloon, and thought of that travesty of a man whose stunted ideas of masculinity had turned him into an aggressive baboon. Our shadow stretched and distorted over rows of shacks, then an old fishing wheel* and finally the wide river. Thoughts of nausea disappeared at the sight of the great, clean expanse of the wilderness, and my heart filled with joy. I was so happy to be going home again, where I could live simply as I had intended, free of all the conflicting emotions that had plagued me of late. Bradley flew low over twisting rivers and creeks, swooping and circling past huge moose lumbering through the snow. We spotted a wolf kill beside Pilot Mountain, and I felt privileged that I had often heard those wolves howling, and that I lived as a guest in their territory. All along the slough I could see sickly yellow patches of overflow. They looked putrid and malevolent and I felt glad of the lift. Yet I was also relieved to see the thin, barely detectable line of my trail, which still clearly existed despite the heavy snow, and would be even better once I had the chance to snowshoe along it.

When we reached a straight part of the slough Brad began to circle sickeningly, and my vomiting worries returned. 'Okay, let's see what the landing is like,' he shouted, and I tried to focus on the horizon as he circled out wide, then swooped down and ran the skis along the surface. We lifted back into the air in a long, banking curve and then came back round again so that Bradley could examine his ski lines in the snow. 'Yeah, we'll put down there,' he said. 'It's over a sandbar – no overflow.' We made another hideous turn, during which I stared at the flimsy roof and prayed that my stomach would hold out, and then dropped down to land. I clenched my fists in anticipation, but it was so gentle and smooth that I barely realised when we touched the ground. We slewed to a gentle halt, and Bradley turned off the engine. A wonderful silence descended, and I sat back feeling deeply relieved as Bradley nipped out and shimmied along one of the skis. He draped a heat-retaining quilt over the engine, and then jumped into the snow and sank to his chest. 'Now this is where I could have done with being just a bit taller!' he shouted.

I jumped out after him, also sinking immediately, and we both

---

* A fishing wheel is an ingenious structure invented by Athabascans – powered by the river it scoops up fish and looks like a mill wheel.

laughed. Fuzzy came next, landing with a 'wumpf' and disappearing entirely. He barked in muffled alarm from the bottom of the hole, but soon managed to snow-swim up to the surface where he shook himself, looking happy to be back. I put on my snowshoes, heaved my kit on to my shoulders and said goodbye to Brad. He taxied for take off, sending a glittering cloud of snow into the air, and Fuzzy and I watched as he turned the little plane into the wind, then revved the engine and tore into the cold sky. He banked round and passed low over me, and I waved with both hands raised above my head like a Zoroastrian greeting the sun. He waggled his wings in return and the sight made me smile as I thought of all the planes I had waved to as a child, and now finally one had waved back. I watched until the plane became a speck, and then disappeared. Silence descended, and I stood soaking it all in. I heard wings beating, and looked towards the riverbank where a big black raven was flying towards the willow-clad sandbar. The sleek black bird gurgled a complex song, dropping its head to examine us with a cold eye as he flew past.

I turned to walk across the slough, noticing as I did so that the snow was shallow, due to wind barreling along its course, piling snow up along the sandbanks. I knew I was about to cross overflow and didn't want to get my snowshoes wet, as they would quickly freeze and clog with ice, making them unbearably heavy and virtually impossible to get off. I took them off, feeling grateful for my US Army 'vapour' boots, which I knew would remain watertight,* and for my clever overalls, which locked over the high boots, ensuring that no water would seep through. I stepped on to the river ice, and immediately cracked through a thin layer on the surface, sinking down through about a foot of water before reaching the solid river ice below. I looked down in dread as the water steamed around my foot in the cold air. It felt scary to crack

---

* After my near frostbite experience when my foot got wet in the overflow, Jenny bought me some US Army 'vapour' or 'bunny' boots, which are made of two layers of rubber. You inflate them before heading out, thus creating a layer of insulating air in between. The colder it gets, the more one inflates, and the result is comical but very effective.

through ice on a fast-flowing river, and I had to keep telling myself that there was no danger of falling through, as the ice below was at least three feet thick. Nevertheless I moved slowly, prodding with my axe as I crossed. At last I reached the other side, and dried Fuzzy's legs with my handkerchief before strapping on my snow-shoes and making my way along the trail. It was getting dark, and yet I felt unafraid, deeply relieved to be home. As I walked I listened to the contented sound of Fuzzy's footsteps behind me, and then began to sing. The trail ahead was full of animal signs due to the recent warm weather, which had been as warm as minus twenty. Yet the clear sky was telling me that cold was coming, and all animals reduce their movements to a minimum when the temperature drops to around minus thirty or below. Native people also reduced their activity to a minimum in these very cold temperatures, and waited, like the animals, for the warm spells. Any man who ventured out in these temperatures would get little sympathy if he lost digits or died. He was making the mistake of being arrogant, and forgetting that he was an animal too.

Back at camp, I poured some food on to the snow for Fuzzy, and then walked over to the cabin, imagining a giant mug of tea. The image fizzled away when I discovered that the door was frozen shut so tightly that I had to kick it open. The beam of my torch shone into the dark room and my heart sank. I had been away for nearly a month, but it might as well have been a thousand years. Inside the cabin everything was white, and looked like the inside of a freezer, with a layer of frost covering everything in cruel, icy sparkles. Already I felt tired at the prospect of bringing warmth into a place that looked like an abandoned cabin from the gold-rush era. I dusted the frost off a bucket of kindling and bunches of birch bark I had left inside the door, and lit the stove, closing the door tightly behind me and hanging up the still-frozen blanket. Then I filled and lit the pressure lamp. The warm yellow light and comforting hiss of that tough old lamp did much for my morale, even though it was clear that it was going to take a long time to thaw the cabin out. The temperature inside stood at minus twenty-eight degrees centigrade, and as I stared at the thermometer I let out an ironic laugh, thinking that our freezer at home was warm by comparison.

I made some tea, then climbed into bed. The logs in the cabin were starting to thaw and their sides were glistening wet, so I pulled my bed into a dryer spot, only to find a steady drip falling from the melting frost on the tin above. The drops splattered on to the canvas cover of my bed roll, and I considered moving again, but decided it was pointless. Effectively I was defrosting a freezer whilst living in it, and the dripping would only increase as the logs warmed up. Nevertheless, I was glad to be back.

37

BRINGING THEM PANT-SNIFFERS HOME

The weather grew colder over the next week or so, and it stopped snowing, which meant that the overflow would be less of a problem. I was keen to get my dog team out while I had the opportunity, and managed to hitch another ride with Brad back to the village. When I got there Don told me that a young Indian man had been killed on the night we went along the Yukon trail – he had fallen from his snow machine, and frozen to death where he fell. I looked down at the white river, marvelling again at its cruelty. 'I wonder how many people that river has killed?'

'Some it kills – but more kill themselves by forgetting to respect it,' Don answered gruffly. 'Now, how you gonna get all them dogs down there? You know I hate messing with dogs, so I hope you're not expecting me to help.'

'No, not at all – I'm going to figure something out.'

'Aha! Like what?'

'Well Glenn says I can borrow the dog box,' I answered. 'Then all I need to do is tie it on to a big wood sled and tow them down in that.'

'Okay, so whose wood sled you gonna use?' he asked with a look of resigned amusement in his eyes.

'Ah, now that is where you might come in . . . Perhaps you could lend me yours?'

'Thought so,' he nodded sarcastically. 'We go tomorrow.'

'We?'

'Yeah, we.' He held up a finger in mock seriousness. 'Think I'm gonna let you trash my wood-sled? But mark my words, this is the only time I'm gonna help with them pant-sniffers. Goddit?'

'Of course Don, but really . . .'

But he had walked away. As he went he said over his shoulder, 'Go away now – I gotta do some work for MY family.'

I watched him walk off, reflecting that this man was the kind that just couldn't let a friend down.

The next day Don and I drove over to Glenn's yard to collect the dogs. While Don secured the dog carrier to his sled, Glenn and I tied the six dogs inside. Then we fixed on the lid, and on top of this lashed the dogs' boxes with their tether chains, bowls, dog feed and rice, as well as booties for their feet and extra lengths of rope for sled line repairs. I also tied on a shovel and rake for cleaning the dog yard, as well as buckets, ladles and a fifty-five gallon drum that I would use to make the dog-pot. Once it was all tied up Glenn placed the birch sled on top of the pile and bungee corded it on, then he turned and looked at me seriously. 'You're on your own now. You be careful, go slow and keep yourself and these dogs in good shape, you hear?'

'I'll try Glenn, and thanks so much for everything. I know I've been a bit of a pain at times, but I am sure you'll laugh about it one day.'

A smile spread beneath his moustache. 'Hey, I'm laughing now!' He raised a hand to both of us, and we watched as he drove off on his snow machine.

'I just can't believe you got me doing this,' Don said, turning to look at the great pile of mushing gear teetering on his wood sled. The dogs were barking and howling, and he shook his head. 'I sure hope no-one sees me today – I'd be mortified if it got out that I'd become a musher.'

We checked everything was secure and set off, Don first, trailing the wood sled behind his snow machine, while I followed behind on the Tundra with Fuzzy nestled between my arms. The weight of the sled compressed the trail further, and it felt good to be flattening newly fallen snow over the sharp, slippery areas of frozen overflow. When the trail passed along a steep contour Don showed his expertise by jumping nimbly to the side of his machine, leaning into the incline and skilfully steering the heavy sled away from danger. I noticed that he drove up on to the sides of the trail rather than staying in the middle. This collapsed the edges, packing down the snow on either side of the trail. When we stopped in the sheltered lee of a riverbank he said, 'Now the kids don't bother much to keep working on one trail – they just charge off all over the place. You gotta keep working at your trails 'cause you live out here, and later on you'll need 'em to hold up when everything is thawing out.'

His advice was wise. In the spring, snow thaws from the bottom up, and the more compressed your trail is the longer it will stay hard.

Several hours later we had made it to the slough and stopped opposite my portage. Don wiped the frost from his moustache. 'You hook 'em up,' he said, 'and I'll cache your stuff here.' Full of nerves I unhitched the dog sled and anchored it in the snow, remembering to take the extra precaution of tying the rope to Don's machine in case the anchor didn't hold. I then rolled out the gangline, straightening each individual tug line and harness ready for its dog. I followed the exact routine that Glenn had taught me, conscious of Don watching me closely. 'Okay,' he said, 'You ready for them dogs?'

I was about to say yes when I suddenly remembered Fuzzy. He had been padding about behind me like a little golden shadow, and had no idea about the arrival of the six new dogs. 'Oh shit!' I said. 'What about Fuzzy?'

'I don't know,' Don shrugged his shoulders. 'I was kinda thinking the same.'

It is a well-known fact that sled dogs and pet dogs do not mix. When I mushed into the village people would grab their dogs before I passed. Sled teams sometimes snatch pets as they run, chewing them up and spitting them out like a giant shredder. I was worried about Fuzzy, yet I also knew that he was a careful dog, and obedient. I would have to impose a new and immediate rule, that whenever the sled was out Fuzzy would remain behind it. If he stayed beside the sled's runners and never came alongside the dogs he would be out of danger.

I discussed the idea with Don. 'Yeah, might work,' he said, 'and heck, them sled dogs might also treat Fuzzy different.'

'What do you mean?'

'Well if they're chained up all day and he gets to walk around with you, in dog language that means he's . . .' He paused, and I saw that familiar teasing glint. 'Means he's the *boss's dog*.' He put particular emphasis on the words, and I knew he was getting at something, but it took a moment before it dawned on me.

'Okay, I get it – you mean the alpha female.'

He raised his hands. 'You said it,' and a wicked grin spread over his face.

I led Fuzzy over to the runners and told him sit and stay. He sat obediently, looking up at me with eyes full of love and happiness, and I knew he was glad to have left the village. I opened the box, and it erupted like a present from the beast of Bodmin Moor. The dogs were in a frenzy of excitement, and the box rocked about as they scrabbled and clawed at the sides, barking and yowling. In the midst of the seething canine bucket one dog stood quite still, gazing up at me with determined incisive eyes. It was Bubbles, my lead dog, and as usual she was showing her leadership abilities. I reached in and unclipped her, and then leaned in to lift her clear. She licked the side of my face once, then hopped on to the snow and stood looking around her as I put her booties on and harnessed her up. She appeared uncertain for a moment, until I said 'Line out!' and pulled her forward by the harness. Immediately she strained against the gangline, raising it up clear of the snow and holding it tight. Fuzzy, standing beside us, was in clear contravention of the rules. 'No!' I said firmly, reaching down and grabbing him by the scruff of his neck, and then dragging him back to the runners. 'Stay!' I said, and he sat down reluctantly, glaring at me indignantly as if to say 'Why? And more to the point, who the hell is she?'

Soon I had the whole team in place, and the river basin resounded with barks and howls. Fuzzy was now staying by the runners as instructed, perhaps realising the danger. I knew that this first run up the portage would be dangerous: Bubbles did not know the trail, which was sinuous in the extreme. I thought of all of the trees and sharply cut back brush, and watched the dogs, leaping and howling and packed full of energy. I had set the team up so that they faced towards the steep cutting that marked the start of the trail, and wished now that we had not driven up to the cabin on the snow machines. The deep snow would have slowed the dogs down on their first run, whereas now they would have firm footing, and would go flat out. Don was unloading more stuff from the sled. 'Going to be very fast,' I said, and he nodded slowly.

'Them dogs is fit and they're raring to go. Over time you'll get them used to a steady working pace, but problem is they're racing dogs.' He took his glove off and shook my hand. 'Good luck.'

He let go of the rope, and the sled trembled with the dogs' collective power, then I pulled the anchor and we were off. Like an unwilling parent on a roller coaster I clung on as we rocketed towards the cutting, but instead of slowing down they surged up it effortlessly, such was the superb traction of four-leg drive. The sled flew on to the narrow trail, and the cottonwoods passed in a blur as we shaved the high sides of the trail. 'Easy!' I shouted, and pushed my foot hard on the brake. To my relief Bubbles fell back into a trot, then gradually the whole thing cranked up again and we galloped on. It felt like taking a Ferrari along a mule track, and the sled bumped and jerked as the dogs swerved along the trail. We shot up a little incline, then dropped down and turned so fast that I slipped off the runners and fell. The dogs kept running and I dragged behind the sled, holding on for dear life: to lose the dogs on their very first outing was too terrible to contemplate. I tried to pull myself back on to the runners, but couldn't quite make it, and ran comically behind until the conveyer belt of snow whipped my feet away again. Finally the sled ran off the trail and lodged in some thick snow-covered bushes. The dogs stopped, and I threw in the anchor and lay panting face down in the snow. Fuzzy jumped on to my back and barked as if to say 'Come on!' and after a moment I got up and straightened the sled. I stood back on the runners, lifted the snow anchor and said 'Okay' weakly, and off we charged again.

Taking a tight corner on a sled in a woodland portage is one of the biggest challenges for any musher, and he has to be anti-instinctive. The length of the team means that when going fast the dogs will have rounded a corner before the sled has reached it, and the musher's instinct will be to brake sharply. If he does so, the gangline suddenly goes tight between the slowing sled and the lead dog, and both sled and musher can be pulled off the trail. They will then be towed through the brush at speed, perhaps wounding or killing dogs along the way and blinding or impaling the musher on sharp tree branches. The musher must therefore overrule rational instinct, and instead of braking on the turn lean back, set his runners firmly at the outside of the bend and hold on, thus allowing the power of the team to rip him around the turn.

I had to face this test time after time as we charged up the portage, but somehow we made it, and when we arrived at camp the relief was so immense that for a moment I was unable to move. My damaged knee ached, yet there was no time for rest as I had to improvise a dog yard that would last until I was able to fetch the rest of the gear next day. The dogs would spend their first night outdoors, but in the beam of my head torch I could see snow falling, so it would be relatively warm. I strapped on my snow-shoes, and cut away the brush surrounding six slender alder trees in a thicket immediately behind the cabin. I then snowshoed around each tree until I'd made a good solid surface, before cutting some spruce boughs for the dogs to lie on. I unharnessed the dogs one by one, and tethered them to the trees. They immediately began pacing in circles, stopping to mark their trees or sniff about. It was a relief to have the dogs tethered safely near the cabin. I poured them each some dog food, which they devoured in seconds and watched them settle down on their spruce beds, curling up into little balls. I felt cold just looking at them, and resolved to get their boxes set up the next day, then groaned at the thought of manhandling the six dog boxes, dog-pot and other bits of gear up to camp. But then I remembered I had dog power – my days as a human mule were over. I had six dogs, each with a pulling power of around two hundred pounds. The idea was exciting, and with it came the realisation that I had moved on just a step. At last, my newly won knowledge was beginning to bear fruit.

I returned to life in the ice-box feeling less despondent, as I knew it would soon thaw out. As I huddled inside my bed-roll, images of my black and white, blurring portage flashed before me: tight, terrifying turns and the arching and stretching backs of six charging dogs. I felt the power again through my hands, holding tight to the birch handle of the sled, and heard the creaking of the rawhide lashings, and the swish and cut of runners through snow. I remembered the speed over parts of the portage where once I had toiled in an endless green purgatory surrounded by a cloud of flies; or walked slowly, parched and tired, back to the lonely, billowing tent.

38

WOLF MANTRA AND LEGEND

By nightfall the next day my cabin had thawed out, and felt like home again. The dogs' homes were in good shape too, and each now had its own snug box. To make them extra warm I piled an insulating layer of snow around and on top of each one, and just behind the cabin I placed the dog-pot, which was simply a fifty-five gallon barrel that had been cut in half. The bottom half held the fire, with an opening cut in the front to allow a good supply of oxygen, and the top half – the pot – sat on top. Keeping this going meant a dramatic increase in my wood consumption, so I spent days cutting eight-foot lengths of wood, and then using the dogs to drag them back to camp. There I would spend endless hours cutting, splitting and stacking the logs ready for use. Once I had worked out a routine the process became almost joyful, and the pulling power of the dogs made a huge difference to what had formerly been heavy and demanding work.

My day would start with hooking up the dogs and letting them charge out on to the lake, where I would run them for ten minutes at full speed to allow them to burn off their pent-up energy. When they had calmed down a bit, and were ready to move in a steady trot, I would take them down to a suitable point on the lake and anchor them very securely using two anchors, one secured to the link between the two front dogs, and the other behind the whole team, stamped in beside the sled. Two anchors were essential; on one occasion Bubbles had wheeled the whole team round to run back past the sled, which had only been anchored to stop it moving forwards. As they shot past the sled the anchor popped neatly out of the snow, the sled swung round and they were off. I ran after them, heart in mouth, knowing that I'd never catch them, and picturing them running and running into eternity, until they got tangled up in the undergrowth and died a horrible death. Fortunately however they got tangled in the gangline and gradually came to a stop. I spent the next half hour threading legs back through knotty snares and unwrapping hard little bodies from tight coils of rope.*

When the sled was firmly anchored I would strap on my snowshoes and haul myself up into the woods beside the lake where there were many good-sized standing dead spruce. I would approach a suitable tree and then figure out the line along which it would fall. The snow on that ridge was deep – up to eight feet or more – and with this in mind I cut brush for it to fall on to. I would fell the tree, then cut it into eight-foot lengths, making sure as I worked that I wasn't building up a sweat. Even when working in temperatures as low as minus fifty, I wore very little, and my spare clothes would hang over a nearby bough, waiting to warm me when the job was done. I would then shoulder the logs and snowshoe back to the sled, hitching on the logs one by one and trailing them back to camp. The dogs were learning to work slowly and steadily, and seemed to enjoy their new role as carthorses, throwing themselves into their harnesses with gusto. At the end of the cutting and dragging, with the dogs back in the yard, I would

---

* Getting caught up in the harness is one of the hazards of being a sled dog, and they are conditioned to stay very calm when this happens, waiting patiently to be disentangled, even when trussed up closely to another dog.

then set about splitting logs, working methodically to ensure I didn't injure myself. I learned to work at a considered, steady rhythm, finding that the work was pleasurable if it wasn't done in a rush. When felling, I would listen for the measured echo of my axe blow, and would wait for it to die away before striking at the frozen trunk again. As I waited my body would cool perfectly, only to warm up gently again at the next stinging strike.

The thought of the cosy cabin waiting for me was always a great comfort, and I would often stop my work and look up towards camp. If it was very cold I would see a column of heat rising up from the stove pipe, even though the fire would be burning slowly with the air vent almost completely closed. Before I went out, I would set a pot of bacon and beans simmering, and the thought of it always cheered me. At the end of the day's work I would travel back slowly along my frozen trails, lit by the light of the moon, stars and sometimes the Northern Lights with frost glittering all around. I would return the dogs to their tethers, and they would go into a frenzy of excitement as I started piling up wood ready to light the dog-pot. Once I'd lit the fire, I would shovel snow in, followed by ladles of rice, dog feed, chopped fish and scraps of grouse.

The fishy smell of the pot would be driving the dogs crazy by this time, and the frozen air would be reverberating with the sounds of barks, yelps and howls. The pot would be like a black, fire-belching demon, lurking beneath a great white cloud of hot air and bitter smoke. I would stand above it stirring, utterly engulfed in the foul-smelling fog like a witch stirring a cauldron, the steam so dense that I couldn't see my arms, never mind the grisly bobbing bits of pike or grouse. When it was ready I would ladle the thick broth into a large bucket, then stir in some snow so as not to scald the animals. As I stirred, the occasional brown dollop would blurp up and stick to my clothing, adding to my already foul personal miasma. The dogs would hang back, darting in and out of their boxes while I ladled the stew into their dishes, and then pounce on it like sharks in a frenzy as soon as I had moved on. Unlike Fuzzy, they didn't make the meal last, and would lap up the liquid in seconds before devouring the chunks in single gulps. Soon there would be nothing left, and they would set about prancing lightly around their tethers, keeping their eyes trained on me like the fixed stares of spinning ballerinas. It was satisfying to see the dogs well fed, and to know that they would enter their boxes for the night with something warm in their bellies. As I watched them refuel I would marvel at their incredible endurance, and wonder how anyone could imagine that horses in the Arctic were a good idea. Even Captain Scott took ponies to Antarctica, only to watch them all die fast. Horses are finicky eaters because they can't vomit – what goes in stays in, and if it doesn't agree with them their intestines go into spasms, wrapping and knotting themselves in an excruciating and sometimes fatal condition called colic. Dogs on the other hand will eat almost anything, and though of course great care should be taken to feed them well, there is comfort in the knowledge that if the food doesn't agree with them they will bring it back up again – frequently going on to re-digest the purged morsel later.

As I crunched back to the cabin, a dog would occasionally start to howl, and then gradually I would hear the tinkle of frosty chains as the others emerged from their boxes to join in. Each dog added a different call to the eerie song, some fading away as others rose high, the sound ebbing and falling into the frozen night. Old-timers called this a 'howlankyou', and said that it came after a good meal, when the dogs felt safe and warm with heavy stomachs. I would creep from the cabin to listen, keeping myself hidden as I knew that if they saw me they would stop. I never got much right in my former life in the corridors of the corporate world, and when I did I felt very little when I was thanked or congratulated. Yet in those great boreal woods, shivering beside my cabin beneath a sky full of stars, I could have cried as I listened to those dogs. Their canine song of gratitude meant more to me than anything else in the world at that moment, as it told me the team was well and happy, and that tomorrow they would run and run and run.

When I had finished setting up the dog yard, and cut enough wood to see us through a few weeks, my thoughts turned to making a winter portage. My old portage was too sinuous for the dogsled, and I knew that if I carried on using it at some point I was going to kill myself, so I worked out a new, straighter route. The winter portage would run down the grass lake, giving me a straight run towards the slough, where I would only have to pass through about half a mile of woodland towards the end. I had to make the portage the old-fashioned way, and each day I snowshoed down the lake towards the willow woods at the far western end, dragging my chainsaw, axe and Sandvik in the hand-pulled sled. I walked slowly, placing each step deliberately, whilst Fuzzy loyally trailed behind me. Overnight my tracks would freeze hard, and the next day I would retrace my steps and widen the trail, returning over subsequent days to compress the newly fallen snow. I would set off in half-light, often returning beneath a vivid moon with ice gathering thickly on my eyelashes.

After a few days hard snowshoeing the portage through the grass lake had a good icy surface, and if I stepped off it I sank into five feet of snow. Next I had to cut through an eerie willow wood near the slough, where the trees had grown in an erratic and haphazard fashion due to being constantly browsed by moose. There was a gothic feel to those woods, like something from *The Legend of Sleepy Hollow*, and the shadows of the gnarled, frozen branches seemed to reach out towards me in the moonlight. Sometimes as I worked my nerves tingled. Stories abounded of 'the woodsman', a primitive man or people who were reputed to be part of a lost tribe that dwelt in the Interior. Most tales involved harassment or the abduction of women by wild men in search of mates.

One particularly dark, moonless night, I was on my way home when I was stopped in my tracks by a strange sound. I crept over to a tree and leaned against it, listening. I was halfway up the grass lake, and the sound seemed to be coming from the direction of my cabin. It was a continuous, low murmuring, that rose every now and then as if about to reach a crescendo, but then pulled back again. It had to be the wolf pack, and I looked down at Fuzzy, who was standing rigid with his hair on end. This was a new sound from the wolves: it sounded like some kind of canine mantra, and had a malevolence that I had never heard before. I listened as if bewitched, and then an image of Bubbles appeared. 'Oh shit! The dogs!' I said, remembering that they were waiting on their tethers, alone and unguarded. Glenn had told me how wolves would attack sled dogs, ripping and pulling them off their tethers, and I started snowshoeing as fast as I could, ready to shoot anything in their defence. The murmuring was growing louder as I got nearer to camp and I entered the dog yard with dread, expecting to find a scene of carnage. To my relief they were unmolested and I heard no more of the wolves that night, yet they must have been very close by, and would certainly have smelled my dogs as well as the acrid, fishy scent of the dog-pot, which wafted through the woods like a dinner invitation to every animal for miles around. Midwinter was a hard time for animals in the Interior, and I felt vulnerable, knowing that my camp was emitting an irresistible scent.

That evening I ate my standard meal of seared grouse breast on a bed of noodles, then poured myself an immense dram before sinking into my bedroll. I lay awake for some time, staring at the purlin above me and thinking about that weird murmuring sound. I assumed it had come from the wolves, but had it? It had been nothing like any sound I had heard from them before. I thought of the dark woods around my little home, and wondered what mysteries lurked in that huge expanse of trackless country. Legends abound in the Interior, and there are some parts where no Indian will go, even to this day. I remembered asking Don about the legend of the woodsman months ago, when I was still living in my wall tent. 'Yeah some guys really believe it,' he had said, 'I don't really, but some do.'

'Have you ever met anyone who has seen the woodsman?' I asked.

'Oh yeah,' he sighed. 'I met plenty.'

There was a silence. 'And?' I asked impatiently.

'Well, mostly they don't take kindly to being laughed at – in fact one of 'em will clear walk out of the room if anyone don't take him seriously. He and his family had to leave their camp 'cause of the woodsman, or so he says.'

'What happened?'

'Well, first he was stealing from the smoke-house, then one night they was eating in the cabin when all of a sudden stones started hitting the roof, so he went outside and saw the woodsman up on high ground, flinging stones at 'em with a sling.'

'But you don't believe it?'

'Well I know that this country is huge, and you should never say never, but I believe in one thing for definite.'

'What's that?'

'Everything that lives has gotta leave a trail, and someday it has to leave a body. I ain't seen neither.'

Later I heard many similar stories, but couldn't help thinking that there may have been an even more sinister explanation; that the woodsman may have provided a useful alibi for the crimes of men. An old musher also told me he thought that people had been mistaking black bears for woodsmen. Bears often stand on two legs and their movements can be very human, and I myself had demonstrated that an unpractised eye could easily mistake one for a man. Then there were the practical jokers, like a friend of Charlie's, who liked to dress up in a gorilla suit and wander around at night. His joke worked on most people, who would swear they'd had a sighting, and even made Glenn Stout jump higher than a gazelle when he suddenly emerged from beneath a tarpaulin on a hunter's boat. Charlie and Don wisely warned him that if he carried on doing it he was likely to be shot as the ultimate hunter's trophy. Yet there were plenty of very experienced, rational men who were certain that they had seen the genuine article, and as I closed my eyes that night I was still thinking about that strange, low murmuring.

39
SETTLING IN

Now that my trails were solid I set about getting the dogs fitter. If they were to be useful, they needed to be able to travel long distances, and certainly as far as the village thirty-five miles away. I used the slough trail as a training ground, venturing a little further each day until I reached the Yukon proper. It took a while to get there, yet I knew that I mustn't overstretch the dogs too early. The dogs enjoyed these journeys, and came back into camp each day with their tails wagging. Gradually I began to get to know them as individuals, forming a relationship with the team that might have been similar to that between a happy class and a friendly school teacher . . . in the 1850s.

The dogs wanted to work for me, and although they liked me and knew that I liked them, they were also just a little bit scared, knowing that I could be, and had been, very stern. Glenn had taught me it was vital to assert my dominance from the start, and when any of the dogs had been caught dawdling or not concentrating they were quickly disciplined. From the start Bubbles and I had got on well, and this was essential as she was the helmswoman to my captain. I called out her commands very gently, and when we traversed tough sections of trail I would encourage her in a high, light voice. The effect was incredible, and with each petite call a forwards surge would ripple through the team, in contrast to occasions when I had shouted or been too strident, when the dogs seemed to lose heart and give up. Thus I learned that when the going was tough it was especially important to be gently positive.

Next to Bubbles ran Sprite, a pure white dog with an immensely positive attitude and a seemingly inexhaustible supply of energy. Her character was fresh and fun, and if she had been a person I imagined her as a good-looking tennis player: not too bright, but full of laughter and very fit. Sprite was rather critical of me at times, and if ever I stopped the team for some reason she would be the first to look back as if saying 'Oh come on! Don't waste our time!' She never gave up, and even in deep snow, a head wind or a blizzard, she just kept going.

Behind Sprite and Bubbles ran the 'team' dogs, Spot and Lefty.* Running on the left was Spot, who was the youngest in the team, and had much to learn. He was incapable of trotting, by far the most economical gait for long distances, and would instead endlessly gallop, jerking his partner and the whole team. Yet I had a soft spot for him, as he had great heart and was still very much a puppy. He had started life with a well-known French musher, who had used him to pull sleds stuffed with tourists along a glacier in the south of Alaska. He had a very thick coat, and so was not best suited to racing, yet his incredible strength and endurance made him ideal for my purposes.

Running on the right, occasionally jumping over the gangline to the left, ran Lefty, the veteran of the team. From the start he fascinated me with his composure, and while the other dogs yelped and barked he would pace wisely, his mouth tight shut beneath a few silvery whiskers. When I unhooked him he would pull towards the sled in anticipation, and once harnessed he would lean hard on the tug-line, looking ahead unflinchingly as the harness strained

---

* If I had a bigger team, the team dogs would be called the 'swing' dogs.

over his iron-hard shoulders. I would stretch the old campaigner before every run, and when I checked his feet never found so much as a scratch on his hard black pads. Lefty had run the Yukon Quest* three times, and had sired numerous first-class pups for Glenn. I was deeply impressed by him, and yet on the odd occasion that I attempted to pet him he would shrink away with a look on his face that said 'I'm here to run. You want touchy-feely? Go get a cat.' Lefty was also a careful guardian of the yard, and would always be the first to step out of his box and bark at some real or imagined enemy. He had seen a lot in his time, and I wondered if his alacrity stemmed from the memory of a wolf skulking wraith-like into some distant dog yard of his youth.

Behind Lefty ran my two 'wheel' dogs, Blackie and Brownie. The wheel dog's position is a hard one in any sled team as they run nearest the sled, acting like canine shock absorbers and taking the strain as the sled jars over miles of uneven trail. Yet Blackie was tiny, slight and shy, and of all the team seemed the least up to the job. I remembered when I first came to her, and how unlike all the other dogs she had shyly retreated into her box. Yet when I knelt and waited she came out and licked my hand, and now had a good deal of trust in me. Despite her slight frame, when she was hooked up she transformed every time into a hard pulling dog, and never, ever gave up.

Brownie was the biggest dog in the team and the most striking. He was the one who was jumped on by the dingo back in Glenn's yard, and was big-boned and strong, with fearsome, dramatic eyes. When harnessed he looked the best in the team, but like Spot he never trotted. Unlike Spot he didn't have the excuse of youth or inexperience, and when the anchor was lifted he would charge off, galloping in great long stretching strides. This was worrying, and my worries were confirmed when he turned out to be what mushers call a 'one day dog', meaning that on the first day he ran well but on the second flaked out completely. One night, as we returned from a run up the slough, I examined each pair of dogs in

* The Yukon Quest is one of the longest sled races in the world, and runs 1,200 miles from Whitehorse, Yukon to Fairbanks, over very tough terrain.

turn in the beam of my head torch. I was happy to see that they were all pulling equally, until I came to Brownie who was running sideways and letting the tired team drag him along. Rage gripped me, and yet I could do nothing about it – if I stopped and put him on the sled he would probably do it the next day, hoping for another lift. I stopped the sled and let them rest for a moment, but saw that this would not help the others, who all stared at me in disgust. I lifted the anchor and we carried on, but then Brownie collapsed completely. I stopped and rested them again, giving Brownie a good rub and stretch while whispering sweet encouragements. When we finally made it back to camp, the other dogs whirled about and barked for their dog-pot while he stood quiet and exhausted in his run. I felt sorry for him, yet knew that sentimentality would do him no good, and that to have any future he would have to improve.

He perked up when I served him his food, and I stood watching him while he ate, wondering why such a strong dog was so appalling as a runner. And then it dawned on me: it was a matter of brains, and clearly Brownie was a very dim dog. The bargain between sled dog and musher is very straightforward: hard work in exchange for food. All the other dogs ran because they knew that when they got to their destination they would be fed – this was obvious as they always sped up as they got closer to home. The one dog who had failed me was Brownie, and it seemed that when he was tired he lost hope, unable to keep the end goal in mind.

Bubbles was showing real ability as a lead dog, and although Glenn told me she was just starting out it was clear that she was skilled. If we came to a fork in the trail where we usually went left, for example, and I cried out 'gee!' for a right turn instead, she would at first instinctively head in our usual direction. I would brake and hold the team, then wait for her to turn to the right, but again she would skip to the left. 'No' I would say firmly, then giving a few light but insistent calls of 'Gee, gee, gee!' She would glance back once, then look right, clearly showing that she had understood. Then I would shout 'Gee!' one more time and off we would go to the right. As we got to know each other she began to make these adjustments faster and faster, so that eventually she just had to look the wrong way, and a quiet 'No' from me would set her on the right course. As the lead dog she was the most important in the team, and was always given slightly more rations than the others because her workload was the greatest. She had to be a superb runner, like the stroke on a rowing boat, and yet she also had to be clever enough to read a trail.

To a large extent I left it to Bubbles to choose our route along the trails, and she always showed impressive athleticism. Sometimes Sprite would challenge her and insist on going the wrong way, and then Bubbles would simply jump over her in a dramatic overrule, chivvying the team to follow her through sheer force of willpower. I was captivated by the exotic sight of my new transport, and would stare down at them, fascinated by the team dynamic and the individual personalities of the dogs. They shat and pissed copiously along the trail, barely breaking pace in the process, and I was grateful for the arctic temperatures, as all that hit me was the occasional yellow crystal or scentless frozen brown clod.

Our training sessions also benefited Fuzzy, who would run tirelessly between the runners of the sled. The meals from the dog-pot were also doing him a lot of good, and his great shaggy blonde coat shone beautifully. Sometimes I would stop to rest the team, and would walk along the gangline, patting each dog and rubbing ice from their happy, open faces. Fuzzy would stay at a safe distance, leaning casually against the sled and chewing ice from his paws, regarding the team with thinly disguised scorn. And he had reason to be cocky. Once, while my attention was distracted, he sneaked into Brownie's run. I was about to retrieve him, but then decided that he had to learn for himself that messing with sled-dogs was not a good idea – especially with Brownie, who was the biggest in the team. I stood back, ready to jump in if necessary, and sure enough heard growls and scuffles, followed by a high-pitched squeal. To my surprise I saw Brownie retreating into his box with a whine, and Fuzzy growling victoriously as he shook frozen spittle from his thick coat. He puffed up his chest and walked calmly towards me, as if announcing to the whole yard: 'That's right. I'm the boss's dog. And don't you ever forget it.'

After a few days our daily runs were up to around sixteen miles, and Fuzzy often proved his worth as tail-end Charlie. Once we were skittering fast over a bumpy section of trail when one of my snowshoes fell off the sled. I braked, but the pedal just slid over the ice. Eventually the sled slowed and the brake just held, but I couldn't risk the anchor, as the holding wasn't good. I looked back at the snowshoe, which lay about fifty yards behind us, then down at Fuzzy. 'Fetch', I said, pointing down the trail, and he looked back at me as if to say, 'I knew you were going to say that'. He dashed back, then spent a few minutes trying to balance the cumbersome snowshoe in his mouth, before galloping back to me with his head held high. I took the shoe from him and tied it on carefully, then said 'I love you Fuzzy, do you know that?' He answered with a loving growl, letting his tongue out and then slurping it in again in that familiar display of affection that I had previously found unbearable. From then on he played an official role as sled retriever, and would collect things without even being asked, passing them to me when we were on the move, like a relay runner passing a baton. There was no doubt about it, this former sworn cat lover had converted to dog power, and without my canine companions my life in the sub arctic would have been much the poorer.

40

CARRY ON UP THE YUKON

I was getting low on provisions, and decided the dogs were fit enough to try their first run to the village. In the morning I heated up the remains of the dog-pot from the night before. This time I put in no chunks, but simply added snow to create a warm, watery, hydrating stew. While the ice gradually thawed in the pot I packed the sled. This journey would be by far my longest, so I had to be prepared. First I tied on my thirty-five litre rucksack, into which I had packed the basics of survival for five days. It contained a complete change of clothing, every means possible of lighting a fire, food for five days plus three US Army ration meals, extra socks, hats and gloves, hand warmers, an emergency 'man over-board' beacon,* map, compass, sleeping bag, bivvy bag and a heliograph. Around the rucksack I tied my snow shovel, spare rope and an axe, as well as the 45/70 rifle, which had a dog's bootie tied over the muzzle to ensure that ice didn't clog the barrel, and was placed in such a way that I could slip it quickly out of its padded

* I used the kind issued to sailors. They can be bought at any yacht chandler.

sleeve. In the outer pockets of my jacket I carried bundles of nylon string of various lengths, spare necklines and clips, and in the inner pockets, which were warmed by body heat, I carried spare batteries and my GPS. In all my pockets there were my usual extra items for making fires.

When I had packed the sled I ladled out the soup for the dogs, then cut chunks of fish and put them in a sack. I cut the fleshiest pieces of fish, as these would be full of water and easy to digest. Finally I packed a long wire tether, which could be tied between two trees or two anchors to hold the dogs if I needed to hole up anywhere overnight – it is not good to leave dogs too long on a gangline, as they will often chew through ropes.

At last it was time to hook up the dogs, and as I did so I noticed how strong and fit they were looking. They were full of energy, and as Bubbles leaned into the gangline the sled creaked with the strain. Once they were all harnessed I let the rope go and held them on the brake, and their pull was so powerful that we ploughed a furrow in the snow as the sled started to edge forward. Knowing there were over thirty miles to travel, I said a small prayer to the god of tenderfoot mushers and hoped for the best. 'Okay,' I said lightly, and lifted the brake, and they reared almost as one on to their hind legs before shooting off along the trail. They had never felt so strong or full of energy, and as we charged down the old portage I realised that I was barely in control. Twice I fell on tight corners, but managed somehow to get back on, and I searched desperately ahead for the winter portage turn. Through iced eyes, in the half-light of the murky winter day, I spotted it coming up very fast ahead. 'Ha!' I cried loudly, and Bubbles swerved to the left, the others following behind her and pulling me along like a bob-sled.

We passed through a series of tight turns as the trail wove in and out of clumps of willow, and each time I set my runners hard and leaned back and we powered through. Sheets of snow flew up from the runners, and the fear began to change to simple, bone-jarring joy. At last we reached the straight of the grass lake and the team opened out, but I cried 'Easy!' and braked to make the point. I had survived the early adrenalin charge, and now managed to settle the dogs into a good steady trot. Some of their energy would now be saved for the long road ahead. We swished and swerved silently through the willows, and I noticed the plump outlines of willow grouse in the trees, but then thirty yards ahead I saw a great black shadow looming on the trail. 'Whoa' I shouted immediately, and slammed the brake down. We stopped in a cloud of snow, and the black shadow moved towards us. It was an immense bull moose, taller than me at the shoulder, and I had met him in the worst possible scenario: square on in the middle of my trail with deep, powdery snow high on either side.

I stamped in the anchor to hold the dogs, who were barking and jumping frenziedly, straining to give chase. The moose stopped and stood square, staring at us, and I slipped the 45/70 from its sleeve, testing the lever to ensure that it wasn't frozen. The dogs barked louder and the moose began to lollop his head up and down. 'Oh shit!' I said to myself, picturing him stamping the dogs into the ground, hooves pumping like the pistons of a steam engine. I decided to try my shouting approach, which had worked last time. 'Go away big man!' I shouted, waving my arms, but he held his ground. In creating the portage I had unwittingly set up this scenario; my trails were used by all the animals, as they no longer had to wade through deep snow. The bull moose lowered his head and then raised it again, and I saw the crescent-shaped whites of his eyes glow vividly in the gloom. I glanced at my rifle, knowing that one heavy round could easily crash through the moose's forehead, and was tempted by the thought of the meat. But then I remembered the regulations: the carcass could not be touched, as it was out of season*. Nevertheless a moose or any animal could be killed in defence of one's life or property, and if the moose charged I would have no choice. I rapidly considered my options: if I had been on foot I could have gone around the moose or turned back, but this was not possible with the dog team, as my trail was not wide enough. On foot I could also have sent Fuzzy off to the moose's right and I could have gone to the left, as if we were

* Regulations surrounding the hunting of moose are strict – moose hunting season ends on 29th September.

stalking him. This often makes a moose back off, as it is reminis-
cent of wolves' approach. I wondered about firing off a warning
round, but worried that the animal might charge at us in response.
All the while I continued shouting, but when after ten minutes he
still had not budged I decided to take a risk, and levered a round
into my rifle and fired into the air. The explosion shattered the
silence, and after a stunned pause the moose turned and lolloped
away through the deep snow at the side of the trail. The dogs
strained after him, but were held firmly by the anchor, and I
packed away my rifle while waiting for the animal to disappear. A
few minutes later I weighed anchor and we were off again,
charging through the woods and down on to the slough trail.

I could see that the clouds were clearing from the sky, and it
promised to be a very cold day. It was tempting to rush as I felt
vulnerable, just a tiny speck on the huge expanse of white river ice
under a dark, looming sky, but I didn't want to push the dogs too
hard this early in the journey. I stopped briefly to put on extra
layers of clothing, including a face mask, scarf, goggles and a hat.
Over the whole lot I pulled the windbreaking hood of my North
Face jacket, and then pushed my gloved hands inside my great
wolf fur mitts. The dogs ran on, their breath freezing and falling
onto their backs as frost, showing that the air was very cold. From
time to time I saw more moose standing still in the snow, watching
as we flashed past, and I knew it was a sign that the wolf pack was
hunting, as the moose were taking refuge on the open expanse of
the slough. On we skittered, past banks of frozen willow osiers,
screening more shadowy shapes of moose bounding through the
snow. The dogs were extremely excited as they could smell the
moose everywhere, and this benefited me as they transferred their
excitement into running still faster.

We had been running for just under two hours when we
approached the mouth of the slough, and ahead I saw an immense
white field, which I knew was the Yukon. I stopped the team, who
stood panting in a cloud of frost, and rubbed and patted each dog
before hastily doling out the fish chunks, wary of letting the dogs
grow cold. In very cold conditions old-timers used to tie rabbit

skins over the dogs' exposed groin areas, with the rabbit fur on the inside to keep them warm. I wished that I had an equivalent for them, but the dogs all seemed happy and wolfed down their fish. I had meant to rest them for as long as they had run, but pretty soon they started to yowl and leap again impatiently. So after thirty minutes I lifted the anchor and we headed east along an immense stretch of river that was five miles wide. To my right I could see eerie windblown shapes etched into the sides of endless snow berms, and I saw the trails of foxes, which appeared blue against the shining white snow. When my face grew cold I did what Don had showed me, and held a fur mitt up to the cold part until it warmed up again. I pushed up my goggles so that I could appreciate the true colours of the snowy landscape, and popped on a pair of steel-rimmed snow glasses, which immediately burnt into my skin. I crushed them into my pocket in disgust, wondering what dumb company had ever thought of using metal frames for snow glasses.

On and on we went, and I would shift my position, at times standing sideways on one runner so I could look at the passing bank, or sometimes leaning forwards on the birch handlebar and staring at the dogs' bodies, which stretched and contracted as they ate up the miles. Between the runners as usual ran Fuzzy, and I could hear his breathing and the icy pounding of his paws. Out there alone, between the dark sky and the frozen river, I felt overwhelmed by my debt to the world, which had chosen to indulge me so far beyond my artificial dream of the wilderness. I shouted out with joy and my tears froze and collected around the ice of my breath that held to my eyelashes. I thought of the hearts of those seven dogs that ran with me, and realised that we formed a bond of trust and mutual reliance, and had truly become a pack. I slowed them, worried that they might be growing tired, and leaned on the handlebar to look up. Night had fallen, and as I watched the Plough begin its circle around Polaris, I thought of my beloved step-father who had died thirteen years before, and of my mother who lived alone on the Isle of Mull having lost the love of her life. I wondered if he was gone completely, or if there was anything more to it all, and then thought of my two little boys whose lives were just beginning.

Six hours after leaving the mouth of the slough I saw some familiar bent, half-fallen spruce trees leaning over the edge of the riverbank, and knew that we had reached Four Mile Point. As I rounded the point I saw the lights of Galena up ahead, and steered towards them. I reached the village, and with a sense of disbelief steered the sled up over the riverbank and into the willow woods, letting the dogs take me along the familiar trail. The village was silent, wrapped in snow and darkness, and we swished silently to Glenn's yard. I tethered the dogs and cooked up some dog-pot, pleased to see that they were in great form, tails wagging and happy. The entire journey had taken just under nine hours, and the dogs seemed unaffected by the journey. I stood watching them for a few minutes, admiring their endurance and strength of character, before stowing away the sled. Then I hoisted my bag and rifle over my shoulder and walked through the scruffy village, feeling happy to see it again but already longing for my cabin.

PART 5

'There is an ecstasy that marks the summit of life, and beyond which life cannot rise. And such is the paradox of living, this ecstasy comes when one is most alive, and it comes as a complete forgetfulness that one is alive.'

JACK LONDON, *THE CALL OF THE WILD*

41

FIRST CATCH YOUR BEAVER

Grub first, then ethics.
BERTOLT BRECHT

The cold kept her grip tight over my forest home throughout January, and the whites of her knuckles were showing. Each time I left camp I armed myself with a cloak of caution, knowing that she would kill me at the slightest chance. A big area of high atmospheric pressure had moved in, and the temperatures dropped as low as minus sixty. I observed the effect of these temperatures with awe, noticing that my logs cracked like melba toast, and wet clothes hung outside became first boards, and then light and fluffy as they freeze-dried. I was losing weight again in the harsh cold, and realised it was time to start hunting for fat meat, which could only mean beaver. In this weather that meant snaring, as hanging around for too long outside was not a good idea. I would have to set my trap in the thin hours of daylight, then get home quickly and wait until the next day to see if I had caught anything.

Throughout the autumn I had watched the family of ten or so

beavers steadily piling up branches of non-resinous wood. They would drag the branches out towards their house, and then pull them underwater to their 'stick-pile'. They needed to make a big enough pile to sustain them through the winter months, when they would be trapped by a thick layer of ice, and would have to live full time in the house. From there, the beavers could swim to the stick-pile whenever they needed to, grabbing a tasty branch and bringing it back to the house. When they had gnawed off all the bark, the beavers, being house-proud, would deposit the leftover stick on their refuse pile, known as the 'bone-yard'. I had no idea really of how to go about trapping beaver, but I spent many hours thinking about them, and how I might be able to intercept them in their ordered routine. Pangs of guilt that I might have felt earlier were quickly dissipated by hunger, and the knowledge that there is no shortage of these mighty rodents in Alaska. I knew they were intelligent animals, however, and that catching one would present quite a challenge.

One morning I wrapped up and, with Fuzzy beside me, set off to collect my 'bait'. I dug away the snow surrounding a delicious-looking cottonwood sapling, and then sawed it as near as possible to its base. I then cut a three-foot long spruce pole and threw everything into my hand-sled, which I dragged over the lake towards the beaver house. As I approached the house I jabbed my pick in front of me, as the constant movement of the industrious beavers underneath the ice meant that caution must always be applied. Above the snug white house a thin trail of heat was rising from the apex as if a fire burned within. It was caused by the heat of their bodies, grouped in the upper chamber, rising up and condensing in the icy air outside, yet it made me feel guilty, as if I were a killer lurking at the gate of a little cottage, planning to murder the family seated cosily around the fireplace. Then I thought of the glorious beaver stews I would cook up, and it hardened my resolve. I tried to remember where I had seen the beavers drag sticks under the water, so I could work out the location of their stick-pile. I was planning to sink the tasty sapling between the pile and the house, hoping to tempt a passing beaver with a fresh bit of bark. The idea was that it would swim for the branch, and in so doing place its head through a wire snare that hung in front of the bait. The beaver's flat tail becomes a drag if it tries to swim backwards, and so it would have no option but to plunge forwards, pulling the snare tight around its neck.

I identified what I thought was a likely spot for the stick-pile, and started to shovel snow. Four feet of hard, wind-packed snow lay on top of the ice, and it was heavy work, especially as I was wearing so many layers of clothing. I dug slowly and methodically, removing the odd piece of clothing, until I reached a layer of nasty brown crunchy ice that had been overflow. I shovelled a clear area around this, and then used the heavy ice pick to start chipping a hole roughly three feet in diameter. I soon realised that shovelling snow had been easy in comparison to this, and I had to stop often to clear away the ice chips that piled up by the hole. After a foot or so I reached a layer of much harder, clearer ice which I knew was the lake ice proper. On and on I picked, my arms and shoulders aching, and my hands numb with cold. Three feet later my pick finally broke through, and I was glad that I had tied it to my hand, or it would have sunk without trace.

Brown water sucked and gushed into the hole, filling the air around me with the stink of a sewer. I chipped on, making the hole wider and being careful not to soak myself. At last the hole was clear, and I stared down through the noxious steam. It smelled so bad that the dog-pot seemed like a rose garden by comparison. Did I really want to eat a creature that lived in there? Suddenly the idea of eating beaver seemed less appealing. Then I saw a branch float up, and reaching into the hole with the ice pick realised that I was right over the stick pile. My heart sank – there was no way that a snare would work with all of those sticks around it, it was too crowded. Methane bubbles rose to the surface and popped like fetid mushrooms, making the stench even worse, and I looked at Fuzzy who was staring into the hole as if about to sample soup in a dog restaurant of the highest order. 'This is going to be like trapping rats in a sewer', I said, and he looked up at me with his tail wagging as if to say 'Count me in!'

I rubbed the frost away from his face and then walked about, trying to figure where next to try a hole. It was dark by the time I had finished cutting the next one, and this time I was relieved to find that I wasn't so close to the stick pile. I sunk the cottonwood sapling down, leaving just the end poking above the hole, and then looped two snares on to the spruce branch, which I laid across the hole in front of the bait. I fiddled about, lowering the loops down through the dark water and feeling that my chances of catching anything were very slim. I stood and looked at the little ribbon of heat rising up against the dark backdrop of spruce trees, and felt another pang of guilt. Hardening my heart, I turned and walked towards my own little house over which a wisp of birch smoke hung in the still air. The first attack was in place.

The next day the temperature held at minus fifty, and I was reluctant to venture out, but the trap had to be checked. I trudged over to the hole, which was buried in windblown snow, and could just see the top of my bait stick poking out. I scooped the snow out of the way and then, with a gloved hand, cleared the ice that had grown over the hole. I was looking for bubbles or chips of bark that would have been evidence of a beaver working away at the bait stick, but I saw nothing. The wind was moaning softly, and snow filled the air like a sandstorm making the visibility almost zero. I trudged a little way off and stood staring down at the snow, trying to think where I should dig a second set. Once I had decided on a spot, I began the tiresome job of digging, shovelling and ice-picking all over again, and then set the bait and snares. I then returned to chip away the ice from the first hole, so that I could see what, if anything, had happened. I quickly discovered that one of the crafty rodents had indeed gone for my bait, and had carefully nibbled its way round the outside, removing the side branches and leaving the main stem intact. I was stumped – this job of remote hunting was hard, and I was working literally in the dark. I cut another branch and reset the snare, then walked back to the cabin feeling doubtful about the whole enterprise.

Over the next week or so I tried every combination of sapling and snare, but always returned to find a perfectly nibbled bait and useless dangling loop of wire. The gentle approach of the early days was long gone now, and with each day both my determination and my hunger grew. It was becoming a vendetta, and I would look hard at the beaver house, watching the steam rising and muttering darkly. My first thought on waking was whether today would be the day, and each day the wily creatures foiled me once again. The snow around the beaver house was peppered with holes, all to no avail: I had to go back to the drawing board. One morning I walked back to my cabin after yet another unsuccessful foray, clutching a gnawed bait branch. I pumped the lamp to shine brightly, then placed the sapling on the floor in front of me and stared at it. The beavers were taking my bait – that was good news – and yet somehow they were missing my snares. Maybe the snares were at the wrong depth, although it seemed I had tried them in every possible position. Then I realised that the beavers' neat line of trimming on the bait sticks could give me just the information I needed, acting as a kind of snare depth gauge and showing me the exact depth at which they were approaching my bait. I returned to the hole and reset the trap.

When I returned the next day I brushed the snow away from the dark window of the frozen-over hole, and for the first time saw something that hinted at food. In the pane of ice little chips of bark hung around a burst of frozen bubbles, as if there had been some kind of suspended underwater explosion. I chipped around the hanging wire of my snare until it hung free of ice. The wire felt tight, and the snare was heavy. I had caught something, and I looked at Fuzzy, who had picked up on my excitement and was whining in anticipation. I stood up and looked at the beaver house, feeling hopeful but responsible, and knowing that if I had at last caught one of the creatures every part of its body must be used. I chipped out the rest of the ice, grabbed the snare and pulled. I couldn't budge it at all. I lifted the spruce pole to which the snare was attached, leant back and pulled with all my strength. Still it didn't move, and I began to wonder if it might be a log. I then took a length of discarded bait and poked it gently into the hole, following the snare wire down into the dark water and feeling around like a blind man. The end of the stick struck something that yielded and had a soft covering of some kind. 'It's a beaver!' I shouted to Fuzzy, who bounded round in circles.

Still I was left with the problem of how to get the creature out of the hole, and I realised that it was stuck fast to the underside of the ice. It was clear that the only way to get it out would be to cut around it through the ice. Two hours later I managed to free the incredibly heavy beaver, weighed down still further by water and ice. It shot up head first through the slushy dark water, almost as if it was leaping out at me, and made me jump. I stared down aghast as two huge and very yellow front teeth glinted in the gloom, framed by a pair of sharp-clawed paws that seemed to clutch out in attack. The snare was set tight around its neck, and I reassured myself that it would have died quickly. As soon as I had it on the ice I cut away a fleshy rear paw, throwing it to Fuzzy as a reward for his steadfastness. I hauled the beast into my sled with some difficulty, and then stood staring at it in disbelief. It was an immense male, about four feet long from head to tail, and must have weighed fifty pounds at least.

The beaver was frozen solid by the time I reached the cabin and I needed to hang the carcass up somewhere warm. The only warm place was inside, and with a sinking heart I strung the giant rat from the purlin nearest the stove, placing my sled underneath to catch the drips as it thawed out. That night, as I sat down to eat my beans, I had to work hard to keep my appetite, distracted by the sight of those yellow teeth glinting reproachfully through the gloom. The beaver took three days to thaw out, and dripped steadily throughout, haunting me like an Alaskan form of water torture. As it dried out it became less ghastly, and I admired the rich brown colour and incredible thickness of its fur.

When the beaver had thawed out completely I hung it from a tree outside then made a cut from its lower lip to its vent, careful not to rupture any of its internal organs. The glossy innards hung out, and I neatly cut its dark liver and placed it in Fuzzy's bowl, where he fell on the meal with complete abandon. I then threw the rest of the innards into the dog-pot. Then I used snow to clean out the internal cavity, and brought the beaver back into the cabin. I was determined not to waste anything, and skinned away the pelt, glad to see that the animal did indeed have a thick layer of fat. Less joyfully, the fat began to melt and run in the warmth of the cabin, and soon my hands were slick with gore. The beaver has something called a castor gland, which is often used as a base for high quality perfume. It has a distinctive musky, almost minty smell, and was also used in the past by indigenous people to lure quarry towards their traps. Every meat eater in the sub-arctic prizes beaver, and the scent of the castor travels for miles in the dry, cold air.

Next I stretched the pelt out on a board, hammering in little nails and leaving it flesh-side out to dry. I had cut off the wide, scaly tail and added it to the dog-pot – although many Indians had told me that the tail is good eating, I was not tempted by the fatty, salmon-pink flesh that showed between the leathery scales. I hung the animal up on my game pole outside, knowing it would freeze solid and I would able to saw off portions of meat as required. I looked at the pole, hung with about eight grouse and now the livid red carcass of the prepared beaver, and then my eyes settled on Fuzzy, who lay nearby chewing on the thick beaver paw. There was no doubt about it: the more adept at living in the wilderness I grew, the more gruesome my camp became.

Later that night I called Don on the satellite phone to tell him of my triumph. He told me that many hunters shaved their beavers to reveal the denser fur under the guard hairs, and we talked about the unique unforgettable smell of a beaver. Back at home this conversation would have been peppered with innuendo, and several times I had to stop myself from making lewd jokes. Don was oblivious. In Alaska a beaver is a beaver. My next challenge was to cook the animal, and as I drifted off to sleep I mulled over recipe ideas, trying all the while to forget that the main ingredient would be rat.

42

PITY THE LITTLE THINGS

Over the coming weeks I caught a few more beaver, and began to see the benefits of the fatty meat for myself and the dogs. I had come up with a few good recipes, particularly for beaver ribs, which I would fry up with paprika and dried onion shavings. Once they were nicely browned I would add some dried split peas, and cover it all with grouse stock. The result was a delicious pea soup. I was now feeling very comfortable with living on my own in the wilderness, but with that ease came a growing preoccupation with home. My dreams were full of Juliet and the children, almost as though my subconscious was reminding me of where my true home was.

One night I hooked up the satellite phone, planning to make a call home. Before I did so I plugged it into my laptop to see if I had any messages, and found one from Juliet titled 'CALL ME NOW!!' I looked at the date and saw it was yesterday's, then dialled without reading the message.

'Hello?' Juliet answered the phone. 'Is that you Guy?'

'Yes it's me,' I shouted. 'Is everything okay?'

'Yes . . .' She sounded hesitant, but even through the crackly line I could hear she was excited. 'Well at least I think it is. I've sold the house!'

'You've what?' I thought I must have misheard her.

'I've sold the house! I'm sorry Guy, I hope it's okay, but I had to make a very quick decision and I couldn't get hold of you.'

A series of images of our little house ran through my mind, and I thought sadly of my vegetable garden, which it seemed I would never see again. Still, this is what happens if you leave your wife to run the ship alone, I thought, and I could hardly protest.

'Well . . . what are we going to do then?' I asked, feeling confused.

'We're going to live on Mull! You know we've discussed it so many times Guy, and it was just too good an opportunity. The boys absolutely love it here, and it would be very hard for them to leave their grandparents after all this time. We'll make things work here – I know we will.'

I was speechless but she was right, and as I put down the receiver at the end of the call I felt happy. Now our fate was sealed, and there was no going back to our old life, whatever happened. Assuming of course that I made it home in one piece.

The dog team were working like a crack squad of legionnaires, and one night in particular they proved their worth. I was travelling along the Yukon, having overruled my instinct to stay in as it was threatening snow. We were on the river's main channel when the blizzard began, and I cursed myself for ignoring my intuition. I had about six miles to go to the mouth of the slough, and then eight miles further to my portage. I was having enough trouble following this well-worn path, and the trail would be much less distinct when I veered off the main channel. The snow grew heavier and a light wind blew it into my face, piling snow up on the sled. Pretty soon I could see nothing: I was caught in a complete white-out on the Yukon river in the middle of the night. I mentally kicked myself for being so stupid, and stopped the sled to think.

The Eskimo solution is to stop and wait for the storm to pass, and I knew that if necessary I could build a snow-shelter. Yet I also knew that it might well snow non-stop for days, and the idea of being holed up in a shelter for a long time so far from home was not appealing. My main concern was finding my turn-off from the main Yukon trail – if I kept going I might over-shoot the turn, floundering on until truly lost. I had no real alternative, however, and decided to proceed carefully, keeping a watch on the time, and hoping that Bubbles would pick up the turn. In the muffled white silence I gingerly gave the order to go, my head torch reflecting feebly back at me in the whiteness. After a while I felt the team swing confidently to the left, and I knew they would not have done this if Bubbles had not made a strong, knowing turn. I trusted that she had found the slough trail, and sure enough a few minutes later I was just able to make out a prominent bank of willow that marked the mouth of the slough. She had done it, and I felt deeply grateful to the clever little dog.

We followed the snow-blown trail as it descended into the bowl of the valley, and then a mile or so later the blizzard grew dramatically worse. These were conditions to die in: nobody in their right mind would travel in such weather. Even Bubbles wasn't up to it, and once or twice she wandered off the trail, pulling the whole team into the soft, powdery snow. On both occasions I managed to salvage the sled, untangling the dogs' harnesses more by feel than sight, but Bubbles was clearly tired, and we were looking at serious trouble if we continued. Through the gloom I saw Lefty glancing back at me casually as if to say 'Okay boss, this is all getting a bit amateurish – let me take it from here.' I took Bubbles off her harness and put the iron-hard veteran in her place, deciding I had no option but to put my trust in him. He strained forwards into the thick snow and pulled the line out beautifully, and I walked along the line of friends, patting each dog and speaking soft words of encouragement. Tails wagged, and they shook the snow from their backs in readiness. I stepped on to the runners and pulled up the anchor, murmuring a soft 'okay.' We set off, not as fast as under Bubble's leadership, but at a slow, steady trot. The wind and snow barrelled into us, and the dogs' heads hung low, yet they continued to steadily pull. I might as well have been blind, and at times could not even see my hands on the handle of the sled before me, yet I felt confident that Lefty would take us home.

Two hours later I caught a glimpse of the familiar high bank of cottonwoods that stood near the entrance to my winter portage, and I knew the old boy had done it. He led us up into the shelter of the willows, and then continued up the portage in his economic way until we reached the cabin. I stepped off the runners with deep relief, and warmly congratulated each of the dogs. When I got to Lefty, he looked up at me with a tired expression that seemed to say 'Yeah, yeah – less of the talk and get on with that dog-pot.'

Soon the dogs were silent except for the occasional slurp as they tucked into their brew of beaver offal, grouse bits, fish and rice, and as I watched them eat my heart soared with pride. No one can grow to love a snow machine, and no machine can ever find its way home. My instinct was still suspect but I had the advantage of six highly tuned animals, whose spirit and natural instincts of self-preservation went a long way toward making up for my own lack of experience.

With relentless predictability the snow cleared, and the temperature plunged to a brutal minus sixty. It hovered there for the next few weeks, sometimes rising to the minus mid-fifties during the day but dropping back at night. It seemed extraordinary that the dogs could survive these conditions, yet I knew huskies thrived in dog yards throughout the Interior, and it gave me still more respect for their endurance. As they ran around their tethers they would sometimes lift a paw and hop along lamely on three legs, then drop it and lift another. In reality they were just warming a pad for a moment by keeping it off the frozen ground. One morning I walked through the yard checking each dog, and saw that Blackie had not emerged from her box. I called her, and she sweetly scurried out to nestle her head between my gloved hands. I looked at her closely then peered into the box. Inside there were two little puppies. I reached in to gently pick one up; they were completely frozen. Glenn had told me she was in pup, but it hadn't showed and I thought she must have miscarried. I sat for a while slumped beside the box, holding the two frozen little puppies in my lap. My fragile defences were under siege as I thought of my own children, and more generally of all the young lives that enter the world only to be cut short. Of all the places in the world for a new life to begin, an Alaskan dog yard in the depths of winter had to be one of the worst.

Sprite leaned over and snatched at the little carcasses, and I quickly stepped out of her reach. I buried them in the snow not far from the cabin, and as I snow-shoed home knew that it wouldn't be long before an animal emerged from the woods to dig them up again. I sat beside the stove, feeling morose and belittled by the harshness of it all, my mood not helped by occasional glimpses of another frozen beaver swinging darkly overhead. I longed for softness, gentleness and compassion, things that didn't exist in this brutal order of things, and knew I could die just as easily as those puppies. When I called home later I found Juliet sounding happy and hopeful, and I didn't mention the frozen pups. As she spoke about their life on the island I realised what a beautiful, gentle place it was, and what a safe haven it had provided for my family. I thanked the lords of luck for Juliet's strength, and knew that whatever happened she would always create a safe home for our children. When we had finished talking the wolves started their lonely chorus on the mountain, and as I listened the lamp oil ran out, the light slowly flickering from yellow to blue and then nothing.

Frigid weeks passed by, and I was kept busy in my daily routine of wood cutting, hunting and dog mushing. Then, sometime around the beginning of March, I noticed that the world had begun to change. Gradually, almost imperceptibly at first, the days were lengthening, and each day the sun held a little more warmth. Light was returning to the sub-arctic, and winter was giving way at last. With spring came the tentative realisation that I had made it through the winter in one of the world's coldest regions, and now I could afford to relax a little. The dogs were exceptionally fit, and as I hooked them up each morning I felt like the coach of an Olympic running team. They had reached their full potential, and with the morale boost of the sunshine they ran still better. Mother nature was now indulging every living thing, as if making up for her mercilessness through the winter, and although it was still cold by British standards, usually in the minus twenties, it felt positively balmy by comparison to what had gone before.

The thaw was still some way off, and my trails remained hard and true.* Most days I would travel up the slough, enjoying the sight of the country moving into spring, and we often stopped at a particular place opposite Bishop Creek, near a long belt of willow osiers. Here the air was filled with the sweet scent of willow sap, and I would breathe deeply, relishing the smell of spring. In the sterility of winter my sense of smell had become highly tuned, and I realised I was picking up the scent of the sap rising.

One day, as we neared the sweet belt of willow, the dogs suddenly picked up speed. They ran with their heads held high, all looking in the direction of the willows. I saw two moose calves, sitting close together in the snow right in the middle of the rust-coloured osiers. I braked and held the excited team, and to my surprise the little calves did not lumber off, but simply lay there chewing contentedly on the sugary willow. The low sun filtered brightly through the red-coloured stems, and the gentle sight of those two young animals captivated me. Bubbles suddenly leapt into the air and whined, and I saw their huge mother appear on the bank above the willows. She looked at me angrily and advanced with a snort of aggression, and I lifted my foot and we shot off. I looked back and saw her standing square, watching us skitter away. I admired her for bringing her brood safely through the coldest months, and wished them well.

Each day as I passed the willow belt the calves were there, sitting like chocolate-brown boulders in snow that shone blue in the sunshine. I always stopped for a moment, holding the team on the brake, and would disappear when the mother looked threaten-

* Thaw arrives late in the Interior, around April/May.

ing. My yearning for my own children had grown to a point where I needed an outlet, and those calves became a kind of touchstone for me that was keeping the fathering instinct alive.

One night I heard the wolves calling out to each other, and knew that they were back in their territory to hunt. I sat beside the stove staring into a tin cup of whisky, thinking of that brave little family amidst the sighing willows. The next day I passed by as usual and stood quietly watching the calves gently chewing the cud. I looked about for their mother, but she was not there, and when I passed by later there was still no sign of her. Days passed, and I grew seriously worried, as the calves had not moved from their snow beds in the willow. I felt sure that the mother must have been taken by wolves, and I felt helpless, knowing they were alone and defenceless.

One afternoon I made a siwash* camp on the sandbar, a mile or so from the willows. I had tethered the dogs out along my wire line, and had built a quinzee to sleep in.† First I piled snow into a ten foot high mound, compressing it as I built by jumping on the mound with my snowshoes. Then I cut foot-long lengths of willow, which I inserted into the mound until their ends were flush with the outside surface. Next I hollowed out an opening, and then started to dig snow out from inside the mound, stopping whenever I reached the end of one of the sticks. The sticks were a way of ensuring that my walls were uniform, and thick enough to keep me warm and not collapse. Immediately inside the quinzee I dug a cold well beside the door, and at the far end created a shelf for sleeping where I laid spruce boughs and my sleeping bag. Cold air would drop into the cold well, and Fuzzy would provide me with a superb pillow. If it grew very cold I could take the whole team in, and in fact old-timers used to talk of 'four dog nights' or 'six dog nights', meaning the number of dogs you would need in your shelter to keep you warm. That night I fed the dogs cold food that I had packed, and cut spruce for each one to lie on. As I lay inside

---

* Siwash is an Indian term that describes the activity of sleeping outside using shelters made from the woods or snow.
† See Notes.

the perfect little snow-house, about to fall asleep, I heard the wolves again, and knew they were nearby. The dogs started barking nervously, and I wished I had brought the shotgun instead of the rifle. There was no howling, but instead I heard that strange group humming again, which I now knew was the sound that wolves make after a kill. I lay wide awake, struggling to comprehend the extraordinary fact that here I was, sleeping in what was effectively a snowball on the Yukon when it was minus thirty-five outside and fourteen powerful wolves were on the prowl. I felt like one of the three little pigs, only I had unwisely built my house out of snow, and there were fourteen big bad wolves instead of just one.

The next morning I lit a fire on a platform of green wood to keep the blaze off the snow, and placed a ball of snow inside a piece of clean cloth, which I hung from a tree branch downwind from the fire. As I checked the dogs over and packed the sled, the heat of the fire melted the snow, and water filtered through the cloth to collect in my coffee jug below. I made some reviving sweet coffee, and then chewed on salmon sticks and a pilot biscuit.* Then I hooked up the dogs. The sun was its brightest yet, and reflected dazzlingly off the wind-polished snow. I headed along the slough towards the calves, and a chill gripped me when I saw the trail was covered in wolf prints, all leading in the direction of the willows. Sleek black ravens had gathered in the cottonwoods on the bank above their hiding place, occasionally swooping down into the willows, and I knew the calves were gone.

I anchored the sled, put on my snowshoes and walked into the willows. There were wolf prints everywhere, and lines made by their flicking paws. I parted the osiers and looked down to see the bodies of the two calves, which lay close together in death as they had in life. They had been utterly rendered by the pack, and fragile rib bones glinted white above hides that looked as though they had been professionally skinned. Everything that could be eaten had been, and all that was left apart from bones was the frozen

* Pilot biscuits are very plain, nearly indestructible biscuits that keep for a long time like ship's hard tack.

contents of their stomachs. I stood looking at the scene feeling gaunt and hollowed out with sadness. I knew that I shouldn't have allowed myself to become so attached to the two little calves, and I knew that the wolf pack had to live, yet it hurt me in a way that was not rational. It was yet more evidence of the harshness of the Interior, and that these young animals had managed against all the odds to survive the winter only added to the pain. As I turned back towards the sled I heard a crunching noise behind me, and spun round, rifle at the ready, to find Fuzzy snacking on a dainty rib. He froze when he saw my expression, but then gave me a nonchalant look as if to say, 'Wake up to reality pal – this is life', and crunched on.

I got back on the sled and continued the journey back to my camp, feeling depressed by it all. Fuzzy followed behind me, clutching a large bone in his jaws as if to emphasise the fact that, here at least, sentimentality was never a good idea. What really rubbed salt in the wounds was the fact that those wolves had been helped in their massacre by my trail, which had led them quickly and directly to the two little calves, peacefully awaiting slaughter in the perfumed shade of the warm willow bank.

43

MY WINTER KINGDOM MELTS

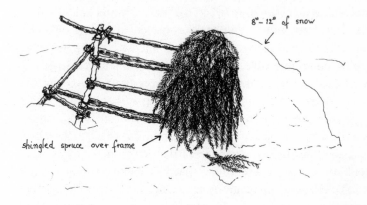

8" – 12" of snow

shingled spruce over frame

It was mid-March, and sun was gradually working away at the foundations of my winter kingdom. In many ways I welcomed it, and there were days of perfect sunshine when I put all tasks aside and sat with my back to a tree, soaking it up and feeling rewarded for the hardships of winter. Yet it was bittersweet, as I knew each warm day brought me closer to the end of my journey. I had achieved my goal of living through the winter, and it was time to start thinking about packing up camp. I was full of conflicting emotions: desperate on the one hand to be reunited with my family, but on the other reluctant to say goodbye to this place which had become my home. It was hard to watch the clean white snow become brown and mushy, and to hear the icicles dripping and sliding from my roof, and I knew that my camp would return to its muddy, pre-winter state. It was also clear that soon travel would be impossible, as the snow was becoming thick and wet. Even walking was difficult, as my snowshoes sank through the surface to a wet slushy layer underneath, clogging the shoes and making them impossibly heavy.

It was at this point that the hard work I had done on my trails over the winter months really began to pay off, as the layers of compressed snow lasted well into the thaw. Gradually the snow levels on either side of the trails dropped down, leaving them standing sometimes three foot proud of the surface, and instead of hedged country lanes they now appeared like raised highways. I had to travel with great care – if we fell off the trail we would sink into slush many feet deep, and getting back on presented serious difficulty. The rivers too had to be treated with immense caution, as the ice was becoming unreliable. At the mouth of the slough a large lead had opened up, and I knew that in places the water below was fathoms deep with a swift current. Looking at that menacing half-acre of open water was to look into the face of death, yet I couldn't avoid the river completely as I had to get the dogs back to the village before the trails melted altogether. I decided to make the journey before sunrise, when everything that had melted during the day would be refrozen and relatively safe. Once I had returned the dogs I would then use Don's old snow machine to ferry tools and equipment back to Galena, and start packing up the cabin and making it safe from bears. Soon the woods would be seething with these bad-tempered animals, crashing about like grumpy adolescents forced to do some housework.

One morning I was outside sorting out my gear when I heard the distant sound of a snow machine. It was coming down the slough, and I knew it would be using my trail. I remembered Don's advice that, in the bush, people were by far the most dangerous visitors. Many people have been murdered in the Interior, and a body shoved through a hole in the Yukon ice will be swept away immediately, and can easily be dismissed as an accident. Following Don's advice I strapped my snowshoes on backwards, so it would look as if I was inside the cabin, then slung the 45/70 onto my back and walked away. I crossed the lake and went up into the trees on the other side where I waited, utterly concealed, yet able to clearly see my visitor. As I lurked in the resiny shadow I felt paranoid, and thought this was surely a sign that I had spent too much time on my own. I stood listening as the machine came up my portage,

Fuzzy barking loyally from his tether. The engine sounded loud and aggressive, and I felt a surge of irrational anger as I did not want anyone to invade my solitude. Yet I was also worried by my own reaction – was I going bushy? The machine drew up in front of the cabin, and the driver took off his goggles and hat. It was an Indian man, and I saw him focus on my snowshoe trail before knocking politely on the door and stepping back.

'Hello there!' I shouted, stepping out of the trees, and he raised a hand in greeting. He'd been passing along the slough trail, and had come up to have a look at the 'Scotsman in the woods'. Clearly I had become a phenomenon, like the abominable snowman or the local loony, and as we sat chatting he looked with interest around my camp. I hadn't had many visitors to my camp, but those that I had had been interesting. A few months before I was out on the lake, gathering snow, when I saw a plane fly low overhead, then bank sharply to come in and land. It hit the ice at speed, almost veering into the trees along the bank, then headed straight for us. Fuzzy and I ran for the trees, where we waited till the plane taxied over. The flimsy door was kicked open, and a native Alaskan man hopped down on to the ice and shook my hand. I was struck immediately by his face, which had been completely burnt in what must have been a terrible accident in his past. Yet even through the fearsome scars, I could see he had kind eyes, and his smile was one of the warmest I had ever seen. We walked over to the cabin and he looked at my camp with what I hoped was approval then, almost as fast as he had come, he was gone. I asked Don about him later, and he told me he'd crashed his plane years ago and escaped unhurt, but then crawled back to rescue a trapped passenger from the flames. He was terribly burned, yet managed to get the injured passenger back to the village, walking through country that many able men would have found impassable. He was clearly a brave man, and I felt privileged to have met him.

After a while we noticed that the day was warming up, and my visitor had to be on his way before the trail got too soft. I watched him go, happy to be alone again, yet knowing that I was getting far too comfortable with silence and the company of dogs. That night I fed the dogs well, and by the time the moon rose the temperature had fallen to minus thirty. The trail would be good in the early morning I thought, and decided to leave for Galena before dawn the next day.

I called home later and Juliet answered the phone, sounding breathless and happier than I had heard her for months. 'Guy! We're counting the weeks. I can't believe you're coming home!'

It was great to hear her sounding so happy, and with a sense of unreality we discussed flights and timetables. I talked to each of the boys, knowing that to them I had become an abstract notion rather than a real father. Luke particularly could have no memory of me at all, as he had been just one year old when I left, and talk of 'Daddy' to him meant photographs and a voice at the end of the phone. 'Daddy,' he said, 'Oo coming home?'

His sweet, pure voice almost brought me to my knees, and my voice was shaking when Juliet came back on the phone. 'What have we done? Why did we do it?' I asked, no longer bothering to hide the tears.

'I know – it's been so hard.' She too was crying, and it was as if we knew that now time was short we could afford to let go for the first time.

'Are we going to be okay do you think?'

'Yes of course we will – our lives will be so much better. The boys love living on Mull, and we can go to the beaches and fish and camp all summer. We'll have lots of time to catch up.'

'Do you think Luke will accept me as his father?'

She paused, and as usual gave me the truth. 'Well, it'll be strange for him at first, but he'll see how Oscar and I are with you and I'm sure it won't take long.'

My throat felt numb, and I hoped I would be able to make up for my long absence and find my way into that little boy's heart. 'I'd better go,' I said, 'I'm taking the dogs back to the village tomorrow – all the snow's melting.'

'Be careful Guy – please, please be careful. It would typical if something happened to you right at the end, and we need you to come home.'

The next morning I woke in pitch darkness at 4am. I felt both sad and excited about the journey, and as I placed each dog in its harness I felt proud that they were so strong. They strained and barked till I said 'okay', and we scythed off through the dark woods. We kept going straight past the winter portage turn, as I wanted to travel along my old portage on our last journey. The dogs moved swiftly, and as we slid along the trail I remembered the backbreaking work and fear of the early days. Back then I had never imagined that I would one day reach the river in just over five minutes, when the walk took a half hour.

Soon we were on the slough, and I let the dogs open up a bit as we flew along the frozen trail. Just before we reached the slough mouth, with no warning, Bubbles suddenly pulled the whole team to a stop. I anchored the sled and walked forward with my axe to see that five yards ahead the trail had collapsed, leaving just a thin sheet of ice below which I could see water. I tapped the ice with my axe and water gurgled through. Bubbles must have smelled the river water, and I looked back at her with deep gratitude – yet again these dogs had saved me from serious trouble. I strapped on my snowshoes and walked a detour around the little lead, carefully prodding ahead of me with my axe. Then I walked back again, stepping harder this time to compress the new trail. I got back on the sled, lifted the anchor and called 'Ha', and Bubbles gingerly placed a paw on the new trail. She sniffed the ground, and then threw herself into her harness with gusto, leading the team through the yielding, slushy snow. They bucked their way around the lead, the sled slipping and sliding behind them until we once more rejoined the firm trail.

As we proceeded the sun rose in the sky, and it was so warm now that I took off my hat and jacket and loosened my scarf. The dogs ran with wonderful power and we were making great time. Halfway through the journey I stopped to give them a long rest, as I knew there was now no danger of them getting too cold, and we all flopped down on the hard trail and lay basking in the sun. Close to Four Mile Point I looked out across the glittering expanse of the Yukon to see a silver mirage, wavering and shifting in a vast curtain that stretched across miles of river ice.* The sun was reclaiming its kingdom, and the mirage looked like a gift from the ice, as if it was begging to stay just a little longer. I smelled green everywhere and it was good to be able to breathe the invigorating air, instead of hiding below layer after layer of material.

On the outskirts of the village we passed a great fat woman picking her way across the slushy ice, leading a tiny dog that nipped about on a long leash. She was dressed entirely in black, and looked utterly out of context, as if she was walking her dog in Central Park instead of a rough little shantytown in the Interior. As she saw me approach she retracted the lead, and teetered to the side of the trail to watch my charging team pass. We shot by with a wave, and I saw that Fuzzy had stopped to greet the little pet. As I watched he lifted his leg and urinated over it, and the woman pulled back in horror. He shook his leg coolly, and, keeping his eyes on us, galloped back into position behind the team. 'I'm so sorry,' I shouted, horrified and embarrassed by Fuzzy's barbaric behaviour. 'It's okay,' she called out tremulously in return, looking down sadly at her little dog, which stood shaking and humiliated by her side. Later I discussed the incident with Don, who said that Fuzzy had been making the greatest possible display of one dog's contempt for another. As a hardened dog of the Yukon, he was showing off his macho prowess, and his total disdain for this animal that he clearly considered a disgrace to his species. Who says snobbery is a human failing?

In no time at all we were up the dyke and clattering along the road. When we reached Glenn's dog yard I braked, and a stream of ice and snow shot up behind me as we slithered to a stop. I held the dogs on the brake, wanting to prolong our last journey for just a moment longer. They looked back at me questioningly, tails wagging and tongues lolling as if to ask what next, but I knew our journeys had come to an end.

I unhooked the dogs and tethered them back beside their old

---

* Mirages are caused by temperature inversion, and in this case cold air lying under warm air caused the light to bend towards the cold air, making the landscape appear to hover above its true location.

running mates in Glenn's yard. Then I walked back to the sled and picked up the gangline, which lay lifeless like a piece of useless old rope. I rolled it around the sled's handlebar and then put the whole lot in the steel container where everything was stored. I had been on the sled for so long that walking felt strange, like a sailor who steps onto the quayside after a long passage. I cooked up some dog-pot and fed the dogs, giving them extra portions as a reward for their long journey. Then I shuffled over to the edge of the yard to look at them one last time. Lefty was in his box, but I could just see his grizzled nose poking out as he leaned out to look at me surreptitiously. Bubbles sat quietly amidst the chaos of the yard, looking at me with steady, intelligent eyes. In all the journeys we had made together she had never let me down, and she was the bravest, most willing dog I had ever known. Beside her, and trotting about as ever, was the unstoppable Sprite. Even after a hard thirty-mile run along a slushy trail she still had energy to burn. At the far end of the yard Blackie had jumped on to the roof of her box and sat neatly, gazing at me with gentle eyes. I remembered her two frozen pups, and how she would irritate us all with her incessant howls and barks whenever we stopped, such was her drive to run. Nearest to me, Spot and Brownie sat staring, ready as ever to leap into action if required. I raised a hand and said goodbye, and then turned away. I would never forget those dogs, and as I walked through the quiet village I fervently hoped they would each have good and long lives. Our silvery sled lines were all melting into the earth now, but I knew they would be forever etched in my heart.

44

THIN ICE AND THE DEATH OF A SHE-WOLF

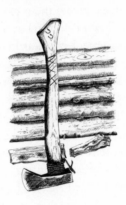

I spent the next couple of weeks ferrying borrowed tools and equipment back to the village using Don's old snow machine. The river was thawing fast, and I travelled either at night or in the early morning to make the most of the cold, towing the wooden sled behind me with a canvas cover tightly covering its load. After many repetitive journeys I finally got everything back to the family and then returned to see out my last few weeks. I set out in the evening, and left the village beneath a huge yellow moon that whitened as it rose. Ahead of me the river trail stood out perfectly above the snow that had sunk all around. The temperature was minus thirty, and I knew it would be colder still in the river basin.

As I reached the lowest point on the trail, where it passes down from a sandbar onto the river ice, I felt the cold tighten around me, gripping at my clothes as if trying to find a way in. I was just thinking that this would be the coldest and worst possible place to break down, when there was a loud crack, and I saw something shoot out the side of the engine. I immediately lost power and slid to a heart-rending stop, then sat for a moment in complete disbelief. Was it some kind of cruel joke?

A profound silence descended, magnifying the loneliness of my situation, and I looked up at the moon, which no longer looked beautiful, but merciless. I lifted the plastic bonnet and peered at the engine, and Fuzzy leaned intelligently by my side, looking first at the engine and then back at me. His eyes were full of righteous indignation; he was clearly unhappy that the metal dog was disobeying me. I saw immediately that the fan belt had snapped, and with relief remembered that I had packed a spare. I slipped off my gloves and reached down to remove the remnants of the broken belt, and my hand stuck immediately to the frigid metal. Cursing, I pulled my hand off, swearing as the skin ripped away, then stood up and pulled my gloves back on. After some tinkering the new belt was fitted, and I pulled the starter cord, but the engine didn't start. I tried several times, each time with no luck, and the moon seemed to grow brighter, as if to accentuate my agony. I looked up angrily – it was as if I was being deliberately set up, and not for the first time I wondered if a malevolent force was at work.

I unscrewed the spark plug and removed the carbon, then opened the fuel cap and dipped the plug in, wetting the contact with petrol. I closed the bonnet and looked up at the icy stars. I said a silent prayer, and this time when I pulled the starter the machine juddered reluctantly into life. I climbed on, calling Fuzzy to jump up in front of me, and gently accelerated.

Eventually we entered the slough, where I made Fuzzy run behind for a while as I knew he was getting cold. I kept my eyes fixed ahead, imagining a crackling stove and coffee with a dash of whisky, and was so deep in thought that at first I barely noticed the wolf. It was running ahead of me on the trail, but I could see immediately that it was badly lame, and would skip along for a few paces before falling over and struggling to its feet again. I could see that its rear leg was dragging behind it, shattered and useless like jelly wrapped in leather. I speeded up until I was about thirty yards behind the wolf, and it tried to run but then stopped and yelped with pain. The injury was probably the result of a kick from a moose, as now the thaw had started the wolves no longer had the upper hand. Earlier they had the advantage as they could run along the surface while the moose floundered in deep snow, but now the tables had turned, and it was far harder for them to avoid a devastating kick.

My heart went out to the wolf, who was clearly frightened and in terrible pain, and I reacted as I would when I came across a terminally wounded animal back at home. Forgetting that I was not dealing with a rabbit with myxomatosis or a run over bird, but rather with a powerful wild animal that could easily kill me, I turned the engine off and looked behind me at the sled, then realised that I had not packed the 45/70, which would have been ideal for the job. All I had was a .357 magnum loaded with 200 grain rounds, and this hung at the front of the snow machine just in case I had to shoot a moose or bear at close range. I pulled the revolver out and shot at the wolf, and it hobbled away, yelping in pain. I missed, and missed again several times, as I was not at all experienced at shooting handguns, but my last shot stopped the animal, and it sat down on the ice.

By now I was feeling pretty desperate – I had no more bullets, but I knew the animal was still alive, and I had to finish the job. My eyes fell upon my boy's axe strapped to the side of the machine, and I took a deep breath and unhooked it. I walked quickly towards the wolf, turning the axe to strike it hard with the heavy back of the blade. The wolf began to growl with a ferocity that made the most vicious dog look like a kitten by comparison. Beneath that cold moon I saw teeth flashing as black gums drew back in a great snarl.

It was then that I realised how naïve I had been: this was no rabbit or half-dead pheasant flapping beside the road. I was face-to-face with a wounded and cornered wolf, the worst of all possible encounters, and I should have left well alone. I wondered if there was any way out, but I was frightened to turn my back. Just then the wolf launched itself at me with a horrible snarling sound. I hit out hard with my axe, landing the blow square on the wolf's head and it fell back, stunned. For a fraction of a second it lay still, and I wondered if it was dead, until it began to struggle to its feet. Before it could get up I delivered two more blows to the head, and this time knew I had killed it. I walked over, still clutching my axe and trembling with shock, and saw it was a female. I felt overpowered by sadness at the sight of the mangy creature. Before her injury she would have been sleek and strong. Now she was terribly thin, unable to hunt, and destined by her injury for a slow, painful death.

I loaded the wolf's body into the sled. In the morning I would set up the satellite phone to call the Alaska Fish and Game Service and report the incident. Had I done the right thing? From the wolf's point of view it was maybe better than a slow death from starvation. From my own point of view it had been foolhardy. I had allowed myself to forget the danger of a wounded animal. I thought of Juliet pleading with me to be careful in these last weeks, and realised that on this occasion I had been anything but.

Life was becoming distinctly less arduous, as I had acclimatised to cold temperatures and thus consumed much less wood. At minus fifteen I would wander about in not much more than a t-shirt. For water I would simply amble down to the slough and dig until I reached the layer of clean thawed snow that lay between the river ice and the snow above. I was feeling very relaxed and comfortable with my surroundings, and had forgotten Don's words of warning about being overconfident. I had also forgotten the importance of listening to my instincts.

Searching for relief from the monotony of beaver and grouse meat my mind had turned vaguely to fishing, and one morning I decided to head down the slough to look around. I started the Tundra easily and passed slowly down my old portage, before turning into the winter portage where the trail was slumping away. I came down off the bank and on to the river, and immediately had an incredibly strong urge to turn back – so strong that I actually turned the machine, making a nice arc in the snow. Overruling my instincts however, and telling myself not to be stupid I completed the circle and carried on. Geese lifted from little pools of snowmelt as I charged along the slough, following the faint outline of a trail that I had not used for months. Suddenly the snow machine slowed down, and I felt a kind of juddering. I looked back at the trail behind me, and where my tracks should have been saw dark, sinister water opening up instead. I knew immediately that this was river water, not run-off or snowmelt, and that it would be deep. 'Shit!' I shouted, realising that the ice had been breaking behind me, and I hadn't heard it over the roar of the engine. Then before I could do anything the ice ahead of me gave way completely, and the machine and I plunged into the water. Some snow machines are so powerful that they can plane across water, and many a life has been saved by their power. The old Tundra was no match for this however, and lurched forwards, turning to the right. With a sickening jolt I realised that it was going to be swept beneath the ice, taking me with it.

I let go of the snow machine and jumped towards the unbroken ice, and in the process felt my ankle give a painful click. The ice broke under my weight, and I fell into the freezing water. The shock hit me hard, and I felt the strong current pulling at my legs. So this is what it feels like to go under, I thought, part of me feeling strangely detached as I held desperately on to the edge of the ice. I reached down to grab my knife from my pocket, and, stretching as far away as possible, jabbed it firmly into solid ice. Then I pulled my second knife out and did the same. With immense effort, I pulled myself up on the knives' handles, spreading my weight and trying to be as light as possible. When I was finally lying flat on my stomach I lay still for a moment, shocked and sodden, before gradually starting to slither away.

When I reached solid ice I turned to see the snow machine bobbing on its side on the fast current. By some miracle it had caught on the downstream end of the hole, but I knew it would soon sink. I had to release my snowshoes, which were tied to the machine and acting like a rudder in the current, so I slithered carefully over and cut them free. I put them on, wincing when I tried my weight on my ankle, and limped over to the more solid ice in the middle of the slough. I wore the shoes unlaced just in case I fell through again, as snowshoes are deadly in deep water. Fortunately I hadn't thrown all caution to the wind, and was still carrying my pack of survival essentials, including a change of clothing. I changed into dry clothes, teeth chattering and shaking as I did so, and then dug out my little stove and brewed tea. All the time I was cursing myself for being so stupid. I had done exactly what Don had told me never to do, and travelled close to the river edge, where the ice was thin and likely to break first.

When I had drunk some tea I dragged myself up the steep snowy riverbank, and then cut some lengths of cottonwood which I planned to use to lever the machine out. Returning to the hole, I slipped them under the heavy machine and heaved as much as I dared, but it just wouldn't budge. I gave up eventually, and pushed a few more boughs underneath to ensure that it wouldn't sink. Then I started the long, painful walk back to camp.

Each step sent a jolt of pain through me, my right knee now hurting as well as my ankle, but I had no alternative but to keep going slowly for as long as it took. After a while I heard the sound of a plane overhead, and looking up recognised Brad's little Cub. The plane swooped down low above me, a guardian angel of canvas and birch, and I could see Brad peering down. He lifted and waggled his wings, then banked and came in to land.

He opened the door of the plane. 'Guy Grieve! Is that your hole in the ice that I've just flown over?'

'I'm afraid so.' I hung my head in shame.

'You okay?'

'Fine apart from my right knee and left ankle.'

He laughed. 'Well something made me fly back this way today – guess I just wanted to see what you were up to, then I saw the hole and followed your tracks.' His face turned serious. 'You came close there I think – can I do anything for you?'

Waves of shame washed over me as I asked him to tell Don what had happened, and that the snow machine was stuck in the river.

'I'll do that,' he said. 'You be careful.' He pulled the door shut, then taxied round and took off. I watched him go, knowing this had been my closest brush with death yet, and I was very lucky to be alive.

Five painful hours later I finally made it back to the cabin. My ankle was swollen to the size of a grapefruit, but I didn't care, as I knew I'd got off lightly. I felt terribly guilty about Don's snow machine, and set up the satellite phone to call him.

'We're comin' out tonight when it's all frozen up,' he said, 'Chris'll come up and collect you.'

I felt ashamed. 'God, I'm so sorry about all this, and about the Tundra – I hope it'll be okay.'

He interrupted: 'Ain't nothin' more important than living. I don't give a shit about that machine as long as you're in one piece. But you know, I warned you about getting too confident. Still, you're lucky – looks like someone was watching out for you.'

It was snowing when Chris arrived, and he gave me a bottle of beer that he had kept warm in his jacket. I jumped on to the back of the machine and we drove down to the slough where Don was waiting. Not once did either of them make me feel guilty, and I realised this was because their priorities were right. Life came before anything else. We managed to get the machine out and loaded on to a sled behind one of their machines. Don walked over. 'You came close to buying the farm there,' he said.

'I know.' I dropped my head, feeling ashamed. 'I really chuffed up.'

'Well you were travelling in exactly the wrong place on the river. You never travel along the sides – that's where the bad ice will be. If you have to go over you got to cross it fast and at right angles, or better still travel way up on the bank – even if there's deep snow, you just go slower.'

'Thanks Don,' I mumbled. 'You're right.'

He reached into his pocket and brought out a chocolate bar, which he pushed into my hand. 'Now don't beat yourself up about it,' he said. 'You know what?'

'What?' I said sadly

'We've all done it. And I'll tell you something else, those that have lived to tell the tale have never travelled on the ice hoping for the best since. You've been lucky enough to learn a lesson through experience – now don't you ever forget it.' He shook my hand in his iron grip then turned back to Chris. 'Let's move!' he shouted, and they were off into the snowstorm. I turned and started hobbling home, knowing that I had miles of shuffling ahead, but I didn't care. Then I heard the sound of a snow machine, and Chris pulled up behind me.

'Hey, I forgot you,' he said. 'Hop on – I'll take you up the portage.'

I shook my head. 'It's okay, Chris. Thanks, but I'm fine.'

'Guy, just get on the fucking machine.'

I climbed gratefully on, and we shot off towards the cabin in a whirl of snow. When we got there he took a swig of Highland Park from the bottle, then turned the machine round ready to go. 'Hey, you know what?' he shouted over the noise of the engine.

'What?' I called back.

'You should get your bear boards up, then stop over for a bit before you go.'

'I might just take you up on that Chris – thank you.'

That night I thought again about Don and his family, wondering what lucky star had led me to them. Today's events had proved once again that friendship was an essential ingredient of survival in the lonely Interior, and when I thought back to my idea of existing completely alone and isolated from everyone it seemed ridiculous. Together, Don, Chris and Charlie had over 130 years of living in the sub arctic, and as well as adding greatly to my whole experience they had taught me almost everything I knew. Don was right – never again would I ignore my instincts, or forget how utterly small and insignificant I was.

45
BEAR BOARDS

A week or so later my ankle had healed, and it was time to close up the cabin. I collected the rolls of insulation and plywood that I had stored for the roof, and piled them inside the cabin, knowing that some day Charlie would put on a proper roof. It was early April, and bears were much in evidence again. The day before I returned the dogs I had encountered a large grizzly. He was on the bank of the slough above my trail, just opposite the mouth of Bishop creek, and stood up on his hind legs to get a good look at me. He was huge, and the low sun shone on his fur, still dark after months of slumber. I stopped the sled and stared, marvelling at the immensity of the beast and imagining what would happen if he charged with an intent to kill. The dogs stayed completely silent, cowering in their harnesses, and there was no cheeky barking and howling now. The sight and smell of that great predator was lodged in all our genetic memories, and our instincts told us to be submissive and still. I had heard horrific accounts of grizzlies attacking sled teams, and ripping dogs from their harnesses, snapping their spines and crushing their skulls, and leaving the musher till last. Glenn had told me a story that particularly stuck in my mind, about a musher who came across a grizzly in early winter. The animal worked its way through his team, snapping the dogs' spines as it approached. He had sunk to his knees behind his sled and was gripping his snow anchor, wishing he had packed his shotgun. As the dogs lay dying, the bear approached the helpless man. It pushed its snout right onto his chest and inhaled deeply, dog blood and saliva dripping from its mouth. The musher sat still, waiting to die, but then at the last moment was saved by one of his wheel dogs. Somehow the dog managed to stagger to its feet and attack the bear from behind, causing it to turn away from the man. After dealing with the dog, it seemed to forget about him, and disappeared into the bush. He had a lucky escape.

All this ran through my mind in a split second, and I stood still, uncertain of what to do. I considered simply lifting the brake and shooting off, but knew that the bear could run at least as fast as we could, and didn't want to risk triggering his chase instinct. Between the bear and the sled there was deep, wind-blown snow and a dense belt of willow, and I knew this would slow him down if he charged, giving me time to grab the 45/70. But the only thing holding my sled still was my footbrake, and to reach the rifle I would need to step off it, whereupon the dogs would shoot off. To reach my gun I would need to set the snow anchor, and this would take two hands – one to hold the sled and the other to reach for the anchor and drop it into position ready to be stamped down. This would take valuable time, and might trigger the grizzly to charge. It was stalemate, and I prayed that the creature wouldn't charge. Seven dogs, one man and a grizzly stared at one another for several minutes. I heard the cries of ravens overhead, and out of the corner of my eye saw them settling heavily in the cotton-woods, like diners arriving early at their table. Suddenly the bear turned away from us, and, dropping on to all fours, bounded off with cat-like speed. A tide of relief flowed over me, and I stood with trembling knees, waiting until he was long gone before letting off the brake. When I came back along my trail a few hours later, it occurred to me that he might be lying in wait, so I levered a round into the rifle's breach and carried it slung over my shoulder, ready for a quick series of shots if necessary. Thankfully he was nowhere to be seen, and the dogs flew past and down on to the river.

The grizzly encounter made me nervous, as I knew that my thawing camp was omitting a range of smells that would be an absolute magnet to bears. I had to get some bear boards up, or pretty soon they would come knocking at my door. I also had to get back to the village before it thawed any more, as soon the river would be impossible for travel, and would remain that way for many weeks.

Bear boards are simply lengths of wood with scores of long nails sticking through. They are fixed over the windows and doorways of vacant cabins with the nails pointing outwards, in the hope of deterring curious bears from breaking and entering. Bears are like the worst kind of party guests, and if they ever do manage to get into a cabin they will completely trash the place. First they will eat every-thing – from packets of sugar to soap – and then they will proceed to defecate all over the cabin before ripping the place to bits. The sickly smell of a bear is almost impossible to get rid of, and sometimes there's no choice but to abandon the cabin altogether after such a visit.

I nailed the bear boards securely up, and then stepped back to look at the place. One thing was certain, there could have been no more final way of saying goodbye to my little log home. I had decided that a fitting end to my time here would be to spend one last night alone beneath the stars, and I snowshoed across the lake and walked on until I reached an area of black spruce trees beneath the mountain which formed a kind of natural amphitheatre. I found a suitable spot for my shelter, where two thin trees grew close together, forming a natural doorway ninety degrees to the prevailing wind. I half cut one tree at about four feet, and then bent it across and tied it to the other before snowshoeing my length back from the doorway to create a floor. I covered the floor with spruce boughs, and then set up a ridgepole which rested on top of the bent tree. Next I attached two purlins, which stretched back from the doorway, and laid sticks all over the frame. Finally I thatched the shelter with spruce boughs, and finished it off with a layer of snow. The result was a snug A-frame shelter: windproof and warm and imbued with the invigorating perfume of spruce.*

* See Notes.

In front of the shelter I laid a platform of green boughs, on top of which I lit a slow-burning fire. In the hot downwind zone beside the fire I melted snow through a sheet, whilst brewing Italian coffee in a fruit tin hung from a pole. That night I snuggled deep into my yielding green shelter, and despite a temperature of minus twenty outside slept only in my bivvy bag. A yellow moon hung low, and as I blew out my candle a gentle wind sighed through the trees and owls hooted mournfully. I felt completely content at that moment, and a great sense of privilege again washed over me.

I woke early the next day to see the spring sunshine streaming across a perfect blue sky. Oats and then strong coffee recharged my batteries, and I packed my bag and headed for the slough. I needed to return to the village before the snow crust began to melt on my trails, which would have left me stuck. Even so, when I reached my lake I couldn't resist pausing to look at the beaver house, and walked up to my cabin to say a last goodbye. The nails glinted in the morning light, and the boarded-up door made a forlorn sight. I stood staring at the honey-coloured logs, thinking that each round told a story, and every notch held a joke or the memory of some ache or pain. I remembered the months of hard work and the times of fear and hopelessness, and also the moments of utter freedom and joy when I knew that I had discovered the ideal existence for my spirit. There was no denying it: I had built a cabin in the wilderness, the dream had become reality and I had survived.

I drove slowly down my portage, savouring every sight and sound and trying to fix it in my mind forever. As I went I thought of the well-known lines by Robert Frost:

> *I shall be telling this with a sigh*
> *Somewhere ages and ages hence:*
> *Two roads diverged in a wood, and I –*
> *I took the one less travelled by,*
> *And that has made all the difference.**

By the time I reached the outskirts of Galena my face was wet with tears and snowmelt.

* Robert Frost, *The Road Not Taken*

46

WELL HELLO – TO THE MAN IN THE DRESS

It was the end of April, and I had just one week left in Alaska which I spent mooching about from house to house. Playing with the children was less painful now as I knew I would soon be reunited with my own. It was also good simply to sit in the sun beside Don's smokehouse, watching the birds returning and filling the sky with their calls where so recently there had been frozen silence. Now my calls home were full of happiness and excitement, and the past months of worry and fear were gone. I was coming home.

A couple of days before I was due to leave, Chris asked me along to a dance in a village called Ruby, fifty-four miles upriver. That night we left the village on two very powerful snow machines, accompanied by some of his friends. All were indigenous Alaskans, and had been driving snow machines since childhood. The trail was frozen and jagged, and after crossing the river the party shot off at enormous speed, until all I could see were distant tail lights. I followed, jolting over icy bumps and then lurching down into dips in a hideous, bone-jarring rhythm, dreading the fifty or so miles that lay ahead. This was a whole different kind of snow machining from what I'd been used to, and night travel Alaskan style was not for the faint hearted. After a while the party stopped for a drink, and I caught them up.* I took a swig of rum, telling them that I was going to fall apart with all the bumps on the trail, and they laughed. 'You go too slow,' a beefy relative of Chris's said: 'You gotta go faster – then you'll fly over all them bumps.'

I took his advice, and made a breakthrough. Now I was travelling at seventy to eighty miles per hour – still slower than the rest, but fast enough to avoid feeling every bump and depression. I skimmed over the surface, exhilarated by the speed and the cold, rushing air.

Two hours later we saw the lights of Ruby approaching, and it reminded me of coming into Tobermory, the main town on the Isle of Mull, from the sea. We paused for another shot of rum, and then thundered on towards town. Set on a hilltop, Ruby is a beautiful village, almost entirely made up of log cabins. It started as a gold boomtown, with a population of over 20,000 that dropped almost to nothing when the gold was exhausted, and now stands around three hundred. Chris and I separated from the rest of the party, and rattled up a steep ice road to a fine log house where we would be sleeping that night. We were greeted at the door by a burly friend of Chris's named Jay, who I could see immediately was wild and rebellious. He had been brought up in a little family mining camp far up a lonely creek, and proved to be great fun.†

Jay's wife Ginger was also a colourful character. She was an amazing cook and as bright as a button, and Jay too, try as he might, could not hide the sharp intelligence that lay beneath his

---

* Drinking whilst driving snow machines is one of the main causes of death amongst young people in Alaska. Laws do exist to restrict drinking and driving, but with lawmen thin on the ground most people happily flout them.

† Gold miners still work the rivers and creeks of the Interior, but mainly collect dust rather than nuggets, and rarely make their fortunes as in days gone by. Now they are more like farmers, working hard all year round for a fairly reliable annual income.

rough exterior. They welcomed us in, and before I knew it Jay had poured me an immense glass of whisky. Across the room, Chris raised his eyebrows at me, looking like John Belushi – clearly there would be no shortage of booze tonight, as Ginger owned the liquor store.

'So, we all goin' to the dance tonight?' Jay slumped on to the sofa with a grin.

'Yup.' Ginger turned around, beaming and clutching an immense bottle of something lethal. 'That okay with you Guy? You're the guest.'

'I'm looking forward to it,' I said. 'I thought I'd wear my kilt.'

Everyone fell silent, and Chris looked concerned. 'Do you think that's a good idea?' he asked.

'Why not? I'd wear it to a ceilidh back home.'

Chris looked at Jay as if about to protest further, but then shrugged. 'Sure, why not.'

Several drinks later I strapped on the tartan and we shot down the hill. Chris and Jay stopped to talk to friends, and I walked alone towards the log hall. A group of teenagers were standing by the entrance, and they turned to look at me as I approached. I raised a hand in greeting, and before I knew it was surrounded by a mass of bored and very drunk young men. 'Why you wearing a dress, man?' one shouted loudly, and I was momentarily stumped, as I expected everyone to recognise that it was a kilt. I told them that I was a visitor from Scotland, and that the 'dress' was in fact a kilt. A strange, yeasty silence settled over the crowd, and the atmosphere felt distinctly unwelcoming.

'Well . . . nice talking to you,' I said, stepping with short-lived relief into the hall, where everything ground to a halt. The mournful band, made up of men who would look more at home holding shotguns than guitars, stopped in mid-tune, and there was a stunned silence. Then the singer leaned into the microphone and said, 'Well hello . . . to the man in the dress'. I raised a hand in feeble greeting, beginning to feel nervous, and sat down beside some elderly native Alaskans. They recognised the kilt, as they had seen Scottish miners during their childhood, and I began to feel a bit better as I talked to them. Then to my amazement a rough-looking adolescent boy approached and dropped his gloves on to my lap.

'Hold these,' he instructed arrogantly, as he put his jacket on. I was stunned by his rudeness, and wondered at the cause, but then realised that he was treating he was treating me as he would a woman, because I was wearing a 'dress'. I felt a twinge of rage.

'I don't want your bloody gloves,' I said, and stuffed them back into his pocket.

He stared at me woozily, clearly trying to look threatening, and I stood up, feeling it might be time to go.

Just then a woman came forward: 'It's great that you've come in your national costume,' she said. 'So good for the kids to meet a man from another culture.' I thanked her, holding back a sardonic laugh at the very thought that the kids might be interested. Sure enough, a few minutes later a large group of very drunk young men appeared, and began circling me like a pack of wolves. One of them started talking to me, and I relaxed a little, but then after a few minutes he fixed me with a playground stare.

'Stop looking at me like that,' he said threateningly.

'But I'm speaking to you – I have to look at you,' I said, in what I hoped was a calming voice.

I watched with fascination as his face moved through a range of expressions, from a death's head grin to black rage and then total blankness. 'I really feel like killing someone tonight,' he said eventually through gritted teeth.

'Well why don't you start with one of your friends over there,' I suggested, and he stalked back to the group. They stood muttering, casting occasional glances towards me, and I decided not to hang around any longer. You don't take any chances on a fight when your opponents are likely to be armed, and I was feeling distinctly jumpy. I glanced around for Chris, and noticed an immensely fat man leering over at me. He was clutching a gallon jug of rum, and it was clear that he had no problem with the idea of a man in a dress – on the contrary, he looked far too friendly. Scenes from *Deliverance* played through my mind, and I decided to abandon Chris and go. On the way out I bumped into the little tough boy again, who glared at me narrow-eyed and muttered a few more threats. I pushed past him and made my way outside. I stood by my snow machine, relieved to have escaped the claustrophobic surroundings of the village hall, but then noticed that the fat man had followed me out. He stood silently watching me, grinning spookily, until I pointed my finger and told him to get lost. He turned back reluctantly, and suddenly I felt sorry for him and all the other gormless hard lads that I had had the displeasure to meet. The next day I learned that the boy who had threatened me was carrying a 9mm hand gun. The whole episode proved yet again that my most dangerous encounters in Alaska had been with humans, not animals, and that the safest place for me out here was the wilderness.

The next morning Jay took Chris and I along the river to some hidden hot springs that only he knew about, and we lay back in the perfect hot water, staring up at a celestial forest of snow-bent birch trees. We stayed there for hours, singing and chatting and swigging from cans of beer while I enjoyed my first proper hot soak for over ten months. We flew back along the snowy river at top speed, and I saw green sun-dogs on either side of the setting sun.* I felt happy and free, thinking of my children and the risks we had taken as a family. The next day I would be leaving to go back to my old life, only it was a new life, and nothing would ever be the same.

---

* Sun dogs are caused by the bending of the sun's light by ice crystals, whose flat sides refract the light as they fall through the sky. They appear when the sun is low in the sky, and on the same horizontal plane as the observer and the ice crystals.

47
I SHALL BE TELLING THIS WITH A SIGH

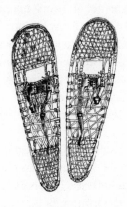

'So, what you gonna do with him?' Don nodded at Fuzzy, who sat with his tongue lolling, ready for orders. I leaned down and rubbed his ears, and he raised his snout and growled gently.

'Can I leave him with you?'

Don nodded slowly. 'Yeah, leave the little guy in my yard for a bit. He can have Pancho's old box till I get another.' We both looked at the little dog in silence for a moment. 'He sure had a great time out there with you,' Don smiled. 'Kinda won his spurs, wouldn't you say?'

'He certainly did.' I gazed down at the little dog sadly, wishing I could take him with me, but he would have to be in quarantine for six months before he could enter the UK. 'Do you think I could come back and fetch him?'

'Well sure, you know we'll always be here. And if it all goes pear-shaped, you know you've got a place here too.'

I looked over at the grizzled, kind man, who had taught me more than he would ever know, and felt bereft at the thought of leaving this family that I had grown to love. The feeling was bittersweet.

Soon I would be wrapped within the sweetness of my own. Yet for just a moment I wished the world were smaller. I called Fuzzy over to Pancho's box and he shot across, raising a paw and looking up at me excitedly as if to say, 'Right boss, what next? Are we going downriver? I'm ready!'

'Not this time Fuzzy, I'm sorry,' I said, and knelt down and clipped the light chain to his collar. I sunk my hands into his blonde shaggy coat and said 'Well, fruitcake, I'm off. You behave and I'll see you soon if luck allows it.' I stood up slowly, keeping my eyes fixed on his, and then took a step back. He jumped up and barked shrilly, leaping on his back legs and pawing the air, and it was clear that he knew I was leaving him for good. Tears pricked and I turned quickly away to begin loading my bags on to the back of Don's pick-up.

Leaving Fuzzy felt like a betrayal, after all we had been through together. As I drove out of the yard I could still hear his high-pitched barking, and I remembered how hopeless he had seemed in the beginning, and then the turning point when I had realised his strength of character. I thought of the time that he dragged the huge moose leg back to camp, of him guarding the camp and running tirelessly behind the sled. We had relied on each other, and now I had abandoned him. I felt terrible.

At the airstrip I met Charlie, who shook my hand. 'Well, you sure made it,' he said. 'No drunk Indians got a chance to shoot you or anything – so you done good!' We laughed, and I thanked him sincerely for all he had done. I would see Don and the rest of the family for the last time in Anchorage the next morning, as they were all going to a family wedding in the south, and would be passing through the airport while I was waiting for the connecting flight to New York.

The plane that had once felt so small now felt immense in comparison to Brad's tiny canvas Cub. It lifted up high over the great brown river, and I looked out over thousands upon thousands of square miles of wilderness, which had looked so alien when I first arrived, but now were familiar. I remembered a time that I had been siwashing in an open area of snow, and was sitting beside my breakfast fire, sipping from a tin, when a large private plane flew overhead. It circled me a couple of times, curious faces peering out through the windows, and I thought how extraordinary it must seem to see a man on his own, drinking from a silver tin beside a spruce shelter and surrounded, seemingly, by nothing. How differently it might have turned out I thought, and remembered Don telling me what happened to the man who had arrived around the same time that I did. He had also planned to spend the winter living alone in the woods, but had been inadequately prepared, and refused to take advice from local people. A few months later a plane spotted a rough SOS that he had marked out in the snow with spruce boughs, and rescuers found him emaciated and frightened, freezing in a cheap canvas tent with no food. He had undoubtedly been foolhardy, but I felt sad rather than smug, and incredibly grateful for my good luck.

The next morning I checked in for the flight to New York, and then went to find the family, who were standing around in a highly polished concourse beside the airline desks. It was strange to see them all without the river behind them, and as I walked towards them I felt I was going to be unable to say goodbye. I hugged Claudette and Jenny, two girls who I wished could have been my sisters, and then Carol, whose stern exterior had turned out to conceal a heart of gold. I said goodbye to each of the children in turn, and with each one the pain welled higher, until last of all I came to Don. 'Good luck,' he said, pressing a piece of river-washed jade into my hand, and I hugged this man who had become a father and friend in that lonely wilderness. He had been patient, kind and even indulgent towards this stranger who came with nothing, yet hoping to learn everything, and he had done more for me than he would ever know. I looked around at them all for a moment, struggling to find the words to articulate what I was feeling, but then couldn't stand it any more and turned to leave. I walked away fast towards the check-in, then found Chris walking alongside me as I struggled to hold back tears. He had become like a brother in the past few months, and when we said goodbye I hugged him too. When I had passed through security I looked back, and saw that Don, ever the woodsman, had followed, and was watching from higher ground while the rush and chaos from which I had run almost a year ago swallowed me up. I closed my eyes as the plane lifted and thought of home, thanking fortune that I had survived. I thought of the huge, silent, wild place that had been my home, and told myself that it was over, over, over.

At New York airport I felt stunned by the sheer hectic chaos of it all, yet something unexpected was happening. Far from resenting the large numbers of people swarming around me, I was enthralled. For seven hours I sat on a shiny steel chair in an airport café, smiling at anyone who looked my way. In the bathroom I turned on the tap, smiling at the luxury of hot water without having to cut wood or gather snow. I stared into the mirror and saw that I was still the same, intact, and nothing had been lost except the part of me that believed he knew it all. The wilderness had taught me the importance of humility, and that residue of certainty from my childish years had gone, but somehow I felt stronger as a result.

As the airport swarmed with busy people preparing to rush across the surface of the earth, I passed a middle-aged Korean woman cleaning the floor. She smiled politely, and then bent to push the mop along the marble aisle, looking through the windows of the many shops as she did so. I wondered what dreams had brought her to America, and suspected that, like me, she would have known little about the reality. How lucky I was that the reality of Alaska had held far more than my dreaming mind could ever have predicted.

My attention turned to some silver-haired men who were glued to a television sitting on a bar. They were watching a game of baseball, and stared at the screen with child-like openness, wide-eyed and lost as they watched the men in pyjamas run around bases in the sand. The sight seemed to me to encapsulate all the strengths and weaknesses of America in one moment: that naïvity and innocence that comes from being cut off from the rest of the world, and can lead to hopeless misconceptions of other people and appalling heavy-handedness. Yet by the same token, there also comes a child's ability to take dreams and dreamers seriously, instead of stamping them down with clever cynicism. I had been lucky that my first steps in the wilderness had been taken in a land that celebrated dreamers and travellers, and that I had encountered at first hand the greatest American of them all: the land. John Muir walked through wild parts of America, bringing rich tales back to his home in Scotland, and countless near-perfect books or works of art owe their power to the central character, America. Even if it would prove to be just once in my life, I was so lucky to have been granted the privilege of living simply and without clutter, free of the many artificial concerns that flood our daily lives, and thus closer to the untouched truth. So many of our good natural instincts are smothered by society, and much of our daily lives are directed by false goals, dictated to us by others. Even in this day and age, with our sophisticated technology and developed culture, it must still be important, just occasionally, to find a wild place, where the land and the animals that move through it speak loudest, and the sun and the moon dictate the rhythm of our lives. Only through this can we remember our proper place in the order of things.

That night I left America as Juliet drove with the children through the Highlands to Glasgow, where my plane would land at 7am the next morning. I sat by the window, replaying image after image of my adventure, and remembering the ups and the downs with equal clarity. As the stewardess handed me a cup of coffee, flashing me a bright smile, I was far away, standing beneath the branches of the frozen birch trees and listening as they rubbed and chimed together in the frozen air. The cabin lights dimmed and I recalled the blizzards that had wrapped me in a cloak of fear, and how I had held the sled tight, trusting that Bubbles would find her way home. I thought of the faces of Don and his family, and of Fuzzy, and wondered if I would ever see them again. I remembered when Don had showed me an atlas of satellite images of the world at night. He flattened out the pages, and with a calloused finger traced the lines and clusters of bright garish light. Britain showed more or less as one big light, so dense is its population, and I had felt waves of claustrophobia as I realised that was my home.

The far north showed as a vast tract of darkness, with only the flare of an occasional forest fire. I thought of the wind singing through the pine cones high in the swaying spruce forests, and swore never to forget my time alone in one of the last sacred dark places of the earth.

The next morning I lifted the plastic window screen and saw the sun rising from the east. It was a beautiful clear dawn, and dark night clouds were still strewn across a pale, duck egg blue sky. 'Good morning ladies and gentlemen,' said the pilot, 'We are now approaching Scotland. Those of you on the left of the plane will have a good view of the islands of the Inner Hebrides, and particularly Mull, which is immediately below.'

I couldn't believe it – I was coming home at last. I craned my neck to look down on the island, and saw the Ross of Mull lying purple in a sea that was being touched by the pale dawn light. I thought of my mother, wrapped up and snug in her bed at her home in Tobermory, and wondered how she must be feeling to know that her son was coming home. And then I thought of Juliet, and the atmosphere there must have been in our car as she drove to the airport with the children.

At Glasgow airport I walked through the corridors to the arrivals lounge in a daze, and they were waiting for me. Oscar was standing with his arms around Juliet's leg, watching eagerly for the first sight of me, and in her arms was Luke, chubby and curious and waiting to see this 'daddy' that Oscar kept talking about. I stood looking at the three of them for a moment. They looked excited, happy and just a bit anxious, and like the most beautiful thing I had ever seen. Only as we embraced, and Oscar and Luke clung to me with all of their strength, did I know that we were safe again. My days as a loner were over, and I knew I was exactly where I should be. People around us stared at the sight of a man with snowshoes tied to his bag, hugging his family and wrapped in tears and smiles of disbelief and joy. It must have looked as if I had survived a disaster, and in many ways I had.

We got in the car and drove towards the Highlands, passing through the grey Glaswegian commuting traffic, which reminded me of that world I had so hated, and then on through landscape that grew gradually more beautiful and remote. At Oban we boarded the ferry for Mull, and sat together in silence as it took us towards the island where Juliet had grown up, and the place that had kept my family going during the hardest, darkest months. I held the boys in my arms and buried my nose in their hair, breathing in their warm, mothered scent, and digesting the fact that I was a father back in his proper place, and at last able to let go of that relentlessly masculine side that had dictated my life for so long. I looked at Juliet and saw the woman I remembered, but also a woman who was more confident and empowered. She too had come to the end of a long hard test, and had pulled through with the same conclusions about the way we should live our lives.

The ferry cut a white, sparkling trail past Lismore Lighthouse across a fresh blue sea, and I remembered how I had replayed this very image over and over in my mind through the darkest days of the winter. It felt so profoundly good to smell the sea and to breathe it all in deeply. This was our home now, and I knew that the pain and sacrifice had all been worthwhile. We would never return to the lives we had before, as we had passed from one way of looking at the world to another, and had dropped our artificial, career-related goals in favour of other, slower values that would stand us in greater stead than any amount of money or status. Sometimes, just sometimes, it pays to refuse to be rational, and to turn our backs on everything that society says we should do. Whether our destiny lies halfway across the world or in the next room, what is certain is that we have only one life, and it must belong to us.

As we sat drinking tea in Juliet's parents' kitchen, it felt impossibly exotic to be able to actually talk to each other, to have the time to speak and to listen without worrying about satellite signals or running low on batteries. As we spoke Juliet's eyes searched mine, looking closely as if making sure that I was her husband and not some impostor.

'It already seems as if it was all a dream,' she said, 'as if you never went away. I mean, look at us!' It was true: we weren't rolling naked through rose petals, screaming each others' names or consuming vast quantities of champagne and caviar. Instead we sat simply at the kitchen table, quietly sipping tea and talking, while the boys pushed toy cars along the floor. It felt so natural, so easy, and completely right.

EPILOGUE

I write these last lines looking out over a sea loch on the island, from the windows of a hut where I write each morning. Often the wind whistles hard and I see grey, foam-topped waves beat against the shore, reminding me never to forget the simplicity of life, and the joy of being able to feel it without clutter. Mull feels gentle and safe by comparison to where I have been, but there is still plenty of wildness to keep my soul alive. One morning I walked out during a gale that touched Force 12 on the Beaufort Scale, and came across a stag and his harem sheltering in a stand of birch trees and bracken. I walked gently towards them, and then watched as they pulled away, the stag holding his proud antlers high. Sometimes I pluck up the courage to swim across the loch, and often a seal follows in my wake, popping his head up as if hoping for a conversation. How life has changed: eighteen months ago, all I saw were grey lines of traffic and the hardened faces of frustrated commuters. I was lost and going nowhere, trapped by a web of debt, living a half-life with time always ebbing away.

It is now six months since I came home from Alaska, and even after writing this entire book I still cannot clearly explain why I went. The reasons are complex, and do not come fast enough for some people who get confused and impatient when I cannot give quick, easily digestible answers to the all-too easily asked question 'why?' What I am able to talk about more lucidly is what I learned. Humility was my greatest ally when living alone in the woods – the realisation that, if I forgot how frail and insignificant I was, I would die quickly. Humility helped me to deal with the pain, loneliness, hardship and hunger, as I believed I deserved nothing more. Every animal had a hard time in the winter, so why should I be any different? In this comfortable, insulated world of ours it is easy to forget that our lives are no more or less significant than that of an ant.

My journey was not based on anything rational, which is why I can't fully explain it. My time in the woods were the result of nothing more than a daydream that gradually became an obsession, until I had no choice but to follow it. What is certain is that I was unhappy before I went into the wilderness, and now I am happy. Sometimes, perhaps, the route to happiness cannot come from our ordered mind or the seemingly sensible world that surrounds us, nor can it come from creating or conforming to an image of oneself. Instead clues lie wrapped and hidden deep within our subconscious, as if hiding from the strident and annoying bark of reason. I would not recommend my course of action to every person, but I would always ask, is most of you happy? And if not, how can you change things? I am not sure what will come next or where life will lead us. Life does not reveal itself to us all in one go, and why should it? Better to seek out happiness now than to waste time scrimping and saving for a future that may not exist, and can never be tamed.

AUTHOR'S NOTES

This is not intended to be a comprehensive list or guide to wilderness living, but simply a few notes from my own experience.

CAMPSITE

Running a campsite over a long period of time, and in the extreme conditions of the Alaskan Interior, was very different to the camping I had done in the UK. Though my campsite was a disaster at first, I quickly learned how to make it comfortable with the help of a few key pieces of equipment.

Wall Tents

I worship these tents – although heavy (a 14 × 16ft tent will weigh around 70lb) for living in over long periods they are superb. I hung a ridgepole between two trees, then stretched the tent out with six poles to form an A shape. To make more space push willow lengths (6–8 feet long) between the ridgepole and the canvas. The willow will flex and push out the canvas, creating a spacious, domed ceiling as opposed to a mean triangle. This makes a great difference, especially if you are under canvas for months. Before winter sets in, hoist up another ridgepole above the first one, then sling over a tarpaulin to cover the whole tent, leaving about a foot between it and the canvas below. Pile snow around the sides of the tent for extra protection from wind. When you cut your spruce for the poles keep the branches or boughs for flooring – they keep you dry and smell good.

Stoves

The beating heart of my campsite was my stove. Lehman's (an American mail order company specialising in equipment that doesn't require electricity) sent me a beautiful 'Alaskan four-dog stove' (a reference to the mushers' description of a cold night, as this was the number of dogs they would need in the tent to keep themselves warm). The stove was 'baffled': a metal shelf between the stovepipe hole and the fire inhibits sparks from flying up the stovepipe, and helps to make a good cooking surface. The stove also had an airtight door, which kept heat in the firebox for up to ten hours. I had a four-gallon aluminium container that slotted on to the side of the stove to heat up water for washing. The stove weighed 58lb, and stood two feet off the floor. If you have a good stove you can survive anything, and some trappers have lived through entire winters in wall tents in the Interior, by keeping their stoves burning red hot.

Cooking

Cooking is an essential survival skill in the bush, and all good woodsmen can rustle up a decent meal. Good food is vital to morale when living in the wilderness over long periods – you don't need much to eat well, but a few key ingredients can make the difference between meals that are just edible, and high quality dining. Dried herbs are easily transportable and keep well, as do salt, pepper, garlic and lemon juice. Of course, in winter there is no problem storing meat, as you just have to open your door to access the freezer. Storing vegetables is more difficult, as most don't freeze well. I used the old timers' trick of cutting a hole in the ice and storing them underwater, which kept them cold but not frozen. My vegetables quickly ran out, however, so to keep myself nourished I took multivitamins. Decent supplies of protein were essential, as was fat, especially when the weather grew colder. Dried beans have always been a great campsite standby, as they are full of protein, can be cooked in many different ways and keep forever. Here are a few of my favourite campsite recipes:

Bacon 'n' Beans

The classic frontier dish. Soak whatever beans you have overnight (close to the stove, as anywhere else they will freeze) and then, after breakfast and before heading out, fry up some fatty bacon pieces in a big solid pot. Add the beans and stir around nicely, and then add stock and gently bring to the boil. Cover and put the pot on a cool part of the stove, then leave to simmer gently. This would be my lunch and dinner, accompanied by sweet tea. My best stock was made from willow grouse, flavoured with salt, black pepper and a pinch of sage. If I was lucky a chopped carrot and celery might find their way in. I made stock once from beaver bones – and did not try again. This recipe can also be made without the bacon, adding garlic and serving with olive oil and bread, or in my case pilot biscuits.

Refried Beans & Meat

Gently fry leftover beans in oil (if you are lucky enough to have butter, add some too) until it all gets nicely dry and almost crunchy in texture. Now push to one side of your big frying pan, and add chunks of grouse/ duck/ swan/goose/squirrel/beaver/moose/caribou/muskrat/lynx/black bear/crane/ salmon/ burbot/pike or whatever meat you have. Seal the meat, and when cooked through (juices run clear) stir in the beans from the side of the pan. Season and serve.

Willow and Spruce Grouse

When times got tough I did occasionally 'pot roast' whole grouse with whatever veg I had to hand, thus ensuring I got the maximum possible nutrition out of the meal, but generally I only ate the breast, keeping the rest for making soup. Willow grouse have perfect white breast meat, and unlike spruce grouse, which feed entirely on pine needles through the winter, a delicate flavour that would not offend even the most finicky person. I would sear the breasts and season with oregano and a few drops of treasured lemon juice sent by my mother, then serve them up with . . . beans. Spruce grouse are powerfully flavoured by their diet of pine, but they are still good. I treated their meat like fillet steak (it was the same colour when cooked) then served it with black pepper and mustard if I had some. It felt like luxury.

Beaver

Not the easiest animal to catch – messing about digging holes in the ice at − 45 and below is not fun. Nevertheless beaver is full of fat, and if one forgets that they are essentially rats, and have come from water that smells like a sewer, they can make good eating. They take a long time to skin, and their thick fat reserves melt in a warm cabin as you prepare them, making for slippery work. Once the pelt was off I would tie the animal to my game pole by its neck and gut it, then cut it into four quarters, removing the tail for later use. The result was a saddle, two large hams and two good-sized forelegs. The meat is dark and nicely marbled, and if you were starving and cold it would save your life fast, as it would be possible to eat large amounts of pure fat. Everything that I did not eat went into the dog-pot. I experimented with all sorts of methods of cooking beaver, and found that it pot roasts quite nicely. In the end though my best recipe was beaver ribs and pea soup. Before cooking, soak the meat for two nights in salt water, changing the water at the end of the first night. Then separate the ribs from the rack, and fry them in oil with some chilli and dried onion. Once well sealed, add dried split peas that have been soaked overnight, and stir around until warmed through. Add stock and cook as per pea soup.

Sour Dough Hotcakes

Old timers used to be called 'sour doughs', because they carried their sour dough 'starter' in a little capsule around their neck to keep it warm against their skin (if the yeast got cold it would die fast). I was fascinated to learn that some sour dough starters have been on the go for over one hundred years, and children sit down to hot-cakes and syrup made from a solution that was carried through blizzards around the necks of their great-grandfathers at the time of the gold rush. When men left their cabins for extended trips they knew that when the fire died everything would freeze, so they took their sour dough starter with them. When they returned to the cabin they would get the stove going, then mix their starter with water and flour and cover it lightly before leaving it by the stove to rise overnight. The next morning revealed a bubbly, yeasty mixture called a sponge that could be cooked on the griddle as hotcakes, or baked to make bread. A little of the mixture was kept aside for the next starter, and so the cycle continued year after year.

The fascinating thing about sour dough is that it relies on first capturing, and then feeding, wild yeast (our ancestors started theirs in caves). Once you have got your little colony going it could last forever. To make your 'starter', mix a cup of warm water (water from boiling potatoes is ideal) with a cup of any kind of unsieved flour in a large bowl. Place the mix in a stone crock, cover and leave in a warm place, and each day take away a cup of the mixture and replace with another half cup of warm water and half cup of flour, to 'feed' the yeast. Over the next three to four days, hopefully, it will froth up, showing the yeast is active. Wait for it to sink again, and then store in a cool place or fridge and feed once a week by the method above. Now you have your very own starter, and a ready source of nourishment that just needs water and flour to be made into a sustaining and tasty meal. For real desperadoes, the starter can also get you nicely drunk: a liquid known as 'hooch' develops and lies on top of it in a yeasty layer. I never tried it, but I'm told it has quite a kick.

Water

Before winter set in, I would collect over five gallons of water each night that it rained, using tarps which angled the water into a bucket with a sheet placed over it to collect debris. I then aerated it by pouring the collected water from jug to jug for a while before pouring it into its holding container. This makes a massive difference to the taste, which is otherwise flat and dull. I used a MIOX purifier for a while, but it didn't provide a large enough quantity of water to keep dehydration at bay. Later I used a 'Katadyn' water purifier, which provided up to 10 litres of water per day. When winter set in I had the luxury of ice and snow all around, and just melted a big pot on my stove. I should have boiled it just in case, but never bothered. I preferred ice, but if there was none available I went for dense, windblown snow.

SIWASHING

Knowing that you can make a shelter from whatever surrounds you and hole up if necessary gives you tremendous security when travelling and living in the bush. I used three main shelters. The 'coffin trench' is the simplest and quickest to build, but claustrophobic, and not ideal for more than one night. The snow cave makes a good home, but must be built only if you have lots of time to do it – otherwise you risk building up a sweat. The spruce A frame worked well and was easy to make, and the insulating layer of snow above spruce boughs makes it warm. The 'igloo' is not authentic – better described as a snow block house. I made a version of this to cover my shithole.

CLOTHING AND KIT

Clothing for Work

Despite the cold in the Interior, I most often found myself wearing relatively light clothing. I was carrying out hard, physical work, and it was crucial that I didn't build up a sweat, as this can drastically reduce one's body temperature, leading to hypothermia. Thus I found a way of felling a large tree, for example, processing it into stove-sized logs and dragging it all the way back to camp without building up a sweat. I achieved this by wearing many layers of clothing and removing a layer whenever my body heat started to build up. The aim is to never allow sweat to dampen clothing, as it will freeze, rendering your clothing useless.

All solo timber work is taxing, but working in snowshoes on 12 feet of snow in incredibly low temperatures was so challenging that it was almost funny (in fact there were moments when I was convinced I was taking part in a Japanese game show!). I tried where possible to carry out essential chores during warm spells (−10 to −25) thus avoiding the additional risk and discomfort of working in the −50s, but there were times when I had no choice. Over time, however, by working slowly and methodically, planning each job carefully and never rushing, each task became a joy. Sometimes I found myself wearing nothing but a thin pair of wool long johns with an icebreaker wool vest, then an MSR thermal suit and over this a North Face all-in-one. My beaver fur hat was often too hot for working, so would be temporarily discarded in favour of a wool forage cap. My North Face Summit Series windbreaker jacket would also be put aside. On my hands I wore a pair of thin wool gloves, warming them occasionally by stuffing inside an immense pair of wolf fur mitts which were wrapped around my waist out of the way. If the weather was particularly cold I added a pair of gardening gloves – demonstrating that not all kit has to be specialised.

Footwear

I wore two types of footwear during the winter. Firstly, my mukluks, which were given to me by Jenny, Claudette and Carol. These boots are exceptionally effective right down to −80, yet they are only effective when it is cold and dry. Mine were made of canvas, with a moose hide sole, felt liner booties and loose insole. The great plus with mukluks is that they give your toes space to move, and, as the sole is not rigid, each step forces your feet and toes to flex and hence generate circulation. At night I took the insoles out and dried them – this is vital. I wore a good pair of 'smart' wool socks inside my mukluks and they made a perfect combination. It felt very odd to put on what looked like a pair of slippers before walking out into one of the coldest regions on earth. To begin with I was sceptical, but they worked very well.

My other mainstays in the foot department were the indispensable US Army vapour or 'Bunny' boots. Given to me by Jenny, they are made of two layers, and have a valve so you can inflate them to whatever level you require (for very cold inflate to maximum, any warmer inflate slightly less and so on). Made of rubber, they are brilliant at any temperature, and will work even if filled with water. The boots look utterly hideous and border on comic in their appearance. But then again – the black and blue of frost-bite doesn't look that good either.

All the locals had a pair of these boots and almost all also carried mukluks. Many visitors came a cropper wearing tight flashy boots with all sorts of brands attached – they might work really well on the ski slopes, but they failed utterly in the Arctic regions. Nothing is sadder than the look of panic on an adventurer's face as he/she realises that they don't have the right kit for the job – particularly if that face is reflected in a mirror!

Clothing for Travel

Here the issue changes, as when you travel you are by necessity relatively inactive, and at the same time exposed to massive wind-chill. When I was travelling by dog sled, I benefited from the fact that mushing is quite active, requiring all sorts of jumping about, holding on etc – I could also get off and run behind the sled if I started to get too cold. Nevertheless, I did wear extra clothing, once again in layers. For a trip at −35 or below I would wear long thick wool underwear (Icebreaker is the best in my experience), MSR thermal all-in-one, Mountain Equipment windbreaker, North Face Gortex outer layer, a big old pair of padded overalls made of 100% thick tightly sewn cotton and over this a North Face Apex top. Finally, I would add a North Face Summit Series windbreaker. On my feet I wore my Bunny boots and any old socks, thick or thin.

How I got dressed was important too, and I was careful to ensure that all my clothes were completely dry. My clothes were all loose-fitting, and I left everything unzipped as I got ready, putting on most of my layers outside to avoid getting into a sweat. When I was ready to go I would don my final layers and zip everything up, then put on my beaver hat and a thick smock around my neck. When really cold I pulled the smock up into its balaclava mode and put my hat over this, then pulled up the hood from the Summit Series and tightened the sides. I also carried a goosedown jacket in my bag in case I needed it – the jacket was too vulnerable to puncture for it to be worn daily. On my hands I wore the ubiquitous wool gloves and my big pair of fur mitts. For my face I wore a neoprene mask that covered my nose and mouth and directed my breath away from clouding goggles.

For snow-machine travel I wore a big down jacket with a large hood over all of the above. Ideally a fur ruff would line the hood, creating a warm space around the face which helps deal with wind-chill.

Kit That Went With Me Everywhere

Wherever I went, I always carried my 35-litre day bag which contained enough supplies to keep me going for five days. Getting caught out was always a very real possibility, and I never allowed myself to feel 'safe', no matter how settled the conditions. My day bag was called a Crux AK47, and was superbly packable, in my sled or on my back, 100% waterproof and made of very tough material. Its one major drawback was that it had no outside pockets. This was a pain, as I had to unpack everything to get one little item – not fun in a blizzard, and bad news at −45 and below where I risked major hand heat loss. This is just one example of those little things that seem minor whilst selecting kit, but become critical in the bush. In the bag I carried the following:

- Hand warmers (for emergency use only) × 12
- Spare heavy gloves × 2
- Spare wool gloves × 2
- MSR pots and pans
- Half a bed sheet and collecting tin (the sheet I used as a water generator – stuff snow inside it, then tightly close the bundle and suspend from a stick downwind of your fire. The snow melts into the tin below, providing about a litre of water per hour)
- Food for five days: tea bags, coffee, oats, sugar, salt, two malt loaves, chocolate, dried salmon, dried moose, powdered milk (Shackleton gave his men hot milk drinks every 4 hours or so)
- Fire making kit: when recovering from falling through ice or getting caught out in a blizzard you need to light a fire fast, not toss about with bootlaces and sticks. I carried strike-anywhere matches in watertight bags and four plastic bottles of anti-freeze, which makes the perfect fuel for quick starting a fire – some locals also carried fuel-soaked rags in watertight bottles. On my body I carried matches in two used shotgun cartridges on which I had filed the brass to create a striking surface. I also carried a magnesium block and spark for last resort stuff, and always had a pocket stuffed with birch bark.
- A heavy duty bivvy bag
- Silva base plate compass and Garmin GPS

- Wool forage hat
- Spare fur hat and scarf
- Change of clothes and socks
- Emergency 'man over board' beacon (which would send an internationally recognised radio distress signal that even high-flying aircraft would pick up)
- Mountain rescue medical bag

Strapped to my day bag I carried a small trapping axe, a length of rope (always coiled) and pieces of string of various lengths and thicknesses. I carried a handkerchief in each pocket: one red, for non-human wipings such as rifles, knives and dogs' faces etc; and one blue, for snot, cuts, frozen breath on face etc. I considered carrying fishing gear, snares etc, but believed that in five days I could walk out of danger. I always carried my snowshoes, so that if I fell off the sled or if the snow machine broke down then at least I could walk back along my tracks.

MEDICAL KIT

I had a superb book entitled: 'A comprehensive guide to Wilderness and Travel Medicine' by Eric A Weiss, MD and hoped that this, along with a supply of medicines good enough to stock a fair-sized pharmacy, would see me through most eventualities. The medicines I had were as follows:

Antibiotics:
- Penicillin, Clarithromycin, Augmentin
- Tetracycline
- Metronidazole
- Ciprofloxacin

Pain Relief:
- Morphine and Diamorphin (Diamorphin is double strength)
- Ibuprofen, Aspirin, Paracetamol

Anti-emetic
- Metoclopramide

Disinfectant
- Surgical alcohol
- Iodine (good for water cleaning too)
- Peroxide

General medical
- Bandages and loads of plasters

- Small mirror for examining eyes and cotton buds, cotton wool rolls and eye wash kits
- Dioralyte for hydration
- Vaseline for burns and calomine lotion for insect bites
- Aloe vera for treatment of dry skin
- For seriously dry skin I have Eucerin which is 10% urea
- A dental emergency kit

Vein access – preparation
- Sterile swabs
- Sterile saline
- Tourniquet
- Tape

Vein access
- Venflon (23 and 21 gauge)
- Butterfly. Nice and quick, in my experience, but not as comfy in the arm as Venflon which leaves a plastic cannula in the vein instead of a rigid bit of metal.
- Tegaderm dressing which goes over IV

I also had bags of saline in case Dioralyte failed orally or there was massive blood loss.

Thankfully I only ever had small cuts, sprains and bangs, and never needed to use anything stronger than spruce sap to treat wounds. My biggest injury was the husky bite, and this happened in Galena, where I could be treated at the medical clinic. Had I not been within reach of medical help, I would have irrigated the wound myself with saline and iodine from a syringe, then removed any obvious dirt and disinfected again with iodine. I would have then lightly bandaged it, and treated with topical antibiotics and possibly oral ones too. If the cut was deep I had suture kits that came with a curved needle already attached to the stitching thread – very useful.

I am relieved that I never had to confront the horror of a serious medical emergency. If I had, however, I am confident that I would have dealt with it to the best of my ability. I think it is important to be mentally prepared to deal with such outcomes, whilst taking every precaution to ensure they do not come to pass. Before leaving Scotland I even went to the length of practicing the insertion of an IV line under the supervision of a doctor friend. Messy, but ultimately successful!

The main conditions that worried me, and that I felt I needed to have some awareness of, were gangrene, cellulitis, pneumonia, high fever, urinary tract infections and – my personal horror – appendicitis. For all of these I made sure that I was familiar with both the symptoms and treatments before I left home.

FIREARMS

Guns were a necessary evil, as far as I was concerned, and I was armed to the teeth almost all of the time. Bears and moose continue to kill people in bush country, and almost all the victims have been unarmed. I took local advice as to the best weapons to use, and was lent a number of useful rifles and one handgun. It is not a good idea to carry weapons unless you have some previous experience, however, not to mention a healthy dose of respect for their hideous lethality. I never let myself forget that a gun is the Devil's right hand, and no substitute for a woodsman's sense. A list of the firearms I used follows:

Winchester Pump Shotgun

This was my summer and autumn 'camp gun', carried for bear defence and foraging. A shotgun can be loaded with shot that is light enough to land a duck for supper, yet can also hold very heavy rounds sufficient to fell an elephant. This particular shotgun carried four rounds, though some can hold an extended magazine of eight rounds, and I carried No 6 shot, No 5 and No 4 for birds. I also had 00 buckshot, and rifled 'slug' rounds for bear. The slugs weighed 550 grains per round (in comparison, a British Army standard issue SA/80 carries rounds that weigh around 50 grains). The buckshot and slug rounds are reliably lethal at up to 50 yards, and give devastating cover at 30–40 yards. The buckshot holds eight balls per cartridge, and is a better round, in terms of hitting the target, than a single slug. I loaded alternate rounds.

Marlin Lever-Action 45/70 Guide Rifle

This was my 'sled gun', shortened for use in bush conditions and fixed with open 'iron' as opposed to scope sights. This makes it ideal for close-range shooting, as a scope will make it impossible to focus if the animal comes up close. This rifle carried four rounds, and was reliably lethal at up to 150 yards, though best at 100 yards. I loaded with 'Corebond' bullets, each weighing 430 grains.

Nylon 66' Semi-Automatic .22 Rifle

This was my winter 'foraging rifle', with a synthetic stock, making it ideal for use in severe sub-zero conditions, and had open iron sights. It is highly accurate, and when hunting I always aimed for the head and neck, so that if I missed it was a clean miss, whilst a hit always killed quickly. Unlike a shotgun this rifle made little noise, allowing me to pick off a number of birds quickly (once I was lucky enough to come home with five grouse, shot quickly from two nearby willow trees). It carries eleven rounds, and though it is best at 100–150 yards, is reliably lethal at up to 300 yards – in good hands (and with scopes) even further.

.357 Magnum 'Security Six' Handgun

This was my 'last resort gun', carried on snow machines and worn on the waist during bear season. It is a handy, tough gun which is safer and more reliable than an automatic, but I was told it was underpowered for Alaskan use. I have no knowledge of handguns and am a hopeless shot with them. It carries six rounds, and I loaded it with 200 grain rounds for bear.

A LAST WORD

Over and above all my kit, the most important factor that got me through my time in the Interior – more than any fancy clothing or piece of hardware – was humility and patience and a complete abandonment of the idiocy of time. I arrived with an absolute readiness to approach everything slowly, and without any macho pride. I was always very careful, and trusted my instincts. On the two occasions that I failed to adhere to this principle I suffered badly – the first time I almost lost a toe (of which I was particularly fond) and the second I nearly lost my life. Yet, on balance, my humble approach to the landscape allowed me to travel with safety on that wonderful road that soon becomes a track, then a game trail, then nothing but wilderness.

ACKNOWLEDGEMENTS

It is hard to properly thank people whom, for no reason other than heart, decided to help me. I wish I could repay them as deeply as that wild place rewarded me, when it allowed me to live in its midst through one long, dark winter. I wish that the busy people who patiently listened to my rambling approaches, and then actually agreed to assist, could be repaid with just one night's gliding behind a dog team along the frozen river, beneath the flickering northern lights. I wish they could experience the joy of returning to a home in the woods, where a stove ticks with heat and fills the cold, still air with the sublime scent of birch smoke. I wish they too could hear wolves calling to each other along the snowbound river; or the loon birds' eerie autumn song hanging in the thick spruce trees that towered over my lake. Sadly I only have words, but I hope they will go some way towards repaying the debt to all those who suspended disbelief on my behalf.

First there is my family, who trusted me enough to let me go, and above all Juliet, who supported me from the beginning. I knew she was strong enough to keep our little family safe while I was gone, and she did so, helping us forge a new life in the process. She has also edited everything that I have written with a thoroughness and ability that is humbling. I also thank her parents, Audrey and James Knight, who have been with us through all the twists and turns of life, always supportive no matter how outlandish our plans. And my mother, Giuliana Ashford, who knew how to nurture a little boy's heart no matter where we landed up in the world.

Then there were those, thousands of miles away, who took a leap of faith by allowing a stranger to become part of their families. Firstly Don and Carol, in their beautiful golden cabin. Without Don's help it is more than possible that I would have died, and I feel privileged to call him a friend. Also their two daughters, Claudette and Jenny, who became like sisters, and Charlie and Chris, their husbands, who could have turned their backs but instead became like brothers. Their bright, mischievous children – Bubba, Bethany, Jack, Noo-Noo, Pearl, Tirzah and Asa – who kept me on the ball, and never let me forget my own boys. Then there was Glenn Stout, who took it upon himself to teach me how to mush. He found me the dogs and lent me everything I needed, as well as putting up with one of the world's most irritating phenomena: the trainee musher. Thanks also to Bradley and Sandy Scotton: he flew a 1940s J-3 Cub and helped out when I got stuck, and she made me a good hat. There were many other people in that riverside village that lent a kind word or pearl of wisdom from time to time, and I thank them for those moments, which were like gold for a tenderfoot. Thanks also to Chuck Sasser and his family in Oklahoma, who gave me hope, and to David Rechter, who helped me in the eleventh hour. The currency was always friendship and trust, and these people made me rich.

It took me four years to find a way of making my escape from cubicle-hell. These are the people who helped me dig the tunnel, and whom I thank with all my heart. At *The Scotsman*, Iain Martin, then Editor, went out on a limb to support me when many had simply laughed. My senior management, Steven Walker, Stephen Tait, Richard Bogie and Alan Boyd also looked out for me, despite the fact that I was the employee from hell. My sponsors, Highland Park Whisky, made the whole thing possible: thanks to Murray Calder, Jason Craig, Sharon McLaughlin, and Emrys Inker, who took a great risk in helping me. I also thank the distillery in Orkney for sending me the best whisky on earth, and for lending me the matches to burn my suit. At Graham Tiso Outdoors, Chris Tiso is a man with a heart as big as a bear, whose friendship has never weakened. He gave me support in the early days when I really needed it, and sent me off with the best outdoor kit currently on the market. Thanks also Louise Ramsay. Once in Alaska, Glenda Lehman Ervin at Lehman's sent me a bounty of wonderful goods including an axe, my stove and snowshoes.

In the days before I left, many came to my rescue at short notice. Amongst these were John Warehand at Inmarsat, who gave me a satellite phone which worked even at $-60°$, and John Macaleenan at Scotsys, who solved my laptop problems within 24 hours. David Watt took the time to help me build my medical kit, as well as giving advice on how to deal with everything from gangrene to dog-bite. Emma Platt spent a bloody few hours teaching me how to self-administer a drip, and her husband David gave me a squeeze-box, which I carried with me everywhere but still haven't had the chance to learn. Angus Bremner spent patient hours with me in front of a computer; Mino Russo suffered the agony of sharing an office with me while I daydreamed – often out loud. Peter Leach gave me last-minute instruction in navigation, for which I still owe him a bottle of whisky.

With respect to this book, I am indebted to Jonathan Lloyd and Euan Thorneycroft, who set me on the road. I also thank Rupert Lancaster and Bob McDevitt at Hodder & Stoughton, for giving me the ink and paper, and dealing with what must be the world's second most irritating phenomena, the first-time author. Thanks to my mother, for her skilled illustrations, and to Dawn Reade, for her beautiful maps. When it came to writing the book, thanks to Douglas Wilson at Inverlussa Shellfish for lending me his portacabin to write in, and to Bob Davis for offering perfect conversation when the words weren't flowing. I also want to thank those two intrepid film-makers, Matt Haan and Ashley Meneely, for braving the journey out to see me, and Tom Roberts and Hamish Barbour for supporting my ideas.

Many friends proved the maxim: 'two-thirds of help is to give courage'. In no particular order I thank Adrian Morgan, Don Galloway, Robert Rattray, Marc Lambert, Bill Melvin, Colin Peter, Richard Megson, Steven Thomas, Justine Watt, John Mackenzie, Sophie and James Manners, Stephen and Nicola Brown, Amy Hardy, Peter Kravitz, Isobel Bathgate and many others who listened as I blathered on and on.

I can't end this without mentioning the dogs that were my companions in that wild place. My six sled dogs – Bubbles, Sprite, Lefty, Spot, Blackie and Brownie – became so much more than just transport, and never let me down. Last but not least, there is Fuzzy, my constant cohort, ally, and fellow learner in the woods. He helped me hunt, guarded camp and ran mile after mile behind my sled – always happy, even when his face was white with frost.

Wild and wide are my borders, ster

for the men who will win me —

as death is my sway, and I wait

and I will not be won in a day